INSTRUCTOR'S MANUAL
WITH TRANSPARENCY MASTERS
AND TEST ITEM FILE

Arthur Aron

STATISTICS

FOR THE

BEHAVIORAL

AND

SOCIAL SCIENCES

A BRIEF COURSE

Arthur Aron
Elaine N. Aron

State University of New York at Stony Brook

PRENTICE HALL, *Upper Saddle River, NJ 07458*

© 1997 by PRENTICE-HALL, INC.
Simon & Schuster / A Viacom Company
Upper Saddle River, New Jersey 07458

ISBN 0-13-651969-5
Printed in the United States of America

Table of Contents

Part I: Teaching the Introductory Statistics Course in the Social and Behavioral Sciences

Chapter A. Teaching Statistics   1

I.   Overall Teaching Issues 1
II. Structuring the Lecture 2
III. Presenting the Lecture 4
IV. Fitting the Course to the Students 6
V.   Supervising Teaching Assistants 7
VI. Some Comments to Teaching Assistants 8

Chapter B. Structuring the Course   11

I.   Selection and Order of Topics 11
II. Assignments 13
III. Exams 13
IV. The Course Syllabus 18

Chapter C. Lecture Examples Based on a Questionnaire Administered to Your Students   23

I.   An Example Questionnaire You Could Use 23
II. How to Record and Send in the Data to Have Lecture Examples Made Up For You 25

Chapter D. Using the Computer in the Statistics Course   27

I.   Advantages and Disadvantages of Using the Computer with this Course 27
II. Computer Software Packages Compatible with this Course 28
III. Facilities and Equipment Needed 28

Part II: Lecture Outlines and Examples Corresponding to Textbook Chapters

Chapter 1. Introduction to the Student and Displaying the Order in a Group of Numbers   29

Instructor's Summary of Chapter 29
Lecture 1.1: Introduction to the Course 30
Lecture 1.2: Frequency Tables 32
Lecture 1.3: Describing a Distribution Graphically 34
Lecture Transparencies 35

Chapter 2. The Mean, Variance, Standard Deviation and Z Scores   43

Instructor's Summary of Chapter 43
Lecture 2.1: The Mean 44
Lecture 2.2: The Variance and Standard Deviation 46
Lecture 2.3: Z Scores 48
Lecture Transparencies 50

Chapter 3. Correlation and Prediction   57

    Instructor's Summary of Chapter 57
    Lecture 3.1: The Scatter Diagram and the Logic of Correlation 58
    Lecture 3.2: The Correlation Coefficient 60
    Lecture 3.3: Bivariate Regression 63
    Lecture Transparencies 65

Chapter 4. Some Key Ingredients for Inferential Statistics:
         The Normal Curve, Probability, and Population versus Sample   77

    Instructor's Summary of Chapter 77
    Lecture 4.1: The Normal Curve 78
    Lecture 4.2: Probability and Sample and Population 82
    Lecture Transparencies 84

Chapter 5. Introduction to Hypothesis Testing   91

    Instructor's Summary of Chapter 91
    Lecture 5.1: Introduction to Hypothesis Testing 92
    Lecture 5.2: Significance Levels and Directional Tests 94
    Lecture Transparencies 96

Chapter 6. Hypothesis Tests with Means of Samples   105

    Instructor's Summary of Chapter 105
    Lecture 6.1: The Distribution of Means 106
    Lecture 6.2: Hypothesis Testing with a Sample of More than One 109
    Lecture Transparencies 111

Chapter 7. Statistical Power and Effect Size   117

    Instructor's Summary of Chapter 117
    Lecture 7.1: Power 118
    Lecture 7.2: Influences on Power 119
    Lecture 7.3: Power in Planning and Evaluating Studies 121
    Lecture Transparencies 123

Chapter 8. The *t*-Test for Dependent Mean   135

    Instructor's Summary of Chapter 135
    Lecture 8.1: Introduction to the *t*-Test 136
    Lecture 8.2: The *t*-Test for Dependent Means 139
    Lecture Transparencies 142

Chapter 9. The *t*-Test for Independent Means   153

    Instructor's Summary of Chapter 153
    Lecture 9.1: Introduction to the *t*-Test for Independent Means 154
    Lecture 9.2: Applying the *t*-Test for Independent Means 156
    Lecture Transparencies 158

Chapter 10. Introduction to the Analysis of Variance   **167**

    Instructor's Summary of Chapter 167
    Lecture 10.1: Introduction to the Analysis of Variance 168
    Lecture 10.2: The Logic and Language of Factorial Designs 170
    Lecture Transparencies 172

Chapter 11. Chi-Square Tests and Strategies When Population Distributions are Not Normal   **183**

    Instructor's Summary of Chapter 183
    Lecture 11.1: The Chi-Square Test of Goodness of Fit 184
    Lecture 11.2: The Chi-Square Test of Independence 186
    Lecture 11.3: Nonnormal Distributions and Data Transformations 188
    Lecture Transparencies 190

Chapter 12. Making Sense of Advanced Statistical Procedures in Research Articles   **203**

    Instructor's Summary of Chapter 203
    Lecture 12.1: Advanced Procedures I 204
    Lecture 12.2: Advanced Procedures II 206
    Lecture Transparencies 208

Part III: Test Item File

Test Bank for Each Chapter in the Text Book   **221**

    Chapter 1 221
    Chapter 2 231
    Chapter 3 241
    Chapter 4 257
    Chapter 5 267
    Chapter 6 279
    Chapter 7 289
    Chapter 8 299
    Chapter 9 315
    Chapter 10 327
    Chapter 11 345
    Chapter 12 367

Part IV: Answers to Practice Problems

Computation Answers to the Practice Problems in the Text Book   **377**

Introduction

This *Instructor's Manual with Transparency Masters and Test Item File* accompanies Aron and Aron's *Statistics for the Behavioral and Social Sciences*. It is designed to help you teach an introductory statistics course using this text.

Section I of this manual includes four chapters (A through D) that discuss general issues in teaching this course: teaching and lecturing about statistics, structuring the course, creating examples based on a class survey of your students, and using the computer with the course. I have organized these chapters in a detailed outline form, in order to make it easy for you to locate and use just that material pertinent to your needs.

Section II includes twelve chapters which correspond to the chapters in the text. For each chapter, I have provided a special chapter summary and lecture outlines. I also included a variety of worked-out examples and other teaching aids to photocopy onto transparencies for use in these lectures.

Section III is a test bank that provides multiple-choice, fill-in, computation, and essay problems for each chapter in the text.

Section IV gives the computation answers for the Practice Problems not answered in the text.

If at any time you have questions or suggestions regarding this course, please feel free to contact me by electronic mail or post:

Electronic Mail: aron@psych.psy1.sunysb.edu

Post: Arthur Aron, Ph.D.
      Psychology Department
      State University of New York at Stony Brook
      Stony Brook, NY 11794-2500

Chapter A
Teaching Statistics

Teaching statistics is a chance to be heroic. Students expect this to be a horrible experience, so if you can make it even bearable, they love you for it.

In this chapter I share with you what I have learned about teaching statistics over the last twenty-five years (as well as what I have learned from reviewing the literature on teaching undergraduate courses and attending various seminars on college teaching). I have organized the chapter into six sections:

I. Overall Teaching Issues
II. Structuring the Lecture
III. Presenting the Lecture
IV. Fitting the Course to the Students
V. Supervising Teaching Assistants
VI. Some Comments to Teaching Assistants

I. Overall Teaching Issues

There are four main issues that make a great deal of difference in the effectiveness of my teaching:

A. Being Organized and Consistent

Students seem reassured by an instructor who has thought out what he or she will do, lets the students know what the plan is, and follows through on the plan. This applies to every aspect of the course: the overall course structure and syllabus, the structure of each lecture, and the content and grading of assignments and exams. If the course includes laboratory or discussion sections, as the overall instructor you must also see that what goes on in the sections is systematically planned and, again, the plan is carried out.

I can not emphasize too strongly that it is not only important to follow an organized plan, but to be sure that the students know, at each point, what this plan is and that you are following it. This is as much an emotional as a rational issue, and applies regardless of whether or not you are feeling organized yourself. My experience is that students need to see order and consistency in you that borders on the compulsive. That way the occasional inevitable error is not taken as a sign of total chaos (something which they may be fearing in themselves).

B. Being Flexible and Responsive to Student Input

On the other hand. Although it is crucial to make and follow a plan, plans do not always work as expected. Teaching requires being alert to whether students are maintaining interest, learning the material, and holding a positive attitude towards the course. There also has to be a sense of compassion coming from you—even mercy—so they can apply that, too, to themselves.

When it is necessary to make changes in the plan, you should plan the changes—perhaps with a discussion with the students (and certainly with any teaching assistants you have)—and then make very clear to everyone just what the changes are and why you have made them. If a change could possibly be interpreted by any students as affecting them adversely, it will be important to address this before they do—preferably by providing some offsetting advantage to those students.

Being responsive to student input also means soliciting it. I encourage students to come to office hours and to send me notes about any suggestions they have about the course (even anonymously, if that is easier for them). In addition, I do two specific things:

1. *Arrive 5-10 minutes early, stay 5-10 minutes late.* I try to be available to students at this time (that is, have all my notes and such prepared and ready before I enter the classroom), and if possible, I actually approach students individually or in small groups and ask them how the class is going. When I know names, that is all the better. But I

make a point to speak to some I don't know—not merely the ones who always speak up in class. Also outside of class, if I see a student of mine at the bookstore or at the drinking fountain, I ask him or her about the course.

2. *In about the fourth week of class, I ask for written evaluations.* My procedure is to ask students to take out a sheet of paper, *not* put their name on the paper, and then answer three questions: (a) What do you especially like about the course? (b) What suggestions do you have? and (c) Do you have any other comments? I make sure to collect these in a way that respects their anonymity. I review the evaluations before the next class and report to them on any issues that have come up. I find it is important not to get defensive, to make changes that are really useful, and to let the class also know how many students are really quite satisfied by reading some of the positives (with appropriate modesty, of course). Students are often surprised that not all the other students responded just as they did (social psychologists call this the "false consensus effect"). I think they also learn to recognize the more generic grumbling-against-authority that sometimes crops up in students. Even when there is some truth in the gripe, they can hear when there is more venom or energy in the attack than an instructor deserves, and so I become more human to them—someone who, like them, is sometimes an underdog.

C. Being Scrupulously Fair

In my experience the one thing that most undermines class morale is when students feel that they are being treated unfairly. In part I try to avert such problems by, again, making the requirements and structure of the course very explicit at the start and sticking to it (point A, above). But problems are also very likely to arise around the grading of exams and assignments, or perhaps around the way you call on students in class, or generally how you are perceived as treating students, both in and out of class. Grades, alas, are often of enormous importance to students. The one or two points that you know are not important for their final grade can be a source of sleepless nights and tearing of hair to them. Once again, it matters not only that things be fair, but that students *perceive* them to be fair.

D. Experimenting and Attending to Your Own Strengths and Weaknesses

Your teaching style is probably based on your best learning experiences. And perhaps you have taken to heart advice of people like me. This is fine, but these suggestions may not make the best use of your personal abilities. Everyone I know who has ever won a teaching award comments that they did not really become a good teacher until they found their own voice, their own style. This meant taking some risks, trying out some new and different ways of doing things—and making quite a few mistakes in the process. In fact, mistakes are an inevitable part of teaching even if you don't experiment at all! But excellent teachers watch more closely to see what does and doesn't work for them and let that shape their teaching style. And when teaching statistics, it really helps to pursue excellence.

II. Structuring the Lecture

Most people who teach this course are pretty confident about the material itself. But this does not guarantee a good lecture. In this section I consider the overall structure of the lecture, then focus on what is the heart of any statistics lecture—the explanation of the concepts and the selection and preparation of examples.

A. Overall Structure of the Lecture

The most important part of an effective lecture structure is that there is a structure! Here are specific suggestions for what makes a good structure:

1. Begin with a statement of this lecture topic and where this topic fits into the overall course. In this context also review what has been covered in the immediately previous lecture or two.

2. *Next, every class period remind students of the relevance of the course to their larger academic and life goals.* They can't escape learning this if they want to be successful in the social and behavioral sciences. They can't fall asleep, much as they'd like to. In other words, you remotivate them about why they need today's lecture—to understand research they will read in later courses; to prepare them for the more advanced statistics courses which will empower them to do sophisticated research on the issues that matter to them; and to sharpen their conceptual abilities, which are not innate, but only developed by patient persistence. Also, when possible, make the relevance of each procedure clear too, by illustrating its application in studies the students are likely to see as relevant to them or to populations they care about.

3. Next give an overview of what this lecture will cover.

4. Make the focus of the lecture a single theme (or a small number of themes) illustrated with several examples.

5. *Focus on the material in the text.* In a statistics course you do not bore the students by covering the same material that is in the text. They need and expect the repetition. Indeed, it is crucial that you use the same symbols, methods, formulas, and language as are used in the book. The lecture is made lively by using some different examples, explaining the concepts in your own words and style (but following the same logic as in the book), your give and take with them through their questions, and by your overall presentation skills.

6. Keep each segment discrete and summarize it before going on to the next.

7. *Plan time for questions at the end of each segment.* I always try to have some extra material to cover if there are very few questions and something near the end that I can leave out if the questions take too long.

8. End with an overview of what was covered and what is coming in the next class. It is very important to leave time for this.

B. Explaining Concepts

The most important thing about explaining concepts is to do it *slowly*, step by step, with simple language, and illustrating each step with an example, analogy, or graphic—anything to make the abstract stick. (Abstract concepts of the kind that are so central to statistics are difficult for most students, who find the language itself very strange.) For example, the idea of the variance has three parts: The deviation of each score from the mean, the square of these deviations, and the average of these squared deviations. My experience is that students have no trouble with the first part, but if I move too fast to the next step, the combination of the first with the second, and then of the first two with the third, it all becomes too much of abstraction laid on abstraction.

Keep in mind short-term versus long-term storage—the extra time and the semantic processing that is required to move an idea from one to the other. Also consider primacy and recency effects, which make the middle idea most easily forgotten—unless you emphasize it.

Finally, since the concepts are the most difficult part of a lecture, they should be given when you and the students are freshest and least likely to be rushed—near the beginning.

C. Preparing Good Examples

Working through examples is the heart of most statistics lectures. *For each major point I make in a lecture, I try to have three examples.* I find it most effective to use one example from the book (this keeps continuity) and two new examples. I usually make one new example that is based on responses to a questionnaire the students themselves completed (see Chapter C of this *Instructor's Manual*) and one other example.

Correspondingly, in the lecture outlines provided in this *Instructor's Manual*, for each major theme I provide transparencies for (a) one example from the text, (b) one based on questionnaires of students from one of my classes (which would be replaced by transparency examples from your own class if you send in the data to me), and (c) one new example.

If you want to make your own examples, here are four suggestions:

1. *An example should not involve unnecessary complexities or idiosyncracies.* The students have enough to do to learn the material without having to deal with examples that are exceptions to rules, include advanced material, involve complicated research designs difficult to understand in their own right, or require learning an unfamiliar theory to understand the rationale of what was done.

2. *The content of the example should be interesting.* If possible select topics relevant to student interests and having interesting results. I try to take mine from real studies (or if I use made-up data, I try to make up examples leading to conclusions supported by actual studies).

3. *Prepare the example in exactly the same format, with exactly the same formulas, steps, and symbols as the examples in the text.* Students are very confused when steps are left out or when faced with formulas or symbols they have not seen before.

4. *Generally avoid showing alternative ways of working a problem.* This can confuse those students having trouble learning it even one way. (Of course, occasionally an alternative approach makes the material come to life.)

III. Presenting the Lecture

Being well prepared is more than half the job. What remains is the way you present. The main issues are the general attitude towards the material you convey, maintaining classroom morale, and style of delivery.

A. *Your General Attitude Towards the Material*

Students will take their cue from you about the value of what they are learning. Thus, I suggest you follow these three principles:

1. *Show them your own excitement (to the degree you genuinely feel it) about the research process and the use of statistics as part of it.*

2. *Don't belittle statistical methods or the research process.* Sometimes, in order to sound more human, an instructor runs down the subject matter being taught. I have learned that this almost always backfires. Students figure that if I feel this way about it, why should they bother to learn it?

3. *Be accurate with logic, formulas, and numbers.* Mistakes are inevitable, but it is important to take great care, especially when working out problems in class. I have all too often heard students complain about statistics professors who can never get the formulas right. It also drives students crazy when half way through a problem they have been laboriously copying down, they have to go back and start over or change every number!

B. *Maintaining Classroom Morale*

I find that my own day-to-day satisfaction with teaching is primarily a function of the feeling atmosphere in the classroom. And I am also convinced that students' learning is seriously impaired by a classroom ambience that is disinterested, chaotic, or hostile. Here are some things I do to keep classroom morale high:

1. *Pay attention to morale.* Ask students how they are doing and respond to grumbling and any challenges in an open, constructive, even eager way. (I resist the temptation to dismiss the discontented as deviant griping swine who do not appreciate the pearls I have spread before them.) Often just acknowledging students' concerns, even if nothing can be done about them, can turn a classroom situation around. But it is also sometimes possible, and necessary, to make real changes, and sometimes to make some special effort (such as an extra review session on your own time, extra handouts, easing requirements, etc.) to show students you will go out of your way for them. But the

main thing is to notice and respond. If things do start to go badly, the longer you let it go on, the harder it gets to do something about it.

2. *Start class on time.*

3. Keep the difficulty of the material you present (and also the difficulty of assignments and exams) at a level that allows everyone to experience success, even if some say later that you went too slow. Remember, your goal is for students to learn—evaluation should always be secondary to this goal. Also, I have found it better not to remind students constantly of how much more there is to learn in statistics and how little of it they are getting in this course, as if this material is really simple and should be a breeze for them. Actually, because of anxiety, for most people it's often the first math courses that seem the hardest.

4. *Avoid saying "clearly," "as is obvious," and the like.*

5. *Be supportive and patient with questions.* A student's attention will never be as consistently on the lecture as yours must be. Students will miss things you said and ask what appear to be stupid questions. It is almost always the case that if one student does not understand something, many others have the same problem but are too shy to speak out. If you are even slightly harsh with a questioner, it will stifle all but the most aggressive students—and also create a fearful (and eventually hostile) climate. Also, don't put the student who asks a question on the hot seat. And repeat the question and give your answer to the whole class.

6. *Don't spoil the experience at the end.* You can do this by getting angry at students' natural tendency to start packing their things a few minutes early. You can do this by expressing your frustration about not having covered everything you intended. And you can do this by trying to cover your last eight points in the last five seconds. (If you are running out of time, recognize it five minutes before the end, leave something out, and allow time to summarize and close graciously.)

7. *Make jokes.*

8. *Let the students know you are a human being.* A personal story now and then goes a long way towards making a connection with your students and adds some random reinforcement during what for some must be very long, dry, difficult lectures.

C. Style of Delivery

Teaching is a performing art. The human performance is what makes it worthwhile for students to attend lectures, as opposed to merely reading the material in a book. Here are some tips for giving a strong performance.

1. *Attend to students' faces to see if they are learning and interested.*

2. *Put variety into your pacing and tone of voice.*

3. *Use your body.* Hand and arm motions, leaning into your points, moving around the room—these all make it easier to follow what you have to say. (You needn't be afraid of being overly dramatic—my experience is that the more outrageous the effort, the more likely students are to pay attention, and that is your goal.) Also, it is generally better to stand if you can, so your motions are less constricted and your level of energy is naturally higher.

4. *Speak to the audience.* Look at individuals, make eye contact, focus on different sections of the audience as you proceed through the lecture. If you are working from detailed notes, look up often—and certainly at the end of each point. Take special care not to spend too much time facing the blackboard or looking down at your notes.

5. *Use simple, clear language.*

6. *Write on the board legibly and in an organized fashion.* (And be sure that the previous material on the board is very thoroughly erased in any area you are working.)

7. *Use diagrams.* Many students do not really grasp concepts such as regression or the normal distribution until they see them visually. However, the diagrams we use in statistics require a bit of explanation and time to digest before they can have the needed impact. So take your time in explaining them and return to them often.

8. *Use transparencies (with an overhead projector).* The chapters in Section II of this *Manual* provide material you can photocopy directly onto a transparency. These are easier for students to read and more attractive than blackboard examples. (Be sure to put the projector back far enough so that those in the back of the room can read the transparency without struggling--if necessary, you may want to enlarge the material on a photocopy machine before making the transparency.) I use one of the special felt-tip pens for writing on transparencies, highlighting points on the transparency as I discuss it. A pointer is also useful. One caution: Many students like to take thorough notes. When you write on the board, they can keep up. But when you project a transparency, you need to allow them ample time to copy it into their notes. Another possibility is to make copies of the transparencies you will use and distribute them to the students at the start of class.

IV. Fitting the Course to the Students

The single biggest difference between new and experienced teachers of statistics is that the latter respond to the reality of the students in front of them. New teachers are more often responding to an unrealistic image of what students ought to be like. Here are some suggestions:

A. *Don't Assume Your Students Are Like Yourself*

Only a tiny proportion of your class will ever be the sort to teach statistics. Very few will even attend graduate school . In your own first statistics class, you were probably among the most interested, motivated, and capable. And if you think back honestly, even you may have been more interested in your love life than in analysis of variance. So don't expect too much of them—the students themselves become discouraged, if not angry.

In this same light it is important not to assume that most of those taking the course are interested in psychology research. The few who will eventually become researchers usually are inspired to do so later in the major. It is your job to start getting them interested. Presuming they already are could open a large gap between you and them.

B. *Assume that Many Will Come to Class Unprepared*

On the one hand, it is not fair to those who do prepare to lower the level of your lecture very much, and doing so also reduces the motivation for students to prepare in the future. On the other hand, you don't want to lose half your audience. One solution is to say to your class, "For those of you who were not able to do the reading, you may well have some trouble following the lecture—just do the best you can and hopefully today's class will make it easier to understand the material when you do the reading." Then I give a lecture geared at a level intended to make sense to a poor student who has done the reading and at the same time to a good student who hasn't.

I try not to berate students too much for not having studied, avoiding comments like, "as you know, *if* you've done the reading, ..." (Many students have legitimate problems preventing them from keeping up. And it is already the students, not you, who suffers most from being behind.)

C. *Monitor How Students Are Doing and Make Adjustments Accordingly*

(See point I. B. above.)

D. Remember that Many Students Are Afraid of (or Loathe) Statistics.

Math anxiety, test anxiety, and a general anxiety about school seem to be common among first- and second-year college students. Box 1.1 in the text discusses some things students can do to cope with these anxieties. One of the most important things *you* can do to help students in this regard is to avoid creating any more additional arousal than necessary. Keep the atmosphere of class calm and noncompetitive. Do not emphasize the evaluation aspects and the consequences of poor performance. The arousal-performance curve—particularly for complex, abstract tasks like learning statistics—quickly peaks. Most students are already highly aroused by their fears of this course (and don't be fooled by an apathetic exterior). Any extra arousal only decreases learning. In addition, extra arousal is likely to manifest itself in classroom behavior that undermines class morale.

It is wise not to demand that students pretend to like the material. I show my own enthusiasm, but respect those who dislike or are even hostile to the need for quantitative methods in the social and behavioral sciences. Indeed, I usually bring this up on the very first day of class. But in doing so, I also point out that it is unfair of them to create an unpleasant atmosphere and undermine the learning of those students who really want to grasp the material.

E. Be Aware of Gender Issues

It is helpful to remind the class at the outset that there is no reliable difference in performance in statistics classes as a function of gender (see our Box 1.2 in the text). Students of both genders all too often hold negative stereotypes about women's statistics abilities—stereotypes that interfere with their performance. Some of the subtle ways instructors unintentionally perpetuate these stereotypes include using masculine pronouns—particularly when describing a person carrying out a data analysis—and using examples mainly of research conducted by men. The stereotype may be reinforced if initially your class's women students ask fewer questions. If that happens, it is worth saying something about this explicitly. Also be sure that when women do raise their hands, they are called upon.

F. Be Aware of Ethnic Differences

Students (and instructors) are also affected by ethnic stereotypes. Those belonging to ethnic groups stereotyped as poor at academics may need extra encouragement. They may also need extra help, since they are often the same ones whose secondary schooling provided an impoverished preparation, especially in math and writing. And students in ethnic groups assumed to be good in math may suffer from unrealistically high expectations. Finally, those who have difficulty with English also deserve your extra help and patience if they need it.

V. Supervising Teaching Assistants

When a course uses teaching assistants (TAs), much depends on the quality of their work with the students. In turn, your relation to your TAs is an important part of the course atmosphere and of your own pleasure in teaching. Here are some suggestions:

A. Plan the Section Activities Yourself

Think in advance about what the TAs should be doing in their lab or discussion sections. Often the section activity is simply taking questions on reading and lecture, going over assignments, and reviewing for exams. If this is what you intend, you should make this clear to the TAs and students. But even with this kind of section, it is wise to have the TAs come prepared with extra examples (a good source of these are the practice problems in the text that were not assigned, or problems from the *Test Bank* that will not be used on an exam). Have them organize each meeting into segments to be sure that time is devoted to each of the major topics covered since the last section meeting.

B. Treat Your TAs as Your Teaching Colleagues

TAs are usually graduate students who will be teaching courses themselves before long. Indeed, they may have TA'd this course more times than you have taught it, or may actually have taught it themselves. You can learn from them. And they are likely to work best with you if you show (and feel) respect for what they can contribute. I find it especially important to show this respect when I interact with my TAs in front of our students. I am also careful not to undermine their relations with students when I am talking to students individually.

I meet with my TAs before the term and give them a chance to review and suggest changes in my draft of the syllabus and my plans for the course. During the course I also discuss with them any changes before I make decisions and announce these to the class.

C. Treat Your TAs as Your Graduate Students

Your TAs are teaching colleagues, but they are also your students, learning how to teach. I provide them with guidance about all the topics in sections I through IV of this Chapter (not just having them read it, but discussing my own and their experience with these issues).

D. Meet with TAs Often

I meet with my TAs weekly, having them report on how their sections are going, taking suggestions, and discussing how the course as a whole is going. We also discuss the material coming up for the next week's sections. If an exam is approaching, we discuss its contents and how grading will be organized. I usually prepare an agenda for each meeting. (These meetings serve as an important source of input about how the students are doing in the course—it is striking the things TAs pick up from students that the students will never reveal to me.)

E. Provide Support and Remember Your TAs Are Human Beings

As graduate students, your TAs have a great many demands on them from their studies and research, as well as undergoing all of the stresses that go along with this period of their life. When a student is unkind to them or if they feel they are not doing an adequate job in their work as a TA, I find it best to provide as much emotional support as I can (a listening and understanding ear) before tackling the specific practical issues of what can be done. Also, I try at the start of each term to learn what special demands each TA may have coming up—such as qualifying exams, proposal dates, or seminar presentations—and to distribute the workload for different parts of the term among the TAs in a way that takes their individual needs into account.

F. Attend Closely to Your TA's Grading of Exams and Assignments

The grading of exams and assignments are crucial determinants of course atmosphere. Inexperienced TAs (like inexperienced instructors) tend to expect too much and grade too hard. They also tend to forget that undergraduates do not welcome unnecessary "constructive criticism." Thus, before my TAs ever grade an exam or assignment, I discuss with them the importance of providing positive feedback on what is done well and not being harsh or heavy handed in noting errors. I also plan with them, as a group, what the grading standards will be, both to be sure I find the standards appropriate and to be sure that all the TAs are using the same standards.

VI. Some Comments to Teaching Assistants

Being a TA for statistics is one of the most useful teaching assignments, for your own professional development, that you will have as a graduate student. First, it will dramatically strengthen your own mastery of statistics—a crucial tool if you plan a career involving research. Second, it will prepare you to teach statistics as an instructor yourself—an ability that will substantively enhance your value on the academic job market as well as make you a much appreciated colleague in many departments.

You also have the opportunity to be especially loved by the students. Students read the material and hear it in class, but often it does not really sink in until they discuss it in the section with you. The result is that you get the credit for the whole learning experience! (This can be hard on the instructor's ego, but good for yours. And if all the credit is not deserved, much of it is, since this does not happen unless you have done a good job with your part.)

My most important suggestions to you are the same as those I made to the instructor in Sections I through IV, above. Here are a few additional points:

A. Prepare for Sections

Don't just walk in and wait for questions. Even if all you will be doing is answering questions on the book and lecture, put an outline on the board of the topics that are involved (and then ask for questions topic by topic). Think out ahead of time one or two examples of things you anticipate students may be having trouble with. Also think out in advance what aspects of what has been covered are most important for the students to master and what aspects are relatively peripheral. This is something that is not obvious to many students, and a place you can really help.

If the section involves covering material not in the lecture (such as teaching them how to use a computer program or covering additional techniques), then you need to prepare just as you would for teaching any class (see the material in Section II above).

Of course, it is crucial that you have done the same reading as the students and have reviewed it again just before class. It is also important to have attended the lectures. If you do not know what the students have been exposed to, how can you help them make sense of it?

B. *Your Relation to Your Students*

You are probably only a little older than most of your students, and younger than some. Nevertheless, the students are taking the course and you are the TA precisely because you know more about the material than they do. This does not necessarily make you a better person or even generally more knowledgeable. But it does mean you are the one in the position to teach and they are in the position to learn (you also learn from them, of course). Thus your role should be one of a consultant, a specialist who is there to help. And if it is also your job to evaluate their performance in the course, you are in the best position to do that. Your duty is simply to be as accurate and even-handed as you can.

C. *Your Relation to the Course Instructor (Who Is Also a Human Being)*

It is the instructor's obligation to treat you with respect and be supportive of you in your role as TA. It is also your responsibility to treat the instructor with respect and to be supportive. In particular, it undermines the course as a whole, as well as the instructor's relation to the students, if you speak negatively to the students about the instructor or the way the course is being taught, or if you complain to them about the way the instructor is treating you or the other TAs. If you feel something is not going well in the course, or the course is not being run properly, you should speak to the instructor about it directly. Or if this is too difficult, send the instructor an anonymous note. You owe that to both the instructor and the students. Also, remember that your instructor is in a political relationship to the rest of the department. If you grumble to your advisor or some other faculty member about something to do with the course (even a casual remark), that could have very large repercussions for the instructor, especially if he or she is untenured.

A Final Word

Statistics is my favorite course to teach. This is partly, as I said at the outset, because I get to be a hero just for making it bearable. But it is also because of the tremendous rewards of seeing students who thought they could never learn statistics become, not just passing students, but knowledgeable ones. Or seeing the more confident types, who nevertheless disdain statistics, suddenly discovering its elegance and utility. If you are teaching statistics for the first time, I welcome you to these teaching pleasures.

Chapter B
Structuring the Course

This chapter discusses issues involved in structuring the course, ending with an example course syllabus. Four topics are covered:

I. Selection and Order of Topics
II. Assignments
III. Exams
IV. The Course Syllabus

I. Selection and Order of Topics

A. *Selection of Topics*

1. *The core material.* The minimum standard coverage of the introductory statistics course in psychology includes frequency tables and histograms, mean, standard deviation, the correlation coefficient, the normal curve, the t-test, analysis of variance, and chi-square. Thus if necessary the second half of Chapter 3 (the part on regression), Chapter 7 (on Power), the second half of Chapter 11 (on data transformations and nonparametric procedures) and Chapter 12 (on advanced procedures) could be omitted. (However, if Chapter 7 is omitted, students should be told to skip the discussions of power at the ends of Chapters 8-11).

2. *Regression.* The second half of Chapter 3 covers bivariate regression and gives a conceptual introduction to multiple regression. This material is difficult for some students and it is not an absolutely necessary part of the course. However, this material is very important for anyone hoping to make sense of journal articles in almost any area of the social and behavioral sciences.

3. *Power and effect size.* These topics, which in recent years have become an increasingly standard part of the basic course material (for the good reason that researchers have come to realize their great importance), are introduced in Chapter 7 and brought up again in every subsequent chapter. However, the coverage of these topics in the subsequent chapters is in a discrete section near each chapter's end, permitting the instructor who chooses to do so to omit Chapter 7 easily.

4. *Data transformations and nonparametric statistics.* Nonparametric methods are very commonly included in the minimum course and data transformations are quite common in today's journal articles. These two topics are covered in the second half of Chapter 11.

5. *Advanced statistical topics.* Chapter 12 offers a conceptual familiarity with many procedures too advanced to be covered in an introductory text, but often encountered in journal articles. In addition to the core material, this chapter requires at least understanding the material on multiple regression in Chapter 3; but does not depend on Chapters 7 or 11.

6 *Reading statistics in journal articles.* Each chapter includes a section on making sense of statistics as they are reported in psychology journal articles. It can be made optional without doing injury to the rest of the course.

7. *Boxes.* Each chapter contains one or two boxes presenting historical or other material intended to show the human side of statistics, or other material we think will interest students. Some instructors may choose to require these, but I prefer leaving them for optional enjoyment.

8. *Computational formulas.* The traditional computational formulas for each technique are provided in a footnote whenever the corresponding conceptual formula is first introduced. These are not at all necessary to any other aspect of the course.

9. *Recommendations about topic coverage.* In my opinion any course should include at least the core material. My additions, in order of preference, would be power and effect size (Chapter 7), regression (second half of Chapter 3), the material on advanced procedures (Chapter 12), and then the material on data transformations and nonparamtric procedures (second half of Chapter 11).

I always require students to know the material in each chapter on reading statistics in journal articles. I never require the boxes--they are intended to be pleasurable study breaks.

In a semester course at an institution with average to above-average ability students, I cover the entire book.

In a semester course with students who might have trouble with the course or a quarter course with average to above-average students, I cover the entire book except the second half of Chapter 4, the second half of Chapter 11, and all of Chapter 12. If the students are of very minimal ability, I would consider leaving out Chapter 7 and the corresponding material on power and effect size in each subsequent chapter, which is of moderate difficulty. Leaving all this out allows much more time for review.

B. *Order of Topics*

1. Prerequisites for chapters. The following table shows which chapters are prerequisites for other chapters.

Chapter	Chapters that must be read first									
1										
2	1									
3	1	2								
4	1	2								
5	1	2		4						
6	1	2		4	5					
7	1	2		4	5	6				
8	1	2		4	5	6	(7)*			
9	1	2		4	5	6	(7)	8		
10	1	2		4	5	6	(7)	8	9	
11	1	2		4	5	6	(7)	8	9	
12	1	2	3	4	5	6		8	9	10

----

*Chapter 7 is in parentheses because it can be omitted as a prerequisite to the chapters if students are told to omit the section on power and effect size in each of these chapters.

2. When to teach correlation and regression. Perhaps the most important implication of the table of chapter prerequisites is that the material on correlation and regression (Chapters 3) can easily be taught either in the order they appear in the book or later on.

The advantages of teaching them where they are in the book are (a) the students have just learned Z scores, which makes Chapter 3 much easier; and (b) correlation and regression are naturally understood as descriptive statistics, the next logical step from the univariate descriptive statistics learned in Chapters 1 and 2.

On the other hand, if Chapters 3 and 4 are taught after some or all of the inferential statistics technique chapters (4-11), then it is easy to include a discussion of the significance of a correlation coefficient when teaching this topic. Finally, the second half of Chapter 3 is relatively taxing. Thus, teaching Chapter 3 early can have advantages spreading out the "hard stuff" and catching students while they are fresh. It can also have disadvantages, discouraging some because of the abrupt jump in difficulty.

We have included the basic material on testing the significance of a correlation coefficient in Chapter 3, in a chapter appendix. If you cover Chapter 3 in the usual order, you may want students to go back to that appendix sometime after covering Chapter 8. If you decide to cover Chapter 3 later in the course (a good place would be right after the *t*-test chapters), then this appendix should be included when teaching the chapter.

II. Assignments

For most students to learn statistics, they need actively to work problems. I also find that the more writing about statistics the better, to engrain it in their minds and provide a solid preparation for the next topic.

A. Amount of Assignments

My policy is to assign about an hour's worth of problems for each class, to be turned in at the start of the next class session. I select a variety of problem types, using those with answers in the back of the book. These permit students to check their answers against those in the back of the book, but I do require them to show their work.

B. Marking Assignments

Unless your institution provides more than the usual funding for readers or TAs, it is not practical to provide much feedback to students on their daily assignments. I ask my TAs to look over the assignments and check that all the different parts were done while spot-checking a few more closely. (If time permits, they may also review more closely the work of students having difficulties, or when a student has specifically expressed concern about their answer to a particular problem.) But in general, the TA just marks the assignment as completed, without giving it further evaluation.

C. Assignment Requirements

I require *all* assignments to be completed to pass the course. I consider the working out of these problems as a central part of learning the course material, which exams can only partially evaluate.

D. Late Assignment Policy

I strongly discourage late assignments. Because the course material is largely cumulative, students who turn in assignments late (and hence probably do not learn that material as well) are going to do poorly on learning subsequent material--and bring down the entire level of class discussion.

I have tried several policies to encourage timeliness without imposing draconian discipline (and the attendant disruption to the course atmosphere from the grumbling of the guilty). The most successful has been a rule that a student is allowed two late assignments during the term without penalty. Each additional late assignment requires a short paper summarizing the statistics in a research article provided to the student by the instructor. (I usually require them to read a short research article, in their major if possible, that uses a topic covered in the course up to that point, and write an explanation to a lay person of the result in the article.)

I also emphasize that "on time" means the *beginning of the class*--otherwise, students miss class to complete the assignment. However, because there are other reasons students can be late, I usually also add the rule that a paper between 5 minutes and 24 hours late counts as half late.

III. Exams

In my experience, exams (and the grading of them) do the most to determine the atmosphere of the course.

A. Objectives of Exams

Below I describe, in what I consider their order of importance, the four objectives of exams in this course:

1. *Incentive for the student.* An exam encourages a concentrated review of the material. It seems to me that, for better or worse, half the learning that takes place in a course occurs in the 48-hour period preceding each exam. I am especially aware of this from the excellent teaching that is called forth from me by desperate students at the long review sessions I hold.

2. *Feedback to the student*. The graded exam gives students a realistic appraisal of how they are doing in the class. This can encourage students by reminding them how much they have learned. It can also be a rude awakening for those who have not mastered the material well, hopefully inspiring them to improve the situation. However, I have found that in statistics most students benefit more from the encouragement of seeing what they have learned than from the shock of seeing what they failed to get. Thus, I make it a priority in structuring exams to be sure that the problems provide average students a chance to demonstrate their accomplishments, even if this means the overall class average is relatively high.

3. *Feedback to the instructor*. The distribution of performance of students on the different parts of the exam provides the instructor valuable information about what the students are and are not learning well. One implication is that it is important to make a separate distribution (I find a histogram most helpful) of class performance for each problem or question and to review these carefully and consider what modifications might be made now and in future courses in light of what has been mastered and what is still shaky. Sometimes I find I need to change the schedule and spend an entire class reviewing some concept, instead of proceeding willy-nilly and leaving much of the class hopelessly behind.

4. *Basis for course grade*. Exams are the primary basis for assigning grades. In my opinion this is the least important value of an exam, and when this value comes in conflict with one of the above three, I give those three priority. Nevertheless, when constructing an exam I make an effort to be sure it will yield a distribution of student accomplishment, tap those aspects of student accomplishment that provide an appropriate basis for assigning a course grade, and be structured so that it can be scored reasonably objectively.

B. How Many Tests to Give?

1. *Advantages of giving a large number of exams*. Giving many exams assures that each segment of the course is mastered before proceeding, gives the student and the instructor ongoing feedback on how much has been learned, and provides a more reliable basis for a final grade. Based on these advantages, some statistics instructors give exams weekly--some even give short quizzes as part of each class.

2. *Disadvantages of giving a large number of exams*. Giving many exams constantly focuses the course on evaluation (and possibly quibbling over grades), takes up a lot of class time, and each exam must be prepared, printed, graded, recorded, and handed back. For these reasons, some statistics instructors give only a single midterm plus a final.

3. *My recommendation*: Compromise by giving four to five mid-term exams, one at the end of each major segment of the course, plus a final.

C. Content of Exams

The *Test Bank* that accompanies this text provides several kinds of test questions. Below I describe the pros and cons of each type, some possible mixes and lengths of exams that would be appropriate for different course situations, and the issue of whether exams should be cumulative.

1. Problem-and-essay questions. I have found the most useful test question is one in which the student is given a description of a study and its result (including data), then asked to carry out the appropriate statistical procedure, draw a conclusion, and explain what was done to a person who has never had a course in statistics. (To shorten the task, I usually modify the essay so that it is written to a person who knows some statistics, but not the material covered since the last exam.)

Advantages: Knowing that there will be this kind of question on the exams focuses the students' studying on the core skills I want them to gain. And their performance on this kind of question provides the most direct feedback to them and me of whether they have indeed gained what matters.

Disadvantages: First, such questions take a long time to answer. This means you cannot ask many of them, which in turn means low reliability (if they miss the point of a problem, a huge chunk of the exam is a zero) and a reduced range of topics that can be tested. Second, they are time-consuming to grade, and thus often impractical for large classes. Third, the grading of essay questions necessarily has a subjective component that can be a source of disruptive student quibbling. Finally, such questions put special emphasis on writing ability, and so special burdens on students with poor writing skills or for whom English is the second-language.

2. *Problem questions.* These are the standard statistics exam fare--the student is given a description of a study and data (or just data) and carries out the statistical computations. (I always require students to show their work at each stage of the problem.)

Advantages: These questions directly examine whether the student has learned the computation of the statistical procedures. If the problem does not indicate which procedure is to be used, such questions also require the student to determine this. (For example, does this problem require a t-test for independent or dependent means?) Since so much of a statistics course necessarily focuses on computation (and usually the assignments very heavily so), including such questions appropriately taps what the students have been studying. Answers are usually relatively brief, so several can be included, and they can be graded fairly rapidly and objectively. Finally, such questions minimally impact those not good at English.

Disadvantages: Problem questions do not necessarily get at underlying concepts, but may show only a rote memorization of a formula and the ability to plug numbers into it. Nor are such problems appropriate for testing vocabulary, for example, or how to read statistics in a research article. In addition, such problems give great emphasis to computational skills. Thus students who understood the ideas, but are not agile on a calculator or facile with numbers, may not be able to show what they have learned. Finally, although problems of this kind take less time to answer and are easier to grade than problems with essays, they are nevertheless moderately time consuming. Thus, you still can only include a relatively small number of such problems in any one exam, which creates low reliability and limits topic coverage. And for large classes, grading problems is still a substantial task.

3. *Reading-statistics essays.* A unique feature of this text is its emphasis on reading and interpreting statistics as they are presented in social and behavioral science journal articles, and the *Test Bank* includes exam questions that evaluate how well students have mastered these skills. These questions consist of a brief description of a study followed by a short excerpt (or table) from the results section. The student is asked to explain what the result means to a person who has never had a course in statistics (or who has only learned the statistics material covered through the last exam).

Advantages: These essays directly assess whether the student has mastered one of the most important objectives of the course. They also tap the student's general mastery of the principles behind the technique. Further, these essays often put special emphasis on evaluating the role of power and effect size in a relatively concrete context.

Disadvantages: These essays share many of the disadvantages of problem/essays: Each takes up a lot of test time, the grading is time consuming and somewhat subjective, and they penalize those with poor writing skills or whose native language is not English.

4. *Multiple-choice questions.* Multiple-choice questions mainly focus on definitions of terms, understanding of concepts, and retention of factual material.

Advantages: The grading is economical and objective--especially important in large classes or where the instructor wants to give daily short quizzes. In addition, studying for multiple-choice questions focuses the student on concepts (as opposed to rote computation). Finally, a relatively large number of multiple-choice items can be included on an exam, making for higher reliability and giving the opportunity to cover a broad range of topics.

Disadvantages: Multiple-choice questions only minimally tap computational skills (which is usually one of the main things students are being asked to do in their assignments) and do not provide any opportunity for student creativity or expression. Students also often report a sense of mechanization about multiple-choice exams, a feeling that they are being treated as numbers. Finally, in my experience, multiple choice exams seem to be most prone to student quibbling about the right answers.

5. *Fill-in-the-blank items.* These items primarily emphasize definitions of terms and knowledge of factual material.

Advantages: Fill-in items share much of the grading advantages of multiple-choice questions, as well as also being rapid for the student to complete. But fill-in items can be superior when they give the student the sense of a more personal connection with the instructor; and they test recall, not just recognition.

Disadvantages: Fill-in items share most of the limitations of multiple-choice questions, are even less well suited to assessing conceptual material, are somewhat less economical and objective to grade, and can be even more troublesome for those with language deficits.

6. *Recommended mixes and exam length.* The main question is whether it is practical to grade essays and problems. If it is, I prefer a mix of one essay (of either type), and two or three problems. I have found that as long as the students know that the exam will include at least one essay--but do not know on which subtopic it will focus--they study the concepts thoroughly. And having this mix, as opposed to all essay-type problems, gives me a chance to cover several different topics (allowing the students to show their competence at each), and to increase the reliability of the overall exam.

For a 50-minute class period, I give one essay and one or two not-very-complex problems. For a 75-minute class, I give one essay and two or three other problems (depending on the complexity of the problems).

If it is not practical to include essays and problems, a mix of multiple choice and fill-in items does a quite good job. Depending on the length of the testing time and the ability level of the students, I would use 20 to 40 multiple choice and 5 to 15 fill-ins.

7. *Should exams be cumulative?* Much of the material in a statistics course is intrinsically cumulative. For example, almost every topic after the start requires a mastery of mean and standard deviation. Nevertheless, I have found that students are better able to focus on mastering what they have just learned if I assure them that the upcoming test will cover only that material, with previous material only acting as a foundation for the current topics.

I do give cumulative final exams. In this case, I want them to review the whole course and be able to identify which methods are appropriate to a given research situation.

D. What to Tell Students in Advance About an Exam

1. *Why tell them anything?* I talk about an exam in advance (a) to reduce their anxiety so that over arousal does not interfere with learning and (b) to focus their attention on what I most want them to master.

2. *What to say?* To achieve the above goals, I usually tell them the kind of exam questions to expect (how many of each type) and the general topics to be covered. If practical, I provide this information on a printed hand out. For example, if the upcoming exam were on Chapter 8-10, I might tell them that there will be three problems, one on each of the three main types of problems (dependent and independent means t-tests and one-way analysis of variance), one of which would either include an essay or be a reading and interpreting essay.

3. *Practice exams.* To relieve anxiety for the first exam, I generally give my students a practice exam, with answers. I make up the practice exam to follow precisely the format of the real exam, using items in the *Test Bank* not used on the actual exam. However, I emphasize, both in class and in print on the practice exam, that the specific content will not be identical. (For example, if it were for Chapters 8-10, the practice exam might include a problem/essay for a one-way analysis of variance, but on the actual exam there might be a reading-statistics essay instead, on either kind of t-test instead of one-way analysis of variance.)

If you have assigned the *Student's Study Guide* (or made it available as an optional text), providing practice exams is especially unnecessary after the first exam (which gives them the chance to see your particular exam format)--though I still give them a list of study question numbers from the study guide that would amount to the equivalent of the upcoming exam.

E. Exam Feedback and Grading

1. Posting answers. As soon as the last person in the class has completed the exam, I post the correct answers outside the classroom. This way students can find out immediately how well they have done. More important, students who have made errors do not go home convinced of the correctness of a mistake. This approach also greatly minimizes upset when the tests are eventually returned, as well as easing the pressure on the instructor or TAs to grade the test rapidly.

2. General grading process. Unless grading is mechanical (as for multiple-choice), I do one problem at a time for all students. If I have TAs doing the grading, I have them divide up the problems rather than each doing the tests of their own students--this way the grading across students with different TAs is standardized.

3. Grading essays. I treat grading essays much like a content analysis. I develop a coding scheme, allotting points for each aspect of the answer and modifying the scheme based on a subset of students' answers--it is often necessary to make further rules along the way. (I go back and regrade the papers in my initial set, to be sure they get the benefit of adjustments made later.) Also as in content analysis, I prefer to have the grading done blind to the student's name, gender, etc. (Identifying tests by student ID number accomplishes this adequately in most cases.) However, although I like to have an organized scheme for grading these essays, with points for each part laid out, I also make adjustments up for someone who has missed some specific point but demonstrated an unusually good grasp of the problem overall.

When grading essay/problems, it is extremely important to focus on the logic, and not to give many points for simply describing the series of computations in words. Unless this grading norm is established on the first test, the essays will be much less effective in ensuring the right kind of studying for exams.

Finally, I try to make as great an effort to note really good answers (and parts of answers) as I do to note errors and confusions.

4. Grading computational problems. I first check if the final answer is correct. If it is not, I look at the steps of computation and take off only a small number of points for an error along the way, provided the rest of the computations are correct leading to that wrong number. However, I take off more points when an error is sufficiently large that, had the student been thinking about the meaning of the numbers, he or she would have realized the error. (For example, if a correlation coefficient comes out greater than 1). In fact, I tell students in advance that if they realize that the numbers are not making sense but cannot figure out where their error is, they should note that on the test and I will take off fewer points.

5. Returning exams. Prior to returning exams or giving students any information about exam distributions, I look at the distributions. If many students have done poorly on a particular problem or question, I reconsider the grading on that item (and may even drop it). If the overall mean is low I may add a constant or percentage to everyone's score. Although this does not in any way affect final grades if a curve is being used, it can have a dramatic impact on how the students feel about their performance and about the course.

I never return exams at the beginning of a class session. Doing so substantially undermines attention to the lecture or discussion. If exams are to be reviewed in class or a section, I return the exam and do this discussion during the last part of the period. If exams are simply returned at the end of class, I do try to arrange to stay after to talk to those who want to discuss the exam (or have the TAs stay), or I arrange an office hour for me or my TAs shortly after the test.

6. Minimizing student disagreements about grading of their exams. The main way I avert disagreements (besides grading carefully) is to post a copy of the exam with the correct answers at the end of the exam so that students are able to determine right away if they disagree with an answer. Any disagreements about the correct answers must be turned in to me, *in writing*, within 48 hours of the exam. (I announce this policy prior to each exam and post it with the correct answers.)

This policy really encourages students to review the correct answers right away, while the material is fresh in their minds. It puts disagreements into writing, where they are less likely to be confrontive. It lessens classroom hostilities. And it gives me a chance to make adjustments prior to finalizing grades. Particularly when multiple choice or fill-in questions are used, this policy averts a great many problems. It also usually leads to at least one changed answer per test (which lets students know you are responsive to their input).

F. Make-up Exams

In any course it is rare not to have at least one student request to make up a missed exam. However, giving a make-up requires creating a new exam, finding a time and place to administer it, grading it, and adjusting scores to match those on the regular exam. Organizing a time can be particularly difficult if there are several students who need to take such an exam. Also, it can be difficult to determine who genuinely deserves the opportunity and who is making up an excuse because they did not feel prepared.

Having tried different policies, I think the following works best: Students who can demonstrate a legitimate medical or similar reason are allowed to miss one exam during the term. Their grade for that exam will be the average of the other exams (not counting the final).

IV. The Course Syllabus

Here is an example course syllabus. The various policies are based on the issues discussed in this chapter. The schedule assumes a 13-week semester, Monday-Wednesday-Friday course, taught to average to above-average students. As noted in Section IA, with less able students or when teaching on a quarter system (and also taking holidays into account), less material would be covered. This example syllabus also does not include computer lab sessions--a topic considered in Chapter D of this *Manual*.

University of North America
Winter, 1997
Introduction to Statistics
for the Social and Behavioral Sciences
MWF 10 AM - Gosset Hall 105

INSTRUCTOR —
Jane Professor, Ph.D.
Office: 308 Gosset Hall
Office Hours: Mondays 11-1
Phone-4208 Email-JPROF@UNA

SYLLABUS

In this course you should gain the following:

1. The ability to understand and explain to others the statistical analyses in reports of social and behavioral science research.
2. A preparation for more advanced courses in statistical methods.
3. The ability to identify the appropriate statistical procedure for many basic research situations and to carry out the necessary computations.
4. Further development of your quantitative and analytic thinking skills.

Methods of learning:

1. Reading the assigned material, which includes following the numeric examples closely and writing down questions about anything not entirely clear to you. Reading statistics requires close study and rereading, not just reading through once as you might an ordinary book.
2. Testing your knowledge and reviewing each lecture using your *Student's Study Guide*.
3. Completing the assigned practice problems (and turning them in on time). Statistics is a skill--it is necessary to DO statistics, not just read and understand.
4. Attending lectures, listening closely, asking questions--be sure to have done the reading *first*. DON'T fall behind!
5. Attending discussion sections led by the teaching assistants--be sure to bring questions from the reading with you. This is your chance to get real help with what is not completely clear and to pursue deeply whatever has excited you (yes, there can be exciting things in statistics!).
6. Studying for, taking, and reviewing answers for exams.

Required texts:

1. Aron, A., & Aron, E. N. (1997). *Statistics for the Social Sciences: A Brief Course*. Upper Saddle River, NJ: Prentice-Hall.
2. Aron, A. (1997). *Student's study guide to accompany Aron and Aron's Statistics for the Social Sciences*. Upper Saddle River, NJ: Prentice-Hall.

Basis of evaluation:

1. Four mid-term exams and a final.
2. Completion of assignments on time.
3. Participation in class and sections.

About exams:

1. Each of the four mid-term exams will cover only the material since the last exam (except to the extent that the previous material is necessary for understanding the new). The final is cumulative.
2. *There will be NO make up quizzes* and *a missed quiz counts as a zero.*
3. Those who provide a *written* medical excuse can drop that quiz. Most other excuses will not be accepted.

About assignments:

1. *All* assignments must be completed by the start of the final exam to pass the course.
2. Assignments are due at the *start* of each class.
3. Assignments turned in between 5 minutes and 24 hours after they are due are 1/2 late.
4. Two late assignments will be allowed.
5. For each additional late assignment you must write a short paper summarizing in your own words the statistical conclusions of a research article assigned by the professor.

Knowledge of mathematics:

The course does not emphasize mathematics. There will be many calculations, but these require nothing more than elementary high-school algebra. The emphasis, instead, is on understanding the LOGIC of the statistical methods. The most important part of each exam will be either (a) a problem in which you use a statistical procedure to analyze the results of a study and then write an essay explaining what you have done to someone who has no knowledge of statistics or (b) a problem in which you are presented with the results of a study and must explain what they mean to a person who has never had a course in statistics.

Calculators:

I *strongly* encourage you to use a hand calculator for doing your assignments, and I *will* permit calculators during tests. I would much prefer you to spend your time developing an understanding of the statistical concepts rather than adding and dividing numbers. A simple calculator that adds, subtracts, divides, multiplies, and takes square roots should be of great help. Since you must show your work on all assignments and exams, calculators that also do statistical calculations will not be of much help, so don't feel any pressure to spend a lot of money. About $10 or less should do.

Wk	Day	Topic	Reading	Assignment Due
		Part I: Descriptive Statistics		
1	Mon	Introduction/Administrative	Intro	
	Wed	Frequency Tables & Graphs	Ch 1	
	Fri	Distribution Shapes	Ch 1	Ch 1: 1, 4
2	Mon	The Mean	Ch 2	
	Wed	Variance and Standard Deviation	Ch 2	Ch 2: 1, 2
	Fri	Z Scores	Ch 2	Ch 2: 5
3	Mon	Correlation I	Ch 3	
	Wed	Correlation II	Ch 3	Ch 3: 1
	Fri	Regression	Ch 3	Ch 3: 6
4	Mon	Review		
	Wed	First Exam		
		Part II: Basics of Inferential Statistics		
	Fri	Normal Curve	Ch 4	Ch 4: 1, 2
5	Mon	Probability	Ch 4	Ch 4: 3, 4
	Wed	Hypothesis Testing Logic I	Ch 5	Ch 5: 1, 2
	Fri	Hypothesis Testing Logic II	Ch 5	Ch 5: 3, 4
6	Mon	Distributions of Means	Ch 6	Ch 6: 2, 4
	Wed	Hypothesis Testing with $N > 1$	Ch 6	Ch 6: 3, 5
	Fri	Power and Effect Size I	Ch 7	Ch 7: 1
7	Mon	Power and Effect Size II	Ch 7	Ch 7: 3
	Wed	Power and Effect Size III	Ch 7	Ch 7: 4, 6
	Fri	Review		
8	Mon	Second Exam		
		Part III: t-test and Analysis of Variance		
	Wed	One-Sample t-Test	Ch 8	Ch 8: 1, 4
	Fri	Dependent Means t-Test	Ch 8	Ch 8: 3, 6
9	Mon	Independent Means t-Test I	Ch 9	Ch 9: 2
	Wed	Independent Means t-Test II	Ch 9	Ch 9: 3, 5
	Fri	One-Way Analysis of Variance	Ch 10	Ch 10: 1
10	Mon	Introduction to Factorial Designs	Ch 10	Ch 10: 2, 4
	Wed	Review		
	Fri	Third Exam		
		Part IV: Additional Topics		
11	Mon	Chi-Square Test of Goodness of Fit	Ch 11	Ch 11: 1, 2
	Wed	Chi-Square Test of Independence	Ch 11	Ch 11: 3, 4
	Fri	Data Transforms/Rank-Order Tests	Ch 12	Ch 11: 7
12	Mon	Advanced Methods I	Ch 12	Ch 12: 1
	Wed	Advanced Methods II	Ch 12:	Ch 12: 4, 7
	Fri	Review		
13	Mon	Fourth Exam		
	Wed	Review		
	Fri	Review		

        Final Exam [Insert date, time, location]

Chapter C

Lecture Examples Based on a Questionnaire Administered to Your Students

On the first day of class, I administer a questionnaire to my students, the data from which I use as the basis of lecture examples throughout the course. Students find such examples particularly engaging since they are based on their own and their classmates' responses.

I have made this procedure very easy for you to use. In this chapter I provide the questionnaire I use in a form you can photocopy. Once you have administered it, you can enter the data onto the computer and compute examples using the methods covered in each chapter. I also provide as part of this manual ready-to-photocopy transparencies of research examples. You can use these as a model for making transparencies based on your own class's data.

If you are teaching a large class (75 or more students), it is even simpler. Just record the data, send it to me, and I will provide (within 1 to 2 weeks) a set of transparencies of lecture examples for several key chapters based on your class's data.

This chapter includes the following two sections:

I. An Example Questionnaire You Can Use
II. For those with Large Classes: How to Record and Send in the Data to Have
   Lecture Examples Made Up For You

I. An Example Questionnaire You Can Use

The questionnaire on the next page comes from one being used in a research project Elaine Aron and I are conducting on the "highly sensitive person" (See E. Aron & A. Aron, "Sensitivity-Processing Sensitivity and its Relation to Introversion and Emotionality," *Journal of Personality and Social Psychology*, 1977). I have used this questionnaire in my statistics classes as a basis for constructing lecture examples because the questions are so varied and interesting to most students. The questions were selected primarily for their usefulness in creating good class examples and give a somewhat skewed impression of the research project; this questionnaire is *not* a measure of the trait.

Permission is hereby granted to anyone who is using the Aron and Aron text in their course to reproduce this questionnaire for administration to the students in that course.

I distribute the questionnaire to students at the very start of the first day of class, while students are arriving and getting settled. After most of the students are done, I ask them to fold their questionnaires in half (to help maintain anonymity) and pass them to the aisles where I collect them. About 10 minutes before the end of class, I collect any remaining questionnaires and explain the purpose of the questionnaires:

This questionnaire consists of items taken from a longer questionnaire being used in a research program on "highly sensitive people" conducted by Elaine Aron and Arthur Aron, the authors of your textbook. I will use your responses in my lectures as data for examples of the various statistical techniques you will be learning in the course. Since this questionnaire has been used in other statistics classes, we will also be able to compare the responses of our class to those of students at other colleges.

The research program for which these questions were developed focuses on people who are very sensitive to sensory stimulation, so that they become uncomfortably over aroused sooner than others by noise, a lot to look at, and so forth. It is a trait that appears to be inherited, to occur in at least twenty percent of the population, and to be about equally common in men and women. (It is not the same as introversion or shyness, although it can lead to these because people are one common source of stimulation in our lives.) This is *not* a measure of sensitivity, but a means of studying its aspects and effects.

The last question is from research on adult attachment style conducted by Cindy Hazan and Philip Shaver (1987). It is intended to assess your typical style of relating to intimate others.

Questionnaire

Your answers to this questionnaire are completely anonymous. Do not write your name on it.

You are not required to complete this questionnaire, and you should not answer any questions that you feel uncomfortable about or prefer not to answer for any reason.

Your answers and those of your classmates in this course will provide data for examples in lectures throughout the term on each of the various statistical methods you will be learning. The data from this class will also be sent to a data base for use in a large personality-psychology research project.

Please answer each question, honestly and accurately, according to the way you personally feel, using the following scale:

1	2	3	4	5	6	7
Not at All			Moderately		Extremely	

1 Are you introverted?
2 Are you easily overwhelmed by strong sensory input?
3 Do you make a point to avoid violent movies and TV shows?
4 Do you find yourself thinking about some movies the next day?
5 Do you avoid crowds (at malls, carnivals, fairs, etc.)?
6 Are you made uncomfortable by loud noises?
7 Did you tend to fall in love in your early school years (from 5 to 12 years old)?
8 Do you tend to fall in love very hard?
9 Were you prone to hide as a child (under beds or tables, in closets, bushes, etc.)?
10 When you must compete or be observed while performing a task, do you become so nervous or shaky that you do much worse than you would otherwise?
11 Would you characterize your childhood as troubled?
12 Were you close to your father?
13 Was your father involved in your family during your childhood?
14 Were you close to your mother?
15 Was your mother fond of infants and small children (liking to hold and cuddle them, have them around her)?
16 Was alcoholism a problem in your immediate family while you were growing up?
17 When you have a lot to do in a short amount of time, do you get "rattled"?
18 Would you prefer to live out in the country with not many people around?
19 Were you sexually or physically abused as a child?
20 To what extent are you a "morning person?"
21 Do you find yourself needing to withdraw during busy days, into bed or into a darkened room or any place where you can have some privacy and relief from stimulation?
22 Are you a tense or worried person by nature?
23 Are you prone to fears?
24 Do you cry easily?
25 Do you startle easily?
26 Do you like having just a few close friends (as opposed to a large circle of friends)?
27 Do you make it a high priority to arrange your life to avoid upsetting or overwhelming situations?
28 A "highly sensitive person" has been defined as someone who is highly introverted and/or easily overwhelmed by sensory stimulation. To what extent are you a highly sensitive person?

Background Questions: Gender   Age   Number of older siblings

[ ]   Check here if you have taken this questionnaire before.

Please read the following three alternatives and decide which best describes your feelings. Then CHECK ONE.

[ ]   I find it relatively easy to get close to others and am comfortable depending on them and having them depend on me. I don't often worry about being abandoned or about someone getting too close to me.
[ ]   I am somewhat uncomfortable being close to others: I find it difficult to allow myself to depend on them. I am nervous when anyone gets too close, and often love partners want me to be more intimate than I feel.
[ ]   I find that others are reluctant to get as close as I would like. I often worry that my partner doesn't really love me or won't want to stay with me. I want to merge completely with another person and this desire sometimes scares people away.

II. How to Record and Send in the Data to Have
Lecture Examples Made Up For You

As soon as I receive the data from your administration of the questionnaire, I will quickly analyze your data and send you a complete set of lecture examples made up for copying onto transparencies. In most cases, I can send these to you within two weeks of receiving your data.

Please send us your data in a computer file of one of the following types:

1. *IBM type (MS-DOS) computer:* Save your data in what is called   "Text," "DOS" or "ASCII" format. (Almost all word processing programs have an option for saving your data in this format.) Mail you disk to me at the following address:

> Arthur Aron, Ph.D.
> Psychology Department
> State University of New York at Stony Brook
> Stony Brook, NY

2. *Any system that you can use to send electronic mail.* (Most college mainframe computers have this capacity. Also, it is usually possible to transfer a file from your personal computer, including Macintosh computers, to the college mainframe). The file should not be encoded in any way. Send the file to me directly at the following electronic mail address:

> ARON@CATS.BITNET

Along with the data, please send a note including:

1. Your return address.

2. Confirmation that you are using the Aron & Aron text in this course.

3.   The dates you plan to cover each chapter.

4. Permission to use your data as part of an international data base being assembled on the highly sensitive person. (Your agreement to this use of the data is not required, but will be much appreciated. We realize that at some institutions you may need approval from a human subjects committee if the data will be used for any purpose other than class demonstration.) Also, please indicate if there is anything about the administration to your class that would make the data not suitable for inclusion in this data base.

The file itself should be typed so that there is one line per student. Within each line, use the layout described in the following table:

Format for Entering Each Line of Data (One Questionnaire per Line)

Column	Entry (what you type into that column)
1-4	Subject Number (a number of your choice)
5	
6	Question 1 Answer (that is, the number they give from 1 through 7)
7	
8	Question 2 Answer
9	
10	Question 3 Answer
11	
12	Question 4 Answer
13	
14	Question 5 Answer
15	

16	Question 6 Answer
17	
18	Question 7 Answer
19	
20	Question 8 Answer
21	
22	Question 9 Answer
23	
24	Question 10 Answer
25	
26	Question 11 Answer
27	
28	Question 12 Answer
29	
30	Question 13 Answer
31	
32	Question 14 Answer
33	
34	Question 15 Answer
35	
36	Question 16 Answer
37	
38	Question 17 Answer
39	
40	Question 18 Answer
31	
32	Question 14 Answer
33	
34	Question 15 Answer
35	
36	Question 16 Answer
37	
38	Question 17 Answer
39	
40	Question 18 Answer
41	
42	Question 19 Answer
43	
44	Question 20 Answer
45	
46	Question 21 Answer
47	
48	Question 22 Answer
49	
50	Question 23 Answer
51	
52	Question 24 Answer
53	
54	Question 25 Answer
55	
56	Question 26 Answer
57	
58	Question 27 Answer
59	
60	Question 28 Answer
61	
62	Gender (use f or m)
63	
64-65	Age
66	
67-68	Number of older siblings (if just one digit, put a 0 first—ex. if number is 1, put "01", and if the number is 0 or it is left blank, enter "00")
69	
70	Put an "x" if they have ever taken the test before, or leave blank otherwise.
71	
72	Final question (enter a 1 if they checked the first paragraph, 2 if they checked the second paragraph, 3 if they checked the third)

NOTE: "Column" refers to the number of spaces across the page, starting from the left margin. The first space on the left edge is column number 1. If nothing is shown under "Entry", leave the column empty. Also, if a student has failed to answer a question, leave the column blank for that item.

Chapter D
Using the Computer in the Statistics Course

This chapter examines issues and provides suggestions regarding using the computer in your course. I have divided the material into four sections:

I. Advantages and Disadvantages of Using the Computer with this Course
II. Computer Software Packages Compatible with this Course
III. Facilities and Equipment Needed

I. Advantages and Disadvantages of Using the Computer with this Course

A. Advantages

1. *It familiarizes students with the way data are analyzed in actual behavioral and social science research.* This serves as an experiential path, giving the student a better sense of what it is like to be inside of the research process. In addition, it prepares the student for advanced courses that use these methods and gives them tools they can use in analyzing student projects of their own.

2. *It provides students the opportunity to conduct analyses quickly.* This permits them to carry out exercises involving variations on data sets that illustrate various statistical principles. It also encourages them to try out alternative data analysis schemes of their own.

3. *It carries a sense of excitement.*

B. Disadvantages

1. *It is time consuming.* Teaching students to use the computer to analyze data usually takes considerable teaching effort. Even today, many students are not even familiar with using the computer for word processing. So they must be made familiar with such issues as handling the keyboard, using disks, and creating and saving files. (If a mainframe is used, accounts must be created and they must be taught about logging on and off and such.) Finally, of course, the software program itself must be taught.

2. *It can be confusing to students.* Learning statistics is hard enough for many students. Learning to use the computer at the same time can make the experience overwhelming. I often find that even half-way through the course a few students are still struggling with handling the menus when they should be working on learning the concepts and methods.

3. *Facilities and equipment are required.*

C. Circumstances Under Which I Recommend Using the Computer

Presuming appropriate facilities and equipment were available, I would use the computer in my course under any of four conditions:

1. *The course includes a substantial laboratory component.* Ideally, this would include about 2 hours of lab time each week (with appropriate unit credit for a laboratory course provided to students).

2. *A small class of very good students.*

3. *Nearly all students are already comfortable using a computer system of the type to be used in the course.*

4. *The course is expected to provide students the skills needed to analyze substantial data of their own.*

II. Computer Software Packages Compatible with this Course

The supplements that accompany the Aron & Aron text include instructions and examples for SPSS 6.1 for Windows. SPSS is one of the most widely used statistical packages in psychology, available at nearly every university, so that familiarity with it is likely to be particularly useful to the student who goes on to graduate school. With some effort, you could modify the material in our supplementary materials to create your own instructions and examples to use with other statistical packages, such as SAS or Minitab. It is also possible that some other instructor has done this already.

III. Facilities and Equipment Needed

Whatever package you use, each student needs access to the package and the appropriate computer system for sufficient time to complete assignments, practice, and attempt some creative uses of their own.

If a personal computer-based system is used and copies of the package are made available to students, some students will be able to work at home on their own machines. However, do not overestimate the number of students who are likely to have the appropriate system for the package you are using. Many students do not have any computer system; many have dedicated word processing systems; some have older or unusual systems that will not run your software.

If students do not each purchase copies of the program (in which case, manuals are included), it is important to arrange for several copies of the manual to be available at the computer lab.

Introduction to the Student
and
Chapter 1
Displaying the Order in a Group of Numbers

Instructor's Summary of Chapter

Difficulty of course. We have never had a student who could pass other college-level social science courses who could not also pass this course--though for many students this course requires more work.

Reasons for social science students to learn statistical methods: Reading the research literature, conducting research, and developing analytic and critical thinking.

How to gain the most from this course: Attend to the concepts (not just the numbers), master each concept before going on to the next, keep up with reading and assignments, study especially intensely during the first half of the course, and study with other students.

Descriptive statistics summarize and make understandable a group of numbers collected in a research study.

Frequency tables organize the numbers into a table in which each of the possible values is listed along the left from highest to lowest, accompanying each value by the number of cases that have that value.

Grouped frequency tables are used when there are a large number of different values. The frequencies are given for intervals which include a range of values. An interval size should be selected so that the total number of intervals is between 5 and 15; the interval size is a common, simple number; and each interval starts with a multiple of the interval size.

Histograms and frequency polygons. A histogram is a kind of bar graph in which the height of each bar represents the frequency for a particular value or interval. In a frequency polygon a line connects dots, the height of each of which represents the frequency for a particular value or interval.

Distribution shapes. The general shape of the histogram or frequency polygon can be unimodal, bimodal, multimodal, or rectangular; symmetrical or skewed; light-tailed or heavy-tailed in relation to the normal curve.

How the procedures of this chapter are reported in research articles. When frequency tables appear in research articles, it is usually in order to compare distributions and often involves frequencies (and percentages) for various categories. Histograms and frequency polygons rarely appear in articles, though the shapes of distributions are occasionally described in words.

Box 1.1. Math Anxiety, Statistics Anxiety, and You: A Message for Those of You Who Are Truly Worried about This Course. Summarizes research and thinking on various kinds of anxiety associated with studying statistics and methods for coping with these anxieties.

Box 1.2. Gender, Ethnicity, and Math Performance. Reviews research and thinking on gender and ethnic differences in math and statistics performance, emphasizing the lack of evidence for differences in underlying abilities.

Lecture 1.1: Introduction to the Course

Materials

Lecture outline
Transparencies of syllabus
Questionnaires
Syllabi
Enrollment forms (as appropriate to your institution)

Outline for Blackboard

[Name and number of course and name of instructor]

I. Complete Questionnaires
II. Why Study Statistics?
III. What Will You Learn in this Course?
IV. Introductions
V. Course Structure and Requirements
VI. Administrative Matters
VII. Review this Class

Instructor's Lecture Outline

I.   Complete Questionnaires
   NOTE: The questionnaire and description of its content are provided in Chapter C of this
      Manual.
   A. Distribute questionnaires as students enter classroom.
   B. Collect questionnaires when nearly all are done (the remainder can finish during class).
   C. Explain briefly content of questionnaire and how it will be used for data for examples
      throughout the course (see material in Chapter C of this *Manual*).

II.   Why Study Statistics?
   A. It is required for social science majors! But why is it required?
   B. Statistical methods are essential tools used in most social science research. Therefore:
      1. This course prepares you for later courses, which usually require reading research articles.
      2. This course prepares you for more advanced statistics courses, which equip you to use statistics in
         research you conduct yourself.
   C. This course often meets a general education requirement in quantitative reasoning. But
      why is there such a requirement, and how does social science statistics fulfill this
      requirement?
      1. Social science statistics involves abstract logical and numeric methods.
      2. Mastering this methods develops your ability to think clearly and very precisely about these kinds of
         abstractions--something every educated person ought to be able to.

III. What Will You Learn in this Course?
  A. How to *understand* statistical methods. Note: The course is not very math-oriented, but is very logic-oriented.
    1. You will write essays describing statistical procedures as well as carrying them out.
    2. We will emphasize "definitional formulas," which express the concepts, rather than "computational formulas," which ease computation but obscure the concepts.
  B. Hand out syllabi and systematically go through goals and topics. [An example syllabus is included in Chapter B of this *Manual*.]

IV. Introductions
  A. Introduce yourself.
  B. Introduce any teaching assistants.
  C. Ask students about themselves using the following categories and any others you think are appropriate (if a small class, each introduces self; if a large class, ask for numbers of students in each category):
    1. What is your major?
    2. Year?
    3. Have you taken statistics before?

V. Course Structure and Requirements: Read and discuss each section of syllabus--be sure to discuss any aspects involving using a computer and any discussion or laboratory sections.

VI. Administrative Matters
  A. Instructor's and teaching assistants' office hours.
  B. Organizational matters such as enrollment, etc., as required by your institution.

VII. Review this Class: Use blackboard outline.

Lecture 1.2: Frequency Tables

Materials

Lecture outline
Transparency 1.1
Questionnaires (for those who missed first class)
Syllabi (for those who missed first class)

Outline for Blackboard

I.   Organizational Matters
II. Roles of Statistics in Research
III. Frequency Tables
IV. Grouped Frequency Tables
V.   Review this Class

Instructor's Lecture Outline

I.   Organizational Matters
   A. Be sure each student has a syllabus; answer questions on course structure, etc.
   B. Arrange for those who missed the first class to complete the questionnaire.
   C. Complete any remaining administrative matters.

II. Roles of Statistics in Research
   A. Describe data--"descriptive statistics." Focus of beginning part of course and foundation of rest of course.
   B. Make inferences based on data--"inferential statistics." Focus of most of course after beginning, but builds on beginning material.

III. Frequency Tables
   A. General question: Given a set of numbers, how can we make sense of them? Show TRANSPARENCY 1.1 top (example of data from horn-honking study) and discuss.
   B. Show TRANSPARENCY 1.1 middle (frequency table for horn-honking study) and discuss:
     1. Key terms:
        a. Frequency: Number of cases in a given category or of a particular score).
        b. Frequency distribution: The pattern of frequencies over different categories or scores.
     2. Points in constructing a frequency table:
        a. Go from highest to lowest.
        b. Meaning of symbols at top.
        c. All cases are included.
        d. Percentages.
        e. Sometimes cumulative frequency is included as an additional column.

IV. Grouped Frequency Tables
   A. Needed to make large distributions more comprehensible.
   B. Show how grouped frequency tables are derived. Show TRANSPARENCY 1.1 bottom
      (grouped frequency table from horn-honking study) and discuss.

V.   Review Class: Use blackboard outline.

Lecture 1.3: Describing a Distribution Graphically

Materials

Lecture outline
Transparencies 1.2 through 1.8

Outline for Blackboard

I.   Review
II. Histograms
III. Frequency Polygons
IV. Shapes of Distributions
V.   Review this Class

Instructor's Lecture Outline

I.   Review
A. Descriptive statistics.
B. Frequency tables.
C. Grouped frequency tables.

II. Histograms
A. Purpose: Provides a picture of the distribution.
B. Show TRANSPARENCY 1.2 top (stress-ratings histogram) and use it to explain steps of constructing a histogram:
 1. Begin with frequency table.
 2. Make a scale of values (lowest to highest) along a line at the bottom of the page.
 3. Make a scale of frequencies along a line rising from left edge of bottom line.
 4. Place a box for each case above its value.

III. Frequency Polygons: Explain principle using TRANSPARENCY 1.2 bottom (stress-rating example from text).

IV. Shapes of Distributions
A. Unimodal, bimodal, and rectangular.
 1. Show TRANSPARENCIES 1.3 and 1.4 (examples of these three shapes) and discuss.
 2. Show TRANSPARENCY 1.2 top (histogram of stress-rating examples) and discuss.
B. Symmetric versus skewed.
 1. Show TRANSPARENCIES 1.5 and 1.6 (examples of these shapes from text) and discuss.
C. Normal versus light-tailed or heavy-tailed distributions.
 1. Show TRANSPARENCY 1.7 (examples of these shapes from text) and discuss.
 2. Show TRANSPARENCY 1.8 (examples of skewed distributions from class questionnaire ratings) and discuss.

V.   Review this Class: Use blackboard outline.

Interpersonal hostility measured as delay in
seconds for 29 cars before honking horn at stalled
car after the light has changed to green.
(Fictional data based on Kenrick & McFarland, 1986)

3.5, 2.0, 0, 5.0, .5, 1.0, 4.0, 3.5
3.0, 1.5, 1.5, 2.0, 2.5, 3.0, 3.0,
3.5, 4.5, 2.0, 2.5, 4.5, 4.0, 3.5,
3.0, 2.5, 2.5, 3.5, 3.5, 4.0, 3.0

Frequency Table

	X	f	%
5.0 - /	5.0	1	3.45
4.5 - //	4.5	2	6.90
4.0 - ///	4.0	3	10.35
3.5 - //////	3.5	6	20.70
3.0 - /////	3.0	5	17.25
2.5 - ////	2.5	4	13.80
2.0 - ///	2.0	3	10.35
1.5 - //	1.5	2	6.90
1.0 - /	1.0	1	3.45
0.5 - /	0.5	1	3.45
0.0 - /	0.0	1	3.45

Grouped frequency table (Interval = 1)

Interval	f
5.0 - 5.9	1
4.0 - 4.9	5
3.0 - 3.9	11
2.0 - 2.9	7
1.0 - 1.9	3
0.0 - 0.9	2

Aron/Aron
Statistics for the Social Sciences

© 1997 by Prentice-Hall, Inc.
Simon & Schuster/A Viacom Company
Upper Saddle River, New Jersey 07458

TRANSPARENCY 1.2

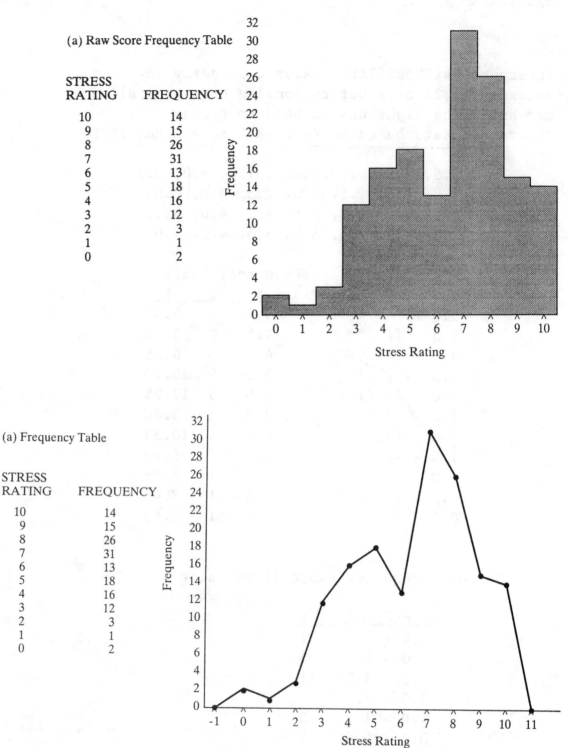

(a) Raw Score Frequency Table

STRESS RATING	FREQUENCY
10	14
9	15
8	26
7	31
6	13
5	18
4	16
3	12
2	3
1	1
0	2

(a) Frequency Table

STRESS RATING	FREQUENCY
10	14
9	15
8	26
7	31
6	13
5	18
4	16
3	12
2	3
1	1
0	2

Aron/Aron
Statistics for the Social Sciences

© 1997 by Prentice-Hall, Inc.
Simon & Schuster/A Viacom Company
Upper Saddle River, New Jersey 07458

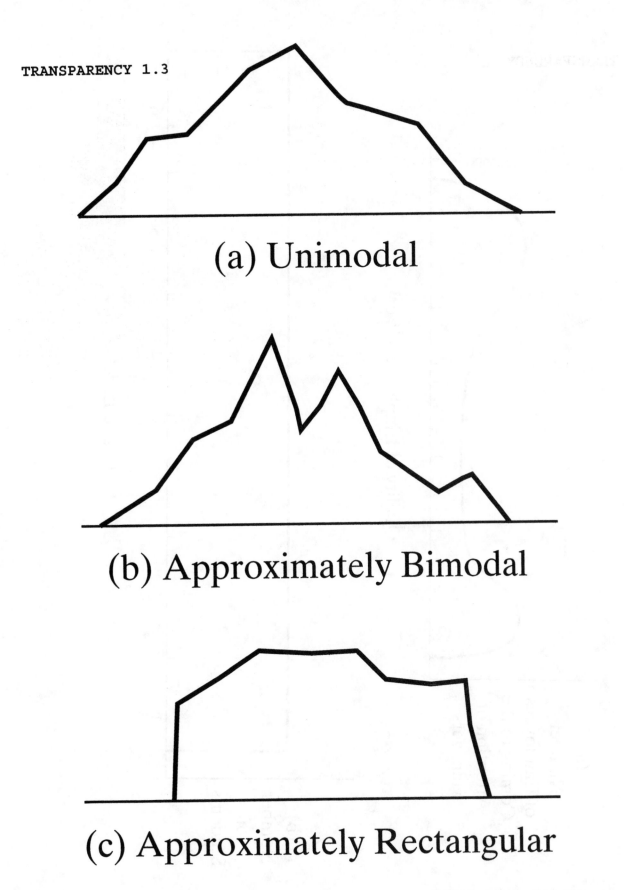

(a) Unimodal

(b) Approximately Bimodal

(c) Approximately Rectangular

Aron/Aron
Statistics for the Social Sciences

© 1997 by Prentice-Hall, Inc.
Simon & Schuster/A Viacom Company
Upper Saddle River, New Jersey 07458

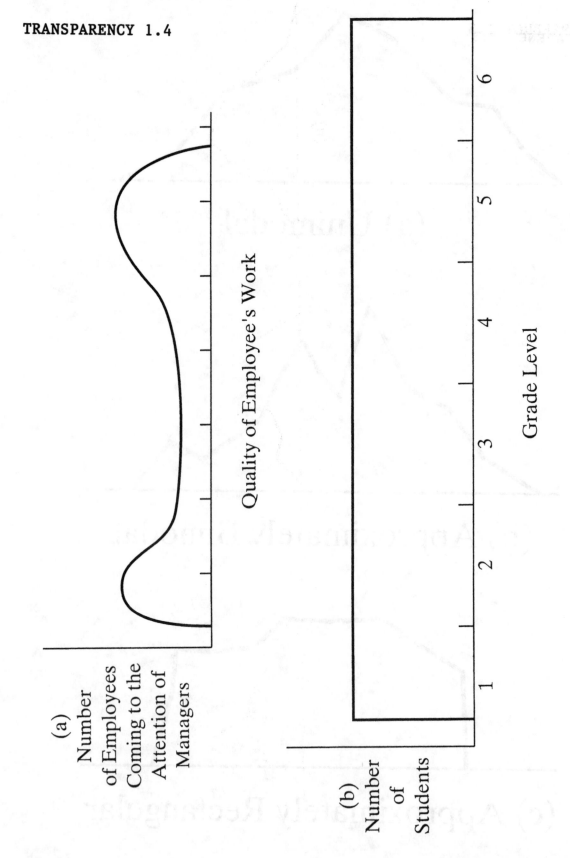

(a)

Number
of Employees
Coming to the
Attention of
Managers

Quality of Employee's Work

(b)
Number
of
Students

Grade Level

Aron/Aron
Statistics for the Social Sciences

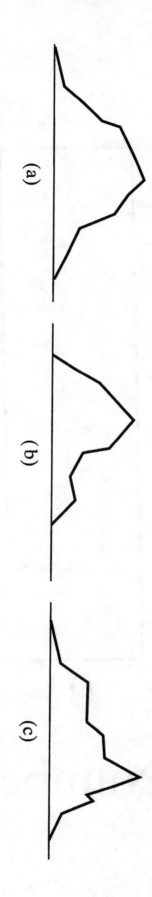

(a)

(b)

(c)

Aron/Aron
Statistics for the Social Sciences

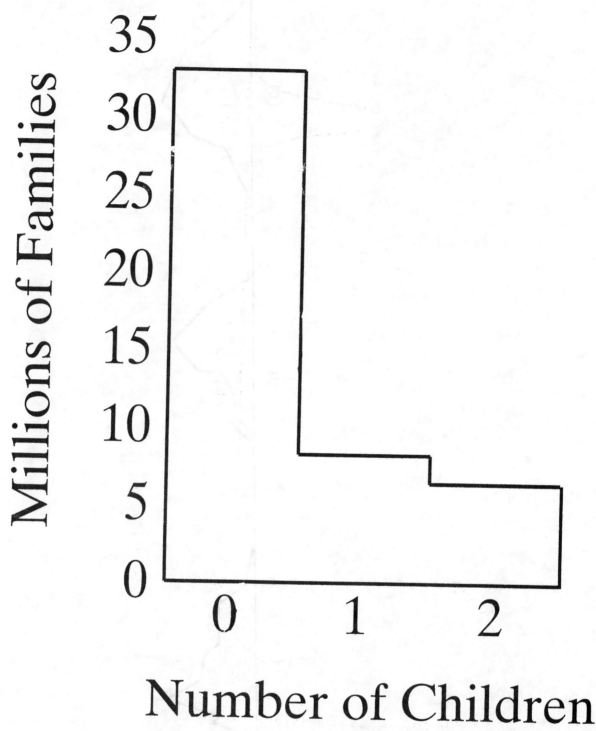

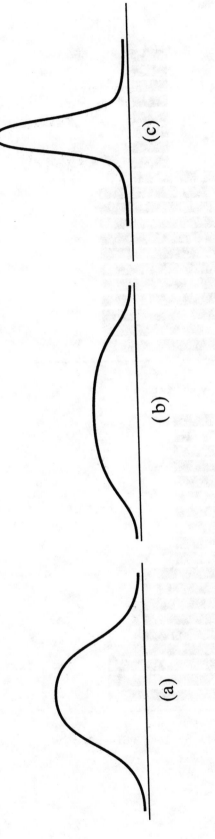

Aron/Aron
Statistics for the Social Sciences

TRANSPARENCY 1.8

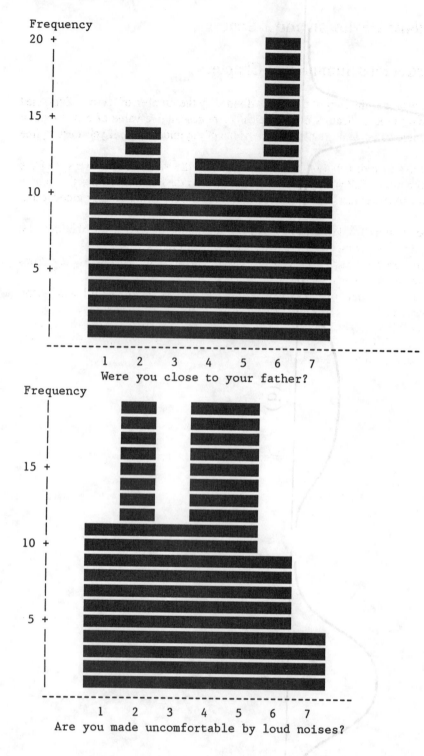

Aron/Aron
Statistics for the Social Sciences

Chapter 2
The Mean, Variance, Standard Deviation and Z Scores

Instructor's Summary of Chapter

Mean. The mean is the ordinary average--the sum of the scores divided by the number of scores. Expressed in symbols, $M = \Sigma X/N$. Less commonly used indicators of the typical or representative value of a distribution include the mode, the most common single value, and the median, the value of the middle case if you were to line up all the cases from highest to lowest.

Variation. The spread of the scores in a distribution can be described by the variance--the average of the squared deviation of each score from the mean: $SD^2 = \Sigma(X-M)^2 / N$. The standard deviation is the positive square root of the variance: $SD = \sqrt{SD^2}$. It can be best understood as an approximate measure of the average amount that scores differ from the mean.

Z Scores. A Z score is the number of standard deviations a raw score is from the mean of a distribution: $Z = (X-M)/SD$. Among other applications, Z scores permit comparisons of scores on different scales.

How the procedures of this chapter are described in research articles. Means and standard deviations (but not Z scores) are commonly reported in research articles; usually in tables.

Box 2.1. The Psychology of Statistics. Some psychologists--especially those associated with behaviorism, humanistic psychology, phenomenology, and qualitative methods--mistrust statistical processes because in the process of creating averages, knowledge about the individual case is lost. Many even holding these viewpoints, however, acknowledge that statistical analysis does play an important role, but argue that when studying any particular topic, careful study of individuals should always come first.

Lecture 2.1: The Mean

Materials

Lecture outline
Transparencies 1.2, 2.1, and 2.2

Outline for Blackboard

    I.   **Review**
    II. **Describing the Average**
    III. **The Mean**
    IV. **Formulas and Symbols:** $M = \Sigma X / N$
    V. **Median and Mode**
    VI. **Review this Class**

Instructor's Lecture Outline

I.   Review

    A. Idea of descriptive statistics and importance for their own right and as a foundation for the rest of the course.

    B. Describing a distribution using frequency tables.

    C. Describing a distribution graphically.

II. Describing the Average

    A. Principle: Summarize a distribution of scores as a single number.

    B. Show TRANSPARENCY 1.2 (stress-ratings example, from text).

    C. Previously we summarized this group of numbers in a table and graph. Now we want to summarize it into a single number.

III. The Mean

    A. Mean is the arithmetic average--sum of scores divided by number of scores.

    B. Example calculation: Show TRANSPARENCY 2.1 top (stress-ratings mean computation).

    C. Mean as balance point: Show TRANSPARENCY 2.1 bottom.

IV. Formula and Symbols

    A. Show TRANSPARENCY 2.1 top (stress-ratings mean computation) and discuss each symbol.

    B. Emphasize value of symbols in statistics and importance of mastering them.

V. Median and Mode

A. Problem with the mean is that it is highly influenced by extreme scores: Show TRANSPARENCY 2.2 (horn-honking and other examples) and discuss computation of mean with and without additional extreme score.

B. The median.
1. An alternative to the mean for describing the typical value of a distribution.
2. The median is the middle score.
3. Computation:
   a. Organize scores from lowest to highest.
   b. Count to middle score.
   c. If an even number of scores, take the average of the middle two.
4. Show TRANSPARENCY 2.2 (horn-honking study and other examples) again and discuss:
   a. Computation of median.
   b. How median is not affected by extreme score in horn-honking study.
   c. How median is not affected by extreme scores as shown in example of 1-1-1-1-1-8-9-9-9-9-9 versus 7-7-7-7-7-8-50-50-50-50-50 (that is, both have same median but not same mean).
   d. Computation of median versus mean in feudal village example.

C. Mode.
1. Another alternative to the mean for describing the typical value of a distribution.
2. The mode is the value with the most scores.
3. Computation:
   a. Make a frequency table.
   b. Find the value with the highest frequency.
4. In horn-honking study it is 3.5.
5. When mode is most useful:
   a. In combination with mean or median to give a fuller description of a distribution.
   b. To describe a modal interval from a grouped frequency distribution.
   c. There are relatively few values.
   d. The values are categories (that is, this is a distribution over a nominal rather than numeric variable).

VII. Review this Class: Use blackboard outline.

Lecture 2.2: The Variance and Standard Deviation

Materials

Lecture outline

Transparencies 2.1 through 2.4

(If using transparencies based on your class's questionnaires, replace 2.2 through 2.5 with 2.2R through 2.5R.)

Outline for Blackboard

I.   **Review**
II. **Variation**
III. **Deviation Scores and Squared Deviation Scores**
IV. **The Variance**
V.   **Formulas and Symbols:** $SD^2 = \Sigma(X-M)^2/N$
VI. **The Standard Deviation:** $SD = \sqrt{SD^2}$
VII. **Review this Class**

Instructor's Lecture Outline

I.   **Review**

   A. Idea of descriptive statistics and importance for their own right and as a foundation for the rest of the course.

   B. Describing a distribution using frequency tables and graphs.

   C. Describing a distribution's typical value as the mean: $M = \Sigma X/N$: Show TRANSPARENCY 2.1 (computation of mean for stress ratings) and discuss.

II. **Variation**

   A. A distribution can be characterized by how much the scores in it vary from each other-- they could all be bunched closely together or very spread out, or anywhere in between.

   B. Knowing the mean and variation in a distribution gives a much more complete sense of how scores are distributed than the mean alone.

   C. Examples of possible situations in which the mean SAT is 600 for entering students at a particular college.
   1. All have almost exactly 600--there is little variation.
   2. About half have SAT's of 400 and half of 800--there is a very great deal of variation.
   3. About equal numbers having SATs of 500, 550, 600, 650, 700--a moderate amount of variation.

   D. In general, the amount of variation and mean are independent of each other.

   E. Show TRANSPARENCY 2.3 (distributions with various means and variances from the text) and discuss.

III. **Deviation Scores and Squared Deviation Scores**

   A. One way of determining the variance numerically focuses on the extent to which scores differ from the mean.

B. A deviation score is the score minus the mean--if a score is 28 and the mean is 25, the deviation score is 3.

C. Over an entire distribution positive and negative deviation scores balance each other out.

D. For this and other more complicated reasons, we emphasize squared deviations.

IV. The Variance

A. A widely used measure of variation in a distribution.

B. The average of the squared deviation scores.

C. But is not the average amount that scores differ from the mean; it is the average amount of *squared* differences of scores from the mean. So it will typically be much larger than the average amount that scores differ from the mean.

V. Formulas and Symbols: $SD^2 = \Sigma(X-M)^2/N$

A. Show TRANSPARENCY 2.1 (stress-ratings example) and discussing the meaning of each symbol in the computation of variance.

B. Show TRANSPARENCY 2.2 (horn-honking study) and discuss the computation of the variance.

VI. The Standard Deviation: $SD = \sqrt{SD^2}$

A. The positive square root of the variance.

B. *Approximately* the average amount that scores differ from the mean in a particular distribution.

C. The most widely used descriptive statistic for describing the variation in a distribution.

D. Show TRANSPARENCY 2.1 (stress ratings example from text) and discuss computation of standard deviation.

E. Show TRANSPARENCY 2.2 (horn-honking study) focusing on computation of standard deviation at bottom.

VII. Review Class: Use blackboard outline and TRANSPARENCY 2.4 (review of mean, variance and standard deviation).

Lecture 2.3: Z Scores

Materials

Lecture outline
Transparencies 2.4 through 2.6

Outline for Blackboard

I.   **Review**
II. **Describing a Score in Relation to the Distribution**
III. **Computing the Z Score: $Z = (X-M)/SD$**
IV. **Transforming Z scores to Raw Scores: $X = (Z)(SD) + M$**
V.   **Review this Class**

Instructor's Lecture Outline

I.   Review

A. Idea of descriptive statistics and importance for their own right and as a foundation for the rest of the course.

B. Describing a distribution using frequency tables and graphs.

C. Describing a distribution's typical value and variation: Show TRANSPARENCY 2.4 (review of mean, variance and standard deviation) and discuss.

II.   Describing a Score in Relation to the Distribution

A. So far we have described distributions, now we turn to describing a single score's location in a distribution.

B. Knowing an individual's score gives little information without knowing where that score stands in relation to the entire distribution.

C. Knowing the mean of the distribution allows you to tell whether a score is above or below the average in that distribution.

D. Example: An individual has a score of 26 on a leadership test.
   1. What does that indicate? Is the person a particularly good leader? A particularly poor leader? About average?
   2. If the mean on this test is 20, then you know that the person is above average in leadership (compared to other people who have taken this test).

E. Knowing the standard deviation of the distribution allows you to tell how much above or below the average that score is in relation to the spread of scores in the distribution.

F. Leadership test example:
   1. Suppose the standard deviation is 3.
   2. The person with a score of 26 is two standard deviations above the mean of 20.
   3. Thus the person is about twice as much above the mean as the average score differs from the mean.
   4. Show TRANSPARENCY 2.5 (graphic illustration of this example) and discuss how the *SD* serves as a kind of unit of measure.
   5. Note that in this example the overall distribution is a normal curve and that when this is the case this approach becomes especially useful, as the students will learn later.

G. Second example: Individual scores 84 on a test of planning ability.
  1. If mean is 90 and standard deviation is 12, this person's score is 1/2 standard deviation below the mean.
  2. Thus the person is below average, but not by a lot--about half as much as the average score differs from the mean.
  3. Show TRANSPARENCY 2.6(graphic illustration of this example) and discuss.
H. The number of standard deviations a score is above or below the mean is called its *Z* score.
I. Show TRANSPARENCY 2.6 again and discuss relation of *Z* scores and raw scores--they are two different ways of measuring the same thing.
J. *Z* scores provide a helpful way to compare scores on measures that are on completely different scales. For example, if a person scored 26 on leadership and 84 on planning, we can say that the person scores much higher than average on leadership and slightly lower than average on planning.

III. Computing the *Z* Score: $Z = (X\text{-}M)/SD$
A. Show TRANSPARENCY 2.5 (leadership test) and discuss computation of *Z* score using the formula.
B. Show TRANSPARENCY 2.6 (planning test) and discuss computation of *Z* score using the formula.

IV. Transforming *Z* scores to Raw Scores: $X = (Z)(SD) + M$
A. Show TRANSPARENCY 2.5 (leadership test) and discuss conversion of *Z* scores to raw scores at bottom.
B. Show TRANSPARENCY 2.6 (planning test) and discuss conversion of *Z* scores to raw scores at bottom.

V. Review this Class
A. Go through blackboard outline.
B. Emphasize importance of knowing *Z* scores thoroughly as preparation for next topics.

Ratings of stress of statistics class students.
(Data from Aron et al., 1993)

Sum of stress ratings = 975
Mean is 975 / 151 = 6.46

$$\underline{M} = \frac{\Sigma\underline{X}}{\underline{N}} = \frac{975}{151} = 6.46$$

$$\underline{SD}^2 = \Sigma(\underline{X}-\underline{M})^2 / \underline{N} = 797.5 / 151 = 5.28$$
$$\underline{SD} = \sqrt{\underline{SD}^2} = \sqrt{5.28} = 2.30$$

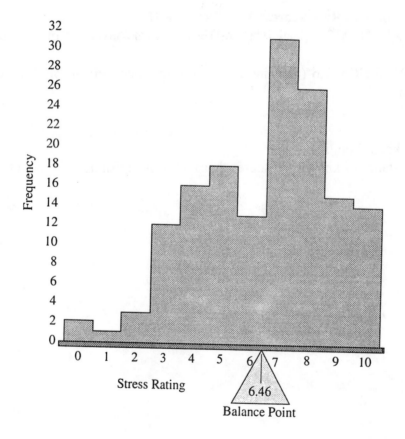

TRANSPARENCY 2.2

Measures of central tendency.
(Fictional data based on Kenrick & McFarland, 1986.)

Seconds honking at stalled car ($\underline{N}$ = 29):

3.5, 2.0, 0, 5.0, .5, 1.0, 4.0, 3.5
3.0, 1.5, 1.5, 2.0, 2.5, 3.0, 3.0,
3.5, 4.5, 2.0, 2.5, 4.5, 4.0, 3.5,
3.0, 2.5, 2.5, 3.5, 3.5, 4.0, 3.0

$\Sigma\underline{X}$ = 82.5 $\underline{N}$ = 29 $\underline{M}$ = $\Sigma\underline{X}$ / $\underline{N}$ = 82.5 / 29 = 2.85

With one additional case of 13 seconds:

$\Sigma\underline{X}$ = 82.5+13=95.5 $\underline{N}$=29+1=30 $\underline{M}$=$\Sigma\underline{X}$/$\underline{N}$=95.5/30 = 3.18

1	0	─┬─
2	.5	│
3	1.0	│
4	1.5	│
5	1.5	│
6	2.0	│
7	2.0	│
8	2.0	│
9	2.5	│
10	2.5	│
11	2.5	│
12	2.5	│
13	3.0	│
14	3.0	│
15	3.0	<===MEDIAN
16	3.0	│
17	3.0	│
18	3.5	│
19	3.5	│
20	3.5	│
21	3.5	│
22	3.5	│
23	3.5	│
24	4.0	│
25	4.0	│
26	4.0	│
27	4.5	│
28	4.5	│
29	5.0	─┴─

Feudal Village Example

50 Families @ $100/Yr = 5,000

1 Family @ $100,000/Yr = 100,000

Village total = $105,000

$\Sigma\underline{X}$ = 105,000 $\underline{N}$ = 51

$\underline{M}$ = $\Sigma\underline{X}$/$\underline{N}$ = 105,000/51 = $2,059

Median = $100   Mode = $100

Median examples:

1-1-1-1-1-8-9-9-9-9-9 --> Median=8

7-7-7-7-8-50-50-50-50-50 --> Median=8

$\Sigma(\underline{X}-\underline{M})^2$: $(3.5-2.85)^2 + (2.0-2.85)^2 + \ldots + (3.5-2.85)^2 = 39.98$

$\underline{SD}^2$ = $\Sigma(\underline{X}-\underline{M})^2/\underline{N}$ = 39.98 /29 = 1.38 $\underline{SD}$ = $\sqrt{\underline{SD}^2}$ = $\sqrt{1.38}$ = 1.17

Aron/Aron
Statistics for the Social Sciences

© 1997 by Prentice-Hall, Inc.
Simon & Schuster/A Viacom Company
Upper Saddle River, New Jersey 07458

TRANSPARENCY 2.3

(a)

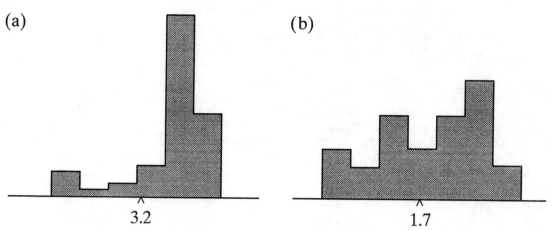

3.2

(b)

1.7

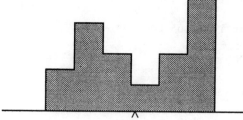

3.2

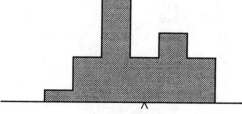

3.2

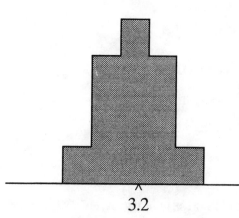

3.2

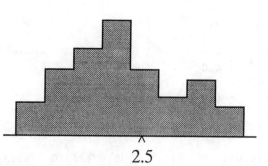

2.5

Aron/Aron
Statistics for the Social Sciences

© 1997 by Prentice-Hall, Inc.
Simon & Schuster/A Viacom Company
Upper Saddle River, New Jersey 07458

TRANSPARENCY 2.4

Review of Mean, Variance, and Standard Deviation

A. Principle: Describe (these are descriptive statistics) by reducing a group of numbers--a distribution--to some simple terms.

B. The mean (arithmetic average):

   RULE: Add up the numbers and divide by the number of numbers

   FORMULA AND SYMBOLS: $\underline{M} = \Sigma\underline{X}/\underline{N}$.

   Mean is most widely used, and generally the best indicator of the typical score.

C. Variation: A single number that describes how much variation there is in a group of numbers—that is, how spread out or narrow a distribution is.

   1. VARIANCE is average of squared deviations from the mean.

      RULE: a. Subtract the mean from each score to get deviation score.
            b. Square each deviation score.
            c. Add up all the squared deviation scores.
            d. Divide by number of cases to get average of squared deviation scores.

      FORMULA AND SYMBOLS: $\underline{SD}^2 = \Sigma(\underline{X}-\underline{M})^2 / \underline{N}$

   2. STANDARD DEVIATION is the positive square root of variance.

      INTUITIVE INTERPRETATION: Standard deviation is roughly the average amount each score differs from the mean.

      RULE: Compute variance and take the square root.

      FORMULA AND SYMBOLS: $\underline{SD} = \sqrt{\underline{SD}^2}$.

Aron/Aron
Statistics for the Social Sciences

© 1997 by Prentice-Hall, Inc.
Simon & Schuster/A Viacom Company
Upper Saddle River, New Jersey 07458

Z score examples for leadership test. (Fictional data.)

M = 20   SD = 3

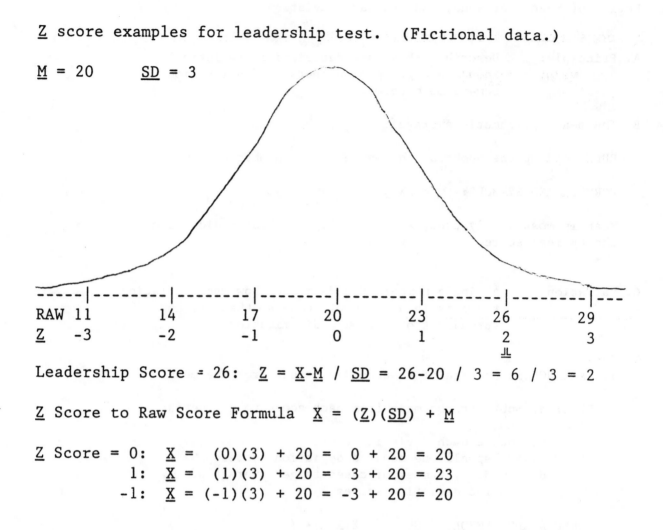

RAW	11	14	17	20	23	26	29
Z	-3	-2	-1	0	1	2	3

Leadership Score = 26: Z = X-M / SD = 26-20 / 3 = 6 / 3 = 2

Z Score to Raw Score Formula X = (Z)(SD) + M

Z Score = 0: X =   (0)(3) + 20 = 0 + 20 = 20
        1: X =   (1)(3) + 20 = 3 + 20 = 23
       -1: X = (-1)(3) + 20 = -3 + 20 = 20

Aron/Aron
Statistics for the Social Sciences

© 1997 by Prentice-Hall, Inc.
Simon & Schuster/A Viacom Company
Upper Saddle River, New Jersey 07458

Z score examples for planning test.   (Fictional data.)

$\underline{M}$=90 $\underline{SD}$=12

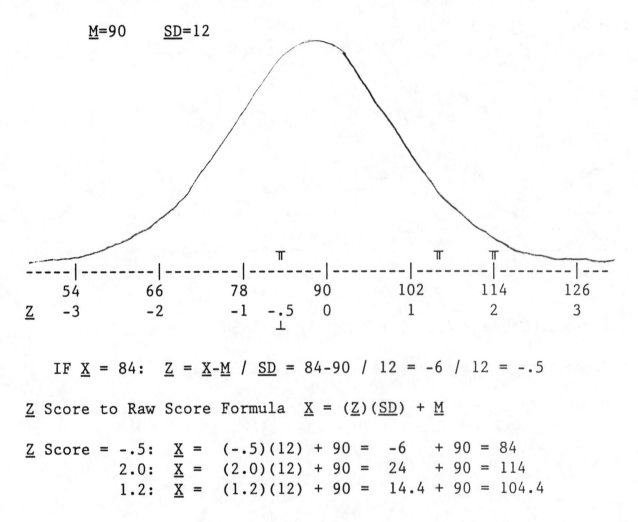

```
     54        66        78        90       102       114       126
Z    -3        -2        -1   -.5    0        1         2         3
                              ⊥
```

   IF $\underline{X}$ = 84: $\underline{Z}$ = $\underline{X}$-$\underline{M}$ / $\underline{SD}$ = 84-90 / 12 = -6 / 12 = -.5

Z Score to Raw Score Formula $\underline{X}$ = ($\underline{Z}$)($\underline{SD}$) + $\underline{M}$

Z Score = -.5: $\underline{X}$ = (-.5)(12) + 90 = -6   + 90 = 84
          2.0: $\underline{X}$ = (2.0)(12) + 90 = 24   + 90 = 114
          1.2: $\underline{X}$ = (1.2)(12) + 90 = 14.4 + 90 = 104.4

Aron/Aron
Statistics for the Social Sciences

© 1997 by Prentice-Hall, Inc.
Simon & Schuster/A Viacom Company
Upper Saddle River, New Jersey 07458

Chapter 3
Correlation and Prediction

Instructor's Summary of Chapter

Scatter diagrams describe the relation between two variables by representing each individual's pair of scores as a dot on a two-dimensional graph of the two variables.

Linear, Curvilinear, Positive, and Negative Correlations. The general pattern of dots in the scatter diagram describe a linear correlation when they roughly fall around a straight line (they describe a positive linear correlation when that line goes upward to the right and a negative when it goes downward to the right). It is a curvilinear correlation when they follow a line other than a simple straight line, and no correlation when they do not follow any kind of line.

The correlation coefficient (r), the standard numeric index of linear correlation, is the average of the cross products of Z scores. r approaches 1 when there is a strong positive linear correlation, because positive Z scores are multiplied by positive and negative Z scores by negative; r approaches -1 when there is a strong negative linear correlation, because positive Z scores are multiplied by negative and negative by positive; and r is zero when there is no linear correlation, because positive and negative Z-score cross products cancel each other out.

Hypothesis testing. A correlation is said to be significant when hypothesis testing procedures (covered in later chapters and the appendix to Chapter 3) applied to your data support the hypothesis that a correlation exists in the larger group your data were intended to represent.

Direction of causality. If X and Y are correlated, X could be causing Y, Y causing X, or a third variable causing both.

Prediction with Z scores. Regression makes predictions about a dependent variable based on knowledge of a person's score on a predictor variable. The best model for predicting a person's Z score on the dependent variable is to multiply the standardized regression coefficient (beta) times the person's Z score on the predictor variable. In this kind of prediction, beta is r.

Prediction with raw scores. Predictions with raw scores can be made by converting the person's score on the predictor variable to a Z score, multiplying it by beta, and then converting the resulting predicted Z score on the dependent variable to a raw score.

Multiple regression. In multiple regression a dependent variable is predicted using two or more predictor variables. In a multiple regression model, each score on the predictor variable is multiplied by its own regression coefficient and the products are summed to make the prediction (a single regression constant is added when using raw scores.) Each regression coefficient indicates the relation of the predictor to the dependent variable in the context of the other predictor variables. The multiple correlation coefficient describes the overall degree of association between the dependent variable and the predictor variables taken together.

How the procedures of this chapter are described in research articles. Correlational results are usually presented either in the text with the value of r or in a correlation matrix.

Box 3.1. Galton: Gentleman Genius. Briefly describes the background and character of Francis Galton and what led him to the work on statistics that eventually resulted in the correlation coefficient.

Lecture 3.1: The Scatter Diagram and the Logic of Correlation

Materials

Lecture outline
Transparencies 3.1 through 3.6

Outline for Blackboard

    I. Review
    II. The Scatter Diagram
    III. Patterns of Association
        A. Linear
        B. Positive linear
        C. Negative linear
        D. Curvilinear and No Relationship
    IV. Review this Class

Instructor's Lecture Outline

I.   Review
    A. Idea of descriptive statistics.
    B. Describing distributions by frequency tables and graphs.
    C. Describing distributions by their mean and standard deviation.
    D. Describing a score within a distribution: The Z score as the number of standard deviations above or below the mean.

II.   The Scatter Diagram
    A. Consider the example from the text of a study of stress level of managers who supervise different number of employees.
      1. Each person has a score on both variables. Are they related?
      2. To see, we can make a graph--show TRANSPARENCY 3.1 (number supervised and stress level, from text) here and throughout the discussion of lecture outline points IIA and IIB.
      3. Note that the general pattern of dots goes up--the more supervised, the more stress. (Draw the approximate regression line with a transparency pen.)
      4. Line is *positive*, highs with highs and lows with lows.
      5. This is just the general trend--almost none of the dots fall exactly on the line and many are a distance away.
      6. A chart like this is called a scatter diagram.
      7. A scatter diagram is a visual description of the relation between two variables.
    B. Making a scatter diagram.
      1. One variable goes on each axis:
        a. If it is clear that one is supposed to be causal (independent), that variable goes on the horizontal axis.
        b. If it is not clear which causes which, it does not matter which variable goes on which axis.
      2. Make the scale go from lowest to highest possible value on the variables being measured.
      3. Place dots in their appropriate location.
      4. Discuss how to handle two dots in the same place.

C. Example 2: Show TRANSPARENCY 3.2 (scatter diagram of fictional data based on Orme-Johnson & Haynes, 1981) and discuss.

III. Patterns of Association
A. Linear correlation.
1. Describes situation where the pattern of dots fall roughly in a straight line.
2. Example: Show TRANSPARENCY 3.1 (supervisor's stress).
B. Positive linear correlation.
1. When the pattern of dots goes up from left to right.
2. Where highs on one variable go with highs on the other, lows on one with lows on the other, and middle scores on one with middle scores on the other.
3. Examples:
a. Show TRANSPARENCY 3.1 (supervisor's stress).
b. Show TRANSPARENCY 3.2 (EEG coherence and creativity).
C. Negative (or inverse) linear correlation.
1. When the pattern of dots goes down from left to right.
2. When highs on one variable go with lows on the other.
3. Example: Show TRANSPARENCY 3.3 (fictional study of marital adjustment and overtime hours worked).
D. No relationship and curvilinear.
1. No relationship: Show TRANSPARENCY 3.4 (creativity and shoe size, from text) and discuss.
2. Curvilinear: Show TRANSPARENCY 3.5 (children's rate of substituting digit symbols and their motivation, from text).

IV. Review this Class: Use blackboard outline.

Lecture 3.2: The Correlation Coefficient

Materials

Lecture outline
Transparencies 2.6, 3.1, 3.2, 3.3, and 3.6

Outline for Blackboard

    I.   Review
    II. Purpose of the Correlation Coefficient
    III. Logic of Computing the Correlation Coefficient
    IV. Formulas and Symbols: $r = \Sigma(Z_X Z_Y) / N$
    V. Interpreting the Correlation Coefficient
    VI. Review this Class

Instructor's Lecture Outline

I.   Review

    A. Idea of descriptive statistics.
    B. Describing a single distribution:
        1. Frequency tables and graphs.
        2. Mean and standard deviation.
    C. Describing a score within a distribution.
        1. The Z score as the number of standard deviations above or below the mean.
        2. Computation: $Z = (X-M)/SD$.
        3. Example: Show TRANSPARENCY 2.6 (Z score examples for leadership test) and review.
    D. Describing the relation between scores in two distributions.
        1. The scatter diagram: Show TRANSPARENCY 3.1 (manager's stress example, from text) and review.
        2. Directions of relationships:
          a. Positive.
          b. Negative.
          c. Curvilinear.

II. Purpose of the Correlation Coefficient

    A. Describes the degree and direction of linear correlation.
    B. Such a measure would be especially useful if it has the following properties:
        1. Numeric on a standard scale for all uses.
        2. A positive number for positive correlations and a negative number for negative correlations.
        3. A zero for no correlation.
        4. A +1 for a perfect positive linear correlation (and a -1 for a perfect negative linear correlation).
        5. The closer a correlation is to perfect, the closer it is to +1 (or -1 if it is negative) and the further from 0.

III. Logic of Computing the Correlation Coefficient
    A. Interpreting correlation in terms of patterns of highs and lows.
        1. A correlation is strong and positive if highs on one variable go with highs on the other, and lows with lows.
        2. A correlation is strong and negative if lows with highs, and highs with lows.
        3. There is no correlation if sometimes highs go with highs and sometimes with lows.
    B. But what is "high" and "low"?
        1. How can we compare scores as high and low that are on completely different scales in completely different distributions?
        2. Solution is to use Z scores.
        3. A high score in a distribution always has a positive Z score.
        4. A low score in a distribution always has a negative Z score.
    C. Multiplying the Z scores of each person's two scores produces the following effects:
        1. With a perfect positive correlation:
          a. Highs always go with highs—multiplying two highs will be multiplying two positive Z scores. Thus the result is always positive.
          b. Lows go with lows—multiplying two lows will be multiplying two negative Z scores. Thus the result is always positive.
        2. With a perfect negative correlation:
          a. Highs on the first variable always go with lows on the second—multiplying a high by a low will be multiplying a positive Z score times a negative Z score. Thus the result is always negative.
          b. Lows on the first variable always go with highs on the second—multiplying a low by a high will be multiplying a negative Z score times a positive Z score. Thus the result is always negative.
        3. With no correlation:
          a. Sometimes highs go with highs and lows with lows, making positive products.
          b. Sometimes highs go with lows and lows with highs, making negative products.
          c. The result over all is that the positives and negatives cancel each other out.
        4. In between degrees of correlation:
          a. To the extent a correlation is positive, there will be more cases of highs with highs and lows with lows than the reverse, making the overall result somewhat positive.
          b. To the extent a correlation is negative, there will be more cases of highs with lows and lows with highs than of both the same, making the overall result somewhat negative.
    D. Each multiplication of a person's two Z scores is called a *cross-product of Z scores*.
    E. The average of the cross-products of Z scores is called the correlation coefficient.
        1. With a perfect positive correlation, the average of the cross-products of Z scores is +1.
        2. With a perfect negative correlation, the average of the cross-products of Z scores is -1.
        3. With no correlation, the average of the cross-products of Z scores is 0.
        4. With a positive correlation that is not perfect, average of the cross-products of Z scores is between 0 and +1.
        5. With a negative correlation that is not perfect, average of the cross-products of Z scores is between 0 and -1.
    F. Show TRANSPARENCY 3.1 (manager's stress example, from text) and discuss how the average of the cross-products of Z scores comes out near +1.
    G. Show TRANSPARENCY 3.3 (fictional study of marital adjustment and overtime hours worked) and discuss how the average of the cross-products of Z scores comes out near -1.

IV. Formulas and Symbols: $r = \Sigma(Z_X Z_Y) / N$
    A. Show TRANSPARENCY 3.2 (EEG coherence and creativity) and discuss each symbol in the formula.
    B. Discuss computation using the formula in TRANSPARENCY 3.3 (marital adjustment and overtime hours).

V. Interpreting the Correlation Coefficient

A. A correlation between two variables does not indicate the direction of causality.

B. Show TRANSPARENCY 3.6 (directions of causality, from text) and discuss the three possible directions of causality.

C. Show TRANSPARENCY 3.3 (marital satisfaction and overtime hours example) and discuss possible directions of causality:

1. Being dissatisfied with one's marriage could make one choose to work more overtime hours.
2. Working more overtime hours could make one less satisfied with one's marriage.
3. Some third factor, such as being very poor, could make one choose to work more overtime hours (to make needed money) and also put excessive stress on the marriage.

VI. Review this Class: Use blackboard outline.

Lecture 3.3: Bivariate Regression

Materials

Lecture outline
Transparencies 3.7 through 3.11

Outline for Blackboard

    I.   **Review**
   II.   **Prediction**
 III. **Prediction with Z Scores**
 IV. **Prediction with Raw Scores**
   V.   **Multiple Regression**
 VI. **Review this Class**

Instructor's Lecture Outline

NOTE: Warn class that this chapter's material is a jump in difficulty, and will require extra effort on their part.

I.   Review
    A. Idea of descriptive statistics and importance for their own right and as a foundation for the rest of the course.
    B. Description of a single distribution in terms of frequency tables, graphs, mean, and standard deviation.
    C. Describing a particular score's relation to the distribution using Z scores.
    D. Describing the relation between two distributions using a scatter diagram.
    E. Describing the relation between two distributions by computing the correlation coefficient (r).
        1. r is the average of the cross-products of Z scores.
        2. r ranges from +1 for a perfect positive linear correlation, to 0 for no correlation, to -1 for a perfect negative linear correlation.

II. Prediction
    A. Psychologists construct mathematical rules to predict a person's scores on one variable from knowledge of their score on another variable. For example, predicting college grades from SAT scores.
    B. Prediction is also called "regression."
    C. Show TRANSPARENCY 3.7 (table from text of names for predictor and dependent variables) and discuss.
    D. We can predict a person's score on a dependent variable using the person's score on a single predictor. Example: Predicting a person's score on college grades from knowledge of their SAT score.

E. In multiple prediction (called "multiple regression") we predict a person's score on a dependent variable using the person's scores on each of two or more predictor variables. Example: Predicting a person's score on college grades from knowledge of their SAT score and their high school GPA.

III. Prediction with Z Scores

A. The basic approach to predicting a person's score on the dependent variable is to multiply a person's Z score on the predictor variable times the *regression coefficient* (beta).

B. Thus a bivariate prediction rule is of the form: Predicted $Z_Y = (\beta)(Z_X)$.

C. $\beta = r$. This is the general rule for predictions with one predictor variable.

D. For example, if the correlation between the predictor and dependent variable is $r = .4$ and a person's score on the predictor variable is 1.8 standard deviations above the mean, then your best prediction for the person's score on the dependent variable is a Z score of .4 times 1.8, which comes out to .72. That is, you would predict their score to be .72 standard deviations above the mean.

E. Show TRANSPARENCY 3.8 (manager's stress example) and explain.

F. Show TRANSPARENCY 3.9 (EEG coherence predicting creativity test score) and discuss Z score predictions.

IV. Prediction with Raw Scores

A. One way to predict from raw scores is to convert the predictor variable to a Z score, make the prediction (of a Z score on the dependent variable), then convert the predicted Z score to a raw score.

B. Show TRANSPARENCY 3.10 (manager's stress example) and discuss.

V. Multiple Regression

A. Principle: Extension of bivariate regression to more than one predictor variable.

B. Regression coefficients.
    1. Raw score (*b*s).
    2. Z score (βs, which are *not* equal to *r*s).

C. With Z scores, predicted value of dependent variable for a particular individual is the sum of each regression coefficient times that person's score on the corresponding independent variable.

D. Show TRANSPARENCY 3.11 (manager's stress example) and discuss.

VI. Review this Class: Use blackboard outline.

Employees Supervised and Stress Level (Fictional Data)

Employees Supervised	Stress Level on Questionnaire
6	7
8	8
3	1
10	8
8	6

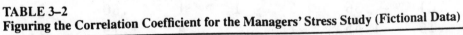

TABLE 3–2
Figuring the Correlation Coefficient for the Managers' Stress Study (Fictional Data)

Number of Employees Supervised (X)				Stress Level (Y)				Cross-Products
X	X – M	(X – M)²	Z_X	Y	Y – M	(Y – M)²	Z_Y	$Z_X Z_Y$
6	–1	1	– .42	7	1	1	.38	–.16
8	1	1	.42	8	2	4	.77	.32
3	–4	16	–1.69	1	–5	25	–1.92	3.24
10	3	9	1.27	8	2	4	.77	.98
8	1	1	.42	6	0	0	0.00	0.00

Σ = 35	SS = 28			Σ = 30	SS = 34		$\Sigma Z_X Z_Y$ = 4.38
M = 7	SD² = 5.60			M = 6	SD² = 6.80		r = .88
	SD = 2.37				SD = 2.61		

Aron/Aron
Statistics for the Social Sciences

Measured creativity using the Torrence Tests and EEG alpha-band coherence in the frontal area in subjects who were practicing Transcendental Mediation. (Fictional data based on Orme-Johnson & Haynes, 1981.)

EEG Coherence	Creativity Test Score
.2	2
.5	6
1.0	7
.8	5
.5	5

```
C
R  8 |
E  7 |                              ■
A  6 |            ■
T  5 |            ■         ■
I  4 |
V  3 |
I  2 |      ■
T  1 |
Y  0 |
      ‾‾‾‾‾‾‾‾‾‾‾‾‾‾‾‾‾‾‾‾‾‾‾‾‾‾
     .0 .1 .2 .3 .4 .5 .6 .7 .8 .9 1.
        EEG COHERENCE
```

	EEG Coherence				Creativity Test Score				Cross-Product of Z Scores
X	dev	dev^2	ZX	Y	dev	dev^2	ZY		ZXZY
.2	-.4	.16	-1.45	2	-3	9	-1.79		2.60
.5	-.1	.01	- .36	6	1	1	.60		- .22
1.0	.4	.16	1.45	7	2	4	1.19		1.73
.8	.2	.04	.73	5	0	0	0		0
.5	-.1	.01	- .36	5	0	0	0		0
Σ 3.0		.38		25		14			4.11
.6	SD^2= .076			5	SD^2= 2.8		r = Σ(ZXZY)/N		
	SD = .276				SD = 1.673		r = 4.11/5 = .82		

Aron/Aron
Statistics for the Social Sciences

© 1997 by Prentice-Hall, Inc.
Simon & Schuster/A Viacom Company
Upper Saddle River, New Jersey 07458

Marital satisfaction and overtime hours.   (Fictional Study)

Marital Satisfaction		Overtime Hours Typical Month		Cross-Products of Z Scores
X	ZX	Y	ZY	ZXZY
8	.67	4	-.74	-.50
9	1.01	4	-.74	-.75
4	-.67	16	1.04	-.70
8	.67	6	-.44	-.29
2	-1.34	24	2.22	-2.97
3	-1.01	9	0	0
9	1.01	0	-1.33	-1.34
2	-1.34	14	.74	-.99
6	0	8	-.15	0
9	1.01	5	-.59	-.60

Σ 60   90   -8.05

$\underline{M}$ 6   9 $\underline{r} = \Sigma(\underline{ZXZY})/N =$

$\underline{SD}=$ 2.98 $\underline{SD}=$ 6.75   -8.05 / 9 = -.81

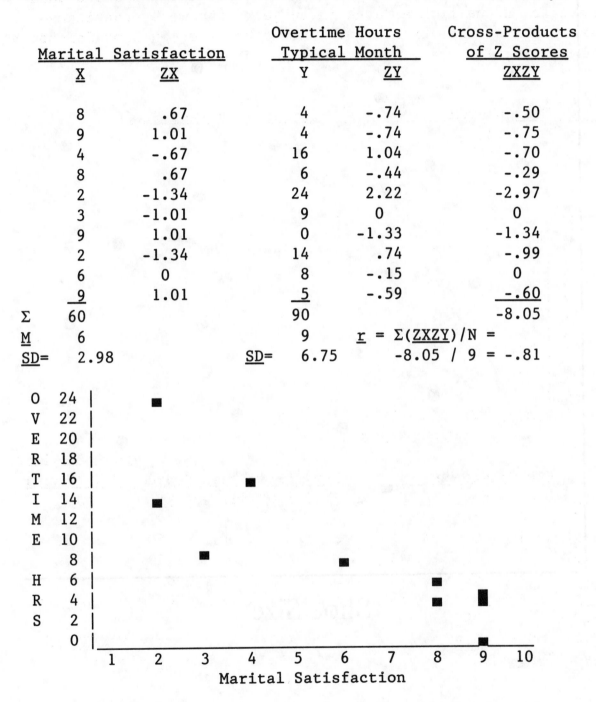

Aron/Aron
Statistics for the Social Sciences

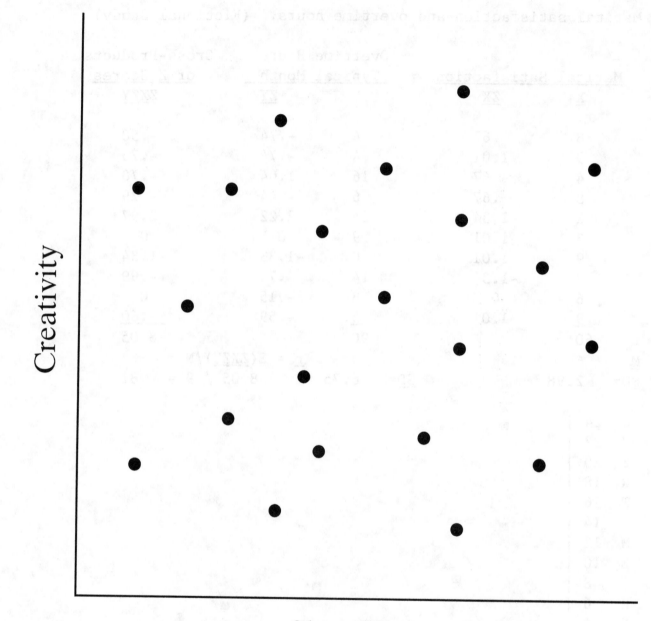

Creativity

Shoe Size

Aron/Aron
Statistics for the Social Sciences

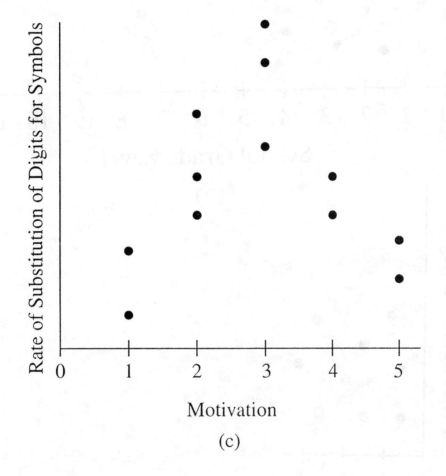

(c)

Aron/Aron
Statistics for the Social Sciences

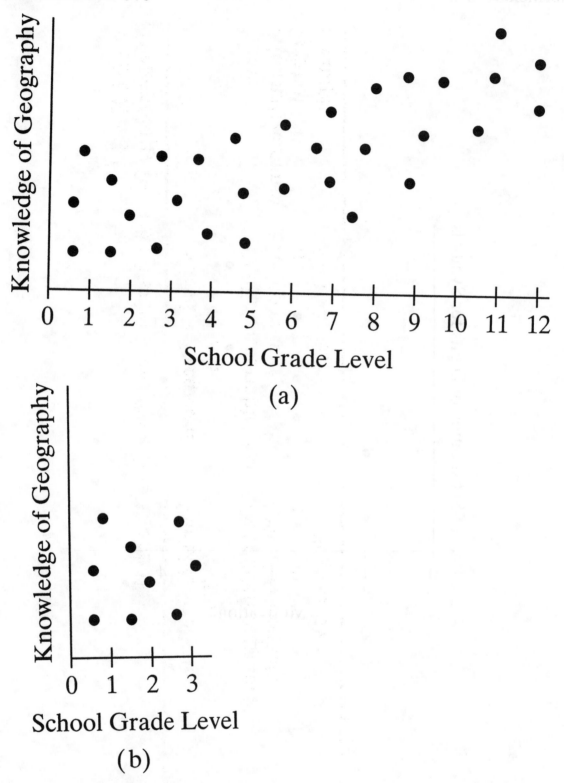

(a)

(b)

Aron/Aron
Statistics for the Social Sciences

TABLE 4-1
Terminology for Two Variables in Bivariate Prediction

	Variable Predicted From	Variable Predicted To
Name	Predictor variable	Dependent variable
Alternative name	Independent variable	Criterion variable
Symbol	X	Y
Example	SAT scores	College GPA

Aron/Aron
Statistics for the Social Sciences

© 1997 by Prentice-Hall, Inc.
Simon & Schuster/A Viacom Company
Upper Saddle River, New Jersey 07458

Manager's stress example.

Number supervised ($\underline{X}$): M = 7   SD=2.37
Stress   ($\underline{Y}$): M = 6   SD=2.61

$$\underline{r} = .88$$

If a manager supervised 10 employees, that manager would have a $\underline{Z}$ score for number supervised of 1.27:

$$\underline{Z}_X = (\underline{X} - \underline{M}_X)/\underline{SD}_X = (10-7)/2.37 = 3/2.37 = 1.27$$

$$\underline{Z}_Y = (\beta)(\underline{Z}_X) = (.88)(1.27) = 1.12$$

If a manager supervised 3 employees, that manager has a $\underline{Z}$ score for number supervised of -1.69:

$$\underline{Z}_X = (\underline{X} - \underline{M}_X)/\underline{SD}_X = (3-7)/2.37 = -4/2.37 = -1.69$$

■

$$\underline{Z}_Y = (\beta)(\underline{Z}_X) = (.88)(-1.69) = -1.49$$

Aron/Aron
Statistics for the Social Sciences

© 1997 by Prentice-Hall, Inc.
Simon & Schuster/A Viacom Company
Upper Saddle River, New Jersey 07458

Examples of bivariate prediction.
(Prediction rule from Orme-Johnson & Haynes, 1981.)

Predicted $\underline{Z}_Y = (\underline{r})(\underline{Z}_X)$

Predicted Creativity $\underline{Z} = (.82)(\underline{Z}$ for EEG Coherence$)$

Example	Example Scores on Predictor Variable EEG Coherence		Correlation r = .82	Predicted Value of Dependent Variable Creativity Test Score
	Raw	Z		Z
a.	.2	-1.45	.82	-1.19
b.	.5	-.36	.82	-.30
c.	1.0	1.45	.82	1.19
d.	.8	.73	.82	.60
e.	.5	-.36	.82	-.30

Aron/Aron
Statistics for the Social Sciences

TABLE 3-5
Summary, Using Formulas, of Steps for Making Raw Score Predictions With Raw-to-Z and Z-to-Raw Conversions, With an Example

Step	Formula	Example
1	$Z_X = (X - M_X)/SD_X$	$Z_X = (3 - 7)/2.37 = -1.69$
2	Predicted $Z_Y = (\beta)(Z_X)$	Predicted $Z_Y = (.88)(-1.69) = -1.49$
3	Predicted $Y = (SD_Y)$ Predicted $(Z_Y) + M_Y$	Predicted $Y = (2.61)(-1.49) + 6 = 2.11$

Aron/Aron
Statistics for the Social Sciences

© 1997 by Prentice-Hall, Inc.
Simon & Schuster/A Viacom Company
Upper Saddle River, New Jersey 07458

Example of multiple regression with $\underline{Z}$ scores.
(Fictional example)

Predicted $\underline{Z}_{\underline{Y}} = (\beta_1)(Z_{\underline{x}}\underline{1}) + (\beta_2)(Z_{\underline{x}}\underline{2}) + (\beta_3)(Z_{\underline{x}}\underline{3})$

Example:

$\underline{Z}_{Stress} = \quad (.51)(\underline{Z}_{Number\ Supervised})$

$+ \quad (.11)(\underline{Z}_{Noise\ Level})$

$+ \quad (.33)(\underline{Z}_{Deadlines/Month})$

Suppose a particular manager whose level of
stress you want to predict had these $\underline{Z}$ scores:

$\underline{Z}$ for Number Supervised = 1.27
$\underline{Z}$ for Noise Level   = -1.82
$\underline{Z}$ for Deadlines/Month   = .94

■
$\underline{Z}_{Stress} = (.51)(1.27) + (.11)(-1.81) + (.33)(.94)$

$= \quad\quad .65 \quad\quad + \quad\quad -.20 \quad\quad + \quad .31 \quad\quad\quad = .76$

Aron/Aron
Statistics for the Social Sciences

© 1997 by Prentice-Hall, Inc.
Simon & Schuster/A Viacom Company
Upper Saddle River, New Jersey 07458

Chapter 4
Some Key Ingredients for Inferential Statistics:
The Normal Curve, Probability, and Population versus Sample

Instructor's Summary of Chapter

The normal curve. Many distributions of variables in psychology research approximately follow a bell-shaped, symmetrical, unimodal distribution called the normal curve. Because it is precisely mathematically defined, there are a known percentage of cases between any two points on a normal curve.

50%-34%-14%-2% rule of thumb. When working with normal curves, 50% of the cases fall above the mean, about 34% between the mean and one standard deviation above the mean, 14% between one and two standard deviations, and 2% beyond two standard deviations.

Normal curve tables give the percentage of cases between the mean and any particular positive Z score. Using such a table, and knowing that the curve is symmetrical and that 50% of the cases fall above the mean, it is possible to determine the percentage of cases above or below any particular Z score, and also the Z score corresponding to the point at which a particular percentage of cases begins.

Probability. Most psychologists consider the probability of an event to be its expected relative frequency, though some treat it as the subjective degree of belief that the event will happen. Probability is usually calculated as the proportion of successful outcomes to the total possible outcomes. It is symbolized by p and has a range from 0 (event is impossible) to 1 (event is certain). The normal distribution can be thought of as providing a way to know the probabilities of scores being within particular ranges of values. (That is, it can be thought of as a probability distribution.)

Sample and population. A sample is an individual or group which is studied--usually as representative of a larger group, the population, which is not practical or possible to study in its entirety. Ideally, the sample is selected from the population using a strictly random procedure.

Sample statistics and population parameters. The mean, variance, and so forth of a sample are called sample statistics; when of a population, they are called population parameters and are symbolized by Greek letters--μ for mean and σ^2 for variance. Most of the techniques in the rest of this book make probabilistic inferences in order to draw conclusions about populations based on information from samples. In this process, populations are usually assumed to be normally distributed.

How the procedures of this chapter are described in research articles. Research articles rarely discuss normal curves (except briefly when the distribution involved seems not to be normal) or probability (except in the context of significance testing, to be covered starting in Chapter 6). However, procedures of sampling, particularly when the study is a survey, are usually described, and the representativeness of a sample when random sampling could not be used may be discussed.

Box 4.1. Surveys, Polls, and 1948's Costly "Free Sample." Discusses the mistaken predictions of the major polling organizations about the 1948 U.S. presidential election and how polling organizations today approximate probability sampling procedures.

Lecture 4.1: The Normal Curve

Materials

Lecture outline

Deck of 90 large index cards made up so that on each is
written a single numeral from one to nine--ten with 1s, ten with 2s, etc.

Transparencies 1.2 and 4.1 through 4.3.

Outline for Blackboard

    I.   **Review**
   II. **Characteristics of the Normal Curve**
 III. **Why Approximations to It Are So Common**
 IV. **Why Some Distributions Are Not Near Normal**
   V. **Normal Curve and Z scores**
 VI. **Review this Class**

Instructor's Lecture Outline

I.   Review

A. Idea of descriptive statistics and brief overview of major types:
    1. Tables, graphs, mean, standard deviation, variance, and Z scores.
    2. Correlation coefficient.

B. Review principle of the histogram and frequency polygon for summarizing a group of data. Show TRANSPARENCY 1.2 (histogram and frequency polygon of student's stress ratings, from text) and explain.

C. Review normal curve as introduced in Chapter 1 as a symmetrical, unimodal distribution.

D. Review Z scores:
    1. Principle: Number of standard deviations above or below the mean.
    2. Raw to Z score: $Z = (X-M)/SD$.
    3. Z to Raw score: $X = M + (Z)(SD)$.
    4. Z score as distance in a histogram or frequency polygon.

II.   Characteristics of the Normal Curve

A. Show TRANSPARENCY 4.1 (normal curve) when discussing points A through C below.

B. Most cases fall near the center, fewer at extremes (that is, it is unimodal).

C. Symmetrical.

D. It is a theoretical distribution:
    1. Precisely mathematically defined by a formula with two variables:
       a. mean--where its center is located.
       b. standard deviation--how spread out the numbers along its base are.
    2. Thus, when using Z scores (where M is always 0 and SD is always 1), the normal curve is always the same.
    3. Does not *exactly* correspond to any distribution in nature (though it certainly does approximately).
    4. The scale has no limit below or above.
    5. It is a smooth curve because, as either a histogram or frequency polygon, the "intervals" of the scale are infinitesimal.

III. Why Approximations to the Normal Curve Are So Common

A. Approximations are extremely common (for each example explain that most cases would fall towards the center with decreasing numbers of cases going out from the center at about equal rates).

    1. Examples:

        a. Scores of a group of people on a test of self-esteem.

        b. Weights of all newborn foals in Kentucky in 1994.

        c. Length of all adult sardines in a particular school of them.

        d. Number of letters in the lines in a particular book.

    2. Ask students to come up with some examples.

B. An intuitive understanding of why it is so common:

    1. Each actual case is influenced by many things, each of which is essentially random.

    2. The combination of these random offsetting events is likely to be a middle score in most cases (making the distribution unimodal).

    3. When it is not a middle score, there are equal chances of an imbalance of the random influences being in either direction (making the distribution symmetrical).

C. The Central Limit Theorem.

    1. Each case representing a combination of random influences producing a normal-shaped curve is called the Central Limit Theorem.

    2. The intuitive understanding given above (in point B) explains only why the normal curve is unimodal and symmetrical, but not why it has its precise shape. However, it can be proven mathematically that taking cases representing a combination of random influences will in the long run produce an exact normal curve.

D. Class demonstration [if time does not permit the entire exercise, omit the version using two cards each]:

    1. On the blackboard draw a base for a histogram with nine intervals, labeled 1, 2, 3, 4, 5, 6, 7, 8, and 9.

    2. Ask three students to volunteer to come to the front of the class. Make one a Shuffler, one a Reader, and one a Grapher.

    3. Show the class the deck of cards and how it consists of 10 ones, 10 twos, etc., through 10 nines.

    4. Have the Shuffler shuffle the deck very thoroughly.

    5. Have the Reader take the top card from the deck, show it and read it to the class, then put the card back in the deck.

    6. Have the Grapher put a box on the histogram for that number.

    7. Repeat this process (Steps 4 through 6) about 20 times and note how the distribution is approximately rectangular and discuss.

    8. Select three new volunteers--this time be sure that the Reader is someone who feels they can figure numbers in their head fairly easily.

    9. Draw a new baseline for a histogram with intervals of 1, 1.5, 2, 2.5, etc., through 9.

    10. Have the Shuffler thoroughly shuffle the cards.

    11. Have the Reader take the top TWO cards from the deck, show them to the class, and speak out their AVERAGE, then put the two cards back in the deck.

    12. Have the Grapher put a box on the histogram for that number.

    13. Repeat this process (Steps 10 through 12) 15-20 times and note how the distribution is now approximately unimodal and symmetrical. (You may have to judge a good point to stop before or after 20 to make this point seem clear.)

    14. Discuss how the result of using two cards demonstrates the Central Limit Theorem and why normal curves are so common in nature. (You might also mention that, when drawing two cards, strictly speaking they should have taken each card out one at a time and put it back before the second--but that for this demonstration it was good enough to approximate equal chances for each possible pair of numbers to arise.)

    15. Repeat whole process again with new volunteers and using three cards each time.

16. Note how curve is more clearly normal—and how it is narrower than when only two were used.
    a. Explain that this principle (that the more cases in each group that are combined, the narrower the curve) will be considered in great detail later in the course.
    b. Note that the idea is that it is unlikely that two cards will BOTH be nines or BOTH ones, making these extremes unlikely. But it is even less likely that THREE cards would all be ones or nines, making these extremes in this case VERY unlikely. But middle scores can be made up of many more combinations--more when there are three cards than when there are two each.

IV. Why Some Distributions Are Not Near Normal
   A. Limits on maximum or minimum score possible:
      1. Ceiling effects. Example: Percent correct on an essay test (maximum=100).
      2. Floor effects. Example: Distribution of SAT scores at college (only those with adequate levels are accepted, so there is a floor effect compared to the whole population).
   B. Limited number of categories, making a noncontinuous distribution (a nonsmooth curve). Example: Number of children in a family.
   C. Growth and time effects. Example: Height of children (will be rectangular if not all at same age).
   D. Direct random effects. Example: Distribution of roulette wheel numbers.

V. Normal Curve and Z Scores
   A. Because the normal curve is an exactly defined distribution, if a distribution is normal then there is an exact relation between any of its Z scores and the percent of cases above and below it. Thus:
      1. If you know the Z score, you can determine the percent of cases above or below that Z score. Example: If a Z score is 2.5, what percent of people have higher scores?
      2. If you know your relative position to others in a distribution (the proportion above or below you), you can determine your Z score. Example: If you are in the top 10% on a test, what is your Z score?
   B. One aspect of the normal curve is that it is perfectly symmetrical around the mean. Thus,
      1. If a person has a Z score of 0, there are exactly 50% of the cases above that person and 50% below.
      2. If a person has 50% of the people below them and 50% above them, there Z score is 0.
   C. 50%-34%-14% Rule of Thumb. Show TRANSPARENCY 4.2 (normal curve showing rule-of-thumb percentages from text) and discuss:
      1. Approximately 34% of cases fall between the mean and one standard deviation. Thus,
         a. If a person has a Z score of 1:
            i.   34% of the people have Z scores between that person and the mean.
            ii. Because 50% of the cases are below the mean, 84% of the people fall below that person.
            iii. Because there is total of 50% of the cases above the mean, 16% of the people fall above that person.
         b. If a person has a Z score of -1:
            i.   34% of the people have Z scores between that person and the mean.
            ii. Because 50% of the cases are below the mean, 16% of the people fall below that person.
            iii. Because there are 50% of the cases above the mean, 84% of the people are above that person.
         c. 64% of the people have Z scores between +1 and -1.

2. Approximately 14% of cases fall between one and two standard deviations from the mean. Thus,
  a. If a person has a Z score of 2:
    i.   14% of the people have Z scores between that person and someone only one standard deviation   above the mean.
    ii. 98% of the cases are below that person (14%+34%+50%)--that is, the person is in the top 2% of the cases.
  b. If a person has a Z score of -2:
    i.   14% of the people have Z scores between that person and someone only one standard deviation   below the mean.
    ii. 2% of the cases are below that person (50%-14%+34%)--that is, 98% of the cases are above that person on this measure.
  c. 96% of the people have Z scores between +2 and -2.
3. Ask class:
  a. If a person has 50% of the people above him or her, what is that person's Z score? [0]
  b. If a person has 50% of the people below him or her, what is that person's Z score? [0]
  c. If a person has 2% of the people above him or her, what is that person's Z score? [+2]
  d. If a person has 2% of the people below him or her, what is that person's Z score? [-2]
  e. If a person has 16% of the people above him or her, what is that person's Z score? [1]
  f. What percent of the people fall between the mean and a Z score of +2? [48%]
  g. What percent of the people fall between a Z score of +1 and a Z score of 0? [34%]
  h. What percent of the people fall between a Z score of -1 and a Z score of 0? [34%]
  i. What percent of the people fall between a Z score of +1 and a Z score of -2? [82%]
4. This procedure can be done with raw scores when you know a distribution's M and SD, because then raw scores can be connected to Z scores and vice versa. Example: If a person has a score of 36 on a test and the mean is 30 and the standard deviation is 6, then that person's Z score is +2, and-- assuming the distribution of scores on this test is normal--that person is in the top 16% of all scorers.

D. Using normal curve tables.
  1. The percent of cases between the mean and any particular Z score can be computed mathematically from the equation for the normal curve.
  2. Because this is quite tedious to do, there are tables.
  3. Show TRANSPARENCY 4.3 (normal curve table) and discuss, giving several examples.

VI.   Review this Class: Use blackboard outline.

Lecture 4.2: Probability and Sample and Population

Materials

Lecture outline
Transparencies 4.1 through 4.6.

Outline for Blackboard

I. **Review**
II. **Probability**
III. **Sample and Population**
IV. **Review this Class**

Instructor's Lecture Outline

I.   Review
  A. Idea of descriptive statistics.
  B. Show TRANSPARENCY 4.1 (normal curve) and discuss key characteristics.
  C. Normal curve and Z scores.
      1. Show TRANSPARENCY 4.2 (normal curve showing rule-of-thumb percentages, from text) and discuss.
      2. Show TRANSPARENCY 4.3 (normal curve table) and discuss.

II.   Probability:
  A. Scientific research does not permit determining the definite truth or falsity of theories or applied procedures.
  B. But inferential statistics are applied to results of research to make probabilistic conclusions about theories or applied procedures.
  C. Probability is a large and controversial topic, but there are only a few key ideas you need to know to understand basic inferential statistical procedures.
  D. Show TRANSPARENCY 4.4 (interpretations of probability) and discuss.
  E. Show TRANSPARENCY 4.5 (computing probability) and discuss.
  F. The normal distribution can also be thought of as a probability distribution: The proportion of cases between any two Z scores is the same as the probability of selecting a case between those two Z scores. Show TRANSPARENCY 4.2 again and discuss.

III.   Sample and Population
  A. Show TRANSPARENCY 4.6 (pot of beans and spoonful, from text) and discuss:
      1. A *population* (like the pot of beans) is the entire set of things of interest.
      2. A *sample* (like the spoonful) is the subset of the population about which you actually have information.
  B. Why samples are studied (instead of populations):
      1. Usually more practical.
      2. Goal of science is to make generalizations or predictions about events beyond our reach.

C. General strategy of psychology research is to study a sample of individuals who are believed to be representative of the general population (or of some particular population of interest).

D. At the minimum, researchers try to study people who at least do not differ from the general population in any systematic way which would be expected to matter for that topic of research.

E. Methods of sampling:

1. *Random selection*: The researcher obtains a complete list of all the members of a population and randomly selects some number of them to study.

   a. Example: Telephone survey using a random numbers table to select from a listing of all residential phone numbers (presuming all people with phones is the population).

   b. Example: Putting all the names of the students in a large class on equal size slips in a hat, shaking up the hat, and taking out 40 names (students in the class are the population).

2. *Haphazard selection*: Selecting whoever is available without any systematic plan. This is likely to yield a biased sample.

   a. Example: Surveying each person you run into in the street. [Ask class and then discuss why not random.]

   b. Example: Selecting students from a class who happen to be sitting in the front row. [Ask class and then discuss why not random.]

3. Ask class for some ideas for doing random sampling when planning research involving each of the following populations. Discuss strengths and weaknesses of each idea:

   a. Presidents of top corporations.

   b. U.S. voters.

   c. Chimpanzees, to be used in a study of language acquisition.

4. In psychology research it is rarely possible to employ true random sampling.

   a. Researchers try to study a sample not systematically unrepresentative of the population in any relevant way.

   b. Researchers often assume that the pattern of relationships will be reasonably unaffected by the particular sample, even though means may differ from sample to sample.

F. Sample statistics include the mean, variance, and standard deviation computed from a known sample. Population parameters are the unknown statistics that are estimated from the sample.

IV. Review this Class: Use blackboard outline.

Aron/Aron
Statistics for the Social Sciences

© 1997 by Prentice-Hall, Inc.
Simon & Schuster/A Viacom Company
Upper Saddle River, New Jersey 07458

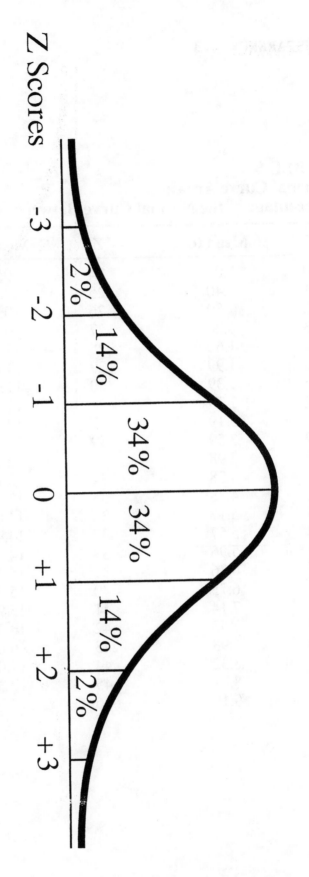

Z Scores

-3 -2 2% -1 14% 0 34% +1 34% +2 14% +3 2%

Aron/Aron
Statistics for the Social Sciences

TABLE B-1
Normal Curve Areas:
Percentage of the Normal Curve Between the Mean and the Z Scores Shown

Z	% Mean to Z	Z	% Mean to Z	Z	% Mean to Z
.00	.00	.24	9.48	.47	18.08
.01	.40	.25	9.87	.48	18.44
.02	.80	.26	10.26	.49	18.79
.03	1.20	.27	10.64	.50	19.15
.04	1.60	.28	11.03	.51	19.50
.05	1.99	.29	11.41	.52	19.85
.06	2.39	.30	11.79	.53	20.19
.07	2.79	.31	12.17	.54	20.54
.08	3.19	.32	12.55	.55	20.88
.09	3.59	.59	22.24	.56	21.23
.10	3.98	.33	12.93	.57	21.57
.11	4.38	.34	13.31	.58	21.90
.12	4.78	.35	13.68	.59	22.24
.13	5.17	.36	14.06	.60	22.57
.14	5.57	.37	14.43	.61	22.91
.15	5.96	.38	14.80	.62	23.24
.16	6.36	.39	15.17	.63	23.57
.17	6.75	.40	15.54	.64	23.89
.18	7.14	.41	15.91	.65	24.22
.19	7.53	.42	16.28	.66	24.54
.20	7.93	.43	16.64	.67	24.86
.21	8.32	.44	17.00	.68	25.17
.22	8.71	.45	17.36	.69	25.49
.23	9.10	.46	17.72	.70	25.80

Aron/Aron
Statistics for the Social Sciences

TRANSPARENCY 4.4

Two interpretations of probability:

1. Long-run relative frequency interpretation:

    Probability is the long run, expected relative frequency of a particular outcome.

    <u>Outcome</u> = result of an experiment or event.

    <u>Frequency</u> = how many times something occurs.

    <u>Relative frequency</u> = number of times something occurs
    relative to the number of times it
    could have occurred.

    <u>Long-run relative frequency</u> = what you would expect to get,
    in the long run, if you were
    to repeat the experiment many
    times.

2. Subjective interpretation:

    Probability is how certain one is that a particular outcome will occur.

Aron/Aron
Statistics for the Social Sciences

© 1997 by Prentice-Hall, Inc.
Simon & Schuster/A Viacom Company
Upper Saddle River, New Jersey 07458

TRANSPARENCY 4.5

Computing probability.

$$p = \frac{\text{Number of possible successful outcomes}}{\text{Number of all possible outcomes}}$$

Examples

Probability of a head (one possible outcome)
on a single coin flip (two possible outcomes)

$$p = \frac{\text{Number of possible successful outcomes}}{\text{Number of all possible outcomes}} = \frac{1}{2} = .5$$

Probability buying a winning ticket for a lottery
(800 winners) in which there are 1,000,000 tickets sold.

$$p = \frac{\text{Number of possible successful outcomes}}{\text{Number of all possible outcomes}} = \frac{800}{1,000,000} = .0008$$

Probability of getting accepted into a class (140 places) in which
400 have applied (assuming acceptance is by a random draw).

$$p = \frac{\text{Number of possible successful outcomes}}{\text{Number of all possible outcomes}} = \frac{140}{400} = .35$$

Aron/Aron
Statistics for the Social Sciences

© 1997 by Prentice-Hall, Inc.
Simon & Schuster/A Viacom Company
Upper Saddle River, New Jersey 07458

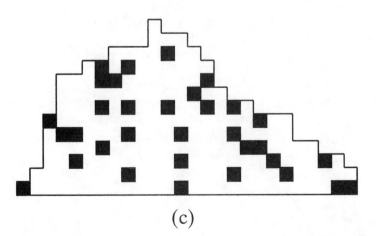

(a)

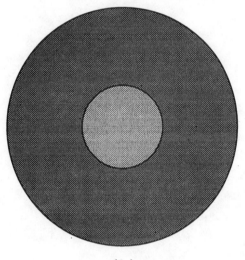

(b)

(c)

Aron/Aron
Statistics for the Social Sciences

© 1997 by Prentice-Hall, Inc.
Simon & Schuster/A Viacom Company
Upper Saddle River, New Jersey 07458

Chapter 5
Introduction to Hypothesis Testing

Instructor's Summary of Chapter

This chapter introduces the logic and key terminology of hypothesis testing, illustrating it with the rare-in-practice research situation in which a sample of one case is being compared to a known population.

The basic principle of hypothesis testing is to examine the probability that the outcome of a study could have arisen even if the true situation was that the experimental treatment made no difference. If this probability is low, this scenario is rejected and the theory from which the treatment was proposed is supported.

Research hypothesis and null hypothesis. The expectation of a difference or effect is the research hypothesis. The hypothetical situation in which there is no difference or effect is the null hypothesis.

Possible conclusions. When an obtained result would be extremely unlikely if the null hypothesis were true, the null hypothesis is rejected and the research hypothesis supported. If the obtained results are not very extreme, the study is inconclusive.

Conventional significance levels and directional and nondirectional tests. Psychologists usually consider a result too extreme if it is less likely than 5%, though a more stringent 1% cutoff is sometimes used. These percentages may apply to the probability of the result being extreme in a single predicted direction, a directional or one-tailed test, or to the probability of it being extreme in either direction, a nondirectional or two-tailed test.

Five steps of hypothesis testing: (1) Reframe the question into a research hypothesis and a null hypothesis about populations. (2) Determine the characteristics of the comparison distribution. (3) Determine the cutoff sample score on the comparison distribution at which the null hypothesis should be rejected. (4) Determine the score of your sample on the comparison distribution. (5) Compare the scores obtained in Steps 3 and 4 to decide whether to reject the null hypothesis.

How the procedures of this chapter are described in research articles. Research articles typically report the results of hypothesis testing by noting that a result was or was not significant, and giving the probability level cutoff (usually 5% or 1%) at which the decision was made.

Box 5.1. Whether and When to Accept the Null Hypothesis. Researchers usually presume that the null hypothesis can not be proven true. Frick (1995) has argued the null hypothesis could be supported in certain situations.

Lecture 5.1: Introduction to Hypothesis Testing

Materials

Lecture outline
Transparencies 4.2, 4.3, 4.5, and 5.1 through 5.6

Outline for Blackboard

   I.   **Review**
   II. **Inferential Statistics**
   III. **Example of Hypothesis Testing**
   IV. **Language and Steps of Hypothesis Testing**
   V. **Additional Examples**
   VI. **Review this Class**

Instructor's Lecture Outline

I.   Review
  A. Idea of descriptive statistics and importance in their own right.
  B. The normal curve.
     1. Approximations to it are common in distributions used in psychology.
     2. Show TRANSPARENCY 4.2 (normal curve showing 50%-34%-14% rules of thumb) and discuss relation of Z scores and percentages of cases when using a normal curve.
     3. Show TRANSPARENCY 4.3 (normal curve table) and discuss using normal curve tables.
  C. Probability: Show TRANSPARENCY 4.5 (calculation of probability) and discuss.
  D. Sample and population.
  E.   Relation of normal curve, probability, sample and population.

II. Inferential Statistics
  A. Involve making inferences about populations based on information in samples (as compared to descriptive statistics, which merely summarize attributes of known data).
  B. Especially important because we use them to draw conclusions about the world in general (i.e., populations we can not measure as a whole) based on results obtained from a particular experiment or study (i.e., a sample).
  C. This and the next few classes use research examples that would almost never really occur in order to introduce the key logic in the simplest possible context. (Later you learn to apply the logic in more realistic research situations.)

III. Example of Hypothesis Testing
  A. A person says she can identify people of above average intelligence with her eyes closed.
  B. The plan is then made to take her to a stadium full of randomly selected people from the general public and ask her to pick someone with her eyes closed who is of above average intelligence.

C. It is known in advance that the distribution of intelligence is normal with $M = 100$ and $SD = 15$.

D. Therefore, we know in advance that if she picks someone with an IQ of, say, 145, that is extremely unlikely to have been by chance. (That is, $Z = +3$, from normal curve table, probability is .13%.)

E. In fact, if she picks someone with an IQ of even 130 ($Z = 2.0$) there is only about a 2% chance and we would probably be convinced.

F. But if she picks someone with an IQ of 115 ($Z = 1$) there is a 16% chance she could have done this by chance and we would probably not be convinced.

G. Thus we set *in advance* a score by which we will be convinced. In this case, maybe 130 (for a 2% chance).

H. Or we might pick, say, a 1% chance (corresponding to a Z score of 2.33 or IQ = about 135).

I. Or for a 5% chance (for a Z score of about 1.64). For an IQ of $(15)(1.64) + 100 = 24.6 + 100 = 124.6$.

J. We then conduct the experiment.
   1. Suppose she picks someone with an IQ of 140? This should convince us that she has done something that would not just result from chance. (That is, she has some special ability, either employing intuition, a hoax, or whatever.)
   2. Suppose she picks someone with an IQ of 90? We would clearly not be convinced.
   3. Suppose she picks someone with an IQ of 115? This result is inconclusive--she did what she said she'd do, but it might have just happened by chance.

IV. **Language and Steps of Hypothesis Testing**
   A. Show TRANSPARENCY 5.1 (steps of hypothesis testing for IQ example) and at each step explain language and logic of this step.
   B. Show TRANSPARENCY 5.2 (normal curve illustration of IQ example) and discuss.

V. **Additional examples:**
   A. Show TRANSPARENCIES 5.3 and 5.4 (millionaire's happiness example from text) and discuss.
   B. Show TRANSPARENCIES 5.5 and 5.6 (stress-reduction method example) and discuss.

VI. **Review this Class: Use blackboard outline.**

Lecture 5.2: Significance Levels and Directional Tests

Materials

Lecture outline
Transparencies 5.3, 5.4, and 5.6 through 5.8

Outline for Blackboard

    I.   Review
    II. Significance Levels
    III. One- and Two-Tailed Tests
    IV. Review this Class

Instructor's Lecture Outline

I.   Review

A. Descriptive and inferential statistics.

B. Basic language and steps of hypothesis testing. Show TRANSPARENCIES 5.3 and 5.4 (millionaire's happiness example from text) and discuss each step.

II. Significance Levels

A. Significance level as percent cutoff in Step 3 of hypothesis testing process.

B. The lower the significance level (smaller percentage), the more sure we are if result is that extreme. Example: If .0001% was used, we would be very sure that if a result was that extreme we are correct in rejecting the null hypothesis.

C. The higher the level (larger percentage), the less likely we are to have to deal with inconclusive results. Example: If 25% was used, almost any result in the direction we predicted would permit us to reject the null hypothesis.

D. Psychologists usually use 5% as a conventional compromise.

E. Some psychologists prefer to use 1%.

F. We consider these issues in much more detail in Chapters 7 and 8.

G. How results are expressed:

    1. A result that is more extreme than the set significance level is said to be "statistically significant."

    2. The 5% level is often expressed as .05 and 1% as .01.

    3. A significant result may be described as $p < .05$.

      a. p is for probability of getting this result if the null hypothesis is true.

      b. $p < .05$ means that the probability of getting this result if the null hypothesis is true is less than .05 (5%).

    4. Sometimes researchers give more extreme (lower percentage) p levels to describe results that are very extreme, even though the original cutoff set was only 5% or 1%.

III. One- and Two-Tailed Tests

A. A researcher's prediction is often that those receiving some experimental treatment will score higher than those not receiving it.

    1. For example, the prediction was that those receiving $1,000,000 would be happier than the general public.

2. This is called a *directional hypothesis* because it predicts a direction of result.

3. It is also called a *one-tailed test* because the hypothesis test looks for an extreme result at just one end (in this case, the high end) of the curve.

4. Example: Show TRANSPARENCY 5.4 (millionaire example figure) and discuss.

5. A study could predict a directional result (that is, involve a one-tailed test) in which the prediction was that the score of the sample receiving the experimental treatment would be *lower*.

6. Example: Show TRANSPARENCY 5.6 (stress-reduction-method example figure) and discuss.

B. Sometimes, however, a researcher predicts that an experimental treatment will make a difference, but does not know whether it will create higher or lower scores.

1. Example: A polluting substance accidentally put in the water in a particular region may be suspected to affect the part of the brain that controls sleep, but it is not known whether it will increase or decrease amount of sleep (or have no effect).

2. This is an example of a *nondirectional hypothesis* because the research hypothesis is that the polluting substance will affect sleep, but no direction of effect is specified.

3. This is called a *two-tailed test* because extreme results at *either* extreme or tail (a lot or a little sleep) would make us want to reject the null hypothesis that the substance did not affect sleep.

4. In setting the cutoff for rejecting the null hypothesis, the overall probability (say 5%) must be divided between the two tails (say 2.5% at each).

5. This dividing means that, to be significant, a score must be more extreme than if a one-tailed test were used.

6. Show TRANSPARENCIES 5.7 and 5.8 (pollution and sleep example) and discuss.

C. When to use one-tailed and two-tailed tests:

1. If you use a one-tailed test and the result comes out in unexpected direction, no matter how extreme, it can not be considered significant.

2. To avoid this problem, researchers generally prefer to use two-tailed tests except where it is very clear that only one direction of outcome would be of interest. Example: Test of new procedure in which if it either did not work or made things worse, it would not be used.

3. Some researchers however use one-tailed tests whenever there is any basis for making the prediction.

IV. Review this Class: Use blackboard outline.

TRANSPARENCY 5.1

Steps of hypothesis testing:

1. Reframe the question into a research hypothesis and a null
   hypothesis about populations.

   Population 1: People chosen by woman with her eyes closed.
   Population 2: People in general.

   Research Hypothesis: Those chosen are more intelligent (Population 1
                        has a higher mean intelligence than Population
                        2).
   Null Hypothesis: Those chosen are not more intelligent (Population 1
                    does not have a higher mean intelligence than
                    Population 2).

2. Determine the characteristics of the comparison distribution.

   Known normal distribution, with Pop. $\underline{M}$ = 100 and Pop. $\underline{SD}$ = 15.

3. Determine the cutoff sample score on the comparison
   distribution at which the null hypothesis should be rejected.

   For 5% probability (top 5% of comparison distribution),
   $\underline{Z}$ needed is 1.64.

4. Determine the score of your sample on the comparison
   distribution.

   Person picks out individual with IQ=140.

   $\underline{Z}$ = ($\underline{X}$-Pop. $\underline{M}$)/Pop. $\underline{SD}$ = (140-100)/15 = 40/15 = 2.67.

5. Compare the scores obtained in Steps 3 and 4 to decide
   whether to reject the null hypothesis.

   Score on 4 (2.67) is higher than score on 3 (1.64).

   Therefore, <u>reject</u> the null hypothesis; the research hypothesis is
   supported.

Aron/Aron
Statistics for the Social Sciences

© 1997 by Prentice-Hall, Inc.
Simon & Schuster/A Viacom Company
Upper Saddle River, New Jersey 07458

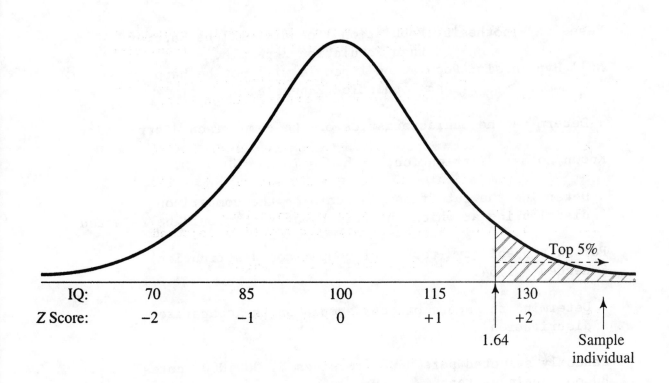

IQ: 70   85   100   115   130
Z Score: −2   −1   0   +1   +2

                                          Top 5%

                                   1.64   Sample
                                                 individual

Aron/Aron
Statistics for the Social Sciences

TRANSPARENCY 5.3

Steps of hypothesis testing:

1. Reframe the question into a research hypothesis and a null hypothesis about populations.

   Population 1: People who 6 months ago received $1,000,000.
   Population 2: People who 6 months ago did not receive $1,000,000.

   Research Hypothesis: Population 1 people will be happier than Population 2 people.
   Null Hypothesis: Population 1 people will not be happier than Population 2 people.

2. Determine the characteristics of the comparison distribution.

   Known normal distribution, with $\underline{M}$ = 70 and $\underline{SD}$ = 10.

3. Determine the cutoff sample score on the comparison distribution at which the null hypothesis should be rejected.

   For 5% probability (top 5% of comparison distribution), $\underline{Z}$ needed = 1.64.

4. Determine the score of your sample on the comparison distribution.

   Randomly selected person who receives $1,000,000 scores 80 on happiness test.

   $\underline{Z}$ = $(\underline{X}-\underline{M})/\underline{SD}$ = (80-70)/10 = 10/10 = 1.0.

5. Compare the scores obtained in Steps 3 and 4 to decide whether to reject the null hypothesis.

   Score on 4 (1.0) is not higher than score on 3 (1.64).

   Therefore, do not reject the null hypothesis; the result is inconclusive.

Aron/Aron
Statistics for the Social Sciences

© 1997 by Prentice-Hall, Inc.
Simon & Schuster/A Viacom Company
Upper Saddle River, New Jersey 07458

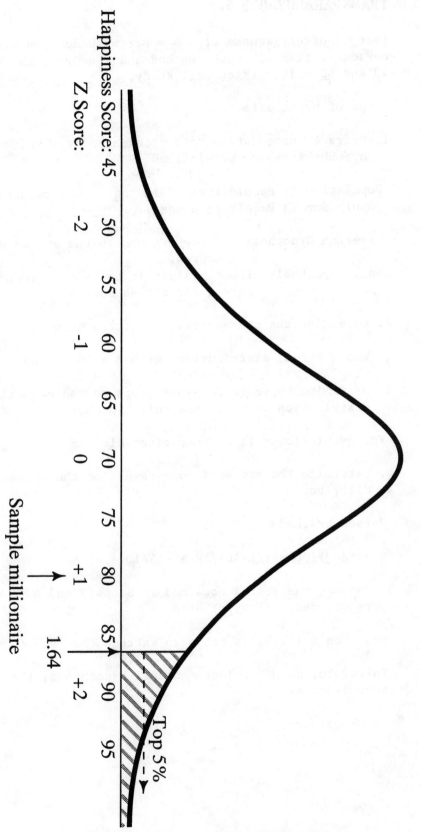

Happiness Score: 45 50 55 60 65 70 75 80 85 90 95

Z Score: -2 -1 0 +1 +2

Sample millionaire

1.64

Top 5%

© 1997 by Prentice-Hall, Inc.
Simon & Schuster/A Viacom Company
Upper Saddle River, New Jersey 07458

TRANSPARENCY 5.5

Test of effectiveness of a new stress reduction method: A randomly selected person is trained in the method and measured; in the general population, M = 40 and SD = 10. (Fictional study.)

Steps of hypothesis testing:

1. Reframe the question into a research hypothesis and a null hypothesis about populations.

   Population 1: People trained in the stress-reduction method.
   Population 2: People in general.

   Research Hypothesis: Those trained in the method do have lower stress scores.
   Null Hypothesis: Those trained in the stress reduction method do not have lower stress scores.

2. Determine the characteristics of the comparison distribution.

   Known normal distribution, with M = 40 and SD = 10.

3. Determine the cutoff sample score on the comparison distribution at which the null hypothesis should be rejected.

   For p<.01 (lower 1% of comparison distribution), Z needed= -2.33.

4. Determine the score of your sample on the comparison distribution.

   Person trained scores 25.

   $Z = (X-M)/SD = (25-40)/10 = -15/10 = -1.5$.

5. Compare the scores obtained in Steps 3 and 4 to decide whether to reject the null hypothesis.

   Score on 4 (-1.5) is not more extreme than score on 3 (-2.33).

   Therefore, do not reject the null hypothesis; the result is inconclusive.

Aron/Aron
Statistics for the Social Sciences

© 1997 by Prentice-Hall, Inc.
Simon & Schuster/A Viacom Company
Upper Saddle River, New Jersey 07458

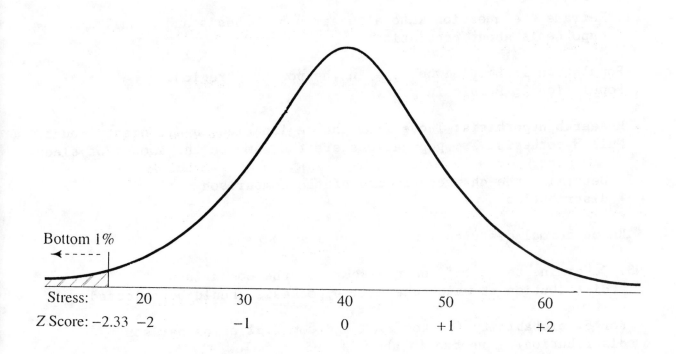

Bottom 1%

Stress: 20 30 40 50 60
Z Score: −2.33 −2 −1 0 +1 +2

Aron/Aron
Statistics for the Social Sciences

TRANSPARENCY 5.7

Study of amount of sleep of person living in a polluted region.
(Fictional data.)

Steps of hypothesis testing:

1. Reframe the question into a research hypothesis and a null
   hypothesis about populations.

   Population 1: People who live in the polluted region.
   Population 2: People in general.

   Research Hypothesis: Those from the region sleep a different amount.
   Null Hypothesis: Two populations are the same on the amount of sleep.

2. Determine the characteristics of the comparison
   distribution.

   Known normal distribution, with $\underline{M}$ = 8 and $\underline{SD}$ = 1.

3. Determine the cutoff sample score on the comparison
   distribution at which the null hypothesis should be rejected.

   For 5% probability (bottom 2.5% and top 2.5% of comparison
   distribution), $\underline{Z}$ needed is above +1.96 or below -1.96.

4. Determine the score of your sample on the comparison
   distribution.

   Person from polluted region sleeps 10.2 hours.

   $\underline{Z} = (\underline{X}-\underline{M})/\underline{SD} = (10.2-8)/1 = 2.2/1 = 2.2$.

5. Compare the scores obtained in Steps 3 and 4 to decide whether
   to reject the null hypothesis.

   Score on 4 (2.2) is more extreme (higher) than high cutoff on 3
   (±1.96).

   Therefore, reject the null hypothesis; the research hypothesis is
   supported.

Aron/Aron
Statistics for the Social Sciences

© 1997 by Prentice-Hall, Inc.
Simon & Schuster/A Viacom Company
Upper Saddle River, New Jersey 07458

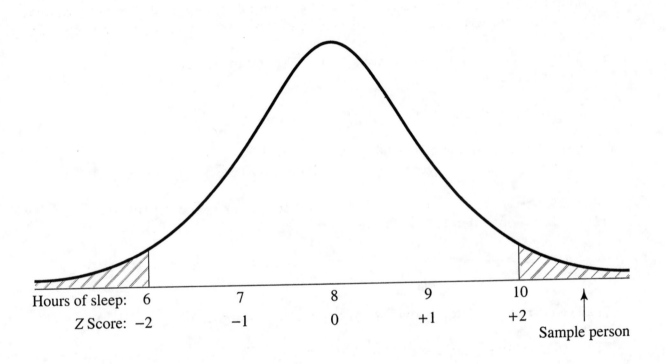

Hours of sleep: 6   7   8   9   10
Z Score: −2   −1   0   +1   +2
                                                    ↑
                                            Sample person

Aron/Aron
Statistics for the Social Sciences

Chapter 6
Hypothesis Tests with Means of Samples

Instructor's Summary of Chapter

The distribution of means. The distribution of means of *all* possible samples (from a particular population) of a given size can be thought of as the result of taking a very large number of samples, each of the same size and each drawn randomly from the population of individual cases, and making a distribution of the means of these samples.

Characteristics of a distribution of means. The distribution of means has the same mean as the population of individual cases. It has a smaller variance because the means of samples are less likely to be extreme than are individual cases--specifically, its variance is the variance of the population of individual cases divided by the size of the sample. Its shape approximates a normal curve if either (a) the population of individual cases is normally distributed or (b) the sample size being considered is of 30 or more.

Hypothesis testing with a single sample with $N > 1$. Hypothesis tests involving a single sample of more than one individual and a known population are conducted in exactly the same way as the hypothesis tests of Chapter 6 (where the single sample was of a single individual), except that the comparison distribution is a distribution of means of samples of that size.

Interval estimates. Sometimes researchers want to estimate a range of values for a population parameter. A confidence interval can be determined using a normal curve table.

How the procedures of this chapter are described in research articles. The standard deviation of the distribution of means—the *standard error* or *SE* is sometimes used to describe the expected variability of means, particularly in bar graphs in which the standard error may be shown as the length of a line above and below the top of each bar (instead of the more common use of the standard deviation for this purpose). Confidence intervals are sometimes reported in survey results.

Box 6.1. More About Polls: Sampling Errors and Errors in Thinking about Samples. Error in an opinion poll is measured with a procedure similar to finding the standard deviation of the distribution of means--the proportion of the population the sample represents is not usually relevant.

Lecture 6.1: The Distribution of Means

Materials

Lecture outline
Transparencies 5.5, 5.6, and 6.1 through 6.3

Outline for Blackboard

I. **Review**
II. **Introduction to the Distribution of Means**
III. **Its Mean**
IV. **Its Variance and Standard Deviation**
V. **Its Shape**
VI. **Summary of How to Determine Its Characteristics**
VII. **Review this Class**

Note to the Instructor

The demonstration described in Lecture 4.1, creating a normal curve, can be used with this lecture instead, or in addition. Just emphasize how the variance of the distribution of means decreases with increasing sample size.

If this demonstration is used here, you will need the appropriate materials (the deck of index cards), as described for that lecture, and the outline should be amended accordingly.

Instructor's Lecture Outline

I. **Review**
  A. Idea of descriptive and inferential statistics.
  B. Basic logic of hypothesis testing:
    1. Show TRANSPARENCIES 5.5 and 5.6 (stress-reduction method example) and go through logic and language.
    2. Highlight role of comparison distribution in this process, noting that *in this case* it is the same as the population distribution, but in material covered later in the course, it usually will not be.

II. **Introduction to the Distribution of Means**
  A. Refer to stress-reduction example:
    1. What if *two* persons were trained in this procedure and *both* scored 25?
    2. Or *twenty* persons were tested and all scored about 25, or averaged 25?
    3. These examples are about hypothesis testing when the sample is greater than one (the situations considered up to now involved samples of one).
  B. The question this situation raises is, "if the null hypothesis is true, what is the probability of randomly selecting a sample of two or more scores with an *average* of some particular number?"

C. The probability of a single individual having a score of 25 is higher than the probability of two individuals both having 25 (or of the two averaging 25).
    1. That is, the probability of a group's average being any particular extreme score is smaller than the probability of an individual's score being that extreme.
    2. This is because if there is, say, a 10% chance of one person getting a score that extreme, for two to get a score that extreme, this thing with a 10% chance would have to happen twice, and the chances of that are certainly less than 10%.
    3. Another example: One is pretty unlikely to win a lottery once, but even more unlikely to win it twice in a row.
D. To determine just what the probability is of a group of a particular size having average scores at various extremes, we need a distribution of averages of groups of this size.
E. Such a distribution is a distribution of all possible means of samples of this size drawn randomly from the population.
F. For short, we call this a *distribution of means*.
G. Statisticians usually call this a *sampling distribution of the mean*. (We avoid that language because students get it mixed up with the distribution of the sample itself.)
H. Developing an intuitive understanding of this distribution, using as an example a distribution of means of all possible samples of 5 cases each:
    1. Start with a population of individual cases.
    2. Select a sample of five cases and compute its mean.
    3. Select another sample of five cases and compute its mean.
    4. Continue this process a very large number of times.
    5. Create a histogram of these means.
    6. This histogram is a distribution of means.
I. At this point remind students of the demonstration in Lecture 5.1 (or carry it out here if it was not done then). Note that in that demonstration they also created a distribution of means, of samples of 1, 2, and 3.
J. An actual distribution of means as used in statistics is not constructed in this way—it would be impractical. But fortunately its characteristics (mean, variance, shape) can be determined mathematically based on the characteristics of the population and the size of the sample.
K. Show TRANSPARENCY 6.1 (three kinds of distributions) and discuss.

III. The Mean of the Distribution of Means
A. The mean of the distribution of means is the same as the mean of the population.
B. This is because there is no reason all these randomly selected sample means should be systematically higher or lower than the population mean.

IV. The Variance and Standard Deviation of the Distribution of Means
A. If each sample has only one case, the distribution of means is the same as the population (in every respect, because it is the same thing).
B. When the sample size is two or more, the variance of the distribution of means is always smaller than the variance of the population.
    1. This is because the probability of getting two or more extreme cases in the same direction is less than getting just one.
    2. This is the same principle we saw in the demonstration in Lecture 4.1 (or in this lecture).

3. This is the reason so many distributions in nature are normally distributed:
    a. The offsetting influences that combine to form each case represent, in effect, an average of a random sample of scores.
    b. That is, most normal curves, in a deep sense, are really distributions of means themselves.
    c. But do not confuse this general sense in which all normal curves can be thought of as distributions of means with the specific distinction between a population as a distribution of single cases and a distribution of means.
C. The more cases in each sample, the smaller the variation.
D. Exact rule: The variance of the distribution of means is the population variance divided by the number of cases in each of the samples.
E. Examples:
    1. Population variance is 12:
        a. Distribution of means of samples of 2 cases each has a variance of 6.
        b. Distribution of means of samples of 3 cases each has a variance of 4.
        c. Distribution of means of samples of 6 cases each has a variance of 2.
        d. Distribution of means of samples of 12 cases each has a variance of 1.
        e. Distribution of means of samples of 24 cases each has a variance of 1/2.
        f. Ask class: What if samples are 4 cases each? [3]
        g. Ask class: What if samples are 36 cases each? [1/3]
    2. Population variance is 50. Ask class, what is variance of distribution of means of samples of the following sizes:
        a. 2? [25]
        b. 5? [10]
        c. 10? [5]
        d. 25? [2]
        e. 50? [1]
        f. 100? [.5]
        g. 500? [.1]

V. The Shape of the Distribution of Means
A. If population is normal, distribution of means is normal.
B. If population is not normal (and $N > 1$):
    1. Distribution of means is still unimodal and symmetrical.
    2. The larger the sample size, the closer the distribution of means is to being normal.
    3. For practical purposes, if $N = 30$ or more, distribution of means can be considered normal.

VI. Summary of How to Determine the Characteristics of a Distribution of Means
A. Show TRANSPARENCY 6.2 (graphic of characteristics of distribution of means, from text) and discuss.
B. Show TRANSPARENCY 6.3 (examples of determining characteristics of distribution of means) and discuss.

VII. Review this Class: Use blackboard outline.

Lecture 6.2: Hypothesis Testing with a Sample of More than One

Materials

Lecture outline
Transparencies 5.5, 5.6, 6.2 and 6.4 through 6.6

Outline for Blackboard

I. **Review**
II. **The Distribution of Means as a Comparison Distribution**
III. **Hypothesis Testing with a Distribution of Means**
IV. **Interval Estimates and Confidence Intervals**
V. **Review this Class**

Instructor's Lecture Outline

I. Review
A. Idea of descriptive statistics and inferential statistics.
B. Basic logic of hypothesis testing:
   1. Show TRANSPARENCIES 5.5 and 5.6 (stress-reduction method example) and go through logic and language.
   2. Highlight role of comparison distribution in this process, noting that *in this case* it is the same as the population distribution, but it is not always.
C. Distribution of means:
   1. Principle: Distribution of means of all possible samples of a given size drawn randomly from the population.
   2. Intuitive understanding as constructed by taking a sample, computing its mean, repeating this many times and then making a histogram of these means.
   3. Show TRANSPARENCY 6.2 (graphic of characteristics of distribution of means) and discuss.

II. The Distribution of Means as a Comparison Distribution
A. The main importance of the distribution of means is that it is the comparison distribution when the sample is greater than one.
B. If you were to use the population distribution for the comparison distribution, you would be seeing where a number representing an average of several cases falls along a distribution of individual cases.
C. The distribution of means is the appropriate comparison distribution because it is the same thing as what is being compared--it is a particular mean being compared by seeing where it falls along a distribution of means.

III. Hypothesis Testing with a Distribution of Means
A. Procedure is the same as all along, except for using this new comparison distribution.
B. Show TRANSPARENCIES 6.4 and 6.5 (stress-reduction method example with $N=20$) and discuss.

IV. Interval Estimates and Confidence Intervals

A. A point estimate is a specific value of a population parameter estimated for an unknown population.

B. An interval estimate of a population mean describes a range of possible means.

C. A wide range that is almost certain to include the population mean is the confidence interval.

D. To determine a confidence interval:

1. Determine the characteristics of the distribution of means.
2. Use the normal curve table to find the Z scores for the upper and lower percentages you want.
3. Convert the Z scores to raw scores. These are the confidence limits for the confidence interval.

V. Review this Class: Use blackboard outline.

NOTE: Warn students that Chapter 7 will take more than the usual attention to master.

TRANSPARENCY 6.1

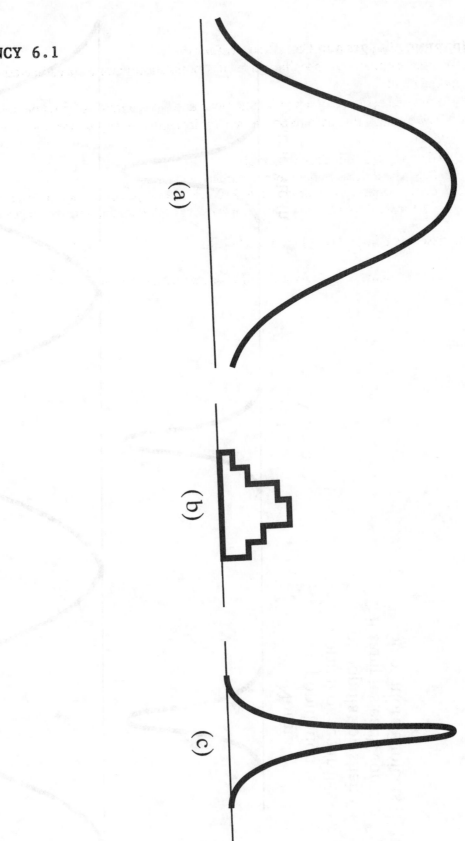

Aron/Aron
Statistics for the Social Sciences

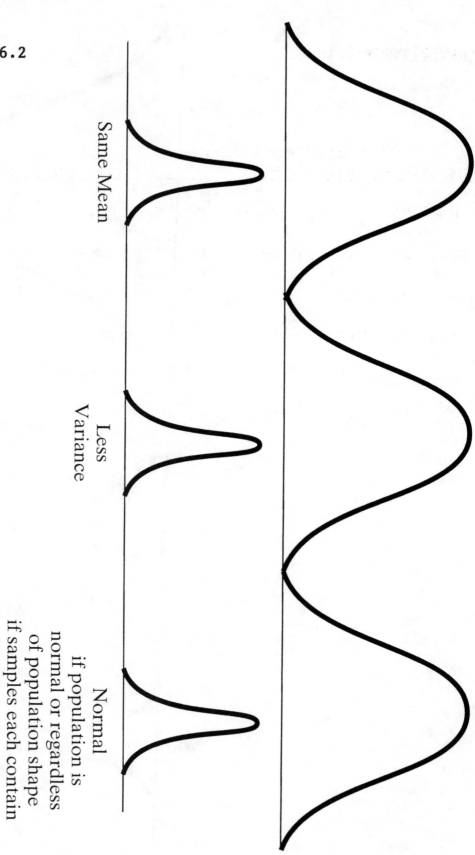

Same Mean

Less Variance

Normal
if population is
normal or regardless
of population shape
if samples each contain
30 or more subjects

TRANSPARENCY 6.3

Population		Sample Size	Population's Shape	Distribution of Means			
$\underline{M}$	$\underline{SD}$	$\underline{N}$	Normal?	$\underline{M_M}$	$\underline{SD_M}^2$	$\underline{SD_M}$	Normal?
109.3	20	10	No	109.3	400/10 = 40	$\sqrt{40}$ = 6.32	No
109.3	20	50	Yes	109.3	400/50 = 8	$\sqrt{8}$ = 2,83	Yes
109.3	20	100	No	109.3	400/100= 4	$\sqrt{4}$ = 2	Yes
28.8	1.6	9	Yes	28.8	25.56/9=2.84	$\sqrt{2.84}$=1.69	Yes
64	11	48	No	64	121/48 =2.52	$\sqrt{2.52}$=1.59	Yes

Aron/Aron
Statistics for the Social Sciences

© 1997 by Prentice-Hall, Inc.
Simon & Schuster/A Viacom Company
Upper Saddle River, New Jersey 07458

TRANSPARENCY 6.4

Stress-reduction-method example from previous lectures, but with 20 subjects. (Fictional data.)

Steps of hypothesis testing:

1. Reframe the question into a research hypothesis and a null hypothesis about populations.

   Population 1: People trained in the stress reduction method.
   Population 2: People in general.

   Research Hypothesis: Those trained in the stress reduction
                         method have lower stress scores.
   Null Hypothesis: Those trained in the method do not have lower
                     stress scores.

2. Determine characteristics of the comparison distribution.

   Population 2: shape = normal; $\underline{M}$ = 40; $\underline{SD}$ = 10.

   Distribution of means: shape = normal;

   $\underline{M}_M$ = 40; $\underline{SD}_M{}^2$ = $\underline{SD}^2/\underline{N}$ = 100/20 = 5; $\underline{SD}_M = \sqrt{\underline{SD}_M{}^2} = \sqrt{5}$ = 2.24.

3. Determine the cutoff sample score on comparison distribution at which the null hypothesis should be rejected.

   For 1% probability (bottom 1% of comparison distribution), $\underline{Z}$ needed is -2.33.

4. Determine the score of your sample on comparison distribution.

   Mean stress score of 20 people trained = 25.

   $Z = (\underline{M}-\underline{M}_M)/\underline{SD}_M$ = (25-40)/2.24 = -15/2.24 = -6.70.

5. Compare the scores obtained in Steps 3 and 4 to decide whether to reject the null hypothesis.

   Score on 4 (-6.70) is more extreme than score on 3 (-2.33).

   Therefore, reject the null hypothesis; the research hypothesis is supported.

Aron/Aron
Statistics for the Social Sciences

© 1997 by Prentice-Hall, Inc.
Simon & Schuster/A Viacom Company
Upper Saddle River, New Jersey 07458

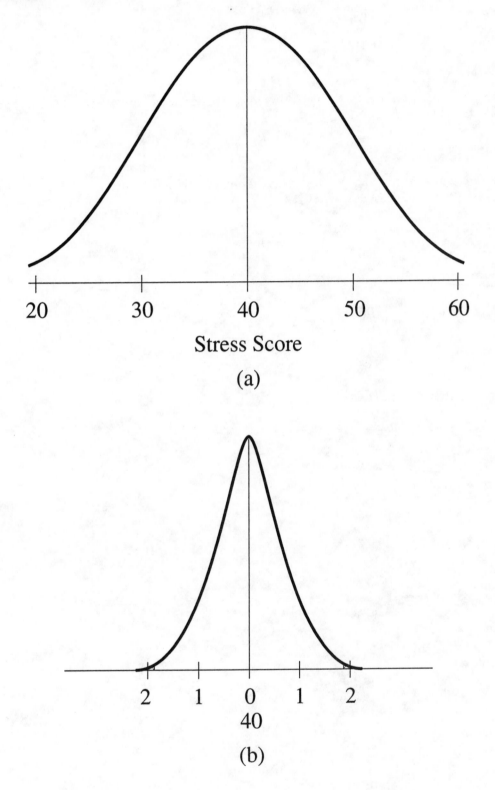

Stress Score

(a)

40

(b)

Aron/Aron
Statistics for the Social Sciences

Chapter 7
Statistical Power and Effect Size

Instructor's Summary of Chapter

Type I and Type II errors. In hypothesis testing in general, there are two kinds of correct outcomes: (a) the null hypothesis is rejected and the research hypothesis is actually true, and (b) the null hypothesis is not rejected and the research hypothesis is actually false. There are also two kinds of errors. A Type I error is when the null hypothesis is rejected but the research hypothesis is actually false. A Type II error is when the null hypothesis is not rejected but the research hypothesis is actually true.

Power. The statistical power of a study is the probability that it will yield a significant result if the research hypothesis is true. It is the probability of not obtaining a significant result even though the research hypothesis is true.

Influences on power. Power is affected by the size of the predicted difference between means, the population standard deviation, the sample size (*N*), the significance level, and whether a one- or a two-tailed test is used. Power is greatest when the predicted difference is large, population *SD* is small, Sample Size (*N*) is large, significance level (alpha) is least stringent, and a one-tailed test is used.

Effect size combines two of the factors influencing power—the predicted difference between means (the greater the difference, the larger the effect size) and Population *SD* (the smaller this is, the larger the effect size). One way effect size can be determined in advance of a study is by using rules of thumb of .2 for a small effect, .5 for a medium effect, and .8 for a large effect. Meta-analysis is a recently developed procedure for systematically combining effects of independent studies, primarily on the basis of effect sizes.

Practical ways of increasing the power of a planned experiment include increasing sample size or increasing effect size--by, for example, reducing variance with a less diverse population or more reliable measures, or increasing the intensity of the experimental treatment.

The importance of power in interpreting a completed experiment is that significant experimental findings with low power may not have practical importance, while nonsignificant experimental results with low power make it possible that important, significant results might show up if power were increased. Further, while it is not possible to "prove" the null hypothesis, with sufficient power a nonsignificant finding may suggest that any true effect is very, very small.

How the procedures of this chapter are described in research articles. When power is directly mentioned in research articles, it is usually in the discussion of results. Effect size is sometimes mentioned, both when comparing results of different studies or different parts of the same study.

Box 7.1. Effect Sizes for Relaxation and Meditation: A Restful Meta-Analysis. Summarizes an example of a meta-analysis study (Eppley, Abrams, & Shear, 1989).

Lecture 7.1: Power

Materials

Lecture outline
Transparencies 6.4, 6.5, and 7.1

Outline for Blackboard

   I.   Review
   II. Possible Outcomes of Hypothesis Testing
   III. What is Power?
   IV. Review this Class

Instructor's Lecture Outline

I.   Review
   A. Idea of descriptive and inferential statistics.
   B. Hypothesis testing with a distribution of means. Show TRANSPARENCIES 6.4 and 6.5 (stress reduction example) and discuss step by step.

II.   Possible Outcomes of Hypothesis Testing: Show TRANSPARENCY 7.1 (table showing four possible outcomes) and discuss using an example like the stress reduction research (TRANSPERENCY 6.4).

III. What is Power?
   A. Ask class, "What is power?"
   B. Meanings of power in ordinary life:
       1. The ability to achieve your goals--presuming these goals are good for you.
       2. Thus, knowledge is power, and the more accurate the knowledge, the more power.
   C. In statistics, we speak of the power of an experiment.
   D. Discuss the definitions of statistical power:
       1. The probability that if the research hypothesis is true, the results of your experiment will support the research hypothesis.
       2. The probability that you will not make a Type II error.
   E. Why power is important (covered in depth in next class):
       1. It helps in planning studies--if power is too low, you can choose not to do the study at all, or to change it to increase power.
       2. It helps when evaluating results of studies, particularly of nonsignificant results.

IV. Review this Class: Use blackboard outline.

Lecture 7.2: Influences on Power

Materials

Lecture outline
Transparencies 7.2 through 7.8

Outline for Blackboard

I. **Review**
II. **Predicted mean difference**
III. **Population Standard Deviation**
IV. **Sample size**
V. **Significance Level**
VI. **One- vs. Two-Tailed Tests**
VII. **Review this Class**

Instructor's Lecture Outline

I. **Review**
A. Idea of descriptive and inferential statistics.
B. Hypothesis testing with a distribution of means.
C. Possible outcomes of hypothesis testing (Type I and Type II Errors).
D. Definitions of Power.

II. **Predicted Mean Difference**
A. Principle:
  1. The greater the predicted mean difference, the more power.
  2. This is because the greater the predicted mean difference, the less overlap between the two distributions of means based on the known and hypothesized populations (they are farther apart).
  3. Show top of TRANSPARENCY 7.2 (overlaps of distributions for different mean differences, from text) and discuss.
B. Examples of effect of different predicted means.
  1. Show TRANSPARENCY 7.3 (stress-reduction example but with predicted mean = 216).
  2. Show TRANSPARENCY 7.4 (same example with predicted mean = 34) and compare to above.

III. **Population Standard Deviation**
A. Principle:
  1. The smaller the population standard deviation, the more power.
  2. This is because the smaller the population standard deviation, the smaller the standard deviation of the distribution of means, and thus the less overlap between the distributions of means based on the known and hypothesized populations (they are each narrower).
  3. Show bottom of TRANSPARENCY 7.2 (illustration of effect of lower standard deviation, from text) and discuss.

119

B. Examples of effect of different population standard deviations:
   1. Show TRANSPARENCY 7.5 (stress-reduction example but with Pop $SD = 5$).
   2. Show TRANSPARENCIES 7.4 (same example with Pop $SD = 10$) and compare to above.
C. Note: The two influences on power considered so far, predicted mean difference and population standard deviation, are often combined in a figure called the effect size, which is considered in the next lecture (Lecture 7.3).

IV. Sample Size (N)
A. Principle:
   1. The larger the sample size, the more power.
   2. This is because the larger the sample size, the smaller the standard deviation of the distribution of means and thus the less overlap between the distributions of means based on the known and hypothesized populations (they are each narrower).
   3. Show bottom of TRANSPARENCY 7.2 (illustration of effect of lower standard deviation, from text) again and discuss--this time pointing out how standard deviation of the distribution of means is affected by *both* variance and sample size.
B. Examples of effect of different sample sizes:
   1. Show TRANSPARENCY 7.6 (stress-reduction example but with sample size = 10).
   2. Show TRANSPARENCY 7.4 (same example with original sample size of 20) and compare to above.

V. Significance Level
A. Principle:
   1. The less stringent the significance level (for example .05 vs. .01), the more power.
   2. This is because the less stringent the significance level, the less extreme is the cutoff score on the lower distribution (the one for the known population), making the corresponding point on the upper distribution (the one for the hypothesized population) less extreme--so that more area is included in the power region.
B. Examples of effect of different significance levels:
   1. Show TRANSPARENCY 7.7 (stress-reduction example but with significance level of $p < .05$).
   2. Show TRANSPARENCIES 7.4 (same example with original significance level of $p < .01$) and compare to above.

VI. One- vs. Two-Tailed Tests
A. Principle:
   1. One-tailed tests have more power than two-tailed tests for a result in the predicted direction.
   2. This is because with a one-tailed test there is a less extreme cutoff score (in the predicted direction) on the lower distribution (for the known population), making the corresponding point on the upper distribution (for the hypothesized population) less extreme--so that more area is included in the power region.
   3. However, there is *zero* power for a result in the opposite-to-the-predicted direction.
B. Show TRANSPARENCY 7.8 (example of power with two-tailed test) and discuss.

VII. Review this Class
A. Use blackboard outline.
B. Emphasize the direction of influence on power of each of the influences considered.

Lecture 7.3: Power in Planning and Evaluating Studies

Materials

Lecture outline
Transparencies 7.9 through 7.12

Outline for Blackboard

    I.   Review
    II. Effect Size
    III. Power in Planning Experiments
    IV. Power in Interpreting Experiments
    V. Review this Class

Instructor's Lecture Outline

I.   Review
    A. Idea of descriptive and inferential statistics.
    B. Principle of hypothesis testing.
    C. Principle of power.
    D. Show TRANSPARENCY 7.9 (influences on power) and discuss.

II. Effect Size
    A. Effect size combines two of the influence on power—predicted mean difference and population standard deviation.
    B. The formula for effect size with a known population and a single sample is
    Effect Size = Population 1 *M* -Population 2 *M* / Population *SD* .
        1. Discuss formula.
        2. Notice it is NOT influenced by sample size.
        3. It is like a *Z* score in that it gives amount of difference between populations without regard to unit of measure.
        4. In this way it provides a standard that can be used to compare results of different studies even if they have different sample sizes, and even if they use different measures.
    C. Cohen's Rules of Thumb for effect size.
        1. Since it is often difficult to determine even a rough idea of the predicted mean, and the population standard deviation may not be known, Jacob Cohen developed rules of thumb that describe overall effect sizes typical of psychology research.
        2. Show TRANSPARENCY 7.10 (effect size conventions) and discuss.

III. Power in Planning Experiments: Show TRANSPARENCY 7.11 (table of practical ways to increase power, from text) and discuss.

IV. **Power in Interpreting Experiments:** Show TRANSPARENCY 7.12 (table of role of significance and sample size, from text) and discuss.

V. **Review this Class:** Use blackboard outline.

TABLE 7-2
Possible Correct and Erroneous Decisions in Hypothesis Testing

	Real Status of the Research Hypothesis (in practice, unknown)	
	True	False
Research hypothesis tenable (reject null hypothesis)	Correct decision	Error (Type I)
Study is inconclusive (fail to reject null hypothesis)	Error (Type II)	Correct decision

Aron/Aron
Statistics for the Social Sciences

© 1997 by Prentice-Hall, Inc.
Simon & Schuster/A Viacom Company
Upper Saddle River, New Jersey 07458

Research hypothesis
situation, based
on Population 1

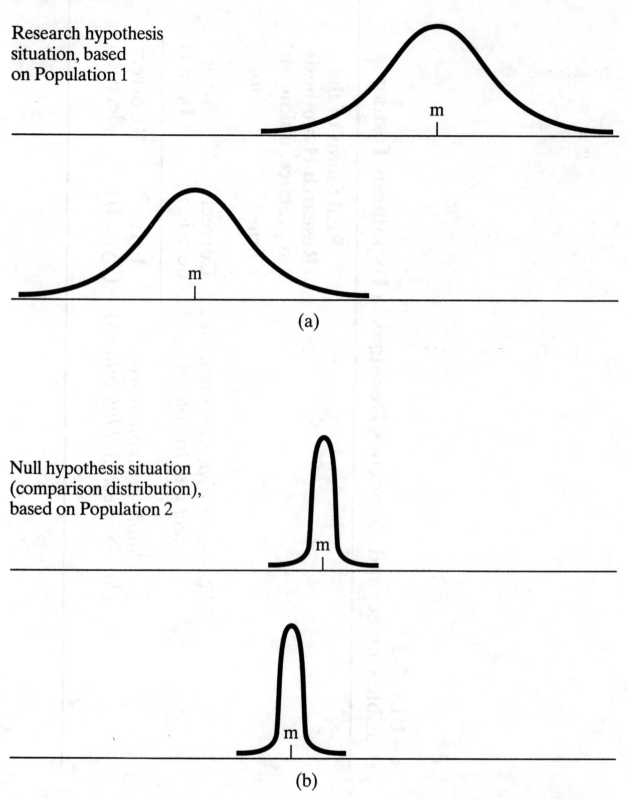

Null hypothesis situation
(comparison distribution),
based on Population 2

Predicted Mean = 32

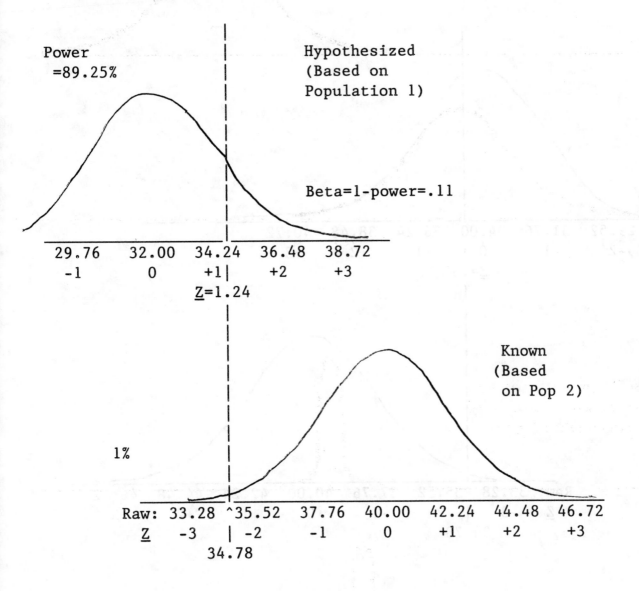

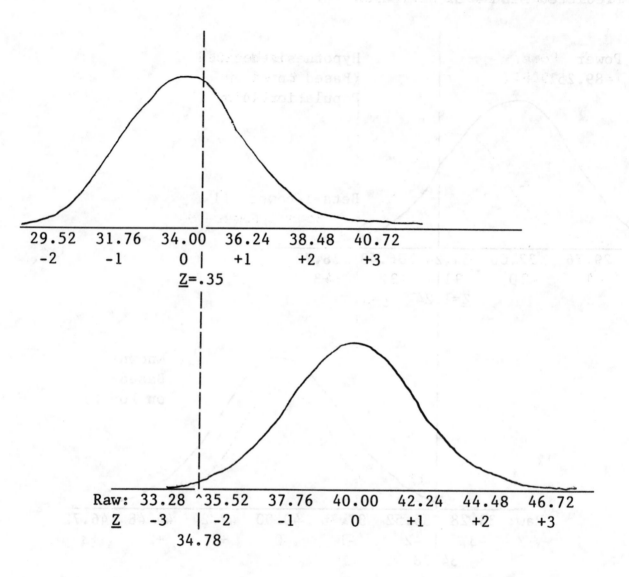

Population standard deviation = 5

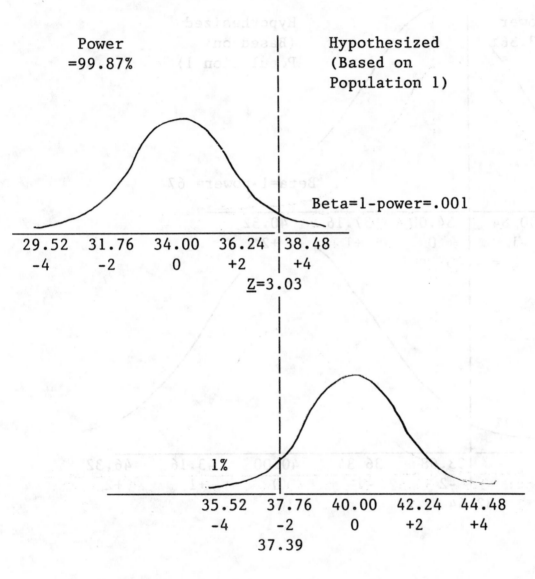

Power
=99.87%

Hypothesized
(Based on
Population 1)

Beta=1-power=.001

| 29.52 | 31.76 | 34.00 | 36.24 | 38.48 |
| -4 | -2 | 0 | +2 | +4 |

$\underline{Z}$=3.03

1%

| 35.52 | 37.76 | 40.00 | 42.24 | 44.48 |
| -4 | -2 | 0 | +2 | +4 |

37.39

Aron/Aron
Statistics for the Social Sciences

$\underline{N}$ = 10 (in original version $\underline{N}$ = 20)

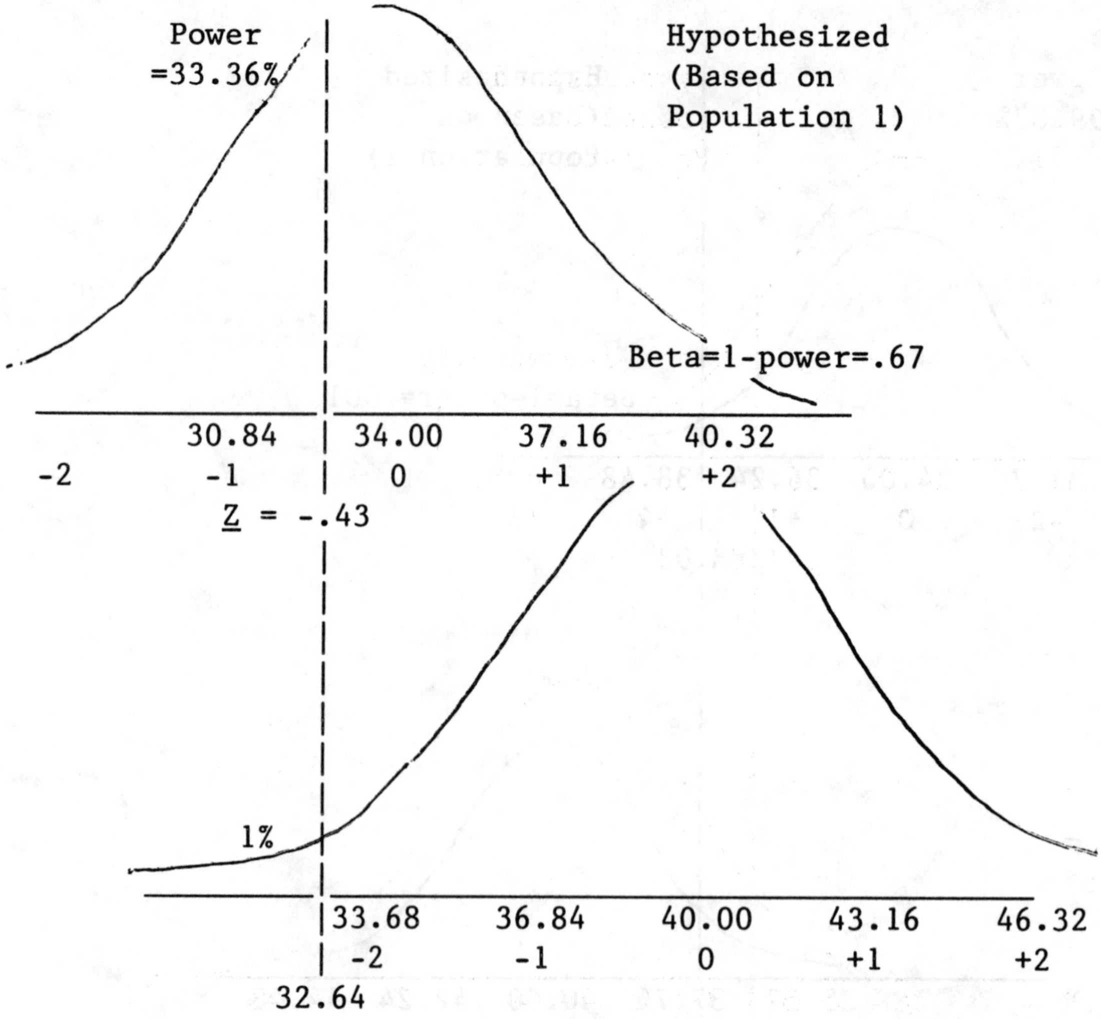

Power
=33.36%

Hypothesized
(Based on
Population 1)

Beta=1-power=.67

30.84	34.00	37.16	40.32
-2 -1	0	+1	+2

$\underline{Z}$ = -.43

1%

33.68	36.84	40.00	43.16	46.32
-2	-1	0	+1	+2

32.64

Aron/Aron
Statistics for the Social Sciences

© 1997 by Prentice-Hall, Inc.
Simon & Schuster/A Viacom Company
Upper Saddle River, New Jersey 07458

alpha = .05 (vs. .01 before)

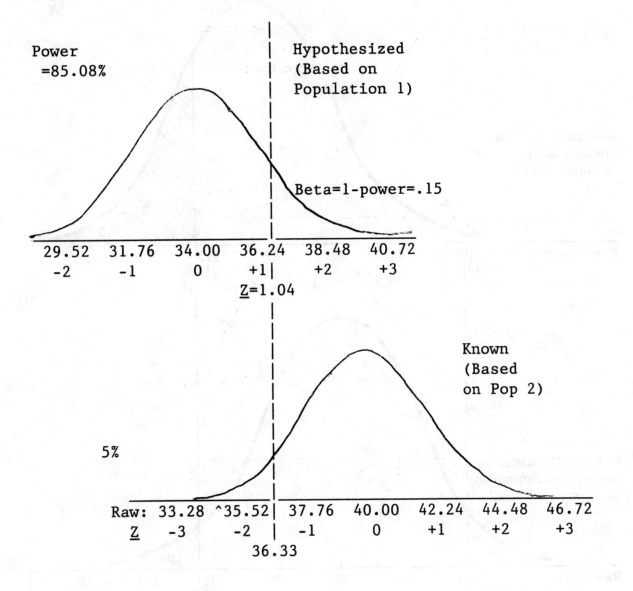

Power
=85.08%

Hypothesized
(Based on
Population 1)

Beta=1-power=.15

| 29.52 | 31.76 | 34.00 | 36.24 | 38.48 | 40.72 |
| -2 | -1 | 0 | +1| | +2 | +3 |

Z=1.04

Known
(Based
on Pop 2)

5%

Raw: 33.28 ^35.52| 37.76 40.00 42.24 44.48 46.72
Z   -3   -2 | -1   0   +1   +2   +3
              36.33

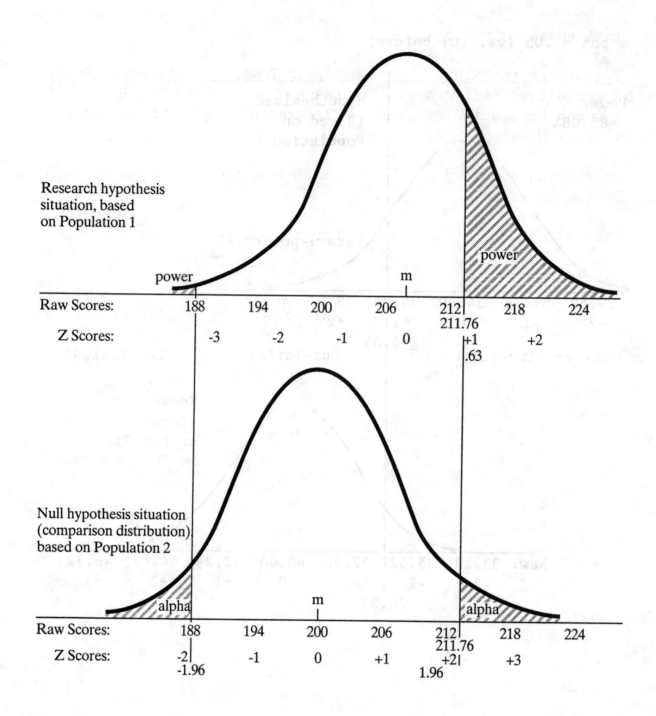

Research hypothesis
situation, based
on Population 1

power

power

Raw Scores:	188	194	200	206	212 211.76	218	224
Z Scores:		-3	-2	-1	0	+1 .63	+2

m

Null hypothesis situation
(comparison distribution)
based on Population 2

alpha

m

alpha

Raw Scores:	188	194	200	206	212 211.76	218	224
Z Scores:	-2 -1.96	-1	0	+1	+2 1.96	+3	

Influences on Power

Feature of the Study	Increases Power	Decreases Power
Hypothesized Difference Between Population Means (Pop. 1 M - Pop. 2 M)	Large Differences	Small Differences
Population Standard Deviation	Small Pop. SD	Large Pop. SD
Sample Size (N)	Large N	Small N
Significance Level	Lenient (5% or 10%)	Stringent (1% or .1%)
One- vs. Two-Tailed Test	One-Tailed	Two-Tailed

Aron/Aron
Statistics for the Social Sciences

© 1997 by Prentice-Hall, Inc.
Simon & Schuster/A Viacom Company
Upper Saddle River, New Jersey 07458

Summary of Cohen's Effect Size Conventions for Mean Differences

Verbal Description	Effect Size (d)
Small	.2
Medium	.5
Large	.8

Aron/Aron
Statistics for the Social Sciences

© 1997 by Prentice-Hall, Inc.
Simon & Schuster/A Viacom Company
Upper Saddle River, New Jersey 07458

TABLE 7–4
Summary of Practical Ways of Increasing the Power of a Planned Study

Feature of the Study	Practical Way of Raising Power	Disadvantages
Predicted difference between population means	Increase the intensity of the experimental procedure.	May not be practical or may distort the study's meaning.
Standard deviation	Use a less diverse population.	May not be available; decreases generalizability.
	Use standardized, controlled circumstances of testing or more precise measurement.	Not always practical.
Sample size	Use a larger sample size.	Not always practical; can be costly.
Significance level	Use a more lenient level of significance (such as .10)	Raises alpha, the probability of a Type I error.
One-tailed versus two-tailed test	Use a one-tailed test.	May not be appropriate to the logic of the study.
Type of hypothesis-testing procedure	Use a more sensitive procedure.	None may be available or appropriate.

Aron/Aron
Statistics for the Social Sciences

© 1997 by Prentice-Hall, Inc.
Simon & Schuster/A Viacom Company
Upper Saddle River, New Jersey 07458

Role of Significance and Sample Size in Interpreting Experimental Results

Outcome Statistically Significant	Sample Size	Conclusion
Yes	Small	Important result
Yes	Large	Might or might not have practical importance
No	Small	Inconclusive
No	Large	Research hypothesis probably false

Aron/Aron
Statistics for the Social Sciences

© 1997 by Prentice-Hall, Inc.
Simon & Schuster/A Viacom Company
Upper Saddle River, New Jersey 07458

Chapter 8
The *t*-Test for Dependent Means

Instructor's Summary of Chapter

One-sample t-test. The same five steps of hypothesis testing described in Chapter 7 apply when the variance of the population is not known, except for the following: (a) The population variance is estimated from the information in the sample using a formula that divides the sum of squared deviations by the degrees of freedom $(df = N-1)$ $S^2 = \Sigma(X-M)^2/df$. (b) The comparison distribution will have the shape of a *t* distribution (for which cutoffs are found in a *t* table). It has more area at the extremes than a normal curve (just how much more depends on how few degrees of freedom were used in estimating the population variance). (c) The number of standard deviations from the mean that a sample's mean falls on the *t* distribution is called a *t* score, $t = (\text{Sample } M - \text{Pop } M)/S_M$.

t-test for dependent means. A study in which there is a group of subjects each having two scores, such as a before score and an after score, are often analyzed using a *t*-test for dependent means. In this *t*-test you first compute a difference score for each subject, then proceed with the five-step hypothesis testing procedure in the same way as if you had only a single sample with an unknown variance, assuming that the null hypothesis is about a population of difference scores with a mean of zero (no difference).

Assumptions. An assumption of the *t*-test is that the population distribution is normal. However, even when the population distribution departs substantially from normal, the *t*-test is usually sufficiently accurate. The major exception in the case of a *t*-test for dependent means is when the population of difference scores appears to be highly skewed and a one-tailed test is being used.

Effect size and power. The effect size of a study using a *t*-test for dependent means can be computed as the mean of the difference scores divided by the estimated population standard deviation of the difference scores. Power and needed sample size for a given effect size can be determined from special tables. The power of studies using difference scores is typically much higher than studies using other designs with the same number of subjects.

How the procedures of this chapter are described in research articles. Research articles typically describe *t*-tests either (a) in the text, using a standard format, such as "$t(24) = 2.8$, $p < .05$," or (b) in a table listing a series of results in which the *t* score itself may be omitted and only a star used to indicate which comparisons are significant.

Box 8.1. William S. Gosset: Alias "Student," Not a Mathematician, but a "Practical Man." Briefly describes the life and character of Gosset, and how he developed the *t*-test.

Lecture 8.1: Introduction to the *t*-Test

Materials

Lecture outline
Transparencies 6.4, 6.5 and 8.1 through 8.6

Outline for Blackboard

I.   Review
II. Estimated Population Variance (S²)
III. *t* Distribution
IV. *t* Table
V.   *t*-Test
VI. Review this Class

Instructor's Lecture Outline

I.   Review
   A. Idea of descriptive and inferential statistics.
   B. Basic logic of hypothesis testing with a single sample and a known population.
   1. Show TRANSPARENCIES 6.4 and 6.5 (hypothesis testing example for a single sample and known population) and discuss.
   2. Show TRANSPARENCY 6.1 (three kinds of distributions) and discuss.
   3. Emphasize that in determining the variance of the distribution of means, we have always begun with a known population variance.

II. Estimated Population Variance (S²)
   A. Show TRANSPARENCY 8.1 (hours/day studied, from text):
   1. Note that this is still a somewhat unrealistic research situation, but we are getting closer to very common ones.
   2. Logic of hypothesis testing is generally same as before--discuss Step 1.
   3. Go to top of Step 2 and note that while it may be reasonable to assume that the population shape is normal, we have no information on its variance.
   B. If the population variance is not known, a solution is to estimate it from the sample's variance.
   1. The only information we have available in this example (and usually in practice) about such a population is the sample.
   2. We assume here (as we have throughout the course so far) that Populations 1 and 2 have the same variance.
   3. If the sample is representative of its population, then its variance should tell us something about the variance of the population it represents:
   a. If the sample has little variance, probably the population it came from has little variance.
   b. If the sample has a lot of variance, probably the population it came from has a lot of variance.
   C. However, the sample's variance can not be used directly as an estimate of the population variance. It can be shown mathematically that a sample's variance will on the average be a bit smaller than its population's.

D. Thus, we make an adjustment to compute the estimated population variance.
1. Ordinarily variance is calculated as the sum of squared deviations from the mean divided by the number of cases: $\Sigma(X-M)^2 /N$.
2. But the estimated population variance is computed as the sum of squared deviations from the mean divided by the number of cases *minus one*: $S^2 = \Sigma(X-M)^2/(N-1)$.
3. N-1 is called the *degrees of freedom* (*df*). It represents the number of scores in the sample that are free to vary when calculating the variance. There are N-1 because when figuring the deviations each score is subtracted from the mean. Thus, if you knew all the deviation scores but one, you could calculate the last one given the mean.
STUDENTS: The idea just presented of *why* degrees of freedom is N-1 is an advanced idea. It is not necessary to understand fully in order to grasp the rest of the material.
4. Show top section of TRANSPARENCY 8.2 (computations of S^2--*not* from ongoing example, in order to present a simple illustration of the process with few numbers) and discuss symbols and the computation of estimated population variance.
5. Show TRANSPARENCY 8.2 bottom (hours studied computations) and discuss.
E. Having estimated the population variance, we can proceed to find the characteristics of the distribution of means.
1. Show rest of Step 2 (up to shape of distribution of means) in TRANSPARENCY 8.1 and discuss computations and symbols.
2. NOTE: Remember that when estimating population variance you divide the sum of squared deviations by the degrees of freedom (N-1), but when computing the variance of the distribution of means you divide the estimated population variance by the full sample size (N).

III. *t* Distribution

A. Estimating the population variance loses some accuracy.
B. We make up for this by setting the cutoff score for significance a little more extreme.
C. In fact, an exact distribution takes this into account. Show TRANSPARENCY 8.3 (*t* distribution) and discuss:
1. Similar to a normal curve, but with fatter tails, making more cases in the extremes so that to include any particular percent of cases (say 5%), the cutoff has to be farther out.
2. This distribution is called a *t*-distribution.
D. There is a different *t* distribution for each number of degrees of freedom.
1. The more degrees of freedom, the closer the *t* distribution is to the normal curve. This is because you are estimating with increasing amounts of information.
2. When there are infinite degrees of freedom, the *t* distribution is the same as the normal curve. This is because your sample is infinitely large and is thus the same as the population, so the estimate is perfect.

IV. *t* Table

A. To determine the cutoffs on the *t* distribution, you use a *t* table.
B. Show TRANSPARENCY 8.4 (*t* table) and discuss:
1. For the hours-studied example there are 15 *df* with a one-tailed test at the .05 level.
2. Thus, cutoff *t* needed is 1.753.
3. If using a normal curve for the distribution of means, the cutoff Z would be 1.64--a more extreme cutoff is required when using a *t* distribution.
C. Show TRANSPARENCY 8.1, bottom of Step 2 and Step 3, and discuss.

V.   *t*-Test. Show rest of TRANSPARENCY 9.1 and discuss.

VI. Review this Class: Use blackboard outline and TRANSPARENCIES 8.5 (comparison of *t*-test to situation with known σ) and 8.6 (steps of conducting a *t*-test for a single sample and known μ).

Lecture 8.2: The *t*-Test for Dependent Means

Materials

Lecture outline
Transparencies 8.1 through 8.11

Outline for Blackboard

I. **Review**
II. **Repeated-Measures Designs**
III. **Change (or Difference) Scores**
IV. **t-Test for Dependent Means**
V. **Assumptions**
VI. **Effect Size and Power**
VII. **Review this Class**

Instructor's Lecture Outline

I. **Review**
    A. Idea of descriptive and inferential statistics.
    B. Hypothesis testing with a single sample and a known population requires knowing population variance.
    C. When population variance is not known, it can be estimated from the scores in the sample. Show TRANSPARENCY 8.2 (computations of S^2) and discuss.
    D. When using an estimated population variance, the shape of the comparison distribution is a *t* distribution and not a normal curve.
        1. Show TRANSPARENCY 8.3 (normal and *t* curves) and discuss.
        2. Show TRANSPARENCY 8.4 (*t* table) and discuss.
    E. Otherwise the hypothesis testing proceeds as usual, but is called a *t*-test and the cutoff and sample Z scores are called *t* scores.
        1. Show TRANSPARENCY 8.1 (hours studied hypothesis testing example) and discuss each step.
        2. Show TRANSPARENCY 8.5 (comparison of *t*-test to situation with known σ) and discuss each step.
        3. Show TRANSPARENCY 8.6 (steps of *t*-test with known μ) and discuss each step.

II. **Repeated-Measures Designs**
    A. Also called "within-subjects" designs.
    B. When same people are tested twice.
        1. Before and after some procedure (sometimes called a "pretest-posttest" design). For example:
            a. Before and after psychotherapy.
            b. Before and after taking a medication.
            c. Before and after exercise.
            d. Before and after leaving home.

2. When there are two conditions to an experiment and the same people are tested under both conditions. For example:
   a. Reading ability under bright versus dim light.
   b. Alertness when alone versus when with a friend.
   c. Answering questions about how anxious you are at home versus about how anxious you are at school.

C. Also considered "repeated measures" when different people can be matched into pairs, as with identical twins, one being tested in each of two conditions. The situation is treated as if the two of them were the same person tested at two different times.

III. Change (or Difference) Scores

A. In these situations, the whole process is much simplified by using change (or difference) scores:
   1. For example, for each subject subtract the before from after score.
   2. Examples:
      a. If before = 8 and after = 6, change = -2.
      b. If before = 39 and after = 10, change = -19.
      c. If before = 80 and after = 60, change = -20.
   3. Ask class:
      a. If before = 30 and after = 40, what is change? [10]
      b. If before = 30 and after = 50, what is change? [20]
      c. If before = 30 and after = 25, what is change? [-5]
      d. If before = 30 and after = 30, what is change? [0]
      e. If before = 100 and after = 100.5, what is change? [.5]
   4. In this way you end up with one score per subject (a change score) rather than two.
   5. In statistical analysis of repeated-measures designs we think entirely in terms of these changes scores:
      a. Population distribution of change scores.
      b. Sample of change scores.
      c. Comparison distribution of change scores.

IV. *t*-Test for Dependent Means

A. A *t*-test for dependent means tests hypotheses about repeated-measures designs of this kind (involving change or difference scores).

B. Usually the situation is that we are interested in whether there is a significant change (or difference).

C. The null hypothesis is that there is no change and the research hypothesis is there is some change (or change in a particular direction).

D. Computation is identical to *t*-test for a single sample, except:
   1. You first convert everything to change scores and do everything from then on working with change scores.
   2. The assumed mean of the Population 2 change scores is ordinarily zero--that is, a population in which there is on the average no change.

E. An example:
   1. Show TRANSPARENCY 8.7 (communication quality before and after marriage, from text), Step 1, and note that emphasis is right away on change.
   2. Show TRANSPARENCY 8.7, Step 2, and note:
      a. Population 2 is assumed to have a zero mean (that is, we are comparing to a population in which there is no change).
      b. The population variance must be estimated since we don't know it. This requires some computations, and first we need change scores.

4. Show TRANSPARENCY 8.8 (computations for communication study example) and discuss.

5. Show TRANSPARENCY 8.7 again and finish discussing each step.

V. Assumptions

A. Assumptions are circumstances that must be true for the logic and mathematics of a statistical procedure to work properly.

B. Major assumption of the *t*-test for dependent means is that the population distribution (of change scores) must be normal.

C. However, usually you need not worry about this unless:

1. There is reason to expect a very large discrepancy from normal in the population of change scores.

2. You have reason to expect that the population of change scores is quite skewed and you are using a one-tailed test.

VI. Effect Size and Power

A. Effect size for the *t*-test for dependent means:

1. It is computed in the same way as we did before: effect size = (Population 1 *M* - Population 2 *M*) / Population *SD*.

2. However, remember we are dealing with change scores and the mean of Population 2 is almost always going to be 0. Thus, in effect, the formula is the mean change divided by the standard deviation of the population of change scores.

NOTE: This standard deviation is not the same as S_M— rather, it is S! This is because effect size is intended to be a measure that is not influenced by N, and S_M is much influenced by N.

3. For example, if the average change is 6 and estimated population standard deviation is 12, then d = 1/2.

4. As before: A small effect size is .20, a medium effect size is .50, and a large effect size is .80.

5. Ask class:

a. If average change is 5 and estimated population standard deviation is 10, what is d? [.5] Is this a small, medium, or large effect? [medium]

b. If average change is 2 and estimated population standard deviation is 10, what is d? [.2] Is this a small, medium, or large effect? [small]

c. If average change is 200 and estimated population standard deviation is 400, what is d? [.5] Is this a small, medium, or large effect? [medium]

d. If average change is 12 and estimated population standard deviation is 10, what is d? [1.2] Is this a small, medium, or large effect? [large]

B. Power.

1. Power can be computed directly from tables. Show TRANSPARENCY 8.9 (power table) and discuss.

2. There is also a table that shows how many subjects are needed to achieve 80% power (a standard desired level). Show TRANSPARENCY 8.10 (number of subjects needed table) and discuss.

VII. Review this Class

A. Use blackboard outline.

B. When summarizing first sections, show TRANSPARENCY 8.11 (steps of conducting a *t*-test for dependent means) and discuss.

TRANSPARENCY 8.1

Hours per day studied by students in your dorm versus students in general at your college. (Example from text)

Steps of hypothesis testing:

1. Reframe the question into a research hypothesis and a null hypothesis about populations.

   Population 1: The kind of students who live in your dorm.
   Population 2: The kind of students at your college generally.

   Research Hypothesis: Population 1 students study more than
                        Population 2 students.
   Null Hypothesis: Population 1 students do not study more than
                    Population 2 students.

2. Determine the characteristics of the comparison distribution.

   Population 2: shape=assumed normal; $\underline{M}$=2.5; $\underline{SD}^2$=unknown; $\underline{S}^2$=.64.

   Distribution of means: shape = $\underline{t}$ ($\underline{df}$=15); $\underline{M}_M$=2.5; $\underline{S}_M$=.2.

   ($\underline{S}_M{}^2$ = $\underline{S}^2/N$ =.64/16 = .04; $\underline{S}_M$ = $\sqrt{\underline{S}_M{}^2}$ = $\sqrt{.04}$ = .2.)

3. Determine cutoff sample score on the comparison distribution at which the null hypothesis should be rejected.

   5% level, 1-tailed, t distribution of $\underline{df}$=15: t needed=1.753.

4. Determine score of your sample on comparison distribution.

   Mean hours/studied in your dorm = 3.2.

   t = (Sample $\underline{M}$ - Population $\underline{M}$)/$\underline{S}_M$ = (3.2-2.5)/.2 = .7/.2 = 3.5.

5. Compare the scores obtained in Steps 3 and 4 to decide whether to reject the null hypothesis.

   t on 4 (3.5) is more extreme than cutoff t on 3 (1.753).

   Therefore, reject the null hypothesis; the research hypothesis is supported (students in your dorm study more than at your college in general).

Aron/Aron
Statistics for the Social Sciences

© 1997 by Prentice-Hall, Inc.
Simon & Schuster/A Viacom Company
Upper Saddle River, New Jersey 07458

TRANSPARENCY 8.2

Computation of estimated population variance based on sample data:

$$\underline{S}^2 = \Sigma(\underline{X}-\underline{M})^2/\underline{N}-1 = \Sigma(\underline{X}-\underline{M})^2/\underline{df}$$

EXAMPLE:

Subject	Score X	Deviation (X-M)	Deviation Squared (X-M)^2
1	8	2	4
2	6	0	0
3	4	-2	4
4	9	3	9
5	3	-3	9

$$\Sigma = 30 \qquad\qquad \Sigma(\underline{X}-\underline{M})^2 = 26$$
$$\underline{M} = 6$$

$$\underline{df}=\underline{N}-1=5-1=4 \qquad \underline{S}^2=\Sigma(\underline{X}-\underline{M})^2/\underline{df}=26/4=6.5$$

+++

Example: Hours per day studied by students in your dorm versus students in general at your college. (Example from text)

Computation of estimated population variance based on sample data:

Subject	Score X	Deviation (X-M)	Deviation Squared (X-M)^2
1	4	.8	.64
2	5	1.8	3.24
.	.	.	.
.	.	.	.
16	3	.2	.04

$$\Sigma = 51 \qquad\qquad \Sigma(\underline{X}-\underline{M})^2 = 9.60$$
$$\underline{M} = 3.2$$

$$\underline{df}=\underline{N}-1=16-1=15 \qquad \underline{S}^2=\Sigma(\underline{X}-\underline{M})^2/\underline{df}=9.6/15=.64$$

Aron/Aron
Statistics for the Social Sciences

© 1997 by Prentice-Hall, Inc.
Simon & Schuster/A Viacom Company
Upper Saddle River, New Jersey 07458

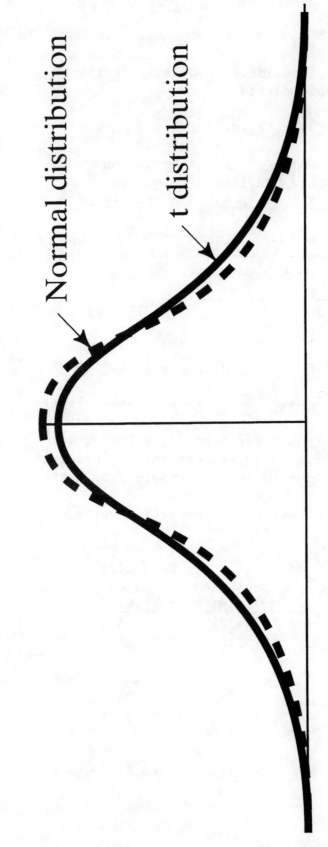

© 1997 by Prentice-Hall, Inc.
Simon & Schuster/A Viacom Company
Upper Saddle River, New Jersey 07458

TRANSPARENCY 8.4

Cutoff Scores for *t* Distributions with 1 Through 17 Degrees of Freedom

	One-Tailed Tests				Two-Tailed Tests		
df	*.10*	*.05*	*.01*		*.10*	*.05*	*.01*
1	3.078	6.314	31.821		6.314	12.706	63.657
2	1.886	2.920	6.965		2.920	4.303	9.925
3	1.638	2.353	4.541		2.353	3.182	5.841
4	1.533	2.132	3.747		2.132	2.776	4.604
5	1.476	2.015	3.365		2.015	2.571	4.032
6	1.440	1.943	3.143		1.943	2.447	3.708
7	1.415	1.895	2.998		1.895	2.365	3.500
8	1.397	1.860	2.897		1.860	2.306	3.356
9	1.383	1.833	2.822		1.833	2.262	3.250
10	1.372	1.813	2.764		1.813	2.228	3.170
11	1.364	1.796	2.718		1.796	2.201	3.106
12	1.356	1.783	2.681		1.783	2.179	3.055
13	1.350	1.771	2.651		1.771	2.161	3.013
14	1.345	1.762	2.625		1.762	2.145	2.977
15	1.341	1.753	2.603		1.753	2.132	2.947
16	1.337	1.746	2.584		1.746	2.120	2.921
17	1.334	1.740	2.567		1.740	2.110	2.898

Aron/Aron
Statistics for the Social Sciences

© 1997 by Prentice-Hall, Inc.
Simon & Schuster/A Viacom Company
Upper Saddle River, New Jersey 07458

Hypothesis Testing Involving a Single Sample Mean When Population Variance Is Unknown (*t* Test) Compared to When Population Variance Is Known

Step in Hypothesis Testing	Difference From When Population Variance Is Known
1. Reframe the question into a research hypothesis and a null hypothesis about the populations.	No difference in method.
2. Determine the characteristics of the comparison distribution:	
Population mean	No difference in method.
Population variance	Estimate from the sample.
Standard deviation of the distribution of sample means	No difference in method (but based on estimated population variance).
Shape of the comparison distribution	Use the *t* distribution with $df = N - 1$.
3. Determine the significance cutoff.	Use the *t* table.
4. Determine score of your sample on the comparison distribution.	No difference in method (but called a *t* score).
5. Compare Steps 3 and 4 to determine whether to reject the null hypothesis.	No difference in method.

Steps for Conducting a *t*-Test for a Single Sample

1. Reframe the question into a research hypothesis and a null hypothesis about the populations.

2. Determine the characteristics of the comparison distribution.

   a. The mean is the same as the known population mean.

   b. The standard deviation is computed as follows:

      i. Compute the estimated population variance: $S^2 = SS/df$.

      ii. Compute the variance of the distribution of means: $S_M^2 = S^2/N$.

      iii. Compute the standard deviation: $S_M = \sqrt{S_M^2}$.

   c. The shape will be a *t* distribution with $N - 1$ degrees of freedom.

3. Determine the cutoff sample score on the comparison distribution at which the null hypothesis should be rejected.

   a. Determine the degrees of freedom, desired significance level, and number of tails in the test (one or two).

   b. Look up the appropriate cutoff in a *t* table.

4. Determine the score of your sample on the comparison distribution: $t = (M - \mu)/S_M$.

5. Compare the scores obtained in Steps 3 and 4 to decide whether or not to reject the null hypothesis.

Aron/Aron
Statistics for the Social Sciences

© 1997 by Prentice-Hall, Inc.
Simon & Schuster/A Viacom Company
Upper Saddle River, New Jersey 07458

TRANSPARENCY 8.7

Example: Olthoff (1989) data of husbands' reported communication quality before and after marriage. (Example from text)

Steps of hypothesis testing:

1. Reframe the question into a research hypothesis and a null hypothesis about populations.

   Population 1: Husbands of the kind included in this study.
   Population 2: Husbands who do not change on their communication quality from before to after marriage.

   Research Hypothesis: Populations are different.
   Null Hypothesis: Populations are the same.

2. Determine the characteristics of the comparison distribution.

   Population 2: shape=assumed normal; M=0; SD^2=unknown; S^2=154.05.

   Distribution of means: shape=t (df=18); M_M=0; S_M=2.85.

3. Determine the cutoff sample score on the comparison distribution at which the null hypothesis should be rejected.

   5% level, 2-tailed, t distribution of df=18: t needed = ±2.101.

4. Determine score of your sample on comparison distribution.

   Mean change from before to after marriage of -12.05.

   t = (Sample M - Pop. M)/S_M = (-12.05-0)/2.85 = -12.05/2.85 = -4.23.

5. Compare the scores obtained in Steps 3 and 4 to decide whether to reject the null hypothesis.

   t on 4 (-4.23) is more extreme than cutoff t on 3 (±2.101).

   Therefore, reject the null hypothesis; the research hypothesis is supported (husbands' reported communication quality decreases from before to after marriage).

Aron/Aron
Statistics for the Social Sciences

© 1997 by Prentice-Hall, Inc.
Simon & Schuster/A Viacom Company
Upper Saddle River, New Jersey 07458

TABLE 8–4
t-Test for Communication Quality Scores Before and After Marriage for 19
Husbands Who Received No Special Communication Training

Husband	Communication Quality		Difference (After – Before)	Deviation of Differences From the Mean of Differences	Squared Deviation
	Before	*After*			
A	126	115	– 11	1.05	1.1
B	133	125	– 8	4.05	16.4
C	126	96	– 30	–17.95	322.2
D	115	115	0	12.05	145.2
E	108	119	11	23.05	531.3
F	109	82	– 27	–14.95	233.5
G	124	93	– 31	–18.95	359.1
H	98	109	11	23.05	531.3
I	95	72	– 23	–10.95	119.9
J	120	104	– 16	– 3.95	15.6
K	118	107	– 11	1.05	1.1
L	126	118	– 8	4.05	16.4
M	121	102	– 19	– 6.95	48.3
N	116	115	– 1	11.05	122.1
O	94	83	– 11	1.05	1.1
P	105	87	– 18	– 5.95	35.4
Q	123	121	– 2	10.05	101.0
R	125	100	– 25	–12.95	167.7
S	128	118	– 10	2.05	4.2
Σ:	2,210	1,981	–229	– .05	2,772.9

For difference scores:

$M = -229/19 = -12.05.$

$\mu = 0$ (assumed as a no-change baseline of comparison).

$S^2 = SS/df = 2{,}772.9/(19 - 1) = 154.05.$

$S_M^2 = S^2/N = 154.05/19 = 8.11.$

$S_M = \sqrt{S_M^2} = \sqrt{8.11} = 2.85.$

t with $df = 18$ needed for 5% level, two-tailed $= \pm 2.101.$

$t = (M - \text{Pop. } M)/S_M = (-12.05 - 0)/2.85 = -4.23.$

Decision: Reject the null hypothesis.

Aron/Aron
Statistics for the Social Sciences

© 1997 by Prentice-Hall, Inc.
Simon & Schuster/A Viacom Company
Upper Saddle River, New Jersey 07458

TRANSPARENCY 8.9

Approximate Power for Studies Using the *t* Test for Dependent Means in Testing Hypotheses at the .05 Significance Level

Scores in Sample (*N*)	Effect Size		
	Small (d = .20)	*Medium* (d = .50)	*Large* (d = .80)
Two-tailed test			
10	.09	.32	.66
20	.14	.59	.93
30	.19	.77	.99
40	.24	.88	*
50	.29	.94	*
100	.25	*	*
One-tailed test			
10	.15	.46	.78
20	.22	.71	.96
30	.29	.86	*
40	.35	.93	*
50	.40	.97	*
100	.63	*	*

*Power is nearly 1.

Aron/Aron
Statistics for the Social Sciences

© 1997 by Prentice-Hall, Inc.
Simon & Schuster/A Viacom Company
Upper Saddle River, New Jersey 07458

Approximate Number of Subjects Needed to Achieve 80% Power for the t Test for Dependent Means in Testing Hypotheses at the .05 Significance Level

	Effect Size		
	Small $(d = .20)$	Medium $(d = .50)$	Large $(d = .80)$
Two-tailed	196	33	14
One-tailed	156	26	12

Aron/Aron
Statistics for the Social Sciences

TABLE 8–6
Steps for Conducting a t Test for Dependent Means

1. Restate the question as a research hypothesis and a null hypothesis about the populations.

2. Determine the characteristics of the comparison distribution.

(a) Make each person's two scores into a difference score. Do all the rest of the steps using these difference scores.

(b) Figure the mean of the difference scores.

(c) Assume a population mean of 0.

(d) Figure the estimated population variance of difference scores:
$S^2 = \sqrt{[\Sigma(X - M)^2 / (N - 1)]}.$

(e) Figure the variance of the distribution of means of difference scores:
$S_M^2 = S^2 / N.$

(f) Figure the standard deviation of the distribution of means of difference scores
$S_M = \sqrt{S_M^2}.$

(g) The shape is a t distribution with $df = N - 1$.

3. Determine the cutoff sample score on the comparison distribution at which the null hypothesis should be rejected.

(a) Decide the significance level and whether to use a one-tailed or a two-tailed test.

(b) Look up the appropriate cutoff in a t table.

4. Determine the score of your sample on the comparison distribution:
$t = (\text{Sample } M - \text{Population } M)/S_M.$

5. Compare the scores from Steps 3 and 4 to decide whether to reject the null hypothesis.

Aron/Aron
Statistics for the Social Sciences

© 1997 by Prentice-Hall, Inc.
Simon & Schuster/A Viacom Company
Upper Saddle River, New Jersey 07458

Chapter 9
The *t*-Test for Independent Means

Instructor's Summary of Chapter

Distribution of differences between means. The main difference in procedure between a *t*-test for independent means and a *t*-test for a single sample is that the comparison distribution is now a distribution of differences between means of samples. This distribution can be thought of as arising in two steps: (a) each population of individual cases produces a distribution of means, and then (b) a new distribution is created consisting of differences between pairs of means selected from these two distributions of means.

Mean and shape of the distribution of means. The distribution of differences between means has a mean of 0 and will be a *t* distribution with degrees of freedom equal to the total degrees of freedom contributed by each sample.

Standard deviation of the distribution of means (and the pooled estimate of the population variance). Its standard deviation is determined in several steps: (a) each sample is used to estimate the population variance; (b) since the populations are assumed to have the same variance, a pooled estimate is computed by simple averaging of the two estimates if the numbers in each sample are equal, or by a weighted average if they are not (multiplying each estimate by the proportion of the total degrees of freedom its sample contributes and adding up the products); (c) the pooled estimate is divided by each sample's number of cases to determine the variances of their associated distribution of means; (d) these two variances are added to produce the variance of the distribution of differences between means; and (e) the square root is taken.

Assumptions. The *t*-test for independent means assumes the populations are normal and have equal variances, although it works if these assumptions are only moderately violated.

Effect size and power. Effect size (*d*) for a *t*-test for independent means is the difference between the means divided by the population standard deviation. For a given number of subjects, power is greatest when sample sizes of the two groups are equal.

How the procedures of this chapter are reported in research articles. *t*-tests for independent means are reported in a standard format--e.g., $t(29)=3.41$, $p < .01$, where the number in parentheses is the degrees of freedom. Results may also appear in a table, each significant difference indicated merely by an asterisk.

Box 9.1. Two Women Make Their Point about Gender and Statistics. An interview with Linda Fidell, coauthor of an influential multivariate statistics text. The focus is on the role of women in statistics.

Lecture 9.1: Introduction to the *t*-Test for Independent Means

Materials

Lecture outline
Transparencies 8.6, 8.11, and 9.1 through 9.5

Outline for Blackboard

    I.   **Review**
    II. **Between-Subject Designs**
    III. **Estimating Population Variance (S_{Pooled}^2)**
    IV. **Distribution of Differences Between Means**
    V. **Conducting the Hypothesis Test**
    VI. **Review this Class**

Instructor's Lecture Outline

I. Review

    A. Idea of descriptive and inferential statistics.
    B. Show TRANSPARENCY 8.6 (steps of conducting a *t*-test for a single sample) and discuss.
    C. Show TRANSPARENCY 8.11 (steps of conducting a *t*-test for dependent means) and discuss.
    D. Show top of TRANSPARENCY 9.1 (basic calculations for *t*-test for dependent means) and discuss.

II. Between-Subject Designs

    A. Principle: A study with two different groups of subjects, such as an experimental and a control group.
    B. Show TRANSPARENCY 9.2 (performance under quiet vs. noisy conditions) and discuss (without considering computations now):
        1. This is a new situation: You can't just take difference scores as they are not the same subjects.
        2. In fact, in the example there are not even the same number of subjects in the two conditions.
    C. The hypothesis testing question is whether the means of these two groups are different enough to permit us to conclude that the two populations they represent have different means.
    D. The procedure for testing such a hypothesis is the *t*-test for independent means.
    E. Populations and hypotheses: Show TRANSPARENCY 9.3 (hypothesis testing, quiet-noisy study) and discuss Step 1.

III. Estimating Population Variance (S_{Pooled}^2)

    A. This is part of Step 2 of the hypothesis testing process.
    B. We assume that both populations have the same variance when doing a *t*-test for independent means.

154

C. Thus we can estimate the variance from each sample.
D. We then average the two estimates.
E. However, if the sample sizes are different, the larger sample provides a more accurate estimate.
F. Thus we use a weighted average, giving emphasis in proportion to the degrees of freedom each sample contributes.
G. This estimate based on the weighted average of the two estimates is called the pooled estimate.
H. Show TRANSPARENCY 9.2 (computations for quiet-noisy example) and discuss computations of S_{Pooled}^2.

IV. Distribution of Differences Between Means

A. The crucial result of a study comparing two groups is a difference between the means of the two samples.
B. Thus the comparison distribution has to be a distribution of differences between means of all possible samples from the two populations.
C. This is called a distribution of differences between means.
D. Show TRANSPARENCY 9.4 (illustration of logic of construction of distribution of differences between means) and discuss each step:
1. Create two distributions of means, one for each population.
2. Take a mean from each distribution of means, compute the difference.
3. Do this many times and make a distribution of these differences.
E. Its mean will be 0--since under the null hypothesis, the means being subtracted from each other come from populations with the same mean.
F. Its variance is computed as follows:
1. Find variance of each distribution of means in usual way.
2. Sum these variances to get $S^2_{Difference}$
3. Show TRANSPARENCY 9.2 (computations for quiet-noisy example) and discuss computations of S_{DIF}^2.
F. It will be a t distribution because it is based on estimated population variance. Its df is the total df on which that estimate is based.
G. Show TRANSPARENCY 9.3 (hypothesis testing for quiet-noisy example) and discuss Step 2.

V. Conducting the Hypothesis Test: Show TRANSPARENCY 9.3 (hypothesis testing for quiet-noisy example) and review each step, noting slight changes from previous t test procedures, and emphasizing how much is the same.

VI. Review this Class: Use blackboard outline and show TRANSPARENCIES 9.3 (hypothesis testing, quiet-noisy example), 9.4 (illustration of logic of distribution of differences between means), and 9.5 (computations for a t-test for independent means).

Lecture 9.2: Applying the *t*-Test for Independent Means

Materials

Lecture outline
Transparencies 9.2 through 9.9

Outline for Blackboard

I. Review
II. Assumptions
III. Effect Size and Power
IV. Review this Class

Instructor's Lecture Outline

I. Review
A. Idea of descriptive and inferential statistics.
B. Basic logic of the *t*-test for independent means:
   1. Show TRANSPARENCIES 9.4 (logic of construction of the distribution of differences between means) and discuss.
   2. Show TRANSPARENCY 9.6 (steps of conducting a *t*-test for independent means) and discuss.
C. Show TRANSPARENCIES 9.2 and 9.3 (quiet-noisy example) and discuss.
D. Show TRANSPARENCY 9.5 (computations for *t*-test for independent means) and discuss.

II. Assumptions
A. As with *t*-test for dependent means, populations are assumed be normal. Usually this is only a problem if both populations dramatically skewed in opposite directions.
B. In addition, populations must have same variance. Usually this is only a problem if the variances are extremely different.
C. It can also be a problem if both assumptions are violated.

III. Effect Size and Power
A. Effect size:
   1. Effect size = (Population 1 M - Population 2 M)/ Population SD
   2. For a completed study, estimated as effect size = $(M_1 - M_2)$ /. S_{Pppled}
   3. As before, a small effect size is .20, a medium effect size is .50, and a large effect size is .80.
B. Power.
   1. Power can be determined directly from table in the text: Show TRANSPARENCY 9.7 (power table) and discuss.
   2. Needed N for 80% power for a given effect size can also be determined from a table in the text: Show TRANSPARENCY 9.8 (needed number of subjects table) and discuss.

3. For the same overall number of subjects, power is greatest with equal Ns.
   a. For unequal Ns, effective N for computing power is closer to the lower N (it is the harmonic mean.)
   b. Show TRANSPARENCY 9.9 (harmonic mean formula and example computations) and discuss.

IV. Review this Class: Use blackboard outline and TRANSPARENCY 9.6 (steps of conducting a t-test for independent means).

Necessary calculations for a $\underline{t}$-test for dependent means.

1. Compute difference scores:

    Each difference score =
    each after score - its before score

2. Compute $\underline{M}$ (mean of sample of difference scores):

    $\underline{M} = \Sigma \underline{X} / \underline{N}$

3. Using difference scores, compute S^2 (estimated variance of population of difference scores):

    $S^2 = \Sigma(\underline{X} - \underline{M})^2 \, / \, (\underline{N}-1)$

4. Compute $\underline{S}_M$ (standard deviation of comparison distribution--the distribution of means of samples of difference scores):

    $\underline{S}_M{}^2 = S^2 / \underline{N}$ $\underline{S}_M = \sqrt{\underline{S}_M{}^2}$

5. Calculate $\underline{t}$ score for sample's mean of difference scores:

    $\underline{t} = (\underline{M}-0)/\underline{S}_M$

Aron/Aron
Statistics for the Social Sciences

© 1997 by Prentice-Hall, Inc.
Simon & Schuster/A Viacom Company
Upper Saddle River, New Jersey 07458

TRANSPARENCY 9.2

Experiment comparing task performance of subjects tested under quiet conditions versus of subjects tested under noisy conditions. (Fictional data.)

Data and computations:

Quiet Condition		Noisy Condition	
Subject	Score	Subject	Score
RX	22	KA	17
BL	20	BI	15
JC	23	OF	16
DM	21	BK	20
FM	19		

$$M_1 = 21 \qquad\qquad M_2 = 17$$
$$S_1^2 = 2.5 \qquad\qquad S_2^2 = 4.67$$
$$df_1 = 4 \qquad\qquad df_2 = 3$$

$$d_{Total} = df_1 + df_2 = 4 + 3 = 7$$

$$S_{Pooled}^2 = \frac{df_1}{df_{Total}}(S_1^2) + \frac{df_2}{df_{Total}}(S_2^2)$$

$$= \frac{4}{7}(2.5) + \frac{3}{7}(4.67)$$

$$= (.57)(2.5) + (.43)(4.67)$$
$$= \quad 1.43 \quad + \quad 2.01 \quad = 3.44$$

$$S_{M1}^2 = S_{Pooled}^2 / N_1 = 3.44/5 = .69$$

$$S_{M2}^2 = S_{Pooled}^2 / N_2 = 3.44/4 = .86$$

$$S_{Difference}^2 = S_{M1}^2 + S_{M2}^2 = .69 + .86 = 1.55$$

$$S_{Difference} = \sqrt{(S_{Difference}^2)} = \sqrt{1.55} = 1.24$$

Aron/Aron
Statistics for the Social Sciences

© 1997 by Prentice-Hall, Inc.
Simon & Schuster/A Viacom Company
Upper Saddle River, New Jersey 07458

TRANSPARENCY 9.3

Experiment comparing task performance of subjects tested under quiet conditions versus of subjects tested under noisy conditions. (Fictional data.)

Steps of hypothesis testing:

1. Reframe into a research hypothesis and a null hypothesis about populations.

   Population 1: People tested under quiet conditions
   Population 2: People tested under noisy conditions

   Research Hypothesis: Those tested under quiet conditions score better (that is, Pop. 1 has higher mean.)
   Null Hypothesis: Those tested under quiet conditions do not score better.

2. Determine the characteristics of the comparison distribution.

Estimated population variance = Weighted Average $\underline{S}^2$ = $\underline{S}_{Pooled}^2$ = 3.44.

Comparison distribution (distribution of differences between means):

   Mean = 0; $\underline{S}_{Difference}$ = 1.24; Shape = $\underline{t}$ ($\underline{df}$ = 7).

3. Determine the cutoff sample score on the comparison distribution at which the null hypothesis should be rejected.

 5% level, 1-tailed, t distribution of $\underline{df}$=7: t needed=1.895.

4. Determine score of your sample on comparison distribution.

$\underline{t}$ = $(\underline{M_1}-\underline{M_2})/\underline{S}_{Difference}$ = (21-17)/1.24 = 4/1.24 = 3.23.

5. Compare scores obtained in Steps 3 and 4 to decide whether to reject the null hypothesis.

$\underline{t}$ on 4 (3.23) is more extreme than cutoff $\underline{t}$ on 3 (1.895).

 Therefore, reject the null hypothesis; the research hypothesis is supported (people perform better under quiet conditions).

Aron/Aron
Statistics for the Social Sciences

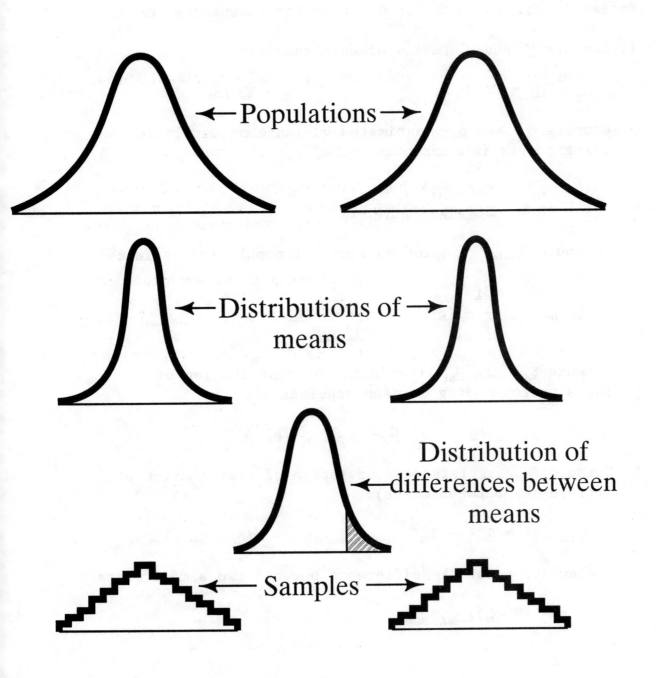

Populations

Distributions of means

Distribution of differences between means

Samples

TRANSPARENCY 9.5

Necessary calculations for a $\underline{t}$-test for independent means.

1. Compute $\underline{M}_1$ and $\underline{M}_2$ (means of each sample):

$$\underline{M}_1 = \Sigma\underline{X}_1/\underline{N}_1 \qquad\qquad \underline{M}_2 = \Sigma\underline{X}_2/\underline{N}_2$$

2. Compute $\underline{S}_1{}^2$ and $\underline{S}_2{}^2$ (estimated variance of population) using scores in each sample:

$$\underline{S}_1{}^2 = \Sigma(\underline{X}_1-\underline{M}_1)^2 \ / \ (\underline{N}_1-1)$$
$$\underline{S}_2{}^2 = \Sigma(\underline{X}_2-\underline{M}_2)^2 \ / \ (\underline{N}_2-1)$$

3. Compute $\underline{S}_{Pooled}{}^2$ (pooled estimate of population variance):

$$\underline{S}_{pooled} = \frac{\underline{df}_1}{\underline{df}_{Total}}(\underline{S}_1{}^2) \ + \ \frac{\underline{df}_2}{\underline{df}_{Total}}(\underline{S}_2{}^2)$$

4. Compute $\underline{S}_{M1}{}^2$ and $\underline{S}_{M2}{}^2$ (variances of distribution of means corresponding to each population):

$$\underline{S}_{M1}{}^2 = \underline{S}_{Pooled}{}^2/\underline{N}_1 \qquad \underline{S}_{M2}{}^2 = \underline{S}_{Pooled}{}^2/\underline{N}_2$$

5. Compute $\underline{S}_{Difference}$ (standard deviation of distribution of differences between means):

$$\underline{S}_{Difference}{}^2 = \underline{S}_{M1}{}^2 + \underline{S}_{M2}{}^2 \qquad \underline{S}_{Difference} = \sqrt{(\underline{S}_{Difference}{}^2)}$$

6. Calculate $\underline{t}$ for the difference between two sample means:

$$\underline{t} = (\underline{M}_1-\underline{M}_2)/\underline{S}_{Difference}$$

Aron/Aron
Statistics for the Social Sciences

© 1997 by Prentice-Hall, Inc.
Simon & Schuster/A Viacom Company
Upper Saddle River, New Jersey 07458

TABLE 9–3
Steps for Conducting a t Test for Independent Means

1. Restate the question into a research hypothesis and a null hypothesis about the populations.

2. Determine the characteristics of the comparison distribution.

    a. Its mean will be 0.

    b. Compute its standard deviation.

       i. Compute estimated population variances based on each sample (that is, compute two estimates).

       ii. Compute a pooled estimate of population variance:

$$S^2_{Pooled} = \frac{df_1}{df_{Total}}(S^2_1) + \frac{df_2}{df_{Total}}(S^2_2)$$

$$(df_1 = N_1 - 1 \text{ and } df_2 = N_2 - 1; df_{Total} = df_1 + df_2)$$

       iii. Compute the variance of each distribution of means: $S^2_{M1} = S^2_{Pooled}/N_1$ and $S^2_{M2} = S^2_{Pooled}/N.$

       iv. Compute the variance of the distribution of differences between means:
$S^2_{Difference} = S^2_{M1} + S^2_{M2}$

       v. Compute the standard deviation of the distribution of differences between means:
$S_{Difference} = \sqrt{S^2_{Difference}}$

    c. Determine its shape: It will be a t distribution with df_{Total} degrees of freedom.

3. Determine the cutoff sample score on the comparison distribution at which the null hypothesis should be rejected.

    a. Determine the degrees of freedom (df_{Total}), desired significance level, and tails in the test (one or two).

    b. Look up the appropriate cutoff in a t table. If the exact df is not given, use the df below.

4. Determine the score of the sample on the comparison distribution: $t = (M_1 - M_2)/S_{Difference}$

5. Compare the scores obtained in Steps 3 and 4 to decide whether to reject the null hypothesis.

Aron/Aron
Statistics for the Social Sciences

© 1997 by Prentice-Hall, Inc.
Simon & Schuster/A Viacom Company
Upper Saddle River, New Jersey 07458

Approximate Power for Studies Using the *t* Test for Independent Means Testing Hypotheses at the .05 Significance Level

Number of Subjects (*N*)	Effect Size		
	Small (d = .20)	*Medium (d = .50)*	*Large (d = .80)*
One-tailed test			
10	.11	.29	.53
20	.15	.46	.80
30	.19	.61	.92
40	.22	.72	.97
50	.26	.80	.99
100	.41	.97	*
Two-tailed test			
10	.07	.18	.39
20	.09	.33	.69
30	.12	.47	.86
40	.14	.60	.94
50	.17	.70	.98
100	.29	.94	*

*Nearly 1.

Note. Based on Cohen (1988), pp. 28–39.

Aron/Aron
Statistics for the Social Sciences

© 1997 by Prentice-Hall, Inc.
Simon & Schuster/A Viacom Company
Upper Saddle River, New Jersey 07458

Approximate Number of Subjects Needed in Each Group (Assuming Equal Sample Sizes) to Achieve 80% Power for the *t* Test for Independent Means, Testing Hypotheses at the .05 Significance Level

	Effect Size		
	Small (d = .20)	*Medium* (d = .50)	*Large* (d = .80)
One-tailed	310	50	20
Two-tailed	393	64	26

Aron/Aron
Statistics for the Social Sciences

Harmonic mean.

$$\text{Harmonic Mean} = \frac{(2)(\underline{N}_1)(\underline{N}_2)}{\underline{N}_1 + \underline{N}_2}$$

Example with 6 subjects in one group and 34 in the other.

$$\text{Harmonic Mean} = \frac{(2)(6)(34)}{6 + 34} = \frac{408}{40} = 10.2$$

Example with 3 subjects in one group and 37 in the other.

$$\text{Harmonic Mean} = \frac{(2)(3)(37)}{3 + 37} = \frac{222}{40} = 5.55$$

Aron/Aron
Statistics for the Social Sciences

© 1997 by Prentice-Hall, Inc.
Simon & Schuster/A Viacom Company
Upper Saddle River, New Jersey 07458

Chapter 10
Introduction to the Analysis of Variance

Instructor's Summary of Chapter

Analysis of variance (ANOVA) is used to test hypotheses involving differences among means of several samples.

The two variance estimates. The analysis of variance compares two estimates of population variance: (a) a "within-group estimate," determined by pooling the variance estimates from each of the samples and (b) a "between-group estimate," based on the variation among the means of the samples.

The F ratio is computed by dividing the between-group by the within-group estimate. If the null hypothesis is true, so that all the samples come from populations with the same mean, the F ratio should be about 1, since the two population-variance estimates are based on the same variation, the variation within each of the samples. But if the research hypothesis is true, so that samples come from populations with different means, then the F ratio should be larger than 1, since the between-group estimate is now influenced by both the variation within the samples and between them, while the within-group estimate is still only affected by the variation within each of the samples.

Computations of the two variance estimates. When there are equal sample sizes, the within-group population-variance estimate is the average of the estimates of the population variance computed from each sample; the between-group population variance estimate is computed by first finding the estimate of the variance of the distribution of means, then multiplying this estimate by the sample size to make it comparable to the variance of a distribution of individual scores.

The F distribution and the F table. The distribution of F ratios under the null hypothesis is known, and significance cutoff values are available in tables that are used by providing the degrees of freedom for each population variance estimate--the between (or numerator) estimate being based on the number of groups minus one, and the within-group (or denominator) estimate being based on the sum of the degrees of freedom in each sample.

Assumptions. The assumptions for the analysis of variance are the same as for the *t*-test--the populations must be normally distributed, with equal variances--and like the *t*-test, the analysis of variance can still be used when these assumptions are only moderately violated.

Effect size and power. Effect size in the analysis of variance can be estimated from the elements involved in computing the analysis of variance or from the F and number of subjects in each group in a completed study. Power depends on effect size, number of subjects, significance level, and number of groups.

Protected t-tests. Comparing each group to each other group is done with a series of *t*-tests call protected *t*-tests. They help a researcher determine if the overall analysis of variance was truly significant for all groups.

Factorial analysis of variance. In a factorial research design, participants are put into groupings according to the combinations of the variables whose effects are being studied. Such designs mean that you can study the effects of two variables without needing twice as many participants and also that you can study the effects of combinations of the two variables (interaction effects). An interaction effect is when the effect of one variable depends on the presence or absence of the other variable. A main effect is the effect of one variable, ignoring the effect of the other variable.

How the procedures of this chapter are reported in research articles. Analysis of variance results are reported in research articles using a standard format--e.g., $F(3,38)=3.41, p < .05$. Factorial analysis of variance results usually are reported by giving the information for each main and interaction effect in the text and by showing a table with the cell means and sometimes the marginal means.

Box 10.1. Sir Ronald Fisher, Caustic Genius of Statistics. Summarizes the life and work of Fisher, inventor of ANOVA.

Lecture 10.1: Introduction to the *Analysis of Variance*

Materials

Lecture outline
Transparencies 9.6 and 10.1 through 11.11

Outline for Blackboard

  I.   **Review**
  II. **Basic Logic**
  III. **Computations**
  IV. **The *F* Distribution**
  V.   **Example**
  VI. **Assumptions**
  VII. **Effect Size and Power**
  VIII.**Review this Class**

Instructor's Lecture Outline

I.   Review

A. Idea of descriptive and inferential statistics.

B. Basic logic of the *t*-test for independent means. Show TRANSPARENCY 9.6 (steps of computing a *t*-test for independent means) and discuss, emphasizing:
  1. Overall logic of hypothesis testing.
  2. *t* distribution and *t* table.
  3. Pooled population variance estimate.

II. Basic Logic

A. Procedure capable of analyzing studies with more than two groups.

B. Example (from text): Subjects rate guilt of defendant either knowing defendant has a criminal record, has no criminal record, or not having any information about he defendant's criminal record.

C. Null and research hypothesis: Show top of TRANSPARENCY 10.1 (logic of analysis of variance) and discuss.

D. Population variance can be estimated based on scores in each sample--the *within-group population variance estimate.*
  1. Estimate from each sample uses usual procedure.
  2. We assume all populations have equal variances.
  3. Thus we can average estimates. (In this class we are dealing only with situations with equal *N*s, so no weighting is necessary.)

E. Population variance can also be estimated based on variation among means of groups--the *between-group population variance estimate.*
  1. If null hypothesis is true, all populations have same mean. Thus, variation among means of samples can only reflect variation within populations.
  2. If null hypothesis is not true, populations have different means. Thus, variation among means of samples reflects both variation within populations and variation between them.

F. If null hypothesis is true, both estimates are reflecting same variance. Their ratio would be 1 to 1.

G. If null hypothesis is false, the between-group estimate is reflecting more than the within, and thus the ratio of the between to the within will be more than 1 to 1.

H. Show rest of TRANSPARENCY 10.1 (logic of analysis of variance) and discuss each step.

III. Computations: Show top of TRANSPARENCY 10.2 (main analysis of variance computations with equal Ns) and discuss.

IV. The F Distribution

A. Can be thought of as constructed this way:
   1. Assume the null hypothesis is true and all populations have same mean.
   2. Draw a sample from each population and compute the F ratio for the set of samples.
   3. Repeat a large number of times and make a distribution of the resulting F rations.

B. Can also be derived mathematically.

C. Shape: Show top of TRANSPARENCY 10.3 (F distribution) and discuss. Exact shape depends on how many samples you take each time and how many scores are in each sample.

D. Table of F values requires knowing significance level and two degrees-of-freedom values. (Note that there are no one-tailed tests possible.) Show bottom of TRANSPARENCY 10.3 (F table) and discuss.

V. Example. Show TRANSPARENCIES 10.4 and 10.5 (criminal-record example, from text) and discuss.

VI. Assumptions

A. All populations are assumed to be normally distributed and have the same variance.

B. The analysis of varaince is still useful if these assumptions are only moderately violated.

VII. Effect Size and Power

A. Effect size (f):
   1. For a completed study, estimated effect size $= S_M / S_{Withn}$.
   3. For a study in an article in which only F and the number of scores in each group are available: estimated effect size $= (\sqrt{F})/(\sqrt{n})$.
   4. Cohen's conventions: Small $f = .10$; medium $f = .25$; large $d = .40$.

B. Power.
   1. Power can be determined directly from table in the text.
   2. Needed N for 80% power for a given effect size can also be determined from a table in the text.

VIII. Review this Class: Use blackboard outline and TRANSPARENCY 10.6 (summary of steps of conducting an analysis of variance).

I. Lecture 10.2: The Logic and Language of Factorial Designs

Materials

Lecture outline
Transparencies 10.7 through 10.11

Outline for Blackboard

I. **Review**
II. **Factorial Designs**
III. **Identifying Effects from Cell Means**
IV. **Identifying Effects Graphically**
V. **Example**
VI. **Review this Class**

Instructor's Lecture Outline

I.   Review
    A. Idea of descriptive and inferential statistics.
    B. Review of types of situations addressed so far in course:
        1. One-group t-test (including special case of t-test for dependent means).
        2. Two-group t-test--t-test for independent means.
        3. More than two groups--analysis of variance.
        4. All of the above involved comparisons on one independent variable.

II.   Factorial Designs—two or more groups and two or more variables.
    A. Example: Burnkraut & Unnava (1989) examined the influence of various factors in changing attitudes, specifically:
        1. Strength of argument made.
        2. Whether subject was encouraged to think about the arguments in terms of self ("self-referencing").
    B. These researchers could have studied each separately, but instead did both together, randomly assigning subjects to one of four conditions.
    C. Show TRANSPARENCY 10.7 and discuss:
        1. Greater efficiency (two hypotheses tested with a single set of subjects).
        2. Permits testing of the interaction effect--joint effect over and above sum of two effects.
        3. Called a factorial research design.
        4. Indicate main and interaction effects.

III.   Identifying Main and Interaction Effects from Tables of Cell Means: Show TRANSPARENCY 10.8 (tables of means from text) and discuss various examples to illustrate:
    A. Structure of table and computation of marginal means.
    B. Main effects recognized from differences in marginal means.
    C. Interaction effects indicated by variations in the pattern of differences across different rows.

IV. **Identifying Main and Interaction Effects Graphically:** Show TRANSPARENCY 10.9 (graphs of previous tables of means from text) and discuss various examples to illustrate:
   A. Identifying interaction effects by nonparallel lines.
   B. Identifying one main effect by different average heights of lines.
   C. Identifying other main effect by average slope of lines being non-horizontal.

V. **Example**
   A. Show TRANSPARENCIES 10.10 and 10.11 (various outcomes on mental health by nationality--French vs. U.S.--and by profession--comedians vs. actors) and discuss.

VI. **Review this Class:** Use blackboard outline and TRANSPARENCIES 10.8 and 10.9.

TRANSPARENCY 10.1

Logic of the analysis of variance.

Null Hypothesis: All groups are randomly drawn
                  from identical populations

Research Hypothesis: Groups are drawn from population
                      with different means

IF null hypothesis is true, two equally good ways to
estimate population variance:

1. WITHIN-GROUPS ESTIMATE: Based on the variation of
                             the scores within each group

2. BETWEEN-GROUPS ESTIMATE: Based on the variation of
                             the means of the groups

	VARIATION WITHIN POPULATIONS	VARIATION BETWEEN POPULATIONS

__Null Hypothesis True__

Within-group estimate reflects	X	
Between-group estimate reflects	X	

__Research Hypothesis True__

Within-group estimate reflects	X	
Between-group estimate reflects	X	X

Therefore:

If null hypothesis true: Two estimates are equal
                          Ratio of Between/Within = About 1

If research hyopth true: Between group estimate is larger
                          Ratio of Between/Within > 1

Ratio of Between/Within called $\underline{F}$ ratio

Aron/Aron
Statistics for the Social Sciences

© 1997 by Prentice-Hall, Inc.
Simon & Schuster/A Viacom Company
Upper Saddle River, New Jersey 07458

Main analysis of variance computations with equal $\underline{N}$s.

Within-Group Population Variance Estimate:

1. Estimate variance of each population: $\underline{S}^2 = \Sigma(\underline{X} - \underline{M})^2 / \underline{df}$

2. $\underline{S}^2_{\text{Within}} = \dfrac{\underline{S}_1^2 + \underline{S}_2^2 + \ldots + \underline{S}^2_{\text{Last}}}{\underline{N}_{\text{Groups}}}$

Between-Group Population Variance Estimate:

1. $\underline{S}_M^2 = (\underline{M} - \underline{GM})^2 / (\underline{N}_{\text{Groups}} - 1)$

2. $\underline{S}^2_{\text{Between}} = \underline{S}_M^2 \times \underline{n}$

F Ratio

$\underline{F} = \underline{S}^2_{\text{Between}} / \underline{S}^2_{\text{Within}}$

Aron/Aron
Statistics for the Social Sciences

© 1997 by Prentice-Hall, Inc.
Simon & Schuster/A Viacom Company
Upper Saddle River, New Jersey 07458

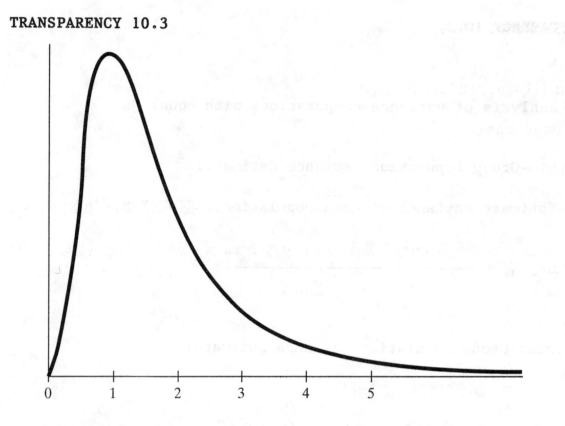

Cutoff Scores for the *F* Distribution (Portion)

Denominator Degrees of Freedom	Significance Level	Numerator Degrees of Freedom					
		1	*2*	*3*	*4*	*5*	*6*
10	.01	10.05	7.56	6.55	6.00	5.64	5.39
	.05	4.97	4.10	3.71	3.48	3.33	3.22
	.10	3.29	2.93	2.73	2.61	2.52	2.46
11	.01	9.65	7.21	6.22	5.67	5.32	5.07
	.05	4.85	3.98	3.59	3.36	3.20	3.10
	.10	3.23	2.86	2.66	2.54	2.45	2.39
12	.01	9.33	6.93	5.95	5.41	5.07	4.82
	.05	4.75	3.89	3.49	3.26	3.11	3.00
	.10	3.18	2.81	2.61	2.48	2.40	2.33
13	.01	9.07	6.70	5.74	5.21	4.86	4.62
	.05	4.67	3.81	3.41	3.18	3.03	2.92
	.10	3.14	2.76	2.56	2.43	2.35	2.28

Aron/Aron
Statistics for the Social Sciences

© 1997 by Prentice-Hall, Inc.
Simon & Schuster/A Viacom Company
Upper Saddle River, New Jersey 07458

Criminal-record study.

Computations:

$\underline{df}_{Between}$ = $\underline{N}_{Groups}$ - 1 = 3-1 = 2

$\underline{df}_{Within}$ = $\underline{df}_1$ + $\underline{df}_2$ + . . . + $\underline{df}_{Last}$ = 4 + 4 + 4 = 12

$\underline{F}$ needed for significance at .05 level with $\underline{df}$=2,12 = 3.89.

Criminal-Record Group			Clean-Record Group			No Information Group		
Rating	Dev	Dev^2	Rating	Dev	Dev^2	Rating	Dev	Dev^2
10	2	4	5	1	1	4	-1	1
7	-1	1	1	-3	9	6	1	1
5	-3	9	3	-1	1	9	4	16
10	2	4	7	3	9	3	-2	4
8	0	0	4	0	0	3	-2	4
40		18	20		20	25		26

$\underline{M}$ = 40/5 = 8 $\underline{M}$ = 20/5 = 4 $\underline{M}$ = 25/5 = 5

$\underline{S}^2$ = 18/4 = 4.5 $\underline{S}^2$ = 20/4 = 5.0 $\underline{S}^2$ = 26/4 = 6.5

$$\underline{S}^2_{Within} = \frac{\underline{S}_1^2 + \underline{S}_2^2 + \ldots + \underline{S}^2_{Last}}{\underline{N}_{Groups}} = \frac{4.5+5.0+6.5}{3} = \frac{16.3}{3} = 5.33$$

Sample means $\underline{M}$	Deviations from Grand Mean (M-GM)	Squared Deviations from Grand Mean (M-GM)^2
4	-1.67	2.79
8	2.33	5.43
5	- .67	.45
17 ($\underline{GM}$ = $\Sigma\underline{M}/\underline{N}_{Groups}$ = 17/3 = 5.67)		8.67

$\underline{S}_M^2$ = $\Sigma(\underline{M}-\underline{GM})/\underline{df}_{Between}$ = 8.67/2 = 4.34.

$\underline{S}^2_{Between}$ = $(\underline{S}_M^2)(\underline{n})$ = (4.34)(5) = 21.7

$\underline{F}$ = $\underline{S}^2_{Between}/\underline{S}^2_{Within}$ = 21.7/5.33 = 4.07

Aron/Aron
Statistics for the Social Sciences

© 1997 by Prentice-Hall, Inc.
Simon & Schuster/A Viacom Company
Upper Saddle River, New Jersey 07458

TRANSPARENCY 10.5

Criminal-record study.

Steps of hypothesis testing:

1. Reframe into a research hypothesis and a null hypothesis about populations.

   Population 1: Jurors told defendant has a criminal record.
   Population 2: Jurors told defendant has a clean record.
   Population 3: Jurors given no information on defendants' record.

   Research hypothesis: The three populations have different means.
   Null hypothesis: The three populations have the same mean.

2. Determine the characteristics of the comparison distribution.

   F distribution with 2 and 12 degrees of freedom.

3. Determine the cutoff sample score on the comparison distribution at which the null hypothesis should be rejected.

   5% level, $F(2,12)$ needed = 3.89.

4. Determine score of your sample on comparison distribution.

   Within-group population variance estimate =   5.33.
   Between-group population variance estimate = 21.70.
   F ratio = 21.7/5.33 = 4.07

5. Compare scores obtained in Steps 3 and 4 to decide whether to reject the null hypothesis.

   F on 4 (4.08) is more extreme than cutoff F on 3 (3.89).

   Therefore, reject the null hypothesis; the research hypothesis is supported (information available to subjects about criminal record makes a difference in ratings of guilt).

Aron/Aron
Statistics for the Social Sciences

© 1997 by Prentice-Hall, Inc.
Simon & Schuster/A Viacom Company
Upper Saddle River, New Jersey 07458

TABLE 10–5
Steps for Conducting an Analysis of Variance (When Sample Sizes Are Equal)

1. Restate the question as a research hypothesis and a null hypothesis about the populations.
2. Determine the characteristics of the comparison distribution.
   (a) The comparison distribution is an F distribution.
   (b) The numerator degrees of freedom is the number of groups minus 1:
   $df_{Between} = N_{Groups} - 1$.
   (c) The denominator degrees of freedom is the sum of the degrees of freedom in each group (the number in the group minus 1): $df_{Within} = df_1 + df_2 + \ldots + df_{Last}$.
3. Determine the cutoff sample score on the comparison distribution at which the null hypothesis should be rejected.
   (a) Determine the desired significance level.
   (b) Look up the appropriate cutoff in an F table, using the degrees of freedom from Step 2.
4. Determine the score of the sample on the comparison distribution. (This will be an F ratio.)
   (a) Calculate the between-group population variance estimate ($S^2_{Between}$).
      (i) Calculate the means of each group.
      (ii) Calculate a variance estimate based on the means of the groups:
      $S^2_M = \Sigma(M - GM)^2/df_{Between}$.
      (iii) Convert this estimate of the variance of a distribution of means to an estimate of the variance of a population of individual scores by multiplying it times the number of scores in each group: $S^2_{Between} = (S^2_M)(n)$.
   (b) Calculate the within-group population variance estimate S^2_{Within}.
      (i) Calculate population variance estimates based on each group's scores: For each group, $S^2 = \Sigma(X - M)^2/(n - 1)$.
      (ii) Average these variance estimates: $S^2_{Within} = (S^2_1 + S^2_2 + \ldots + S^2_{Last})/N\text{Groups}$.
   (c) Calculate the F ratio: $F = S^2_{Between}/S^2_{Within}$.
5. Compare the scores from Steps 3 and 4 to decide whether to reject the null hypothesis.

Aron/Aron
Statistics for the Social Sciences

© 1997 by Prentice-Hall, Inc.
Simon & Schuster/A Viacom Company
Upper Saddle River, New Jersey 07458

TRANSPARENCY 10.7

Design and results of study by Burnkraut and Unnava (1989).

<u>Design</u>:

Dependent measure: Attitude towards product

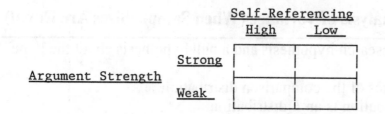

4 Groups: A. Strong argument, high self-referencing
          B. Strong argument, low self-referencing
          C. Weak argument, high self-referencing
          D. Weak argument, low self-referencing

<u>Results</u>:

	Self-Referencing		
Argument Strength	<u>High</u>	<u>Low</u>	<u>Average</u>
<u>Strong</u>	4.94	5.58	5.26
<u>Weak</u>	4.46	3.74	4.10
<u>Average</u>	4.70	4.66	

Main Effects:

Argument Strength: Means: 5.26 vs. 4.10,
$\underline{F}(1,44) = 21.78$, $\underline{p} < .001$.

Self-Referencing: Means: 4.70 vs. 4.66,
$\underline{F}(1,44) < 1$, <u>ns</u>.

Interaction Effect (Argument Strength X Self-Referencing):
$\underline{F}(1,44) = 7.76$, $\underline{p} < .01$.

Reference: Burnkraut, R. E., & Unnava, H. R. (1989). Self-
            referencing: A strategy for increasing
            processing of message content. <u>Personality
            and Social Psychology Bulletin</u>, <u>4</u>, 628-338.

Aron/Aron
Statistics for the Social Sciences

© 1997 by Prentice-Hall, Inc.
Simon & Schuster/A Viacom Company
Upper Saddle River, New Jersey 07458

Possible Means for Results of a Study of the Relation of Age and Education to Income (Fictional Data, Thousands of Dollars)

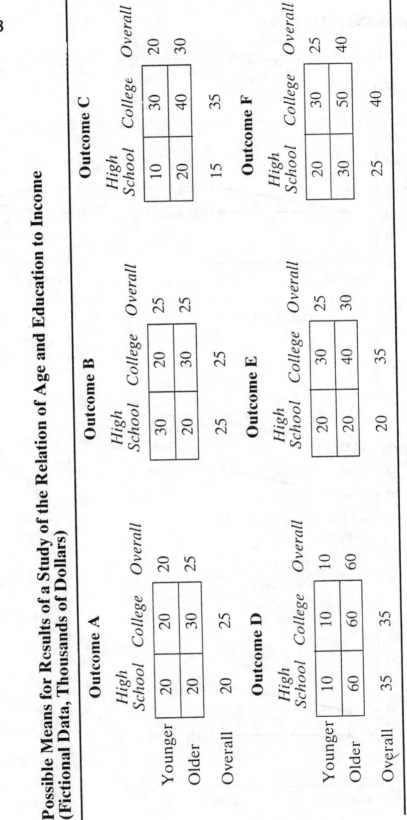

Outcome A

	High School	College	Overall
Younger	20	20	20
Older	20	30	25
Overall	20	25	

Outcome B

	High School	College	Overall
Younger	30	20	25
Older	20	30	25
Overall	25	25	

Outcome C

	High School	College	Overall
Younger	10	30	20
Older	20	40	30
Overall	15	35	

Outcome D

	High School	College	Overall
Younger	10	10	10
Older	60	60	60
Overall	35	35	

Outcome E

	High School	College	Overall
Younger	20	30	25
Older	20	40	30
Overall	20	35	

Outcome F

	High School	College	Overall
Younger	20	30	25
Older	30	50	40
Overall	25	40	

Aron/Aron
Statistics for the Social Sciences

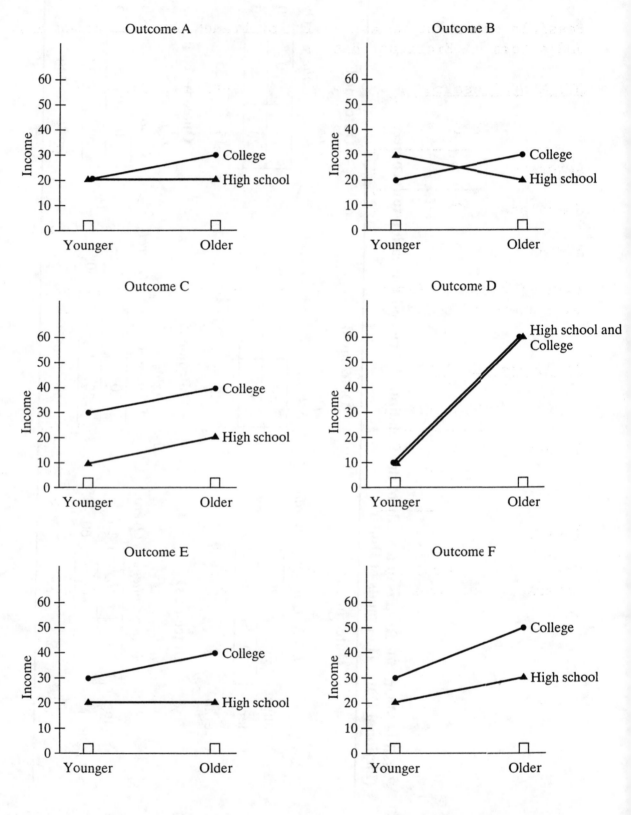

TRANSPARENCY 10.10

Possible means for mental health of French and U.S. comedians
and actors. (Fictional data.)

<u>DV: Mental Health</u>   ***Insert lines***

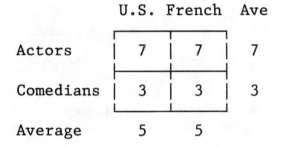

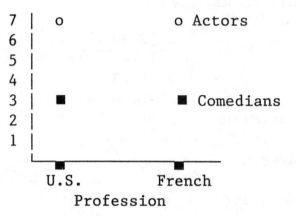

Main effects: profession only
Interaction: none

<u>DV: Mental Health</u>

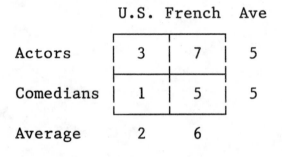

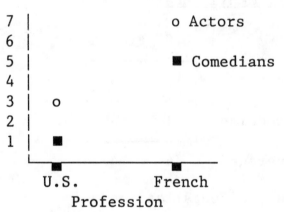

Main effects: profession & nation
Interaction: none

Aron/Aron
Statistics for the Social Sciences

© 1997 by Prentice-Hall, Inc.
Simon & Schuster/A Viacom Company
Upper Saddle River, New Jersey 07458

Additional possible means for mental health of French and U.S. comedians and actors. (Fictional data.)

DV: Mental Health

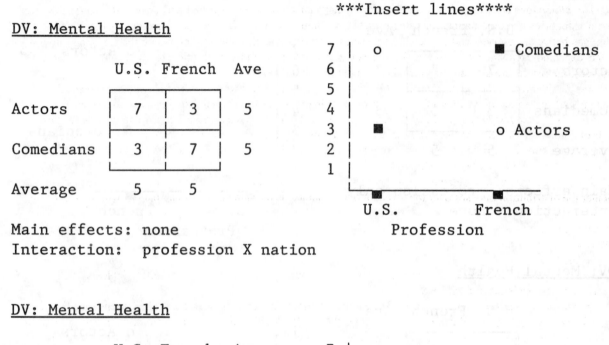

	U.S.	French	Ave
Actors	7	3	5
Comedians	3	7	5
Average	5	5	

Insert lines*

Main effects: none
Interaction: profession X nation

DV: Mental Health

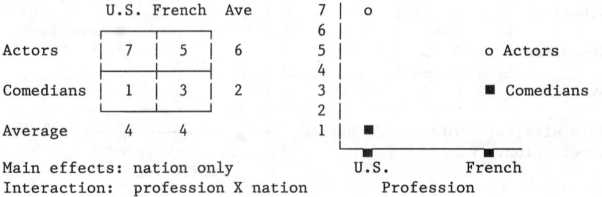

	U.S.	French	Ave
Actors	7	5	6
Comedians	1	3	2
Average	4	4	

Main effects: nation only
Interaction: profession X nation

Aron/Aron
Statistics for the Social Sciences

© 1997 by Prentice-Hall, Inc.
Simon & Schuster/A Viacom Company
Upper Saddle River, New Jersey 07458

Chapter 11
Chi-Square Tests and Strategies When Population Distributions are Not Normal

Instructor's Summary of Chapter

The chi-square statistic reflects the amount of discrepancy between expected and observed frequencies over several categories or combinations of categories. It is computed by finding for each category or combination the difference between observed and expected frequencies, squaring this difference (to eliminate the sign), and dividing by the expected frequency (to help make the squared differences more proportionate to the number of cases involved); the results are then added over all categories or combinations.

The distribution of the chi-square statistic is known and significance-level cutoffs for various degrees of freedom (Df) (based on the number of categories or combinations free to vary) are listed in a chi-square table.

The chi-square test for goodness of fit tests hypotheses about whether a distribution of frequencies over the levels of a nominal variable matches an expected distribution. (These expected frequencies are usually based on theory or on a known distribution in another study or circumstance). Hence, in this test, the expected frequencies are given in advance. Df = number of categories - 1.

The chi-square test of independence tests hypotheses about the relationship between two nominal variables-- whether the distribution of cases over the levels of one variable has the same proportional pattern within each of the levels of the other variable. The data are set up in a contingency table, in which the two variables are crossed. The frequency expected for a given cell if the two variables are independent is the percentage of all the scores in that cell's row times the total number of cases in that cell's column. Df = number of columns minus 1 times number of rows minus 1.

Assumptions. Chi-square tests make no assumptions about normal distributions of their variables, but do require that independence of each case.

Indexes of association and effect size. The estimated effect size for a chi-square test of independence (i.e., the degree of association) for a 2 X 2 contingency table is the phi (ϕ) coefficient (the square root of the result of dividing the computed chi-square by the number of cases), and for larger tables, Cramer's phi (the square root of the result of dividing the computed chi-square by the product of the number of cases times the degrees of freedom in the smaller dimension of the contingency table). These coefficients range from 0 to 1 and can be interpreted in approximately the same way as a correlation coefficient. A phi of .10 is considered a small effect, .30 a medium effect, and .50 a large effect.

Normal distribution assumption in standard parametric tests. The *t*-test, analysis of variance, and the significance tests for correlation and regression all assume that populations are normally distributed. While these parametric statistical tests seem to work over many types of moderate violations of this assumption, when the population is severely non-normal they can permit too many Type I or Type II errors. It is difficult to assess from the sample whether a population is normal, but outliers are clearly a problem, as is a ceiling or floor effect.

Data transformations. One approach when the populations appear nonnormal is to transform the scores mathematically, such as taking the square root, log, or inverse of each score so that the distribution of transformed scores appears to represent a normally distributed population; the ordinary hypothesis-testing procedures can then be applied.

Rank-order methods. Another approach is to rank all of the subjects based on their scores on a variable. Special rank-order statistical tests ("nonparametric" or "distribution-free" tests) exist which use simple principles of probability to determine the chance of the ranks being unevenly distributed across experimental groups. However, in many cases using the rank-transformed data in an ordinary parametric test produces an acceptable approximation.

How the procedures of this chapter are reported in research articles. Chi-square tests reported in research articles often include all information about numbers in each category or cell. The computed chi-square and its significance are also usually reported, following a standard format--for example, "$X^2(3, N = 217) = 8.81, p < .05$." Data transformations are usually described and justified at the beginning of the Results sections, and rank-order methods are described much like any other kind of hypothesis test.

Box 11.1. Karl Pearson, Inventor of Chi-Square and Center of Controversy. Summarizes the life and work of Pearson, inventor of the chi-square test.

Lecture 11.1: The Chi-Square Test of Goodness of Fit

Materials

Lecture outline
Transparencies 11.1 through 11.6

Outline for Blackboard

- I. **Review**
- II. **Nominal Variables**
- III. **Expected and Observed Frequencies**
- IV. **Chi-Square Statistic**
- V. **Chi-Square Distribution**
- VI. **Steps of Hypothesis Testing**
- VII. **Review this Class**

Instructor's Lecture Outline

I. Review
A. Idea of descriptive and inferential statistics.
B. Analysis of variance as looking at means over different categories.
C. Assumptions in analysis of variance.

II. Nominal Variables
A. Principle: Variable measured in levels or categories with no systematic numerical or rank order relationship among levels.
B. Examples: Hair color, religion, which school you attend, major, profession, ethnic group, attachment style.

III. Expected and Observed Frequencies: Show TRANSPARENCY 11.1 (distribution of attachment styles in psychology statistics students, compared to that found in the general public, based on Hazan & Shaver, 1977) and discuss:
A. Key idea is the comparison of observed and expected frequency in each category.
B. *Observed frequency* is the number of cases in the category in the sample data.
C. *Expected frequency* is the number of cases in the category expected based on the population to which we are comparing our sample.
   1. Computed by multiplying the proportion in the population to which we are comparing times the number in the sample.
   2. Note: Sometimes a population distribution is not given and the comparison is to equal percentages in the categories.

IV. Chi-Square Statistic (continue showing TRANSPARENCY 11.1)
A. A measure of degree of discrepancy over all categories.
B. The discrepancy in each category is squared, in part to eliminate the problem of signs.

184

C. The squared discrepancy in each category is divided by the expected frequency to keep these discrepancies in proportion to the number of cases that would have been expected.

D. The chi-square statistic is the sum, over the categories, of the each squared discrepancy divided by its expected frequency.

V. **Chi-square Distribution: Show TRANSPARENCY 11.2 (chi-square distribution) and discuss:**

A. Principle: If samples are randomly taken from a population and a chi-square statistic computed on each, these chi-squares follow a mathematically defined distribution (the chi-square distribution).

B. The distribution is skewed with the tail to the right.

C. The distribution's exact shape depends on the degrees of freedom.

D. For a chi-square test of goodness of fit, df = number of categories - 1.
   1. This is the number of categories with frequencies free to vary, given that the frequency over all categories is fixed.
   2. In the current example, $df = 3 - 1 = 2$.

E. The cutoff chi-square values for various significance levels are given in standard tables.
   1. A chi-square table is included in Appendix B of the text.
   2. In the example with $df = 2$, at the .05 level, cutoff chi-square is 5.992.

VI. **Steps of Hypothesis Testing:**

A. Show TRANSPARENCY 11.3 (hypothesis testing steps for attachment-style example) and discuss each step.

B. Example 2: Show TRANSPARENCIES 11.4 and 11.5 (Fictional example of whether distribution over year in school of students who attend political demonstrations is different from the distribution of students over years in general at the same university) and discuss.

VII. **Review this Class: Use blackboard outline and TRANSPARENCY 11.6 (steps of conducting a chi-square test for goodness of fit).**

Lecture 11.2: The Chi-Square Test of Independence

Materials

Lecture outline
Transparencies 11.6 through 11.9

Outline for Blackboard

- I. Review
- II. Contingency Tables
- III. Independence and Expected Frequencies
- IV. Computing Chi-Square
- V. Degrees of Freedom
- VI. Effect Size (Degree of Association)
- VII. Hypothesis Testing
- VIII. Review this Class

Instructor's Lecture Outline

I. Review
A. Idea of descriptive and inferential statistics.
B. Idea of nominal variables.
C. Show TRANSPARENCY 11.6 (steps of conducting a chi-square test for goodness of fit) and discuss each step.

II. Contingency Tables
A. Breakdown of frequencies across levels of two nominal variables in which each individual is categorized on both variables.
B. Examples:
1. Hair color and eye color.
2. Religious affiliation and ethnic group.
3. Religious affiliation and eye color.
4. Personality type of self and partner.
C. Show top of TRANSPARENCY 11.7 (fictional example of married women with and without children who rent vs. own their home) and discuss:
1. As example of contingency table. (Note that it doesn't matter which variable goes on which dimension of the table.)
2 Cell and marginal frequencies.

III. Independence and Expected Frequencies:
A. Distribution of frequencies over categories on one variable is independent of the distribution of frequencies over categories on a second variable.
B. In example, independence would mean that whether young married women do versus do not have children is unrelated to whether they rent or own their home. Show TRANSPARENCY 11.7 and discuss.

C. Expected frequencies are what would be expected if two variables were independent.

D. If the two variables are independent, then the expected frequencies for a given cell is the proportion of its row's observed frequency of the total observed frequency, times the observed frequency for its column.

E. Show TRANSPARENCY 11.7 and discuss.

IV. Computing Chi-Square

A. Same principle as with chi-square test for goodness of fit except that you add up over cells instead of categories.

B. Show next section of TRANSPARENCY 11.7 and discuss.

V. Degrees of Freedom

A. What is free to vary?

B. If marginal totals are known, only a small number of cells need be known to determine the rest.

C. Formula is $df = (N_R - 1)(N_C - 1)$.

B. Show next section of TRANSPARENCY 11.7 and discuss.

VI. Effect Size (Degree of Association)

A. For a 2 X 2 contingency table:
   1. $\phi = \sqrt{(X^2/N)}$.
   2. ϕ is like r.
   3. Show next section of TRANSPARENCY 11.7 and discuss.

B. For a larger than 2 X 2 contingency table:
   1. Cramer's $\phi = \sqrt{[X^2/(N)(df_L)]}$.
   2. df_L is the degrees of freedom corresponding to the smaller dimension of the contingency table.
   3. Also interpreted like r.

VII. Hypothesis Testing. Show TRANSPARENCY 11.8 (hypothesis testing for rent-own X children-or-not example) and discuss.

VIII. Review this Class: Use blackboard outline and TRANSPARENCY 11.9 (steps of conducting a chi-square test for independence).

Lecture 11.3: Nonnormal Distributions and Data Transformations

Materials

Lecture outline
Transparencies 11.10 through 11.13

Outline for Blackboard

I. **Review**
II. **Assumptions for Parametric Tests**
III. **Solutions to Suspected Nonnormal Populations**
IV. **Data Transformations**
V. **Rank-Order Tests**
VI. **Review this Class**

Instructor's Lecture Outline

I. **Review**
   A. Idea of descriptive and inferential statistics.
   B. Major inferential statistical techniques (parametric tests):
      1. t-test.
      2. Analysis of variance.
      3. Significance test for correlation and regression.

II. **Assumptions for Parametric Tests**
   A. Assumptions are requirements for the statistical procedure to work properly. They are built into the logic or mathematics.
   B. Two main assumptions:
      1. Normal populations--if not met, then comparison distribution (t or F) is not the shape it is supposed to be (and thus tabled values are wrong).
      2. Equal population variances for each group--if not met, then the idea of pooling does not work and we can't compute a single estimate.
   C. Almost never met exactly in practice, but close is good enough--in most cases, these techniques are robust.
   D. Main emphasis has been on normal distribution assumption and the problems of skew, outliers, and ceiling and floor effects.
   E. How to know if a population is normal based on sample data?
      1. Show TRANSPARENCY 11.10 (sample histograms from normally distributed populations, from text) and discuss.
      2. Principle: If sample not highly non-normal, we assume population is normal. (Innocent until proven guilty.)

III. **Solutions to Suspected Nonnormal Populations**
   A. Data transformations.
   B. Rank-order methods.

IV. Data Transformations

A. Principle: If the distribution is not normal, change the scale of the scores so that the distribution is closer to normal.

B. Example: Show TRANSPARENCY 11.11 (History vs. English majors on love for classical music) and discuss:
  1. Need for transformation.
  2. Method of carrying out transformation.
  4. Result of transformation.
  5. Next step would be to carry out the *t*-test for independent means in the usual way.

C. Legitimacy:
  1. Underlying numerical meaning of scale is arbitrary.
  2. Done in advance of data analysis and to all scores in all groups, so there is no systematic bias in favor of the researcher's hypotheses.
  3. Does not alter the order of the scores.

D. Methods of transformation.
  1. Each of the major methods we consider is used when there is positive skew. (When there is negative skew, other transformations can be used, or the scores can be first reflected.)
  2. Show TRANSPARENCY 11.12 (effects of transformations on distribution shape, from text) and discuss three kinds of transformations mentioned: square root, log, inverse.

V. Rank-Order Tests

A. Basic approach:
  1. Transform scores to ranks.
  2. This creates a distribution with known characteristics (it is rectangular, with mean and variance depending only on how many cases are ranked).
  3. Thus, the possibility of any particular distribution of ranks (such as a particular mean or ranks in one group, or a particular high correlation of ranks) can be computed exactly by principles of probability.
  4. Specific tests exist for the computations involved in computing the ranks and the cutoff means or sums or correlations of ranks for various hypothesis testing situations. Show TRANSPARENCY 11.13 (table of rank-order tests, from text) and discuss.

B. Simply applying standard parametric statistics to ranked data provides acceptable approximations.

VI. Review this Class: Use blackboard outline.

TRANSPARENCY 11.1

<u>Expected Distribution</u> (from studies by Hazan & Shaver, 1987):

Secure: 56%   Avoidant: 24%   Anxious/Ambivalent: 20%

<u>Observed, Actual Frequencies</u> (from class questionnaire)

Secure: 51   Avoidant: 23   Anxious/Ambivalent: 16

<u>Expected frequencies</u> (expected percent times number in sample)

Secure: Avoidant: Anxious/Ambivalent:
(56%)(90) = 50.4   (24%)(90) = 21.6   (20%)(90) = 18

<u>Chi-Square Statistic</u>   (indicates overall degree of discrepancy between   observed and expected)

$$X^2 = \Sigma \frac{(O-E)^2}{E} = \frac{(51-50.4)^2}{50.4} + \frac{(23-21.6)^2}{21.6} + \frac{(16-18)^2}{18}$$

$$= \frac{.6^2}{50.4} + \frac{1.4^2}{21.6} + \frac{-2^2}{18}$$

$$= \frac{.36}{50.4} + \frac{1.96}{21.6} + \frac{4}{18}$$

$$= .007 + .091 + .222 = .32$$

Aron/Aron
Statistics for the Social Sciences

© 1997 by Prentice-Hall, Inc.
Simon & Schuster/A Viacom Company
Upper Saddle River, New Jersey 07458

TRANSPARENCY 11.2

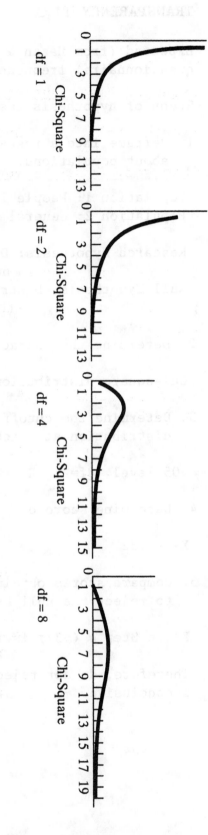

Portion of a Chi-Square Table

df	Significance Level		
	.10	*.05*	*.01*
1	2.706	3.841	6.635
2	4.605	5.992	9.211
3	6.252	7.815	11.345
4	7.780	9.488	13.277
5	9.237	11.071	15.087

Aron/Aron
Statistics for the Social Sciences

© 1997 by Prentice-Hall, Inc.
Simon & Schuster/A Viacom Company
Upper Saddle River, New Jersey 07458

TRANSPARENCY 11.3

Expected (from Hazan & Shaver, 1987) and observed (from class questionnaire) frequencies of students in each attachment style.

Steps of hypothesis testing:

1. Reframe into a research hypothesis and a null hypothesis about populations.

   Population 1: People like students in this class.
   Population 2: General public.

   Research Hypothesis: Distribution of cases over categories differs between the two populations.
   Null Hypothesis: Distribution of cases over categories is the same in the two populations.

2. Determine the characteristics of the comparison distribution.

   Chi-square distribution with two degrees of freedom.

3. Determine the cutoff sample score on the comparison distribution at which the null hypothesis should be rejected.

   .05 level, $\underline{df}$=2: $X^2 = 5.992$.

4. Determine score of your sample on comparison distribution.

   $X^2 = .32$.

5. Compare scores obtained in Steps 3 and 4 to decide whether to reject the null hypothesis.

   X^2 in Step 4 (.32) is less extreme than Step 3 cutoff (5.992).

   Therefore, do not reject the null hypothesis; the study is inconclusive.

Aron/Aron
Statistics for the Social Sciences

© 1997 by Prentice-Hall, Inc.
Simon & Schuster/A Viacom Company
Upper Saddle River, New Jersey 07458

Expected (all students attending a particular university) and observed (students attending political demonstrations at that university) frequencies of those in different years. (Fictional example.)

Year	Observed Frequency	Expected Percent	Frequency	
First	30	15%	45	[(15%)(300)]
Second	20	15%	45	[(15%)(300)]
Third	90	30%	90	[(30%)(300)]
Fourth	120	30%	90	[(30%)(300)]
Graduate	40	10%	30	[(10%)(300)]
TOTAL	300	100%	300	

$\underline{df}$ = 5 categories - 1 = 4 $X^2 = \Sigma \dfrac{(O-E)^2}{E}$

$$= \frac{(30-45)^2}{45} + \frac{(20-45)^2}{45} + \frac{(90-90)^2}{90} + \frac{(120-90)^2}{90} + \frac{(40-30)^2}{30}$$

$$= \frac{225}{45} + \frac{625}{45} + \frac{0}{90} + \frac{900}{90} + \frac{100}{30}$$

$$= \quad 5 \quad + \quad 13.9 \quad + \quad 0 \quad + \quad 10 \quad + \quad 3.3 \quad = \quad 32.2$$

Aron/Aron
Statistics for the Social Sciences

© 1997 by Prentice-Hall, Inc.
Simon & Schuster/A Viacom Company
Upper Saddle River, New Jersey 07458

TRANSPARENCY 11.5

Expected (all students attending a particular university) and observed
(students attending political demonstrations at that university)
frequencies of those in different years. (Fictional example.)

Steps of hypothesis testing:

1. Reframe into a research hypothesis and a null hypothesis about
   populations.

   Population 1: Students at this university who attend political
                 demonstrations.
   Population 2: Students at this university in general.

   Research Hypothesis: Distribution of cases over categories differs
                        between the two populations.
   Null Hypothesis: Distribution of cases over categories is the same in
                    the two populations.

2. Determine the characteristics of the comparison distribution.

   Chi-square distribution with four degrees of freedom.

3. Determine the cutoff sample score on the comparison distribution
   at which the null hypothesis should be rejected.

   .01 level, <u>df</u>=2: X^2 = 13.277.

4. Determine score of your sample on comparison distribution.

   X^2 = 32.2.

5. Compare scores obtained in Steps 3 and 4 to decide whether to
   reject the null hypothesis.

   X^2 in Step 4 (32.2) is more extreme than Step 3 cutoff (13.277).

   Therefore, reject the null hypothesis; the research hypothesis is
   supported (those attending political demonstrations appear to have a
   different distribution of year in school than do students at this
   university in general).

Aron/Aron
Statistics for the Social Sciences

© 1997 by Prentice-Hall, Inc.
Simon & Schuster/A Viacom Company
Upper Saddle River, New Jersey 07458

TRANSPARENCY 11.6

How to conduct a chi-square test for goodness of fit.

1. Reframe the question into a research hypothesis and a null hypothesis about populations.

   A. Populations:

      1. Population 1 are people like those in the study.
      2. Population 2 are people who have the hypothesized distribution over categories.

   B. Hypotheses:

      1. Research hypothesis: The two populations have different distributions of cases over categories.
      2. Null Hypothesis: The two populations have the same distribution of cases over categories.

2. Determine the characteristics of the comparison distribution:

   A. Chi-square distribution.
   B. <u>df</u> = Number of categories minus 1.

3. Determine the cutoff sample score on the comparison distribution at which the null hypothesis should be rejected.

   A. Determine the desired significance level.
   B. Look up the appropriate cutoff on a chi-square table, using the degrees of freedom calculated above.

4. Determine the score of your sample on the comparison distribution.

$$X^2 = \Sigma \frac{(O-E)^2}{E}$$

5. Compare the scores obtained in Steps 3 and 4 to decide whether to reject the null hypothesis.

Aron/Aron
Statistics for the Social Sciences

© 1997 by Prentice-Hall, Inc.
Simon & Schuster/A Viacom Company
Upper Saddle River, New Jersey 07458

TRANSPARENCY 11.7

Young married women who have versus do not have children (first nominal variable) and rent or own their home (second nominal variable). (Fictional data.)

Contingency Table:

	Rent	Own	Total	
Have Children	5	11	16	40%
No Children	20	4	24	60%
Total	25	15	40	

Expected Frequencies:

$E = (R/\underline{N})(C)$ or $E = $ (Row's Percent)(Column Total)

Have Children-Rent = (40%)(25) = 10
Have Children-Own = (40%)(15) = 6
No Children-Rent   = (60%)(25) = 15
No Children-Own   = (60%)(15) = 9

Table with Observed (and Expected) Frequencies:

	Rent	Own	Total
Have Children	5(10)	11(6)	16(16)
No Children	20(15)	4(9)	24(24)
Total	25(25)	15(15)	40(40)

$$X^2 = \Sigma \frac{(O-E)^2}{E} = \frac{(5-10)^2}{10} + \frac{(11-6)^2}{6} + \frac{(20-15)^2}{15} + \frac{(4-9)^2}{9}$$

$$= \frac{25}{10} + \frac{25}{6} + \frac{25}{15} + \frac{25}{9}$$

$$= 2.5 + 4.17 + 1.67 + 2.78 = 11.12$$

Degrees of Freedom:

	Rent	Own	Total
Have Children	5		16
No Children			24
Total	25	15	40

NOTE: Given $\underline{N}$ of <u>one</u> cell and marginal totals, all other cells' $\underline{N}$s are determined.

<u>df</u>=(Number of Rows-1)(Number of Columns-1)=(2-1)(2-1)=1

$\phi = \sqrt{(X^2/\underline{N})} = \sqrt{(11.12/40)} = \sqrt{.28} = .53$, large effect size.

Aron/Aron
Statistics for the Social Sciences

© 1997 by Prentice-Hall, Inc.
Simon & Schuster/A Viacom Company
Upper Saddle River, New Jersey 07458

TRANSPARENCY 11.8

Young married women who have versus do not have children (first nominal variable) and either rent or own their home (second nominal variable). (Fictional data.)

Steps of hypothesis testing:

1. Reframe into a research hypothesis and a null hypothesis about populations.

   Population 1: Young married women like those surveyed.
   Population 2: Young married women for whom renting or owning their home is independent of whether they have children.

   Research Hypothesis: Two populations are different (renting or owning is not independent of having children).
   Null Hypothesis: Two populations are the same (renting or owning is independent of having children).

2. Determine the characteristics of the comparison distribution.

   Chi-square distribution with one degree of freedom.

3. Determine the cutoff sample score on the comparison.

   .05 level, $\underline{df}=1$: $X^2 = 3.841$.

4. Determine score of your sample on comparison distribution.

   $X^2 = 11.12$.

5. Compare scores obtained in Steps 3 and 4 to decide whether to reject the null hypothesis.

   X^2 in Step 4 (11.12) is more extreme than Step 3 cutoff (3.841).

   Therefore, reject the null hypothesis; the research hypothesis is supported (among young married women like those surveyed, renting or owning appears not to be independent of having children).

6. Examine effect size and interpret.

   $\phi = .53$, a large effect size.

Aron/Aron
Statistics for the Social Sciences

© 1997 by Prentice-Hall, Inc.
Simon & Schuster/A Viacom Company
Upper Saddle River, New Jersey 07458

TRANSPARENCY 11.9

How to Conduct a Chi-Square Test for Independence

1. Reframe the question into a research hypothesis and a null hypothesis about populations.

    A. Populations:

        1. Population 1 are people like those in the study.
        2. Population 2 are people whose distribution of cases over categories on the first variable is independent of the distribution of cases over categories for the second variable.

    B. Hypotheses.

        1. Research hypothesis: Two populations have different distributions of cases over categories.
        2. Null Hypothesis: Two populations have the same distributions of cases over categories.

2. Determine the characteristics of the comparison distribution:

    A. Chi-square distribution.
    B. $\underline{df} = (\underline{N}_{Columns}-1)(\underline{N}_{Rows}-1)$.

3. Determine the cutoff sample score on the comparison distribution at which the null hypothesis should be rejected.

    A. Determine the desired significance level.
    B. Look up the appropriate cutoff on a chi-square table, using the degrees of freedom calculated above.

4. Determine the score of your sample on the comparison distribution.

$$X^2 = \Sigma \frac{(O-E)^2}{E}$$

5. Compare the scores obtained in Steps 3 and 4 to decide whether to reject the null hypothesis.

6. Examine effect size and interpret.

    A. If a 2 X 2 table:
        1. $\phi = \sqrt{(X^2/\underline{N})}$
        2. Rules of thumb: small=.10, medium=.30, large=.50.

    B. If greater than a 2 X 2 table
        1. Cramer's $\phi = \sqrt{(X^2/[\underline{N}][\underline{df}_L])}$
        2. Rules of thumb depend on $\underline{df}_L$.

Aron/Aron
Statistics for the Social Sciences

© 1997 by Prentice-Hall, Inc.
Simon & Schuster/A Viacom Company
Upper Saddle River, New Jersey 07458

TRANSPARENCY 11.10

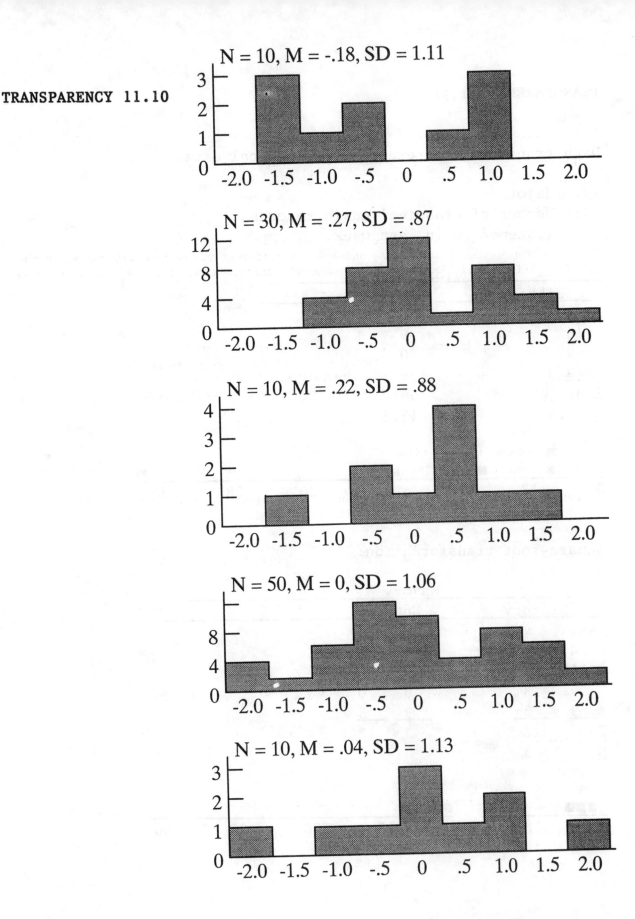

Data transformation example. (Fictional data.)

IV: Major
DV: Number of classical music records
     listened to in last week

	Major	
History	English	
4	36	
16	9	
9	0	
9	9	
Σ 38	54	
$\underline{M}$ 9.5	13.5	

Square-root transformation:

	Major			
History		English		
Raw	$\sqrt{}$	Raw	$\sqrt{}$	
4	2	36	6	
16	4	9	3	
9	3	0	0	
9	3	9	3	
Σ	12		12	
$\underline{M}$	3		3	

Aron/Aron
Statistics for the Social Sciences

© 1997 by Prentice-Hall, Inc.
Simon & Schuster/A Viacom Company
Upper Saddle River, New Jersey 07458

Before   After

(a)

(b)

(c)

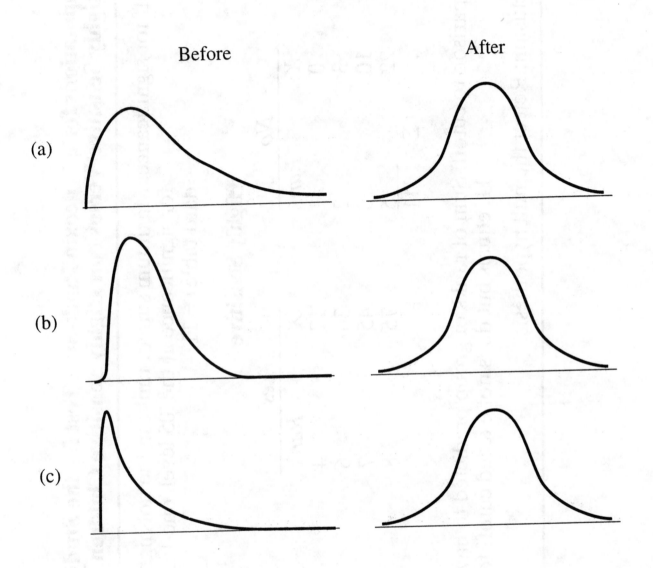

Aron/Aron
Statistics for the Social Sciences

© 1997 by Prentice-Hall, Inc.
Simon & Schuster/A Viacom Company
Upper Saddle River, New Jersey 07458

Computations for a Wilcoxin Rank-Sum Test for the Study of Books Read by Highly Sensitive Versus Not Highly Sensitive Children (Fictional Data)

Cutoff for significance: Maximum sum of ranks in the not highly sensitive group for significance at the .05 level, one-tailed (from a standard table) = 11.

Highly Sensitive

No			Yes	
X	Rank		X	Rank
0	1		17	4
3	2		36	6
10	3		45	7
22	5		75	8
Σ:	11			

Comparison to cutoff: Sum of ranks of group predicted to have lower scores, 11, equals but does not exceed cutoff for significance.

Conclusion: Reject the null hypothesis.

Aron/Aron
Statistics for the Social Sciences

Chapter 12
Making Sense of Advanced Statistical Procedures in Research Articles

Instructor's Summary of Chapter

This chapter introduces various widely-used advanced procedures in order to give the student an appreciation of the basic idea and issues sufficient to make sense of research articles employing these procedures.

Hierarchical multiple regression: Predictor variables are included in a prediction rule in a planned sequential fashion, permitting the researcher to determine the relative contribution of each successive variable over and above those already included.

Stepwise multiple regression: An exploratory procedure in which potential predictor variables are searched in order to find the best predictor, then the remaining variables are searched for the predictor, which in combination with the first produces the best prediction. This process continues until adding the last remaining variable does not provide a significant improvement.

Partial correlation: The degree of correlation between two variables while holding one or more other variables constant.

Reliability coefficients: Measures of the extent to which scores on a test are internally consistent (e.g., Cronbach's alpha) or consistent over time (test-retest reliability).

Factor analysis: Identifies groupings of variables that correlate maximally with each other and minimally with other variables.

Path analysis: Examines whether the correlations among a set of variables is consistent with a systematic model of the pattern of causal relationships among them. A diagram describes these relationships with arrows pointing from cause to effect, each with a path coefficient indicating the influence of the hypothesized causal variable on the hypothesized effect variable. Path coefficients are standardized regression coefficients from a multiple-regression prediction rule in which the variable at the end of the arrow is the dependent variable and the variable at the start of the arrow is the predictor, along with all other variables to that dependent variable.

Latent-variable modeling: A sophisticated version of path analysis that includes paths involving latent, unmeasured theoretical variables (each of which consists of the common elements of several measured variables.) It also permits a kind of significance test and provides measures of the overall fit of the data to the hypothesized causal pattern.

Analysis of covariance: An analysis of variance that controls for one or more variables.

Multivariate analysis of variance: An analysis of variance with more than one dependent variable; multivariate analysis of covariance is an analysis of covariance with more than one dependent variable.

How to read results involving unfamiliar statistical techniques. It is usually possible to extract the general meaning of an unfamiliar statistical technique by its context; in general a p is reported if it is a significance test, and most indicators of effect size fall on the scale of 0 to 1 of a correlation.

Box 12.1.The Golden Age of Statistics. Discusses the relations among Galton, Gossett, Pearson, and Fisher, and the circumstances that may have contributed to the rapid development of statistics.

Lecture 12.1: Advanced Procedures I

Materials

Lecture outline
Transparencies 12.1 through 12.7

Outline for Blackboard

I. Review of Multiple Regression/Correlation
II. Types of Advanced Statistical Techniques
III. Hierarchical Multiple Regression
IV. Stepwise Multiple Regression
V. Partial Correlation
VI. Reliability Coefficients
VII. Review this Class

Instructor's Lecture Outline

I. Review of Multiple Regression/Correlation
A. Show TRANSPARENCY 12.1 (multiple regression formula and worked-out example, from text).
B. The correlation between the set of independent variables and the dependent variable is called a multiple correlation (R).

II. Types of Advanced Statistical Techniques
A. Those that focus on associations among variables (these are variations and extensions of correlation and regression).
B. Those that focus on differences among groups (these are variations and extensions of analysis of variance).

III. Hierarchical Multiple Regression
A. Show TRANSPARENCY 12.2 (outline of procedure, and falling-in-love fictional example) and discuss.
B. Show TRANSPARENCY 12.3 (analysis of hypothesized predictors of tendency to avoid crowds) and discuss.

IV. Stepwise Multiple Regression
A. Purpose: Exploratory procedure to determine which predictor variables of many that have been measured usefully contribute to the prediction.
B. Show TRANSPARENCY 12.4 (outline of stepwise procedure) and discuss.
C. Show TRANSPARENCY 12.5 (predictors of job success at ABC Enterprises) and discuss.
D. Caution: The prediction formula that results is the optimal small set of variables for predicting the dependent variable, *as determined from the sample studied*--when tried with a new sample, somewhat different combinations often result.

V. Partial Correlation

A. The degree of association between two variables, over and above the influence of one or more other variables.

B. Variable(s) over and above which the partial correlation is computed are said to be *held constant*, *partialed out*, or *controlled for*. (These terms are interchangeable.)

C. You can think of a partial correlation as the average of the correlations between two variables, each correlation computed among just those subjects at each level of the variable being controlled for.

D. Partial correlation is often used to help sort out alternative explanations in a correlational study.

    1.   If correlation between two variables dramatically drops or is eliminated when a third variable is partialled out, it suggests that the third variable was behind the correlation.

    2.   If correlation between two variables is largely unaffected when a third variable is partialled out, it suggests that the third variable is not behind the correlation.

E. Show TRANSPARENCY 12.6 (associations among marital satisfaction, passionate love, and marriage length— fictional data based on pattern of results in Tucker & Aron, 1993) and discuss.

VI. Reliability Coefficients

A. Reliability, the accuracy and consistency of a measure, is the extent to which, if you were to give the same measure again to the same person under the same circumstances, you would obtain the same result.

B. Test-retest reliability:
    1. The correlation between the scores of the same people who take a measure twice.
    2. Often impractical or not appropriate, since having taken the test once would influence the second taking.
    3. Show TRANSPARENCY 12.7 (IOS Scale study example) and discuss.

C. Reliability as internal consistency.
    1. Split-half reliability is the correlation between two halves of the same test.
    2. Cronbach's alpha can be thought of as the average correlation for all possible divisions of a test into halves.

D. In general a test should have a reliability of at least .7, and preferably closer to .9, to be considered useful.

VII. Review this Class: Use blackboard outline.

Lecture 12.2: Advanced Procedures II

Materials

Lecture outline
Transparencies 12.8 through 12.13

Outline for Blackboard

    I.   **Review**
    II. **Factor Analysis**
    III. **Causal Modeling**
    IV. **ANCOVA**
    V. **MANOVA and MANCOVA**
    VI. **Review this Class**

Instructor's Lecture Outline

I.   Review

    A. Types of Advanced Statistical Techniques

        1. Those that focus on associations among variables (these are variations and extensions of correlation and regression):

           a. Hierarchical multiple regression
           b. Stepwise multiple regression
           c. Partial correlation
           d. Reliability coefficients
           e. Factor analysis (to be covered this class)
           f. Causal models (to be covered this class)

        2. Those that focus on differences among groups--variations and extensions of analysis of variance (to be covered this class).

II. Factor Analysis

    A. Widely used procedure applied when a researcher has measured people on a large number of variables.

    B. Identifies groupings of variables (called *factors*) such that those within each group correlate with each other and not with variables in other groupings.

    C. The correlation between a variable and a factor is called the variable's *factor loading* on that factor.

    D. Show TRANSPARENCY 12.8 (IOS Scale factor analysis example, from Aron et al., 1992) and discuss.

III. Causal Modeling

    A. Path analysis.

        1. Focuses on a diagram with arrows connecting the variables, indicating the hypothesized pattern of causal relations among them.

        2. Show TRANSPARENCY 12.9 (religious well-being, social desirability, and marital satisfaction, from Leong, 1989) and discuss.

B. Structural equation modeling.
1. Also widely known as *latent variable modeling* or as *LISREL*.
2. An extension of path analysis with several advantages:
   a. Produces an overall measure of how good the model fits the data.
   b. Includes a significance test--null hypothesis is that the model fits.
   c. Permits modeling of latent variables (as assessed by a set of measured variables).
3. Path diagram:
   a. Measured variables shown in squares.
   b. Latent variables shown in circles.
   c. The measurement model, the relation of the manifest to the latent variables they assess, usually involves arrows from each latent to its associated manifest variables.
   d. The path diagram usually involves arrows showing the relations among the latent variables.
4. Show TRANSPARENCY 12.10 (confirmatory factor analysis for measures of closeness in cross-validation sample, from Aron et al., 1992) and discuss.
5. A well-fitting model that is not a significantly bad fit is still only one of the possible models that could fit the data.

IV. Analysis of Covariance (ANCOVA)
A. Same as an ordinary ANOVA, except one or more variables are partialled out.
B. The variable partialled out is called a covariate.
C. The rest of the results are interpreted like any other analysis of variance.
D. Show TRANSPARENCY 12.11 (attractiveness of communicator on attitude change, posttest scores controlling for pretest) and discuss.

V. Multivariate Analysis of Variance (MANOVA) and Multivariate Analysis of Covariance (MANCOVA)
A. Multivariate statistical techniques involve more than one dependent variable. (Like ANOVA, etc. these can have one or more IVs.)
B. The most widely used multivariate techniques are MANOVA and MANCOVA.
C. MANOVA is simply an analysis of variance in which there is more than one dependent variable.
D. MANOVA tests each main and interaction effect of the independent variables on the combination of dependent variables.
E. Show TRANSPARENCY 12.12 (closest relationship, IV, and measures of closeness for other in that relationship, DVs; from Aron et al., 1992) and discuss.
F. MANCOVA is a MANOVA in which one or more variables are partialled out of the analysis.

VII. Review this Class: Use blackboard outline and show TRANSPARENCY 12.13 (table of methods, from text).

Multiple regression formula.

Predicted $Z_y = (\beta_1)(Z_{\underline{X}1}) + (\beta_2)(Z_{\underline{X}2}) + (\beta_3)(Z_{\underline{X}3})$

Example:

$$Z_{Stress} = \quad (.51)(Z_{NumberSupervised})$$
$$+ \quad (.11)(Z_{Noise})$$
$$+ \quad (.33)(Z_{Decisions/Month})$$

Aron/Aron
Statistics for the Social Sciences

© 1997 by Prentice-Hall, Inc.
Simon & Schuster/A Viacom Company
Upper Saddle River, New Jersey 07458

TRANSPARENCY 12.2

Hierarchical regression.

<u>Procedure</u> (based on hypothesized order of influence):

Step 1: R^2 for Y with X_1

Step 2: R^2 for Y with X_1 and X_2

    What is the improvement in prediction over X_1 alone?
    Is the improvement significant?

Step 3: R^2 for Y with X_1, X_2, and X_3

    What is the improvement in prediction over X_1 and X_2 alone?
    Is the improvement significant?
    Etc.

<u>Example</u>:

Study of influences on falling in love (fictional):

    Predicted order of influence:

        X_1 = Readiness to fall in love
        X_2 = Other having desirable characteristics
        X_3 = Perception that other likes self

Step 1: R^2 for Y with X_1 = .08 (p < .05)

Step 2: R^2 for Y with X_1 and X_2 = .17

    Increment = .09 (p < .01)

Step 3: R^2 for Y with X_1, X_2, and X_3 = .23

    Increment = .06 (p < .05)

Aron/Aron
Statistics for the Social Sciences

© 1997 by Prentice-Hall, Inc.
Simon & Schuster/A Viacom Company
Upper Saddle River, New Jersey 07458

Study of hypothesized predictors of tendency to avoid crowds.

Dependent Variable: $\underline{Y}$ = Tendency to avoid crowds

Predicted order of influence:

$\underline{X}_1$ = "Are you a tense or worried person by nature?"

$\underline{X}_2$ = "Do you make it a high priority to arrange your life to avoid upsetting or overwhelming situations?"

$\underline{X}_3$ = "Are you made uncomfortable by loud noise?"

Hierarchical Multiple Regression ($\underline{N}$ = 102)

Predictor Variables	Betas			Overall Model		Increment	
	β_1	β_2	β_3	$\underline{R}^2$	$\underline{F}$	$\underline{R}$	$\underline{F}$
$\underline{X}_1$	-.01			.002	.02	.002	.02
$\underline{X}_1$ and $\underline{X}_2$	-.04	.32		.999	5.50*	.097	10.96**
$\underline{X}_1$, $\underline{X}_2$, and $\underline{X}_3$	-.05	.19	.34	.201	8.26**	.102	3.96*

*$\underline{p}$ < .05; **$\underline{p}$ < .01

Aron/Aron
Statistics for the Social Sciences

© 1997 by Prentice-Hall, Inc.
Simon & Schuster/A Viacom Company
Upper Saddle River, New Jersey 07458

The Process of a Stepwise Multiple Regression

Step 1: Search all potential predictor variables and find the best in correlation with the dependent variable.

Step 2: Test significance.

If not significant, **STOP.**

If significant, include this variable in all further steps, and **CONTINUE.**

Step 3: Search all remaining potential predictor variables for the best single variable to combine with those already included for predicting the dependent variable.

If no addition is significant, **STOP.**

If an addition is significant, include this variable in all further steps, and **REPEAT STEP 3 TO SEARCH FOR THE NEXT BEST REMAINING PREDICTOR VARIABLE.**

Aron/Aron
Statistics for the Social Sciences

TRANSPARENCY 12.5

Predictors of job success at ABC Enterprises. (Fictional study.)

Dependent Variable: $\underline{Y}$ =   Rating of job success after 3 months of employment for clerical employees.

Potential predictors:

1. Typing test score
2. General clerical skills test score
3. Language test score
4. Psychological stability test score
5. Previous job history (rated by personnel officer)
6. Letters of recommendation (rated by personnel officer)
7. Social skills (rated by interviewer)
8. Personal integrity (rated by interviewer)
9. Efficiency/energy (rated by interviewer)

Stepwise Regression for Predicting Job Success

Step	Variable Added	Overall Model $\underline{R}^2$	$\underline{F}$	Increment $\underline{R}$	$\underline{F}$
1	Previous job history	.09	4.20**	.09	5.20**
2	Typing test score	.16	5.98**	.07	4.11**
3	Social skills	.24	6.21**	.05	3.88*
4	Language test score	.26	6.35**	.02	1.39

*$\underline{p}$ < .05; **$\underline{p}$ < .01

Aron/Aron
Statistics for the Social Sciences

© 1997 by Prentice-Hall, Inc.
Simon & Schuster/A Viacom Company
Upper Saddle River, New Jersey 07458

Marital satisfaction, passionate love, and length of marriage.
(Fictional data based on pattern of results in Tucker & Aron, 1993.)

Correlation:

Marital satisfaction and marriage length: $\underline{r}$ = -.31, $\underline{p}$ < .01.

Partial correlation:

Marital satisfaction and marriage
length controlling for passionate love: Partial $\underline{r}$ = -.03, $\underline{ns}$

Correlation:

Passionate love and marriage length: $\underline{r}$ = -.34, $\underline{p}$ < .01.

Partial correlation:

Passionate love and marriage length
controlling for marital satisfaction: Partial $\underline{r}$ = -.27, $\underline{p}$ < .01.

Implications:

1. The correlation between marital satisfaction and marriage length
is mainly accounted for by passionate love.

2. The correlation between passionate love and marriage length is not
mainly accounted for by marital satisfaction.

3. Therefore, passionate love is the primary variable associated with
length of marriage.

Aron/Aron
Statistics for the Social Sciences

Inclusion of Other in Self (IOS) Scale administered to undergradua students twice over a 2-week period, each time describing their relationship with the person with whom they have the closest, most intimate relationship. (From Aron, Smollan, & Aron, 1992.)

Please circle the picture below which best describes your relationship

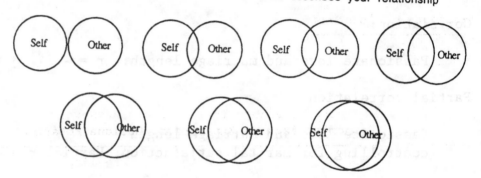

Correlation between two testings (test-retest reliability):

Those rating closeness to a family member (n = 13): r = .85.

Those rating closeness to a nonromantic friend: (n = 31): r = .86.

Those rating closeness to a romantic partner: (n = 48): r = .85.

Aron/Aron
Statistics for the Social Sciences

© 1997 by Prentice-Hall, Inc.
Simon & Schuster/A Viacom Company
Upper Saddle River, New Jersey 07458

Closeness measures administered to undergraduate students, describing their relationship with the person with whom they have the closest, most intimate relationship. (From Aron, Smollan, & Aron, 1992.)

Correlations Among Closeness Measures (N = 208)

	RCI			Subjective	Sternberg
	Frequency	Diversity	Strength	Closeness	Intimacy
IOS Scale	.09	.16*	.36**	.34**	.45**
RCI-Frequency		.71**	.18**	-.01	-.04
RCI-Diversity			.27**	.08	.05
RCI-Strength				.26**	.13
Subjective Closeness					.64**

*p < .05; **p <.01

Factor Loadings for Closeness Measures
(Principal Factors Extraction, Oblique Rotation)

	Feeling Close	Behaving Close
Sternberg Intimacy Scale	.78	-.09
Subjective Closeness Index	.77	.00
IOS Scale (sense of interconnectedness)	.72	.21
RCI-Strength (other's influence on me)	.55	.43
RCI-Frequency (Time spent together)	-.00	.89
RCI-Diversity (number of shared activities)	.13	.91

Aron/Aron
Statistics for the Social Sciences

© 1997 by Prentice-Hall, Inc.
Simon & Schuster/A Viacom Company
Upper Saddle River, New Jersey 07458

Path analysis for predicted pattern in which religious well-being is seen as a cause of marital satisfaction, and two correlated aspects of social desirability (measured by the Crowne-Marlowe and Edmonds tests) are seen as causes of both religious well-being and marital satisfaction. (From Leong, 1989.)

Correlations Among Measures (N = 56)

	Social Desirability		Religious	Marital
	Crowne-Marlowe	Edmonds	Well-Being	Satisfaction
Crowne-Marlowe (CM)				
Edmonds (E)	.10			
Religious Well-Being (RW)	.03	.16		
Marital Satisfaction (MS)	.14	.76**	.41**	

**p < .01

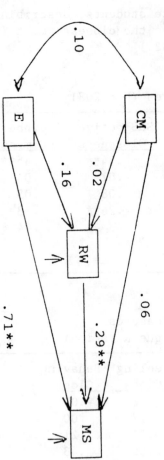

Aron/Aron
Statistics for the Social Sciences

© 1997 by Prentice-Hall, Inc.
Simon & Schuster/A Viacom Company
Upper Saddle River, New Jersey 07458

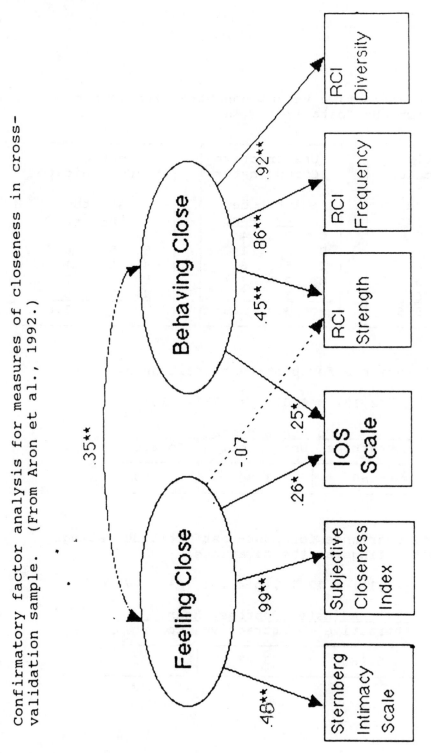

Confirmatory factor analysis for measures of closeness in cross-validation sample. (From Aron et al., 1992.)

Aron/Aron
Statistics for the Social Sciences

Influence of attractive versus nonattractive communicators on attitude change. (Fictional data.)

Attractive Communicator		
	Attitude	
S	Pre	Post
A	4	7
F	1	2
G	5	8
J	2	5
K	4	6
M	3.2	5.6

Unattractive Communicator		
	Attitude	
S	Pre	Post
C	3	4
D	2	1
I	5	6
M	2	2
O	5	6
M	3.4	3.8

Control (No Communicator)		
	Attitude	
S	Pre	Post
B	4	3
E	5	6
H	1	1
L	3	3
N	7	6
M	4.0	3.8

Analysis of variance for post-test attitude ratings:

$$F(2,12) = 1.07, \text{ ns}, R^2 = .15$$

Posttest Means		
Attractive	Unattractive	Control
5.60	3.80	3.80

Analysis of covariance for post-test attitude ratings, with pretest ratings as the covariate:

$$F(2,11) = 12.73, p < .01, R^2 = .70$$

Adjusted Posttest Means		
Attractive	Unattractive	Control
5.98	3.27	3.95

Aron/Aron
Statistics for the Social Sciences

© 1997 by Prentice-Hall, Inc.
*Simon & Schuster/A Viacom Company
Upper Saddle River, New Jersey 07458*

Relation of type of closest relationship (family, friend, romantic; independent variable) to the combination of three questionnaire measures of closeness about that relationship (intimacy, subjective closeness, and interconnectedness; the dependent variables). (From data collected in Aron et al., 1992.)

Univariate analysis of variance for Sternberg Intimacy Scale:

$F(2,194) = 1.20$, ns, $R^2 = .012$

Closest Relationship		
Family	Friend	Romantic
6.35	6.23	6.10

Univariate analysis of variance for Subjective Closeness Scale:

$F(2,194) = 0.02$, ns, $R^2 = .000$

Closest Relationship		
Family	Friend	Romantic
6.03	6.00	6.02

Univariate analysis of variance for interconnectedness (IOS Scale):

$F(2,194) = 2.41$, $p = .09$, $R^2 = .024$

Closest Relationship		
Family	Friend	Romantic
4.35	4.58	4.94

Multivariate analysis of variance for all three dependent variables taken together:

Wilks' $F(6,384) = 2.37$, $p < .05$, effect size (1-Lambda) = .070

Aron/Aron
Statistics for the Social Sciences

© 1997 by Prentice-Hall, Inc.
Simon & Schuster/A Viacom Company
Upper Saddle River, New Jersey 07458

TABLE 12–4
Major Statistical Techniques

Association or Difference	Number of Independent Variables	Number of Dependent Variables	Any Variables Controlled?	Name of Technique
Association	1	1	No	Bivariate correlation/regression
Association	Any number	1	No	Multiple regression (including hierarchical and stepwise regression)
Association	1	1	Yes	Partial correlation
Association	Many, not differentiated		No	Reliability coefficients Factor analysis
Association	Many, with specified causal patterns			Path analysis Structural equation modeling
Difference	1	1	No	One-way analysis of variance; t test
Difference	Any number	1	No	Analysis of variance
Difference	Any number	1	Yes	Analysis of covariance
Difference	Any number	Any number	No	Multivariate analysis of variance
Difference	Any number	Any number	Yes	Multivariate analysis of covariance

Multiple-Choice Questions

1.   Researchers use statistics to help them
 *   a. make sense of the numbers they collect.
      b. generate hypotheses.
      c. generate theories.
      d. design experiments.

2.   An education researcher collects data on how many students are on
     scholarship at different schools. The researcher then constructs a
     frequency table to summarize the data. The researcher is using
      a. a measure of central tendency.
 *   b. a descriptive statistical method.
      c. an intuitive statistical method.
      d. an inferential statistical method.

3.   A student theorizes that performance on statistics exams will be related
     to the number of hours spent studying statistics. Since this student
     has read the first chapter of your text book he or she knows that _____
     will be required to test the theory.
      a. common sense
      b. reasoning by analogy
 *   c. inferential statistics
      d. intuition

4.   The two branches of statistical methods are
      a. theoretical and inferential.
      b. intuitive and observational.
      c. descriptive and intuitive.
 *   d. descriptive and inferential.

5.   The value of putting numbers into a frequency table is that
 *   a. it makes the pattern of numbers clear at a glance.
      b. it is easier to draw inferences from tables.
      c. they are required by many journals.
      d. none of the above.

6.   A psychologist is interested in studying aggressive tendencies in
     people and develops a measure of this personality characteristic.
     The characteristic of aggression has become a(n) _____ in the
     psychologist's study.
      a. abstract concept
 *   b. variable
      c. descriptive statistic
      d. invariable construct

Test Bank

7.   Each of several employees are rated for their degree of job
     satisfaction. If a particular employee's job satisfaction is rated 8 on
     a 20-point scale, 8 represents that employee's
     a. frequency.
     b. variable.
*   c. score.
     d. mean.

8.   An intelligence test includes 12 items. Thus, a person could get
     any number correct between 0 and 12. Each of these numbers
     correct (0 to 12) that a person could possibly get is called a
*   a. value.
     b. variable.
     c. rating.
     d. mean.

9.   A researcher wishing to summarize data for a variable in a study
     creates a frequency table, but finds that there are so many values for
     the variable that the table is too cumbersome to be useful. The next
     step would be to make a
     a. histogram.
     b. frequency polygon.
*   c. grouped frequency table.
     d. bar chart.

10. A researcher measures 50 subjects' eye movements as they read
     ambiguous words embedded in sentences. Since subjects' eye
     movements are measured in milliseconds, and there are likely to
     be many different times measured, the researcher reasons that a
     _____ will best help make sense of the data.
     a. frequency polygon
     b. histogram
*   c. grouped frequency table
     d. bar chart

11. When making a frequency table, the list down the side should
*   a. include all possible values, starting from the highest and ending
        with the lowest.
     b. include all possible values, starting from the lowest and ending
        with the highest.
     c. begin with 0% at the top and go down to 100% at the bottom.
     d. begin with 100% at the top and go down to 0% at the bottom.

12. A frequency table lists
     a. the times per second that variations occur in various wave bands.
*   b. the number of scores at each value.
     c. the intensity of a variable over all the subjects studied.
     d. the average value of each variable.

13. When making a grouped frequency table, if possible each interval should
     be
     a. half the range.
*   b. 2, 3, 5, 10, or a multiple of these.
     c. half the size of the preceding interval.
     d. all of the above.

14. When making a grouped frequency table, there should be a total of about how many intervals?
   a. 1 to 3
   b. 2 to 10
 * c. 5 to 15
   d. 10 to 100

15. What is generally the smallest number of intervals you would want in a grouped frequency table?
   a. 1
   b. 2
   c. 3
 * d. 5

16. A histogram looks most like
 * a. a skyline of a city.
   b. a large wave.
   c. a silhouette of mountains.
   d. a pattern of iron filings.

17. A histogram is most closely related to which of the following kinds of graphs?
   a. Pie
   b. Line
   c. Tree
 * d. Bar

18. In a histogram, the vertical (up and down) dimension represents
   a. possible values the variable can take.
   b. intensity of the variable.
   c. mean score.
 * d. frequency.

19. In a histogram, the horizontal (across) dimension represents
 * a. possible values the variable can take.
   b. intensity of the variable.
   c. mean score.
   d. frequency.

20. When making a histogram, it is easiest if you begin with
   a. a list of all the scores in order.
 * b. a frequency table.
   c. a knowledge of the general shape of the distribution.
   d. a normal curve table.

21. A difference between a histogram and a frequency polygon is that the frequency polygon
   a. represents grouped values.
   b. represents individual values.
   c. covers the full range of values.
 * d. starts and ends with a frequency of zero.

Test Bank

22. A frequency polygon looks most like
    a. a skyline of a city.
    b. a large wave.
  * c. a silhouette of mountains.
    d. a pattern of iron filings.

23. A frequency polygon is most closely related to which of the
    following kinds of graphs?
    a. Pie
  * b. Line
    c. Tree
    d. Channel

24. Social scientists use frequency tables, histograms, or frequency
    polygons to demonstrate
    a. the conclusions they draw from the numbers they collect.
    b. the reasoning behind experiments.
    c. hypotheses.
  * d. how the numbers they collect are distributed.

25. The distributions of the data psychologists collect in their research
    are usually
  * a. unimodal.
    b. bimodal.
    c. multimodal.
    d. rectangular.

26. A researcher examining the empathy people feel for strangers asks
    judges to rate subjects' empathic responses to strangers' distress on a
    scale of 1 to 10. An examination of the distribution of scores reveals
    that judges rate most subjects at either 3 or 7. How would this
    distribution be described?
  * a. Bimodal
    b. Unimodal
    c. Rectangular
    d. Normal

27. A professor collects data on the exam scores of students in an
    introductory statistics class and discovers that most students did very
    well and only a few did poorly (including a few who did very poorly).
    How would the professor describe the distribution of test scores?
    a. Symmetrical
  * b. Negatively skewed
    c. Having a floor effect
    d. Positively skewed

28. A professor gives an exam in an introductory statistics class and after
    making a frequency distribution discovers that most students got a
    perfect score. This is an example of a
    a. symmetrical distribution.
    b. positively skewed distribution.
  * c. ceiling effect.
    d. both b and c.

29.   When a distribution is positively skewed, it means that
        a. there are more scores piled up at the high end of the range.
        b. the scores are evenly distributed.
*   c. there are more scores piled up at the low end of the range.
        d. there is a ceiling effect.

30.   When a distribution is negatively skewed, it is likely that
        a. there is a floor effect.
        b. there are more scores piled up at the low end of the range.
        c. the distribution is approximately normal.
*   d. there is a ceiling effect.

31.   When a distribution is heavy-tailed it means that
*   a. it is more flat or peaked than a normal curve.
        b. it is positively skewed.
        c. it is negatively skewed.
        d. b or c.

32.   A frequency table is most likely to be included in a research
        article when
*   a. nominal variables are involved.
        b. there are a very small number of scores.
        c. a correlation is being reported.
        d. there are only two values for the variable.

33.   If you suffer from test anxiety, some useful advice is to
*   a. overprepare for tests (at least at first).
        b. do everything you can to increase your motivation to do well.
        c. use stimulants (such as coffee) just before the exam.
        d. all of the above.

34.   Which of the following is supported by research cited in your text?
        a. Women generally do worse in statistics classes because they have
           lower expectations for themselves.
        b. Women generally do worse in statistics classes because others have
           lower expectations of them.
        c. Women generally do worse in statistics classes because instructors
           tend to call on them less often.
*   d. Women generally do as well as men in statistics classes.

Fill-In Questions

35.   Social scientists use _____ to summarize and make
        understandable a group of numbers collected in a research study.

        Answer: descriptive statistics

36.   _____ are used to draw statistical conclusions that go beyond the
        numbers actually collected in the research.

        Answer: Inferential statistics

Test Bank   225

37. A listing that shows how many times each value of a variable occurs among a particular group of scores is called a(n) _____.

Answer: frequency table

38. A test of social skills is administered to all the professors at a particular college. The _____ of a particular professor is 81.

Answer: score

39. In a study of hospitalized psychotic patients, the _____ of interest (which is a rating that can take values from 0 to 7) is the extent to which the patients can take care of their rooms, as rated by the nurses.

Answer: variable

40. When making a frequency table, the values are listed in the first column and the _____ corresponding to each value in the second column.

Answer: frequency

41. A business researcher set up a(n) _____ that lists the number of employees for each level of earnings, from the level of $80,000 to $99,999, going down to the level of $20,000 to $29,999.

Answer: grouped frequency table

42. Suppose the scores for a particular group ranged from 2 to 11. The researcher set up a grouped frequency table (properly) in which the lowest interval was 2 to 3.99 and the highest interval was _____.

Answer: 10 to 11.99

43. A way to simplify a frequency table when there are a large number of possible values is to group the scores into 5 to 15 _____.

Answer: intervals

44. A(n) _____ is like a bar graph of frequencies in which the bars are put right next to each other.

Answer: histogram

45. A frequency table, histogram, or frequency polygon describes a _____.

Answer: frequency distribution, distribution of scores

Test Bank

46.   The histogram of a(n) _____ distribution has one of the bars
        higher than all the others.

        Answer: unimodal

47.   In a study of exercise behavior, a researcher found that the shape of
        the distribution of the number of hours exercised was _____ because
        one large group of people did not exercise at all while another large
        group all exercised approximately three hours per week.

        Answer: bimodal, multimodal

48.   Researchers have found that distributions of certain tests are
        _____, such that when you make a histogram of them they have
        several clear peaks.

        Answer: multimodal, lumpy

49.   The number of times the various numbers on a roulette wheel come up, in
        the long run, form a(n) _____ frequency distribution.

        Answer: rectangular, symmetrical

50.   A distribution is called _____ when the shape of the distribution
        on the two sides of the middle are mirror images of each other.

        Answer: symmetrical

51.   A distribution that is lopsided is said to be _____.

        Answer: skewed

52.   On a particular test of reading ability (in which high scores mean high
        reading ability), the distribution of adults is _____ skewed
        because most adults have fairly good reading ability, but a small number
        of people are nearly illiterate.

        Answer: negatively

53.   A survey of the noise in various studying environments of students
        yielded a distribution in which, due to a(n) _____, the scores
        tended to pile up at the low end because no environment could be more
        quiet than no noise at all.

        Answer: floor effect

54.   The distributions of data collected in psychology research studies often
        approximate a(n) _____.

        Answer: normal curve

Test Bank

55. A rectangular distribution, in addition to being symmetrical, would be an example of a _____.

Answer: heavy-tailed distribution

Problems and Essays

56. Explain the difference between descriptive statistics and inferential statistics.

57. Explain why a grouped frequency table can sometimes be more useful than an ordinary frequency table in describing a group of numbers.

58. Explain what it means to have a ceiling effect in a distribution of scores. Give an example.

59. Draw a normal distribution. A bimodal distribution. A positively skewed distribution. A heavy-tailed distribution.

60. Make up an example of a distribution that would be much more peaked than usual.

61. Make up a study that would produce a distribution that was bimodal.

62. A sociologist interested in the social behavior of older people surveyed sixteen single senior citizens living in private apartments. Each subject completed a questionnaire on the number of people with whom he or she had had conversations in the last day. Their answers were as follows: 5,0,2,1,1,9,0,1,0,3,1,1,4,3,4,7.
    a. Make a frequency table.
    b. Make a histogram based on the frequency table.
    c. Describe in words the shape of the histogram.

Answer:

X	f	%
9	1	6.3
8	0	0.0
7	1	6.3
6	0	0.0
5	1	6.3
4	2	12.5
3	2	12.5
2	1	6.3
1	5	31.3
0	3	18.8

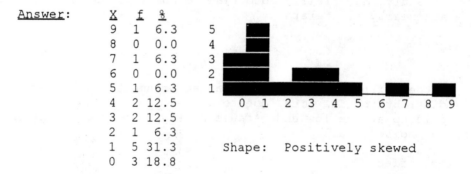

Shape: Positively skewed

Test Bank

63. A prison researcher recorded the numbers of rule infractions for 12 prison inmates over a 6-month period and found them to be 1,3,0,1,0,6,8,2,0,1,0,2.
   a. Make a frequency table.
   b. Make a histogram based on the frequency table.
   c. Describe in words the shape of the histogram.

Answer:

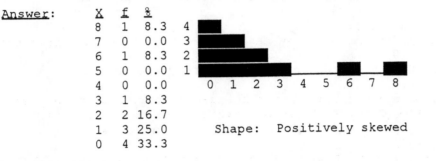

X	f	%
8	1	8.3
7	0	0.0
6	1	8.3
5	0	0.0
4	0	0.0
3	1	8.3
2	2	16.7
1	3	25.0
0	4	33.3

Shape: Positively skewed

64. A study recorded the number of units produced per hour by 15 factory workers. The results were as follows: 8,10,4,9,9,10,1,9,8,5,9,9,8,7,8.
   a. Make a frequency table.
   b. Make a frequency polygon based on the frequency table.
   c. Describe in words the shape of the frequency polygon.

Answer:

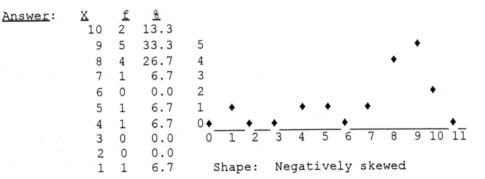

X	f	%
10	2	13.3
9	5	33.3
8	4	26.7
7	1	6.7
6	0	0.0
5	1	6.7
4	1	6.7
3	0	0.0
2	0	0.0
1	1	6.7

Shape: Negatively skewed

65. A survey was administered to 20 active members of a small political action group about how many hours they put into the group's activities each week. The results were as follows: 24,41,1,41,14,2,40,58,2,1,41,2,41,30,0,41,3,3,41,49.
   a. Make a grouped frequency table.
   b. Make a histogram based on the grouped frequency table.
   c. Describe in words the shape of the histogram.

Answer (example):

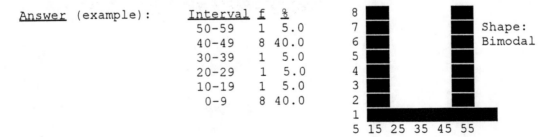

Interval	f	%
50-59	1	5.0
40-49	8	40.0
30-39	1	5.0
20-29	1	5.0
10-19	1	5.0
0-9	8	40.0

Shape: Bimodal

66. A psychologist studied the time it took infants of a particular age to pick up a particular attractive new toy that was placed in the playpen. The minutes for 20 infants are as follows:
19,8,13,12,15,4,19,14,16,3,2,7,11,17,4,6,10,12,8,9.
a. Make a grouped frequency table.
b. Make a frequency polygon based on the grouped frequency table.
c. Describe in words the shape of the frequency polygon.

Answer (one example):

Interval	f	%
18-19.9	2	10.0
16-17.9	2	10.0
14-15.9	2	10.0
12-13.9	3	15.0
10-11.9	2	10.0
8-9.9	3	15.0
6-7.9	2	10.0
4-5.9	2	10.0
2-3.9	2	10.0

Shape: Approximately rectangular

```
3                  ♦      ♦
2      ♦   ♦   ♦      ♦      ♦   ♦   ♦
1
0 ♦                              ♦
   1  3  5  7  9 11 13 15 17 19 21
```

Multiple-Choice Questions

1. A researcher collects the following data on the number of times four 5-year-old boys exhibit aggression during a 6-hour long school day: 2,4,6,12. What is the mean number of aggressive acts for this group of four children?
    a. 4
    b. 5
*   c. 6
    d. 9

2. Five people completed a test of product recognition. Their scores were 0, 1, 2, 4, and 8. What is their mean score on this test?
    a. 2
*   b. 3
    c. 4
    d. 5

3. What is the mean of the following four scores? 1,1,1,5
    a. 1
    b. 1.5
*   c. 2
    d. 3

4. What is the measure of central tendency obtained by computing the average of a group of numbers?
    a. Median
*   b. Mean
    c. Standard deviation
    d. Mode

5. Based on the scores 1, 9, 3, 6, 2, 2, 6, 1, 2, and 6, a score of 4 is the
    a. mode.
    b. median.
*   c. mean.
    d. standard deviation.

6. Which of the following is the correct formula for the mean?
*   a. $\underline{M} = \Sigma\underline{X}/\underline{N}$.
    b. $\underline{M} = \Sigma\underline{X}^2/\underline{N}$.
    c. $\underline{M} = (\Sigma\underline{X})^2/\underline{N}$.
    d. $\underline{M} = \Sigma(\underline{X}-\underline{M})^2/\underline{N}$.

7. In statistical formulas, what does $\underline{N}$ stand for?
    a. The number of different values possible on the variable
*   b. The number of cases
    c. The normal curve
    d. The normalized $\underline{Z}$ score

Test Bank

8. If you were to compute the mean of the scores 1, 1, 8, and 10, what would ΣX equal?
   a. 4
   b. 4.5
   c. 5
 * d. 20

9. A group of researchers examined maternal responsiveness to infants in the United States, France, and Japan. As a part of their study, these researchers collected data on the rate at which infants in the three societies vocalized distress. Below are three sets of scores that approximate the data collected. Which group of infants exhibited the highest mean rate of distress vocalization over the 45-minute observation period?
   US 9,9,10,13,8,8,11,11,10,7,13,6,18,9,9,12,13,10,5,14
   Fr 15,15,16,19,14,14,17,17,16,13,19,12,18,10,10,15,15,2,2,5
   Ja 4,6,20,17,15,30,18,18,25,2,29,17,16,35,19,1,30,25,16,15
   a. French infants
   b. U.S. infants
   c. French and Japanese infants vocalized distress equally.
 * d. Japanese infants

10. The most common single number in a distribution of scores is the
 * a. mode.
   b. mean.
   c. median
   d. average.

11. What is the mode of the following scores?   3,4,6,7,10,10,30
   a. 3
   b. 7
   c. 8.5
 * d. 10

12. Based on the scores 1,2,3,4,5,6,8,8,8,9,10, a score of 8 is the
   a. mean.
   b. median.
 * c. mode.
   d. standard deviation.

13. A statistics professor discovers that the mean score and the mode score for the latest class exam are the same. This would be possible for which of the following distribution shapes?
   a. Skewed
 * b. Normal
   c. Bimodal
   d. Both a and c

14. The middle value in a set of scores lined up from lowest to highest is the
   a. mean.
   b. mode.
   c. average.
 * d. median.

15. What is the median of the scores 1,2,4,4,4,6,7,8,8,9,10?
    a. 4
    b. 5.7
 * c. 6
    d. 8

16. What is the median of the scores 0,0,0,2,5,6,8?
    a. 0
 * b. 2
    c. 2.5
    d. 3

17. A researcher finds that the number of state representatives a group of
    voters can name are 3,3,3,4,4,5,6,7,8,9,10,35. Upon examination of these
    data, the researcher would probably decide that the most useful measure of
    central tendency would be
    a. the mean.
 * b. the median.
    c. the mode.
    d. none of the above.

18. Which statement is true for the scores 1,2,3,4,5,5,7,8,9,10?
    a. The mode is greater than the median.
    b. The median is greater than the mean.
 * c. The mean is greater than the median.
    d. The mean is less than the mode.

19. When a distribution is positively skewed,
    a. the median is greater than the mean.
    b. the mean and the median are the same.
 * c. the mean is greater than the median.
    d. the mean and the median are equal.

20. The median is greater than the mean in a distribution that is
    a. symmetrical.
    b. positively skewed.
    c. normal.
 * d. negatively skewed.

21. The variance of a set of scores is the same as the
 * a. average of the squared deviations.
    b. sum of the squared deviations.
    c. average of the absolute deviations.
    d. sum of the absolute deviations.

22. If the variance of a set of scores is 9, what is the standard deviation of
    that set of scores?
    a. 18
    b. 81
 * c. 3
    d. 4.5

Test Bank

23. If the standard deviation of a set of scores is 4, what is the variance?
     a. 2
     b. 4
     c. 8
   * d. 16

24. A researcher conducts a survey of job satisfaction among laborers and
    white-collar workers. (Job satisfaction is rated on a scale from 1, low
    satisfaction, to 10, high satisfaction.) The findings are that laborers
    have a mean job satisfaction score of 4 and a variance of 1; white-collar
    workers have a mean job-satisfaction rating of 7 and a variance of 10.
    Which statement best describes what these numbers mean?
     a. White-collar workers are more satisfied than laborers.
     b. White-collar workers and laborers are about equally
        satisfied.
     c. Laborers generally are less satisfied than white-collar
        workers, but laborers are just as likely to be highly
        satisfied as white-collar workers are to be highly
        dissatisfied.
   * d. Laborers are less satisfied than white-collar workers
        and most laborers are about equally dissatisfied while
        there is more variation in the satisfaction of white-
        collar workers.

25. In order to compute the variance of a set of scores, the sum of squared
    deviations is divided by
   * a. N.
     b. the mean.
     c. the standard deviation.
     d. the average Z score.

26. What is the variance of the three scores, 1, 4, and 7?
     a. 3
     b. 4
   * c. 6
     d. 9 .

27.What is the variance of the four scores, 0, 1, 1, and 2?
     a. .25
   * b. .5
     c. $\sqrt{.5}$
     d. 1

28. In a distribution of Z scores, the mean is always
     a. 10
     b. 1.
   * c. 0.
     d. 50.

29. Which of the following is NOT an advantage of Z scores?
     a. You can compare scores from scales with different ranges.
     b. You can easily tell if a score is above or below the mean.
     c. You can easily tell how far above or below the mean a score is.
   * d. You can easily tell the shape of the scores' distribution.

30. A positive $\underline{Z}$ score means its raw score was greater than the mean of the raw scores
   a. when the distribution is normal.
   b. when the distribution is positively skewed.
   c. when the distribution is negatively skewed.
* d. in all cases.

31-32 A statistics student wants to compare his final exam score to his friend's final exam score from last year. However, the two exams were scored on different scales. Suddenly, he remembers what he learned about the advantages of $\underline{Z}$ scores! He asks his friend for the mean and standard deviation of her class on the exam as well as her final exam score. He has the same information about his own exam. But he has lost his book and cannot remember the $\underline{Z}$ score formula. Can you help him out? Here is the information:

   Our student: Final exam score = 85;
                 Class--$\underline{M}$ = 70; $\underline{SD}$ = 10.
   His friend: Final exam score = 45;
               Class--$\underline{M}$ = 35; $\underline{SD}$ = 5.

   31.   Compute the $\underline{Z}$ score for our statistics student and his friend.
   *   a. Our student, $\underline{Z}$ = 1.50; his friend, $\underline{Z}$ = 2.00.
         b. Our student, $\underline{Z}$ = -1.07; his friend, $\underline{Z}$ = -1.14.
         c. Our student, $\underline{Z}$ = 1.07; his friend, $\underline{Z}$ = -1.14.
         d. Our student, $\underline{Z}$ = 1.07; his friend, $\underline{Z}$ = 1.50.

   32.   In relation to the other people in their classes, who had the better exam score?
         a. Our statistics student
   *   b. His friend
         c. They were equal
         d. It is not possible to say without more information

33. A $\underline{Z}$ score of 2.0 came from a distribution which had a mean of 80 and a standard deviation of 10. What is the corresponding raw score?
   a. 82
   b. 90
* c. 100
   d. 170

34. A person's raw score is 7, the mean is 13, and the standard deviation is 3. What is the person's $\underline{Z}$ score?
* a. -2
   b. -1
   c. 1
   d. 2

35. A researcher wishing to study the sociological implications of cultural diversity within a society decides to conduct a few lengthy interviews with members of various cultural communities. What kind of method is this sociologist using?
   a. Behavioral techniques
   b. Quantitative techniques
* c. Qualitative techniques
   d. Positivistic

Test Bank

36. Which of the following was a behavioral psychologist who was opposed to the use of statistics in psychology?
    a. Cohen
    b. McCracken
    c. Cronbach
  * d. Skinner

37. Which statistic is least likely to be reported in journal articles?
  * a. A $\underline{Z}$ score.
    b. A mean.
    c. A standard deviation.
    d. The number of cases studied.

Fill-In Questions

38. $\Sigma\underline{X}/\underline{N}$ is the formula for the _____.

    Answer: mean

39. The ordinary arithmetic average is called the _____.

    Answer: mean

40. The mean of 2, 2, 2, and 6 is _____.

    Answer: 3

41. _____ is a Greek letter that means "add up all the scores that follow."

    Answer: Σ

42. If a group of scores is 6, 7, 7, and 8, what is $\underline{N}$? _____

    Answer: 4

43. The _____ is the value with the most scores.

    Answer: mode

44. If a group of scores is 2, 2, 4, 8, and 9, what is the mode? _____

    Answer: 2

45. If a group of scores is 2, 2, 4, 8, and 9, what is the median? _____

    Answer: 4

46. If you line up all the scores from highest to lowest, _____ is the median.

Answer: the middle score

47. If a group of scores is 2, 81, 82, 82, and 84, _____ is an outlier.

Answer: 2

48. A measure of central tendency that is not much affected by outliers is the _____.

Answer: mode, median

49. The variance of a group of scores is the average of the _____.

Answer: squared deviations from the mean, squared deviations

50. The average of the squared deviations from the mean is called the _____.

Answer: variance

51. If a group of scores is 1, 7, and 13, the variance is _____.

Answer: 24

52. The first step in copmputing the variance involves finding each_____ (the difference between the score and the mean).

Answer: deviation score, deviation

53. In symbols, a deviation score is _____.

Answer: $\underline{X-M}$

54. The _____ is approximately the average that a score differs from the mean.

Answer: standard deviation

55. The standard deviation is _____ the variance.

Answer: the square root of, the positive square root of

56. A _____ is the number of standard deviations a score is above or below the mean.

Answer: $\underline{Z}$ score

57. If a raw score is 28 and $M = 20$, $SD = 2$, then the Z score is _____.

Answer: 4

58. The formula for converting a Z score to a raw score is _____.

Answer: $X = (Z)(SD) + M$

59. Behaviorists such as B. F. Skinner sometimes object to the use of statistics in psychology research because averages can distort the pattern of information revealed from observing the behavior of _____.

Answer: each individual case

Problems and Essays

60. List the three most widely used ways to describe a typical or representative value and explain what each tells a researcher.

61. It is historically interesting that the original formula for figuring IQ scores had a serious flaw: although scores for any one age group would always form a normal curve, the variance would be different depending on the age group. Explain why this would be a problem. (By the way, the formula was changed so that the standard deviation is always 15 or 16 on modern versions of the test.)

62. Researchers interested in the relation between maternal power-assertive parenting and daughters' rough play report that the average number of times girls engage in rough play (as observed in 25-minute play periods over 4 weeks) is 4 ($SD = 3$). They further report that daughters of power-assertive mothers engage in an average of 6 rough plays over that time period, while daughters of non-power-assertive mothers engage in an average of 4 rough plays over the same time period. In order for these scores to make sense, what must be true about the variances for the two groups of daughters?

63. How might researchers combine quantitative and qualitative methodologies to improve psychological research?

64. Five high-school English teachers were given a grammar test. Their scores were 17, 19, 14, 20, and 20.
   a.   Compute the mean, variance, and standard deviation.
   b.   Explain what you have done and what the results mean to a person who has never had a course in statistics.

Computation answers: $M = 90/5 = 18$;
                       $\Sigma(X-M)2 = 1+1+16+4+4 = 26$;
                       $SD2 = 5.2$; $SD = \sqrt{SD2} = 2.28$.

65. An education researcher had a teacher rate the grade level in reading ability of six fourth-grade children participating in a special math program. The grade-level ratings were as follows: 3, 3, 2, 8, 4, and 4.

    a.   Compute the mean, variance and standard deviation.
    b.   Explain what you have done and what the results mean to a person who has never had a course in statistics.

Computation answers: $M = 24/6 = 4$;
                               $\Sigma(X-M)2 = 1+1+4+16+0+0 = 22$;
                               $SD2 = 3.67$; $SD = 1.92$.

66. A curator interested in people's responses to art had eight people indicate their liking for a particular piece of Egyptian sculpture. Their ratings were 2, 4, 4, 5, 6, 7, and 7.
    a.   Compute the mean, variance, and standard deviation.
    b.   Explain what you have done and what the results mean to a person who has never had a course in statistics.

Computation answers: $M = 35/7 = 5$;
                                 $\Sigma(X-M)2 = 9+1+1+0+1+4+4 = 20$;
                               $SD2 = 2.86$; $SD = 1.69$.

67. After attending an anxiety-reduction therapy session, a wife's anxiety score is 75, while her husband's is 80. Overall, a woman's average anxiety score after the sessions is 70 ($SD = 10$) and a man's average anxiety score after the sessions is 85 ($SD = 5$).
    a.   Relative to others of their own gender, who has the lower anxiety score after the session?
    b.   Explain your answer to someone who has never had a course in statistics.

Computation answers: Wife's $Z = .5$; Husband's $Z = -1$. Thus,
                                     wife is more anxious relative to her gender.

68. A business researcher has to decide which of three employees to put into a particular job that requires a high level of perceptual-motor coordination. All three employees have taken tests of perceptual-motor coordination, but each took a different test. Employee A scored 15 on a test with a mean of 10 and a standard deviation of 2; Employee B scored 350 on a test with a mean of 300 and a standard deviation of 40; and Employee C scored 108 on a test with a mean of 100 and a standard deviation of 16. (On all three tests, higher scores mean greater coordination.)
    a.   Which employee has the best perceptual-motor coordination?
    b.   Explain your answer to someone who has never had a course in statistics.

Computation answers: Employee A's $Z = 2.5$;
                                   Employee B's $Z = 1.25$;
                                   Employee C's $Z = .5$.
                                   Thus, Employee A has the best
                                   perceptual-motor coordination.

69. A clinical psychologist administered a standard test that assesses symptoms of three different behavioral disorders to a new patient at a particular mental health clinic. On the scale that measures Disorder F (in the general public, $M = 60$, $SD = 8$), the person's score is 62. On the scale that measures Disorder H (in the general public, $M = 32$, $SD = .5$), the person's score is 34. And on the scale that measures Disorder K (in the general public, $M = 83$, $SD = 12$), the person's score is 89.
    a.   For the symptoms of which disorder or disorders does this person score substantially higher than the general public?
    b.   Explain your answer to someone who has never had a course in statistics.

Computation answers: Disorder F, $Z = .25$; Disorder H, $Z = 4$; Disorder K, $Z = .5$. Thus, only on Disorder H are the person's symptoms substantially higher than the general public.

70. Based on an analysis of personnel records, an organizational specialist reports that for her company, "during the last year, the mean number of sick days taken by shop employees was 7.3 with a standard deviation of 6.1." Explain what this result means to a person who has never had a course in statistics.

71. A survey is conducted at a particular college, during the winter, of the number of hours spent outside on weekends. The survey reports that for students from cold-weather climates, $M = 8$, $SD = 1.5$. For students from warm-weather climates, $M = 5$, $SD = 4.2$. Explain what these numbers mean, and the conclusions one should draw from this study, to a person who has never had a course in statistics.

Multiple-Choice Questions

1. A variable that is considered to be a cause is called a(n)
    a. dependent variable.
    b. positive variable.
    * c. independent variable.
    d. criterion variable.

2. An independent variable can also be called a
    a. dependent variable.
    b. criterion variable.
    c. positive variable.
    * d. predictor variable.

3. Suppose that you want to conduct a study to see if the number of friends a person has is associated with how self-confident the person is. The research is based on a theory that having friends is a cause of self-confidence. In this case, self-confidence would be considered the
    * a. dependent variable.
    b. predictor variable.
    c. independent variable.
    d. causal variable.

4. A graph that permits you to see, at a glance, the degree and pattern of the relation of two variables is a
    a. histogram.
    * b. scatter diagram.
    c. frequency polygon.
    d. box plot.

5. Which of these statements is true when drawing a scatter diagram?
    a. The highest number should start where the axes meet.
    b. The predictor variable goes on the vertical axis.
    * c. The predictor variable goes on the horizontal axis.
    d. The dependent variable goes on the horizontal axis.

6. What is the difference between a positive correlation and a negative correlation?
    a. In a negative correlation high scores go with high scores and low with low; in a positive correlation high scores go with low scores and low with high.
    b. Negative correlations are curvilinear, whereas positive correlations are straight lines.
    c. Negative correlations represent a weak relationship, whereas positive correlations represent a strong relationship.
    * d. In a negative correlation high scores go with low scores and low with high; in a positive correlation high scores go with high scores and low with low.

Test Bank   241

7. When the dots on a scatter diagram seem to form a straight line that goes upward to the right, this is called
*   a. a positive linear correlation.
        b. a negative linear correlation.
        c. a curvilinear correlation.
        d. no correlation.

8. Suppose that in general it turned out that if people eat a certain fruit before a test, the more fruit eaten, the better people will do on the test; but beyond a certain point, the more fruit eaten, the worse people do on the test. The relation between amount of fruit eaten and how well people do on the test is an example of
        a. a positive linear correlation.
*   b. a curvilinear correlation.
        c. a negative linear correlation.
        d. no correlation.

9. Which of the alternatives below best describes the data on this scatter diagram?

        a. No correlation
        b. Curvilinear correlation
*   c. Positive linear correlation
        d. Negative linear correlation

10. Which of the alternatives below best describes the data on this scatter diagram?

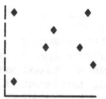

*   a. No correlation
        b. Curvilinear correlation
        c. Positive linear correlation
        d. Negative linear correlation

11. All of the following are reasons why Z scores are used to help determine the degree of linear correlation EXCEPT
        a. Z scores give a standard indication of just how high or low each score is.
        b. the sum of the cross-products of Z scores gives you a large positive number if there is a positive correlation and a large negative number if there is a negative correlation.
*   c. because of the nature of Z scores, the cross-product will be positive in all cases.
        d. using Z scores allows you to compare scores on different measures.

12.   When you compute the average of the cross-products of Z scores, it turns
       out that it is
*   a. never more than +1.0 or less than -1.0.
       b. never more than +10.0 or less than -10.0.
       c. never more than +1.0 or less than 0.
       d. never more than +10.0 or less than 0.

13.   When is the correlation coefficient zero?
       a. It is never zero.
*   b. When there is no linear correlation.
       c. When there is a perfect positive linear correlation.
       d. When there is a perfect negative linear correlation.

14.   Suppose that you are interested in the relation between the number of
       years working for a particular company and loneliness at work. You
       survey 40 workers at this company and compute a correlation between
       these two variables of -.90. This is considered a
       a. weak positive linear correlation.
       b. weak negative linear correlation.
       c. strong positive linear correlation.
*   d. strong negative linear correlation.

15.   Suppose you conduct a study in which you measure two personality traits
       and find a correlation of +.07. This is considered a
*   a. weak positive linear correlation.
       b. weak negative linear correlation.
       c. strong positive linear correlation.
       d. strong negative linear correlation.

16.   When there is no linear correlation, the correlation coefficient equals
       a. +1.0.
       b. -1.0.
*   c. zero.
       d. it depends on the scale of measurement.

17.   The Pearson correlation coefficient is calculated by dividing the sum of
       the cross-products of Z scores by
       a. the number of cases minus one.
       b. the number of Z scores.
       c. the number of Z scores minus one.
*   d. the number of cases.

18.   When you take the sum of the cross-products of Z scores and divide it by
       the number of cases, you are computing
*   a. the Pearson correlation coefficient.
       b. the proportionate reduction in error.
       c. Kendall's tau coefficient.
       d. the raw scores.

19. It is a good idea to construct a scatter diagram before computing the correlation coefficient because
   a. there is no point in computing the correlation if you can see a clear line formed on the graph.
   b. there are different procedures depending on whether there appears to be a positive or a negative correlation.
 * c. it permits you to estimate the degree and direction of correlation to provide a check on your eventual computations.
   d. you should only compute a correlation coefficient if you see a clear curvilinear correlation.

20. We say that a correlation is significant if
   a. the dots appear to form a straight line on the scatter diagram.
 * b. there is a small probability, such as 5% or 1%, that we could have obtained a correlation this big if in fact there had been no correlation in the population at large.
   c. the correlation is .05 or greater (or below -.05 if negative).
   d. there is a large probability (.95 or larger) that this correlation is greater than that computed in standard tables of what is called the $\underline{t}$ distribution.

21. If two variables, $\underline{X}$ and $\underline{Y}$, have a significant linear correlation, under what conditions can the direction of causality be determined just from knowing the correlation coefficient?
   a. When the correlation is negative.
   b. When the correlation is positive.
   c. When there is high power.
 * d. None of the above.

22. Which of the following is the most likely way for the correlation coefficient to be presented in a research article?
   a. $\underline{p}$ = .05, $\underline{r}$ < .52
   b. $\underline{p}$ > .05, $\underline{r}$(.52)
   c. $\underline{r}$(.52), $\underline{p}$ < .05
 * d. $\underline{r}$ = .52, p < .05

23. If a research article reports that a study examining weight and eating habits found a significant correlation using the .01 significance level, how would this be presented in the article if the correlation coefficient was .43?
 * a. r = .43, p < .01
   b. r = .43, significant
   c. r(.43) = significant
   d. p = .01, r = .43

24. Which of the following is NOT usually included in a results section for correlation?
   a. The value of r
   b. The significance level
 * c. The $\underline{Z}$ scores
   d. A correlation matrix

25. Who is given credit for inventing the statistic called correlation?
    a. Ronald Fisher
 * b. Francis Galton
    c. William Gossett
    d. Ralph Rosnow

26. The invention of the correlation coefficient occurred as part of research being conducted for which ultimate purpose?
    a. Military strategy decisions
    b. Environmental influences (such as types and quantities of manure) on crop growth
    c. Determining insurance fire insurance rates
 * d. Selective breeding of human beings

27. Suppose that you want to be able to predict college grades from information about high school grades. In this case, the college grades would be called the
    a. predictor variable.
 * b. dependent variable.
    c. independent variable.
    d. causal variable.

28. Suppose that you would like to predict a person's college GPA from the person's SAT score. In this situation, the SAT score is called the
 * a. predictor variable.
    b. dependent variable.
    c. criterion variable.
    d. positive variable.

29. A person's predicted Z score on the dependent variable is found by multiplying that person's Z score on the predictor variable by a particular number called a
    a. coefficient of redundancy.
    b. regression constant.
    c. proportionate reduction in error.
 * d. standardized regression coefficient.

30. In the equation predicted Z_Y = (ß)(Z_X), ß is the symbol for the
    a. correlation coefficient.
 * b. standardized regression coefficient.
    c. proportionate reduction in error.
    d. regression constant.

31. Suppose that the beta in a particular situation for predicting college grades from high school grades is .4 and that a person had a GPA that was 1 standard deviation above the mean (Z score = +1) in high school. What would the predicted Z score for that person's GPA in college be?
 * a. Predicted Z_Y = (.4)(1) = .4.
    b. Predicted Z_Y = .4/(1+.4) = 1/1.4 = .71.
    c. Predicted Z_Y = .4 + 1 = 1.4.
    d. Predicted Z_Y = 1/.4 = 2.5.

Test Bank   245

32. In prediction with one predictor variable, the optimal number to use for beta (the standardized regression coefficient) is the
   a. proportionate reduction in error.
   * b. correlation coefficient.
   c. sum of squared errors.
   d. regression constant.

33. Suppose you are in a situation where you are making predictions about people's poetry ability based on scores on a general writing-ability test. However, you also happen to have information about their creativity based on a creativity test and you would like to include the creativity information when making your predictions. What is it called when you make a prediction using both pieces of information?
   a. ridge regression
   * b. multiple regression
   c. bivariate regression
   d. proportion of variance accounted for

34. Which of the following is the Z-score multiple-regression formula with two predictor variables?
   a. Predicted $\underline{Z}_Y = (\text{ß}_1 / \underline{Z}_x 1) + (\text{ß}_2 / \underline{Z}_x 2)$
   b. Predicted $\underline{Z}_Y = (\text{ß}_1 / [\underline{Z}_x 1 + \underline{Z}_x 2]) + (\text{ß}_2 / [\underline{Z}_x 1 + \underline{Z}_x 2])$
   * c. Predicted $\underline{Z}_Y = (\text{ß}_1)(\underline{Z}_x 1) + (\text{ß}_2)(\underline{Z}_x 2)$
   d. Predicted $\underline{Z}_Y = (\text{ß}_1 / \text{ß}_2) + (\underline{Z}_x 1 / \underline{Z}_x 2)$

35. Computing the multiple correlation coefficient ($\underline{R}$) allows you to
   a. Look at the correlation between different predictor variables, ignoring the dependent variable.
   b. Look at each predictor variable separately and correlate it with the dependent variable.
   c. Correlate more than two predictor variables with more than two dependent variables.
   * d. Look at the overall correlation between a number of predictor variables and the one dependent variable.

Fill-In Questions

36. If $\underline{X}$ is considered to be the cause of $\underline{Y}$, $\underline{Y}$ is called the _____ variable.

   Answer: dependent

37. A variable that is considered to be a cause is called a(n) _____ variable.

   Answer: independent

38. A(n) _____ is a graphic display of the pattern of relationship between two variables.

   Answer: scatter diagram

Test Bank

39.   In a scatter diagram, the predictor variable goes on the _____ axis.

Answer: horizontal

40.   In a scatter diagram of the relation between hearing sensitivity and love of music (in which hearing sensitivity is considered to be the cause of love of music), a dot located at 4.5 across and 8 up means the person had a score of 4.5 on _____.

Answer: hearing sensitivity

41.   A scatter diagram shows a pattern of dots in which the dots generally go up and to the right. This pattern is an example of a(n) _____ correlation.

Answer: positive, positive linear

42.   A scatter diagram shows a pattern of dots in which the dots generally go down and to the right. This pattern is an example of a(n) _____ correlation.

Answer: negative, negative linear

43.   A scatter diagram in which the pattern of dots go reasonably straight across and then about half-way across start going down is an example of a(n) _____ correlation.

Answer: curvilinear

44.   A scatter diagram in which the dots form a kind of upside down "U" shape is an example of a(n) _____ correlation.

Answer: curvilinear

45.   A study finds that the more scary the movie a person is watching, the more popcorn the person will eat. This relation between scariness of movies and popcorn is an example of a(n) _____ correlation.

Answer: positive, positive linear

46.   A study finds that the longer a book, the less willing children are to read it. This relation between book length and children's interest is an example of a(n) _____ correlation.

Answer: negative, negative linear

47.   In a perfect linear correlation, the dots in a scatter diagram all fall _____.

Answer: on a straight line

48. Multiplying a person's $\underline{Z}$ score on one variable times the person's $\underline{Z}$ score on another variable creates what is called a(n) _____ of $\underline{Z}$ scores.

   Answer: cross-product

49. When using $\underline{Z}$ scores, the cross-product of a high score with a high score will always be _____.

   Answer: positive

50. When using $\underline{Z}$ scores, the cross-product of a high score with a low score will always be _____.

   Answer: negative

51. When using $\underline{Z}$ scores, the cross-product of a low score with a low score will always be _____.

   Answer: positive

52. The average of the cross-product of $\underline{Z}$ scores will be positive when high scores go with _____ scores and low scores go with _____ scores.

   Answer: high; low

53. A correlation coefficient will tend be negative when high scores go with _____ scores and low scores go with _____ scores.

   Answer: low; high

54. When high scores go with high scores, and low with low, the correlation coefficient will be between _____ and _____.

   Answer: 0; 1

55. If a research article reports that a score is statistically significant, this means that it is unlikely that a correlation this high would have been observed in the group studied if the correlation were in fact zero for _____.

   Answer: people in general, the general population

56. When a research article reports $\underline{r}$ = .35, $\underline{p}$ < .05, the "$\underline{p}$ < .05" means that the result is statistically _____.

   Answer: significant

57. A(n) _____ is a table showing the correlations among several variables.

   Answer: correlation matrix

58. Although the correlation coefficient is named after Pearson, it was actually invented by _____.

Answer: Galton

59. _____ is the number you multiply by the Z score of the independent variable to obtain the predicted Z score on the dependent variable.

Answer: Standardized regression coefficient, Beta, ß, r, Correlation coefficient

60. The standardized regression coefficient is the number you multiply by the Z score of the independent variable to obtain the _____ on the dependent variable.

Answer: predicted Z score

61. In a multiple regression situation with two predictor variables, it has been found that $\beta_1 = .4$, $\beta_2 = .6$. A particular subject's Z score on the first predictor variable is 2, and this subject's Z score on the second predictor variable is 3. This subject's predicted Z score on the dependent variable is _____.

Answer: 2.6

The essays called for in many of these problems ask students to explain the logic behind the analysis to someone unfamiliar with the material covered since Chapter 2--that is, they can assume the reader is familiar with mean, standard deviation, and $\underline{Z}$ scores. Instructors may prefer, particularly on a final exam or on any exam covering the material in both Chapters 2 and 3, to ask for an explanation "to a person who has had no exposure to statistics at all." (Of course, such essays take students longer to write.)

62. A researcher conducted a study of the relation between income and generosity. The researcher observed the amount of money given to a panhandler and the wealth of the person being asked (wealth was measured by a rating of the clothing worn). The results for the first four people observed were as follows:

Wealth of Giver	Dollars Given
4	0
6	1
8	3
2	0

a. Make a scatter diagram of the raw data.
b. Describe the general pattern of the data in words.
c. Compute the correlation coefficient.
d. Indicate plausible directions of causality in terms of the variables involved.
e. Explain your result to a person who is familiar with mean, standard deviation, and $\underline{Z}$ scores, but not with correlation.

Computation answers:

	Wealth of Giver Raw	$\underline{Z}$	Dollars Given Raw	$\underline{Z}$	Cross-Product of Z Scores
	4	-.45	0	-.82	.37
	6	.45	1	0	0
	8	1.34	3	1.64	2.20
	2	-1.34	0	-.82	1.10
Σ	20		4		3.67
$\underline{M}$	5		1		$\underline{r}$ = .92
$\underline{SD}$	2.24		1.22		

63. A researcher conducted a study of the relation of dominance behavior to size in a particular species of bird. The results for the first three birds observed were as follows:

Size of Bird	Dominance Behavior
14	82
18	82
10	70

a. Make a scatter diagram of the raw data.
b. Describe the general pattern of the data in words.
c. Compute the correlation coefficient.
d. Indicate plausible directions of causality in terms of the variables involved.
e. Explain your result to a person who is familiar with mean, standard deviation, and Z scores, but not with correlation.

Computation answers:

	Size of Bird Raw	Z	Dominance Behavior Raw	Z	Cross-Product of Z Scores
	14	0	82	.71	0
	18	1.22	82	.71	.87
	10	-1.22	70	-1.41	1.72
Σ	42		234		2.59
M	14		78		r = .86
SD	3.27		5.66		

64. A health researcher conducted a study of the relation of number of hours exercised each week to number of days reporting sick per year. The results for four individuals studies are as follows:

Weekly Exercise Hours	Sick Days per Year
4	6
4	7
0	10
8	5

a. Make a scatter diagram of the raw data.
b. Describe the general pattern of the data in words.
c. Compute the correlation coefficient.
d. Indicate plausible directions of causality in terms of the variables involved.
e. Explain your result to a person who is familiar with mean, standard deviation, and Z scores, but not with correlation.

Computation answers:

	Weekly Exercise Hours Raw	Z	Sick Days per Year Raw	Z	Cross-Product of Z Scores
	4	0	6	-.53	0
	4	0	7	0	0
	0	-1.41	10	1.60	-2.26
	8	1.41	5	-1.07	-1.51
Σ	16		28		-3.77
M	4		7		r = -.94
SD	2.83		1.87		

Test Bank

65. A study examined the relation of math ability to belief that math ability was innate. The data for the first three subjects are shown below:

Math Ability	Belief that Math Ability is Innate
66	7
70	4
50	10

a. Make a scatter diagram of the raw data.
b. Describe the general pattern of the data in words.
c. Compute the correlation coefficient.
d. Indicate plausible directions of causality in terms of the variables involved.
e. Explain your result to a person who is familiar with mean, standard deviation, and Z scores, but not with correlation.

Computation answers:

Math Ability Raw	Z	Belief that Math Ability is Innate Raw	Z	Cross-Product of Z Scores
66	.46	7	0	0
70	.93	4	-1.22	-1.13
50	-1.39	10	1.22	-1.70
Σ 186		21		-2.83
M 62		7		$r = -.94$
SD 8.64		2.45		

66. A researcher studying the structure of intelligence found the following scores for verbal reasoning and numerical ability for six women (Z scores are also given):

Subject	Verbal Raw	Z	Numerical Raw	Z
A	1.4	-1.20	2	-.81
B	6.1	.77	4	.07
C	1.8	-1.03	3	-.37
D	3.3	-.41	1	-1.25
E	4.8	.22	5	.52
F	8.2	1.64	8	1.84

a. Make a scatter diagram of the raw data.
b. Describe the general pattern of the data in words.
c. Compute the correlation coefficient.
d. Indicate plausible directions of causality in terms of the variables involved.
e. Explain your result to a person who is familiar with mean, standard deviation, and Z scores, but not with correlation.

Computation answers: $r = (.97 + .05 + .38 + .51 + .11 + 3.02)/6 = 5.04/6 = .84$.

67. A longitudinal study reported the following data for eight children on their age at first walking (in months) and their first grade teachers' ratings of athletic ability (on a 9-point scale):

Child	Age Walking Raw	Age Walking Z	Athletic Rating Raw	Athletic Rating Z
A	12	-.13	5	.51
B	10	-1.17	4	-.08
C	10	-1.17	6	1.11
D	16	1.95	7	1.70
E	12	-.13	2	-1.26
F	11	-.65	2	-1.26
G	13	.39	3	.67
H	14	.91	4	-.08

a. Make a scatter diagram of the raw data.
b. Describe the general pattern of the data in words.
c. Compute the correlation coefficient.
d. Indicate plausible directions of causality in terms of the variables involved.
e. Explain your result to a person who is familiar with mean, standard deviation, and Z scores, but not with correlation.

Computation answers: $r = (-.07+.09-1.30+3.32+.16+.82+.26-.07)/8$
$= 3.21/8 = .40.$

68. A researcher interested in advertising effects conducted a survey of people's memory for various jingles as well as the amount of exposure they had to the jingles and their interest in the product. The researcher reported the following results: "The correlation between memory for the jingles and exposure was substantial ($r = .48$, $p < .01$); but there was essentially no association of memory for the jingles and interest in the product ($r = .06$, ns)." Explain this result to a person who is familiar with mean, standard deviation, and Z scores, but not with correlation. (Discuss the statistical-significance aspect only in a very general way. ns means not significant.)

69. College students who were currently in a romantic relationship were asked to rate how important each of four different aspects of the relationship was to them. In the article reporting the results, the following correlation matrix was provided:

	Intimacy	Social Status	Self-Esteem
Companionship	.53**	.14	.07
Intimacy		.09	.11
Social Status			.63**

** $p < .01$

Explain this result to a person who is familiar with mean, standard deviation, and Z scores, but not with correlation. (Discuss the statistical-significance aspect only in a very general way.)

70. A researcher studying the relation of length of court trials to length of time for juries to come to a decision reports the following data for the first four trials considered.

Trial	Trial Length (Days)		Jury's Hours of Deliberation	
	X	ZX	Y	Z Y
I	5	-.55	8	.17
II	20	1.65	12	1.52
III	8	-.11	6	-.51
IV	2	-.99	4	-1.18
	M=8.75 SD=6.83		M=7.5 SD=2.96	r = .91

a. Give the Z score prediction formula for predicting length of jury deliberation from length of trial.

b. Predict the hours of deliberation for a jury where the trial lasted for 10 days.

c. Explain what you have done to a person who is familiar with correlation but not with regresssion.

Computation answers:

a. Predicted $\underline{Z}Y$ = (.91)(ZX).

b. $\underline{Z}X$ = (10-8.75)/6.83 = .18; predicted $\underline{Z}Y$ = (.91)(.18) = .16; predicted $\underline{Y}$ = 7.5+(.16)(2.96) = 7.97 hours.

71. A researcher conducts a study of familiarity with certain unusual words and the time it takes a subject to press a button indicating whether the word is singular or plural. All subjects are given the same words. They rate their familiarity with these words (after the reaction-time part) on a 7-point scale (high = familiar). Below are the scores for the first three subjects. That is, for Subject A, average familiarity of the words used was 6 and average reaction time was 1.25 s.

Person Tested	Familiarity		Reaction Time	
	X	ZX	Y	Z Y
A	6	1.37	1.25	-1.04
B	2	-.98	3.16	1.35
C	3	-.39	1.84	-.30
	M=3.67 SD=1.70		M=2.08 SD=.80	r = -.87

a. Give the Z score prediction formula for predicting reaction time from familiarity.

b. Predict the reaction time for a person who rates his or her familiarity as a 5.

c. Explain what you have done to a person who is familiar with correlation but not with regresssion.

Computation answers:

a. Predicted $\underline{Z}Y$ = (-.87)(ZX).

b. $\underline{Z}X$ = (5-3.67)/1.70 = .78; predicted $\underline{Z}Y$ = (-.87)(.78) = -.68; predicted $\underline{Y}$ = 2.08+(-.68)(.80) = 1.54 seconds.

72. A health researcher conducts a study of the relation of proportion of fat in a person's diet to proportion of time the person uses a seat belt. (The idea is that those who practice one kind of health-related behavior may be more likely to practice another kind.) Here are the data for three subjects.

Person Tested	% Fat in Diet		% Seat Belt Usage	
	X	ZX	Y	ZY
K	25	-1.14	70	1.34
L	35	-.16	50	-.27
M	50	1.30	40	-1.07

M=36.67 SD=10.27 M=53.33 SD=12.47 r = -.96

a. Give the Z score prediction formula for predicting seat belt usage from fat in diet.
b. Predict the seat belt usage of a person who has 40% fat in their diet.
c. Explain what you have done to a person who is familiar with correlation but not with regresssion.

Computation answers:
a. Predicted $\underline{Z}Y$ = (-.96)($\underline{Z}X$).
b. $\underline{Z}X$=(40-36.67)/10.27=.32; predicted $\underline{Z}Y$=(-.96)(.32) = -.31; predicted $\underline{Y}$ = 53.33+(-.31)(12.47) = 49.46% seat belt usage.

73. A psychologist studying the relation of similarity to attraction reported the following results for four subjects.

Person Tested	Similarity		Attraction	
	X	ZX	Y	ZY
J.L.	1	-1.17	3	-1.18
K.M.	6	1.43	5	-.39
L.B.	2	-.65	6	0
R.C.	4	.39	10	1.57

M=3.25 SD=1.92   M=6 SD=2.55   r = .36

a. Give the $\underline{Z}$-score prediction formula for predicting attraction from similarity.
b. Predict the attraction to a person for whom the similarity is rated as a 5.
c. Explain what you have done to a person who is familiar with correlation but not with regresssion.

Computation answers:
a. Predicted $\underline{Z}Y$ = (.36)($\underline{Z}X$).
b. $\underline{Z}X$ = (5-3.25)/1.92 = .91; predicted $\underline{Z}Y$ = (.36)(.91) = .33; predicted $\underline{Y}$ = 6+(.33)(2.55) = 6.84.

74. An organizational specialist administered questionnaires to three new employees, assessing psychological rigidity and adjustment to their new job. The scores are as follows.

Person Tested	Rigidity		Adjustment to Job	
	X	ZX	Y	ZY
A	7	1.06	10	-.61
B	4	-1.34	21	1.41
C	6	.26	9	-.80
	M=5.67 SD=1.25		M=13.33 SD=5.44	r = -.92

a. Give the Z score prediction formula for predicting adjustment to retirement from scores on the rigidity scale.
b. Predict the adjustment to a new job for a person who scores 8 on the rigidity scale.
c. Explain what you have done to a person who is familiar with correlation but not with regresssion.

Computation answers:
a. Predicted ZY = (-.92)(ZX).
b. ZX = (8-5.67)/1.25 = 1.86; predicted ZY =(-.92)(1.86)= -1.71; predicted Y = 13.33+(-1.71)(5.44) = 4.03.

75. A researcher surveys a group of working married women and reports the following results for the first four surveyed:

Person Tested	% Contribution to Household Income		% Contribution to Housework	
	X	ZX	Y	ZY
C1	60	1.34	70	-1.15
F3	30	-1.34	100	1.61
B8	40	-.45	80	-.23
J2	50	.45	80	-.23
	M=45 SD=11.18		M=82.5 SD=10.9	r = -.92

a. Give the Z score prediction formula for predicting proportion of housework done from proportion of income contributed.
b. Predict the contribution to housework for a woman who provides 90% of the income.
c. Explain what you have done to a person who is familiar with correlation but not with regresssion.

Computation answers:
a. Predicted ZY = (-.92)(ZX).
b. ZX = (90-45)/11.18 = 4.03; predicted ZY =(-.92)(4.03)= -3.71; predicted Y = 82.5+(-3.71)(10.9) = 42.06%.

Test Bank

Multiple-Choice Questions

1. If you were looking at a graph of a normal distribution, which of the following would best describe it?
    a. It is bimodal and roughly symmetrical.
    * b. It is unimodal, roughly symmetrical, and bell-shaped.
    c. It is skewed to the right.
    d. It is a roughly symmetrical U-shape.

2. Suppose that the mean score on a creativity test is 20 and the standard deviation is 5. You are told that the distribution is normal. Using the approximations for normal curves, how many people would get a score between 15 and 25?
    a. 34%
    b. 14% + 34% = 48%
    c. 50%
    * d. 34% + 34% = 68%

3. Suppose that the mean score on a stress scale is 5 and the standard deviation is 2. You are told that the distribution is normal. Using the approximations for normal curves, how many people would get a score between 5 and 9?
    a. 34%
    * b. 34% + 14% = 48%
    c. 50%
    d. 34% + 34% = 68%

4. Using the approximations for normal curves, what percentage of scores fall between the mean and one standard deviation below the mean?
    a. 14%
    b. 50% - 34% = 16%
    * c. 34%
    d. 50%

Test Bank

5.   Suppose that a person received a test score that was in the top 20% of all the cases. This person's Z score must be at least
      a. .53.
   * b. .84.
      c. 5.03.
      d. 5.34.

6.   Suppose that a person received a test score that was in the top 32% of all the scores. This person's Z score must be at least
   * a. .47.
      b. .56.
      c. .74.
      d. .92.

7.   What percentage of cases fall between the Z score of 1.29 and the Z score of 1.49?
      a. .54
   * b. 3.04
      c. 7.49
      d. 83.34

8.   Suppose that a person received a score that was in the bottom 42% of the scores. What is the highest Z score this person could have?
      a. -1.41
      b. -.94
   * c. -.20
      d. +.25

9.   According to a standardized scoring system, a particular nation has a human rights score of 41 which equals a Z score of 1.3. What is the percentage of cases above this score?
      a. 40.32% - 50% = -9.68%
   * b. 50% - 40.32% = 9.68%
      c. 100% - 40.32% = 59.68%
      d. 50% + 40.32% = 99.68%

10.   What Z score would a person have to receive to be in the top 4% of their class on a particular test?
      a. 4% - 50% = -46%, which corresponds to a Z score of -1.75.
      b. 50% - 46% = 4%, which corresponds to a Z score of .10.
   * c. 50% - 4% = 46%, which corresponds to a Z score of 1.75.
      d. 34% + 14% - 4% = 44%, which corresponds to a Z score of 1.55 or 1.56.

11.   What Z score would a person have to receive to be in the top 5%?
      a. 5% - 50% = -45%, which corresponds to a Z score of -1.64.
      b. -5%, which corresponds to a Z score of -.12.
      c. 5%, which corresponds to a Z score of .12.
   * d. 50% - 5% = 45%, which corresponds to a Z score of 1.64.

12. Suppose that a person got a score of 4.78 on a test, which turned out to be a $\underline{Z}$ score of +1.5. What percentage of cases are above this score?
     d. 43.32% - 50% = -6.68%
*   b. 50% - 43.32% = 6.68%
     c. 100% - 43.32% = 56.68%
     a. 50% + 43.32% = 83.32%

13. Relative frequency is defined as
     a. the expected number of times one will receive a particular outcome in an experiment.
     b. how frequently a result occurs when you repeat an experiment.
     c. what result you expect if you repeat an experiment frequently.
*   d. the number of times something occurs relative to the number of times it could have occurred.

14. If you decided to roll a 6-sided die an infinite number of times you would expect to get a one 1/6 of the time, a two 1/6 of the time, etc. This illustrates which interpretation of probability?
     a. Subjective
     b. Objective
*   c. Long-run relative-frequency
     d. Bayesian

15. Suppose that you think that there is a pretty good chance that when you leave your class you will see your friend who has a class across the hall at the same time as you. You might say that there is about a 90% chance you will see your friend. This is an example of which interpretation of probability?
*   a. Subjective
     b. Objective
     c. Long-run relative-frequency
     d. Bayesian

16. Suppose that you randomly select one person from a group of 12. Two of those in the group were born in Iowa. What is the chance you will pick a person born in Iowa?
     a. 1/12 = .08
*   b.   2/12 = .17
     c. 12/2 = 6
     d. 12 X 2 = 24

17. In a particular housing project there are 350 households in which English is usually spoken, 50 in which Spanish is usually spoken, and 100 in which the language is other than English or Spanish. If a researcher approaches a house at random to conduct an interview, what is the chance that the usual language in that household will not be English?
     a. 1/500 = .002
     b. 50/350 = .14
*   c. 150/500 = .3
     d. 150/350 = .43

18. The fact that probabilities are proportions means that they
    a. have to be larger than one.
    *   b. can't be lower than zero or more than one.
    c. can't be lower than zero or more than 100.
    d. can be either a positive or a negative number.

19. Suppose that you have a fish tank full of tropical salt-water fish and you need to know the exact salt content of the water. To test it, suppose you take a cup and scoop some of the water out. In statistical language, the scoop of water is a
    a. population.
    b. parameter.
    *   c. sample.
    d. population distribution.

20. A researcher conducts extensive interviews with 40 workers at a particular large factory in order to examine the morale among workers in general at that factory. In this example, what is the population?
    a. The 40 workers interviewed.
    b. All workers in the factory except the 40 interviewed.
    *   c. All workers in the factory.
    d. None of the above--the term population only applies when there is a known normal distribution.

21. Suppose you wanted to study the general amount of drug use at your school and you were given a complete list of the students. If you then put all the names into a big box and had a blindfolded person select as many people as you needed, this would be called
    *   a. random selection.
    b. haphazard selection.
    c. specified selection.
    d. type B selection.

22. Suppose that you wanted to conduct a study of the physical effects of caffeine. To recruit participants for your experiment you post a sign-up sheet for anyone who would be willing to participate to sign up. This is an example of
    a. random selection.
    *   b. haphazard selection.
    c. stratified selection.
    d. type B selection.

23. Which of the following statements is most accurate about research articles for social science experiments?
    *   a. Normal curves and method of selection are occasionally mentioned and probability is rarely discussed except in terms of statistical significance.
    b. Normal curves and probabilities are rarely mentioned, but the method of sampling is almost always stated as well as how a list of the population was acquired.
    c. Normal curves and probabilities are almost always mentioned, whereas the populations and samples are rarely mentioned.
    d. Normal curves, probabilities, samples, and populations are all almost always mentioned.

24. The Gallop Poll correctly predicted Bush's 1988 victory using only 4,089 interviews. Why, then, did the Gallop poll in 1948 wrongly predict Dewey's victory over Truman when they used 50,000 interviews to make the prediction?
   a. They only interviewed people in one state.
   b. They used multistage cluster sampling.
 * c. They used quota sampling.
   d. They used random sampling.

25. Which of the following statements is true about the probability method of sampling as used in modern opinion polls?
 * a. The interviewers have no choice about who they interview and there is some definite procedure for selecting the sample that involves the planned use of chance.
   b. The interviewers have no choice about who they interview and the door-to-door method is preferred over phoning because people are more responsive.
   c. Strict quotas are placed so that a range of people are polled, but within these specifics the interviewer can choose who they interview.
   d. Strict quotas are placed and the interviewers have no choice about who they interview.

Fill-In Questions

26. In a normal curve approximately _____ percent of the cases fall between one and two standard deviations above the mean.

   Answer: 14

27. In a normal curve approximately _____ percent of the cases are lower than two standard deviations below the mean.

   Answer: 2

28. On a normal curve approximately 68% of the cases fall between a Z score of -1 and a Z score of _____.

   Answer: +1

29. A(n) _____ shows the percentage of cases falling between the mean and any particular Z score.

   Answer: normal curve table

30. Probability is the _____ relative frequency of a particular outcome.

   Answer: expected, long-run

31. _____ is the expected relative frequency of a particular outcome.

   Answer: Probability

Test Bank

32. In the context of probability, a(n) _____ is the result of an experiment (or virtually any event, such as a coin coming up heads or it raining tomorrow).

Answer: outcome

33. The _____ interpretation of probability is the understanding of probability as the proportion of a particular outcome you would obtain if you were to repeat the experiment many times.

Answer: long-run relative-frequency

34. The _____ interpretation of probability is the understanding of probability as the degree of one's certainty that a particular outcome will occur.

Answer: subjective

35. "_____ = .5" expresses in symbols that the probability is fifty-fifty that something will happen. (Give a symbol.)

Answer: p

36. The scores of the entire group of subjects to which a researcher intends the results of a study to apply is called a(n) _____.

Answer: population

37. A(n) _____ refers to the larger group to which a researcher makes inferences based on the particular set of subjects studied.

Answer: population

38. A(n) _____ refers to the scores of the particular set of subjects studied that are intended to represent the scores in some larger population.

Answer: sample

39. _____ selection is a procedure of selecting a sample of individuals to study such that each individual in the population has an equal chance of being selected.

Answer: Random, Probability

40. In _____ sampling, the researcher often begins with a complete list of all the members of the population.

Answer: random, probability

Test Bank

41. If you conduct a survey by giving out a questionnaire to the people you meet (and who are willing to take your questionnaire) on a given evening, you are using _____ selection.

Answer: haphazard

42. The mean, standard deviation, and variance of a population are called population _____.

Answer: parameters

43. The mean, standard deviation, and variance of a sample are called sample _____.

Answer: statistics

44. Inferential statistics is the branch of statistics that draws conclusions about _____ based on information in _____.

Answer: populations; samples

45. Today, survey sampling uses complex methods in order to insure a close approximation to true _____ sampling.

Answer: random, probability

46. Fifty years ago opinion polls often used the _____ method of sampling, which is now largely discredited.

Answer: quota

Problems and Essays

> The essays called for in many of these problems ask students to explain the logic behind the analysis to someone who is familiar with the material covered in previous chapters. Instructors may prefer, particularly on a final exam, to ask for an explanation "to a person who has had no exposure to statistics at all." (Of course, such essays take students longer to write.)

47. Suppose that it is known that for a particular measure of writing ability, college students in general have a mean of 60 and a standard deviation of 8.
   a. Approximately what percentage of college students have writing ability scores above 68? Above 76? Below 52? Between 52 and 60? (Use the normal curve approximation rules.)
   b. Explain your conclusion and procedure to a person who is familiar with mean, standard deviation, and Z scores, but is not familiar with the normal curve or normal curve areas.

Computation answers: 16%; 2%; 16%; 34%.

48. On a test of physical fitness, 18-year-olds' scores are normally distributed with a mean of 140 and a standard deviation of 25.
   a. Approximately what percentage of husbands have scores above 190? Below 165? Below 115? (Use the normal curve approximation rules.)
   b. Explain your conclusion and procedure to a person who is familiar with mean, standard deviation, and $\underline{Z}$ scores, but is not familiar with the normal curve or normal curve areas.

   Computation answers: 2%; 84%; 16%.

49. The number of words in the active vocabulary of children of a particular age is normally distributed with a mean of 3,000 and a standard deviation of 500.
   a. How many words would a child of this age have to know to be in the top 2%? The top 16%? The top 98%? (Use the normal curve approximation rules.)
   b. Explain your conclusion and procedure to a person who is familiar with mean, standard deviation, and $\underline{Z}$ scores, but is not familiar with the normal curve or normal curve areas.

   Computation answers: 4,000; 3,500; 2,000.

50. The length of conversations between supervisors and workers in a certain type of manufacturing industry has been found to be normally distributed with a mean of 4.0 minutes and a standard deviation of .8 minutes.
   a. What percentage of conversations are longer than 4.4 minutes? Longer than 5 minutes? Longer than 3 minutes? Shorter than 2 minutes? (Use the normal curve table.)
   b. Explain your conclusion and procedure to a person who is familiar with mean, standard deviation, and $\underline{Z}$ scores, but is not familiar with the normal curve or normal curve areas.

   Computation answers: 30.85%; 10.56; 89.44%; .62%.

51. A business has found that on a 7-point scale about satisfaction with the services it provides to clients, the ratings are normally distributed with a mean of 4.8 and a standard deviation of .5.
   a. What percentage of clients rate their satisfaction above a 5? Above a 6? Above 4? (Use the normal curve table.)
   b. Explain your conclusion and procedure to a person who is familiar with mean, standard deviation, and $\underline{Z}$ scores, but is not familiar with the normal curve or normal curve areas.

   Computation answers: 34.46%; .82%; 94.52%

52. On a standard test of optimism, scores of people diagnosed with a particular disease are normally distributed with a mean of 20 and a standard deviation of 5.
   a. How high of a score does such a person need to be among the 5% most optimistic? Among the 20% most optimistic? How low of a score to be among the 10% least optimistic? (Use the normal curve table.)
   b. Explain your conclusion and procedure to a person who is familiar with mean, standard deviation, and $\underline{Z}$ scores, but is not familiar with the normal curve or normal curve areas.

   Computation answers: 28.2; 24.2; 13.6.

53. In a particular community 4,000 of the adults are married, 2,000 have never been married, 2,000 are divorced, and 2,000 are widowed. Suppose you were conducting a survey in this community and telephoned a person at random.
   a. What is the probability that this person would be divorced or widowed?
   b. What is the probability that this person would be either married or divorced?

   Computation answers: a. .4. b. .6.

54. At a particular small college there are 200 students majoring in natural sciences, 300 in social sciences, 250 in humanities, and 250 in other majors. Suppose you are going to select a student at random to interview about the college.
   a. What is the probability this student would be someone majoring in either the social sciences or humanities?
   b. What is the probability that this student would be someone majoring in either natural sciences or social sciences?

   Computation answers: a. .55. b. .5.

55. A sociologist plans to conduct a survey of district attorneys about their attitudes toward the death penalty. What would be the best way to select the sample of district attorneys to study? Explain what you would do and why to a person who is unfamiliar with research methods or statistics.

56. You want to conduct a survey of the students in a particular large dormitory. The survey will involve intensive interviews with each person who participates, so it will not be practical to interview everyone. What would be the best way to select the particular individuals to interview? (Presume that whoever you would ask would be willing to participate.) Explain what you would do and why to a person who is unfamiliar with research methods or statistics.

266

Multiple-Choice Questions

1. Which of the following statements is most accurate about hypothesis testing?
  * a. It is a central theme in the statistical analysis in virtually all research.
     b. It is a simple part of statistics that only applies to three statistical procedures.
     c. It is a fairly uncommon way of using statistics.
     d. It is a kind of statistical procedure that is used mainly as part of descriptive statistics.

2. If you want to know if a new employee incentive program really works, how would you test the hypothesis that it does work?
     a. Try to disprove the hypothesis that it does work.
     b. Try to prove the hypothesis that it does work.
  * c. Try to disprove the hypothesis that it does not work.
     d. Try to prove the hypothesis that it does not work.

3. How do you set up a hypothesis testing problem?
     a. You set it up to test what you predict will happen.
  * b. You set it up to test the opposite of what you predict will happen.
     c. You set up two problems, one to test what you predict and the other to test the opposite.
     d. You set up a test that assumes the two populations are different, regardless of whether that is what you predict or not.

4. Suppose that a researcher wants to know if a new teaching method is more effective than the old one. What would the research hypothesis be?
  * a. The new teaching method is more effective than the old teaching method.
     b. The old teaching method is more effective than the new teaching method.
     c. There is no difference in effectiveness between the old teaching method and the new teaching method.
     d. There is some difference in effectiveness between the old teaching method and the new teaching method, but which is more effective is not predicted.

5. Suppose that a researcher wants to see if there is any difference between how fast people work in the morning versus how fast they work in the evening. What would the NULL hypothesis be?
     a. People who work in the morning work faster.
     b. People who work at night work faster.
     c. There is some difference, but which is faster is not predicted.
  * d. There is no difference in the speed at which people work.

6.   Suppose that a researcher wants to study the effects of a new training
       program. The hypothesis that this new training program will work better
       than the old training program is called the
       a. comparison hypothesis.
   *   b. research hypothesis.
       c. null hypothesis.
       d. There is no name for this kind of a hypothesis.

7.   Suppose that a researcher wants to know if a new type of health
       insurance works better or worse than a standard form of health
       insurance. The hypothesis that there will be no difference between the
       new type of insurance and the old type of insurance is called the
       a. comparison hypothesis.
       b. research hypothesis.
   *   c. null hypothesis.
       d. functional differential.

8.   The characteristics of the comparison distribution are determined in
       order to answer which of the following questions?
       a. Given a particular sample value, what is the probability of
           obtaining it if the research hypothesis is true?
   *   b. Given a particular sample value, what is the probability of
           obtaining it if the null hypothesis is true?
       c. Given a particular population value, what is the probability of
           obtaining it if the research hypothesis is true?
       d. Given a particular population value, what is the probability of
           obtaining it if the null hypothesis is false?

9.   What represents the situation in which the null hypothesis is true?
   *   a. The comparison distribution
       b. The directional distribution
       c. The nondirectional distribution
       d. A one-tailed test

10.   In a hypothesis-testing situation in which a sample is studied to see if
       it represents a population (called Population 1) that is different from
       a known population (called Population 2), the comparison distribution is
       a. the same as the distribution of Population 1.
   *   b. the same as the distribution of Population 2.
       c. a rectangular distribution with the same mean and standard deviation
           as Population 1.
       d. a rectangular distribution with the same mean and standard deviation
           as Population 2.

Test Bank

11-13 Suppose that a researcher is interested in a new kind of exercise. This new exercise can be done by anyone because it does not require any equipment, and therefore could be potentially beneficial, without cost to the person. The researcher is interested in whether this new exercise will reduce the rate of heart attacks in the people who participate in doing it.

11.   What is the research hypothesis?
    a.   People will participate because it does not cost them any money.
    b.   The exercise will make no difference in the rate of heart attacks.
*   c.   The exercise will reduce the rate of heart attacks.
    d.   The exercise will increase the rate of heart attacks.

12.   What is the null hypothesis?
    a.   People will participate because it does not cost them any money.
*   b.   The exercise will make no difference in the rate of heart attacks.
    c.   The exercise will reduce the rate of heart attacks.
    d.   The exercise will increase the rate of heart attacks.

13.   What is the comparison distribution?
    a.   The distribution of those who participate in the exercise program.
*   b.   The distribution of those who do not participate in the exercise program.
    c.   The distribution of those who have heart attacks.
    d.   The distribution of those who do not have heart attacks.

14.   What is the "cutoff on the comparison distribution"?
*   a.   It is the point at which, assuming the null hypothesis is true, it would be extremely unlikely to get a result this extreme.
    b.   It is the point at which, assuming the research hypothesis is true, it would be extremely unlikely to get a result this extreme.
    c.   It is the point at which the comparison distribution ends.
    d.   It is the point at which you accept the null hypothesis if the result is more extreme.

15.   What does it mean if a researcher said she rejected the null hypothesis at the .05 level?
*   a.   It means that there was less than a 5% chance that she would have gotten such an extreme result by chance if the null hypothesis were true.
    b.   It means that there was more than a 5% chance that she would have gotten such an extreme result by chance if the null hypothesis were true.
    c.   It means that there is a 5% chance that there is a difference between the two populations she is testing if the null hypothesis were true.
    d.   It means that there is a 95% chance that the research hypothesis is true.

16. What are the generally accepted cutoff points (or conventional levels of significance) in hypothesis testing in psychology?
    a. .001 and .01
  * b. .01 and .05
    c. .10, .20., and .30
    d. .05, .25, and .95

17. Suppose a researcher says that based on the results of his study, the null hypothesis is rejected, and that it is rejected because the probability of obtaining his result if the null hypothesis were true is less than 5%. How would this be symbolized?
    a. $p = 5\%$
  * b. $p < .05$
    c. $.05 < p$
    d. $p > 5\%$

18. When is a result considered statistically significant?
    a. When the sample value is so extreme that the research hypothesis is rejected.
    b. When the sample value is so extreme that the null hypothesis is accepted.
    c. When the sample value is so extreme that the research hypothesis is rejected.
  * d. When the sample value is so extreme that the null hypothesis is rejected.

19. How do you determine whether or not to reject the null hypothesis?
    a. If the Z score is less than -1 or greater than +1.
    b. If the Z score is greater than +2.5.
  * c. Compare the Z score needed to reject the null to the actual Z score of the sample.
    d. Compare the standard deviation of the sample (SD) to the standard deviation of the population (σ).

20. If the cutoff score on the comparison distribution is ±2.31, you could reject the null hypothesis if the sample value on this distribution was
    a. -2.16.
    b. -1.41.
    c. 2.16.
  * d. 2.83.

21. If the cutoff score on the comparison distribution is 1.64 and the sample value has a score of 1.32 on the comparison distribution, the
  * a. null hypothesis can not be rejected.
    b. null hypothesis is rejected.
    c. research hypothesis is supported.
    d. research hypothesis is rejected.

22. If the null hypothesis is rejected, what can the researcher conclude?
  * a. That the results support the research hypothesis.
    b. That the results prove that the research hypothesis is true.
    c. That the results were inconclusive.
    d. That the results support the null hypothesis.

Test Bank

23.	When the results of a study are not sufficiently extreme to reject the null hypothesis, what can the researcher conclude with reasonable confidence?
	a. The results support the null hypothesis.
	b. The results prove that the null hypothesis is true.
	c. The results support the research hypothesis.
*	d. None of the above--the results are inconclusive.

24.	Which of the following is not a correct statement of one of the five steps of hypothesis testing?
	a.	Reframe the question into a research hypothesis and a null hypothesis about populations.
	b.	Determine the characteristics of the comparison distribution.
*	c.	Determine the cutoff score on the sample distribution at which the research hypothesis should be rejected.
	d.	Compare the scores obtained in Steps 3 and 4 to decide whether to reject the null hypothesis.

25.	Suppose that a researcher wants to know if a new type of exercise improves peoples' health. Would this be a one-tailed or two-tailed test and why?
*	a.	One-tailed because the study is only interested in whether the exercise increases health.
	b.	One-tailed because the study only looks at the effects of exercise and does not take other factors into account.
	c.	Two-tailed because they will have to study healthy and unhealthy people.
	d.	Two-tailed because there is no predicted direction of difference.

26.	Suppose that a researcher wants to know if a new flu drug affects people, either by making them better or worse. Would this be a one-tailed or two-tailed test and why?
	a.	One-tailed because only one issue is discussed--the drug.
	b.	One-tailed because there is only one interaction, which is between the flu and the drug.
	c.	Two-tailed because there are two variables--whether or not people take the drug and how their flu is affected.
*	d.	Two-tailed because there is no predicted direction of the effect of the drug.

27.	A one-tailed test is especially associated with
	a. the research hypothesis.
	b. the null hypothesis.
	c. a nondirectional hypothesis.
*	d. a directional hypothesis.

28. What is the argument for using a two-tailed test even if there is a clear basis for predicting a result in a given direction?
   a. If the null hypothesis is in fact true, a failure to reject it will give stronger evidence in support of it.
   b. One-tailed tests can not be used in almost any real study involving two groups.
   * c. If an unexpected result comes out opposite to what is predicted, it does not have to be ignored.
   d. A two-tailed test gives you a better chance of getting a significant result.

29. What is the argument for using a one-tailed test when there is a clear basis for predicting a result in a given direction?
   a. The underlying mathematics of one-tailed tests are more accurate.
   b. If the result is opposite to the prediction, the researcher can still do a two-tailed test later.
   c. It is more conservative, in the sense that in using a one-tailed test it is harder to reject the null hypothesis.
   * d. A particular theory is being tested, and if the results come out opposite to the theory, that adds no more information than if the result simply had not been significant.

30. What is the problem with using a one-tailed test at the 5% level and then later using a two-tailed test at the 5% level if the result comes out in the direction opposite to what was predicted?
   * a. The null hypothesis could be rejected too often because it is first tested at the 5% level and then at the 2.5% level, making a total of 7.5%.
   b. The null hypothesis could be rejected too often because it can first be rejected at the 5% level and then again at the 5% level, making a total of 10%.
   c. There is no real problem with this, but traditionally it's not done.
   d. There is no problem with this and in fact it is done quite often.

31. Suppose that a researcher reported significant results for a study, noting that ".05 > p." What is not standard about this expression?
   a. ".05" should have been written as "5%."
   b. "p" should be Z.
   * c. ".05 > p" should have been written "p < .05."
   d. Nothing is wrong with this expression (it is correct).

32. Which of the following is a standard way for the significance level of the result of a hypothesis test to be reported in a research article?
   a. p = 5%.
   b. p > .05.
   * c. p < .05.
   d. All of the above are standard.

Fill-In Questions

33. Hypothesis testing is a systematic procedure for determining whether results of an experiment, which studies a sample, provide support for a particular theory, which is thought to be applicable to a _____.

   Answer: population

34. _____ is the most widely used procedure of inferential statistics used in psychology.

Answer: Hypothesis testing

35. In hypothesis testing, a statement about the predicted relation between populations is called the _____.

Answer: research hypothesis

36. In hypothesis testing, a statement that there is no difference between populations is called the _____.

Answer: null hypothesis

37. In hypothesis testing, the opposite of the research hypothesis is called the _____.

Answer: null hypothesis

38. The _____ is a statement that serves as a kind of straw person set up to examine whether it can be rejected as part of the hypothesis-testing process.

Answer: null hypothesis, comparison distribution

39. In hypothesis testing, if the null hypothesis is rejected, this is taken as support for the _____.

Answer: research hypothesis

40. The _____ distribution represents the situation if the null hypothesis is true.

Answer: comparison

41. Before conducting a study, a researcher determines the cutoff sample score on the _____ distribution at which the null hypothesis would be rejected if the sample is more extreme than this cutoff score.

Answer: comparison

Test Bank

42-44 A study is conducted to test a prediction that people who spend a great deal of time on the beach have more eye problems than people in general.

42.   Population 1 refers to _____, Population 2 refers to people in general.

        Answer: people who spend a great deal of time on the beach

43.   The research hypothesis is _____.

        Answer: people who spend a great deal of time on the beach have more eye problems than people in general

44.   The null hypothesis is _____.

        Answer: people who spend a great deal of time on the beach do not have more eye problems than people in general

45-47 A researcher wants to know whether people who listen regularly to radio talk shows are more or less likely to vote in national elections than are people in general.

45.   The _____ is that there is no difference in voting between those who do and do not listen regularly to radio talk shows.

        Answer: null hypothesis

46.   The comparison distribution is based on the distribution of the voting behavior of _____.

        Answer: people in general, Population 2

47.   The researchers would use a _____-tailed test.

        Answer: two

48.   If the value of the sample is more extreme than the _____ on the comparison distribution, then the null hypothesis will be rejected.

    Answer: cutoff

49.   When the null hypothesis is rejected, the results of a study are said to be _____.

    Answer: statistically significant, significant

50.   If the cutoff represents the most extreme 5% of the comparison distribution, then 5% is called the _____ level.

    Answer: significance, alpha

51.   The 1% and 5% levels are _____ levels of significance in social science research.

    Answer: conventional, most commonly used

52. Most social scientists use the _____ significance level, but those wanting to be more conservative commonly use the _____ level.

Answer: .05, 5%; .01, 1%

53. A(n) _____ hypothesis is a research hypothesis predicting that one population will have higher scores than the other.

Answer: directional

54. When testing a directional hypothesis, you use a(n) _____ test.

Answer: one-tailed

55. In a(n) _____, the region of the comparison distribution in which the null hypothesis would be rejected is all on one side of the distribution.

Answer: one-tailed test, test of a directional hypothesis

56. A research hypothesis that does not predict a particular direction of difference between populations is called a(n) _____ hypothesis.

Answer: nondirectional

57. A study is done with a sample of one case. The general population (Population 2) has a mean of 30 and a standard deviation of 5. The cutoff Z score for significance in this study is 1.96. The raw score of the sample is 45. What should you conclude? _____

Answer: reject the null hypothesis, the research hypothesis is supported

58. A study is done with a sample of one case. In the general population (Population 2), $\mu = 100$ and $\sigma = 8$. The cutoff Z score for significance in this study is 1.64. The raw score of the sample is 110. What should you conclude? _____

Answer: do not reject the null hypothesis, the result is inconclusive

59. _____ is a way of saying in symbols that a research result is significant at the .05 level.

Answer: $p < .05$

Test Bank

The essays called for in many of these problems ask students to explain the logic behind the analysis to someone who is familiar with the material covered in previous chapters. Instructors may prefer, particularly on a final exam, to ask for an explanation "to a person who has had no exposure to statistics at all." (Of course, such essays take students longer to write.)

60. A researcher was interested in whether children from lower socioeconomic status (SES) neighborhoods have lower than average test-taking skills. She administered a standard measure of test-taking skills to a randomly chosen child from a low SES neighborhood and found him to have a score of 38. Average on this measure for the population in general is 50 with a standard deviation of 10.
   a. Based on these data, what should you conclude about whether those in low SES neighborhoods have lower test-taking ability? (Use the .05 significance level.)
   b. Explain your conclusion and procedure to a person who is familiar with mean, standard deviation, Z scores, normal curve areas, and probability, but is not familiar with hypothesis testing.

Computational answer:
Cutoff (.05 level, one-tailed--low) = -1.64.
Sample's Z score on the comparison distribution = -1.20.
Do not reject the null hypothesis; study is inconclusive.

61. A researcher was interested in whether the use of computer- assisted instruction could help children with reading difficulties to acquire reading skills at a faster than normal rate. He arranged for one of these children to have access to a set of computer-learning programs instead of his normal reading curriculum for one quarter. At the end of the quarter he tested her on a standardized reading ability test on which the mean for children with reading difficulties is 36 with a standard deviation of 6. His test subject scored 47.
   a. Was this result significant at the .05 level?
   b. Explain your conclusion and procedure to a person who is familiar with mean, standard deviation, Z scores, normal curve areas, and probability, but is not familiar with hypothesis testing.

Computational answer:
Cutoff (.05 level, one-tailed--high) = 1.64.
Sample's Z score on the comparison distribution = 1.83.
Reject the null hypothesis; the research hypothesis is supported.

62. A popular music magazine has speculated that the average length of a song on one of today's popular albums is 3.75 minutes with a standard deviation of .75 minutes. Suppose a randomly selected song of a particular new type of music is 5 minutes.
   a. Based on this one case, what can you conclude about whether this new type of music is longer than popular songs in general? (Use the .05 level.)
   b. Explain your conclusion and procedure to a person who is familiar with mean, standard deviation, Z scores, normal curve areas, and probability, but is not familiar with hypothesis testing.

Computational answer:
Cutoff (.05 level, one-tailed--high) = 1.64.
Sample's Z score on the comparison distribution = 1.67.
Reject the null hypothesis; the research hypothesis is supported.

63. An experimenter was interested in checking the accuracy of a new type of polygraph (lie detector) test. In an experiment designed to test this accuracy, a polygraph operator used the machine on a subject who was told ahead of time to lie about some of the questions being asked. In an average situation of this type, the polygraph test is 75% accurate with a standard deviation of 6.5%. With the new machine the operator correctly identified 83.5% of the false responses.
   a. Is the accuracy of the new polygraph different from the usual ones? (Use the .05 level.)
   b. Explain your conclusion and procedure to a person who is familiar with mean, standard deviation, Z scores, normal curve areas, and probability, but is not familiar with hypothesis testing.

Computational answer:
Cutoff (.05 level, two-tailed) = ±1.96
Sample's Z score on the comparison distribution = 1.31.
Do not reject the null hypothesis; study is inconclusive.

64. A researcher was interested in whether children raised in a communal environment differed from children in general in their ability to recognize emotional expression. The test of emotional expression involves showing a series of pictures of various facial expressions. In this series, the average child in the population in general can identify 14 with a standard deviation of 3. The researcher administers the picture test to a randomly selected child raised in a communal environment and the child is able to identify 16 expressions correctly.

   a. Based on these data, what should you conclude about whether being raised in a communal environment makes any difference in children's ability to recognize emotional expression? (Use the .01 level.)
   b. Explain your conclusion and procedure to a person who is familiar with mean, standard deviation, Z scores, normal curve areas, and probability, but is not familiar with hypothesis testing.

Computational answer:
Cutoff (.01 level, two-tailed) = ±2.58
Sample's Z score on the comparison distribution = -.67.
Do not reject the null hypothesis; study is inconclusive.

Test Bank

65. A researcher was interested in whether people give more money to street performers in certain locations. A street performer was randomly selected and asked to perform in one of these special locations. The researcher found that the person earned significantly more than average and reported this result as "$p < .05$." Explain these results to someone who is familiar with mean, standard deviation, Z scores, normal curve areas, and probability, but is not familiar with hypothesis testing.

66. A psychologist was interested in whether a particular chemical would alter the activity of a particular neurotransmitter in the brain. After obtaining an average level of the neurotransmitter's activity within a particular subject's brain, he administered the chemical and monitored the changed activity level. In his report, he indicated that the response to the chemical was not significant (Z score of $-.34$) at the .05 level. Explain this result to a person who is familiar with mean, standard deviation, Z scores, normal curve areas, and probability, but is not familiar with hypothesis testing.

67. A researcher was interested in reducing the stress level of people on vacation who have been identified as having a "Type A personality." She figured that by taking away the watch of one of these vacationers, his stress level should be reduced. She then recorded the average stress level of all the vacationing Type A people (in order to calculate an average) and compared her test subject to that average. His Z score was -1.93, which was significant at the .05 level. Explain this result to someone who is familiar with mean, standard deviation, Z scores, normal curve areas, and probability, but is not familiar with hypothesis testing.

68. A sociologist was interested in whether a particular film reduced the amount of sex-role stereotyping done by college students. He first obtained a measure of the average amount of stereotyping reported on a particular test among normal college students. He then took a subject who had seen the film and compared that subject's result on the test to the average. The obtained Z score (.23) was not significant at the .05 level. Explain this finding to a person who is familiar with mean, standard deviation, Z scores, normal curve areas, and probability, but is not familiar with hypothesis testing.

69. A researcher who had been studying nonverbal communication became interested in whether he and his lab assistants had begun to use more than the average amount of nonverbal gestures. During a lab presentation, he measured the amount of this type of communication in one of his assistants. He then compared this assistant's score to the average that his research had obtained. He found that his assistant was, in fact, using a significantly higher amount of nonverbal communication (Z score of 4.25, which was significant at the .01 level). Explain this result to someone who is familiar with mean, standard deviation, Z scores, normal curve areas, and probability, but is not familiar with hypothesis testing.

Chapter 6
Hypothesis Tests with Means of Samples

Multiple-Choice Questions

1. The proper comparison distribution for the mean of a sample is   called
   the distribution of means and is used because
   * a. comparing the mean of a sample to a distribution of a whole
         population of scores of individual cases is a mismatch.
     b. the available population parameters are inaccurate and reflect too
         little variance within the population.
     c. the distribution of means is likely to have fewer scores than
         would be represented in the population.
     d. the proper comparison distribution is stated in the null
         hypothesis.

2. Hypothetically, a distribution of means can be constructed by
     a. calculating the mean of all the possible samples and
         dividing it by the variance.
     b. using the sample's mean and variance divided by the
         population's parameters.
     c. randomly estimating the population variance from the various
         samples, and using the sample mean in place of μ.
   * d. randomly taking a very large number of samples from a population,
         each of the same size, and making a distribution of their means.

3. The mean of a distribution of means is
     a. the square root of the original population mean.
     b. the original population mean divided by the sample size.
   * c. the same as the original population mean.
     d. the sample mean multiplied by the variance.

4. The variance of a distribution of means is
   * a. smaller than the original population variance.
     b. the same as the original population variance.
     c. greater than the original population variance.
     d. unrelated to the original population variance.

5. The variance of a distribution of means is less than the original
   population variance because
     a. it is based on fewer cases than the original population.
     b. it is an estimate of the sample parameters rather than the
         original population.
   * c. extreme scores are less likely to affect a distribution of means.
     d. a distribution of means actually has a larger variance than the
         original population.

6. Dividing the variance of the population of individual cases by the
   number of subjects in each sample gives us
     a. the standard deviation of the population.
   * b. the variance of the distribution of means.
     c. an estimate of the sample's standard deviation.
     d. the average deviation of the distribution of means.

Test Bank   279

7.   For a particular known population, M=100 and $SD2$=25. A researcher
      conducts a study in which 10 subjects are exposed to an   experimental
      procedure. To test the hypothesis that the   population these 10
      subjects represent is different from the known population, the
      comparison distribution's characteristics would be
      a. mean=10, variance=2.5.
      b. mean=10, variance=5.
*   c. mean=100, variance=2.5.
      d. mean=100, variance=5.

8.   The standard deviation of a distribution of means is
      a. calculated by subtracting the variance from the sample mean and
          taking its square-root.
*   b. the square root of the variance of the distribution of means.
      c. the population variance divided by the N in each sample.
      d. the same as the square root of the sample variance.

9.   The square root of the variance of the distribution of means is
      a. the estimated sample variance.
      b. the average deviation of the original population.
      c. an unbiased estimate of the population standard deviation.
*   d. the standard deviation of the distribution of means.

10.   In general, the shape of a distribution of means tends to be
*   a. unimodal, symmetrical.
      b. bimodal, symmetrical.
      c. unimodal, skewed.
      d. rectangular, symmetrical.

11.   As the number of subjects in each sample gets larger, the
      distribution of means
      a. begins to look less and less like the normal curve (in terms of
          shape).
*   b. becomes a better approximation of the normal curve (in terms of
          shape).
      c. becomes more positively skewed.
      d. becomes more negatively skewed.

12.   When a researcher has obtained a particular sample mean from a
      study, she or he compares it to
      a. the parameters of the known population distribution.
      b. an estimated distribution calculated by earlier research findings.
      c. the distribution of means of all the possible samples in the
          experimental condition from the research.
*   d. the distribution of means that would arise if the null hypothesis
          were true.

13.   The only difference between creating a Z score from a single score and
      creating one from a sample mean is that
*   a. you use the mean and standard deviation from the distribution of
          means.
      b. the estimated population variance is used.
      c. the difference score is divided by the sample's standard deviation.
      d. only the population's mean is used in the calculation.

14. The $\underline{Z}$ score of the sample mean on the distribution of means is
    a. different from a normal $\underline{Z}$ score because an estimated population standard deviation is used.
    b. smaller than normal due to the reduced variance in the distribution of means.
*   c. conceptually similar to creating a $\underline{Z}$ score from a raw score.
    d. equivalent to the sample mean divided by the population variance.

15-18 A psychologist interested in relationships has developed a scale that measures the degree of affection adult men feel for their father. The data from its development has shown that for the general population the distribution is skewed to the right, the mean degree of affection being 60 with a standard deviation of 16. The researcher now is wondering if men who have themselves just become new fathers will score higher on the scale than men in general. He samples a group of 100 new fathers and finds that their mean is 64.5.

15. What is the research hypothesis?
    a. There will be no significant differences between the two populations.
*   b. The population of new fathers has a higher mean than the mean of the population of men in general.
    c. The sample size will significantly affect the level of affection experienced.
    d. The two populations (of men in general and of new fathers) have different variances.

16. What is the mean of the comparison distribution?
    a. 60/100 = .60
    b. 64.5/100 = .645
*   c. 60
    d. 64.5

17. What is the standard deviation of the comparison distribution?
    a. 16/100 = .16
    b. $\sqrt{(16/100)}$ = .40
    c. 162/100 = 2.56
*   d. $\sqrt{(162/100)}$ = 1.60

18. What is the shape of the comparison distribution?
    a. Skewed to the right
    b. Skewed to the left
*   c. Approximately normal
    d. It can not be determined from the information given.

Test Bank

19-22 A researcher is interested in whether the color of an animal's surroundings affects learning rate and tests 16 rats in a box with colorful wallpaper. Assume that it is known that the average rat can learn to run this particular maze (in a box without any special coloring) in 25 trials, with a variance of 64; the distribution is normal. The mean number of trials to learn the maze for the group with the colorful wallpaper is 11.

19. What is the null hypothesis?
   a. The rate of learning for the sample of rats tested with colorful wallpaper is no different than the population of rats tested under ordinary circumstances.
   b. The rate of learning for the sample of rats tested with colorful wallpaper is faster than the population of rats tested under ordinary circumstances.
 * c. The rate of learning for the population of rats tested with colorful wallpaper is no different than the population of rats tested under ordinary circumstances.
   d. The rate of learning for the population of rats tested with colorful wallpaper is faster than the population of rats tested under ordinary circumstances.

20. What is Population SD_M?
   a. 64/16 = 4.00
 * b. $\sqrt{(64/16)}$ = 2.00
   c. 64/11 = 5.82
   d. $\sqrt{(64/11)}$ = 2.41

21. What is the shape of the distribution of means?
   a. Rectangular
   b. Not rectangular, but flatter than a normal curve
   c. Normal
 * d. It can not be determined from the information given.

22. If the sample mean's score on the comparison distribution is more extreme than the cutoff, what should the researcher conclude regarding the colorful wallpaper?
   a. She should reject the null hypothesis that the rats in the sample will learn faster.
   b. The wallpaper did not have a significant effect on the rate of learning.
 * c. The color of the chamber had a significant effect on the rate of learning.
   d. The results are inconclusive since the null hypothesis can not be rejected.

23. In a research article involving a sample and a known population mean, frequently reported statistics would include
 * a. the standard error and the mean.
   b. the power and the effect size.
   c. T scores and variance.
   d. f scores and the distribution of means.

24. The advantage of a large sample size, like those used in polls, is that they
   a. increase the score needed for a significant result.
   b. increase the probability of a Type I error.
 * c. greatly reduce the standard deviation of the distribution of means.
   d. decrease the probability of correctly rejecting the null hypothesis.

25. Sampling error is usually figured in a large poll
     a. by dividing the variance of the distribution of means by the <u>N</u> of
         each sample.
     b. by squaring the variance.
     c. from the proportion of the population that the sample represents.
*   d. from preconstructed tables indexed by the sample size.

<u>Fill-In Questions</u>

26. A(n) _____ is the comparison distribution when testing a hypothesis
     involving a sample of more than one case.

     Answer: distribution of means

27. A distribution of all possible means of samples of a given size from a
     particular population is known, for short, as a(n) _____.

     Answer: distribution of means

28. When conducting a study involving a sample of several people to see
     whether they represent a population different from some known
     population, the _____ is a distribution of means.

     Answer: comparison distribution

29. The mean of a distribution of means is _____ the mean of the
     population.

     Answer: equal to, the same as

30. There is no reason for the mean of a distribution of means to be larger
     or smaller than the _____.

     Answer: mean of the population

31. Population $\underline{SD2}_M$ stands for _____.

     Answer: the variance of the distribution of means

32. Another name for the standard deviation of a distribution of means is
     the _____.

     Answer: standard error of the mean, standard error

33. The _____ of a distribution of means equals the _____ of the
     population divided by the number of cases in the sample. (Use the same
     word in both places.)

     Answer: variance

Test Bank

34. The variance of a distribution of means equals the variance of the
     population of individual cases divided by _____.

     Answer: the number of cases in the sample, $\underline{N}$, the sample size

35. The standard deviation of a distribution of means is the square root of
     the variance of _____.

     Answer: the distribution of means

36-38 A population is normally distributed with $\underline{M}$ = 50, $\underline{SD}$ = 8. A sample of
     10 is studied.

     36. The mean of the distribution of means = _____.

          Answer: 50

     37. The variance of the distribution of means = _____.

          Answer: 6.4

     38. The shape of the distribution of means is _____.

          Answer: normal

39. A distribution of means will be approximately normal so long as there
     are at least _____ cases in the sample.

     Answer: 30

40. A(n) _____ is the name of the hypothesis-testing procedure used
     when there is a single sample and a known population.

     Answer: $\underline{Z}$ test

41. A(n) _____ is an estimate of a specific value of a population parameter.

     Answer: point estimate

42. The _____ are the upper and lower ends of the confidence interval.

     Answer: confidence limits

43. 95% and 99% are common ranges for _____.

     Answer: confidence intervals

44. The _____ is generally referred to as the standard error ($\underline{SE}$) in
     research articles.

     Answer: standard deviation of the distribution of means

The essays called for in many of these problems ask
students to explain the logic behind the analysis to
someone who is familiar with the material covered in
previous chapters. Instructors may prefer, particularly
on a final exam, to ask for an explanation "to a person
who has had no exposure to statistics at all." (Of
course, such essays take students longer to write.)

45. A school principal was interested in whether a particular group of
students scored above or below the mean grade point average (GPA) at her
school. She calculated the average GPA at the school to be 2.55 with a
standard deviation of .5 and noted that the distribution was
approximately normal. She then took the average of the particular group
of students she felt may vary from the mean. In this group there were
15 students with an average GPA of 2.76.
   a. Did this group represent a population different from students in
       general at this school? (Use the .05 significance level.)
   b. Explain your analysis to a person who is familiar with hypothesis
       testing for studies in which the sample consists of a single case,
       but is unfamiliar with hypothesis testing involving a sample of more
       than one case.

Computation answer:
Cutoff (.05 level, two-tailed) = ±1.96.
Distribution of means: M=2.55, $SD2_M$=.02, SD_M=.14, shape = normal.
Z score for sample on comparison distribution = 1.50.
Do not reject the null hypothesis; study is inconclusive.

46. A professor became curious as to whether the students who turned in
their tests first scored differently from the overall mean on the test.
To examine this possibility, she marked the first 20 tests turned in
during an exam for one of her larger classes. The overall mean score on
the test was 75 with a standard deviation of 10; the scores were
approximately normally distributed. The mean score for the first 20
tests was 78.
   a. Did the people turning in their tests first score significantly
       different from the mean at the .05 level?
   b. Explain your analysis to a person who is familiar with hypothesis
       testing for studies in which the sample consists of a single case,
       but is unfamiliar with hypothesis testing involving a sample of more
       than one case.

Computation answer:
Cutoff (.05 level, two-tailed) = ±1.96.
Distribution of means: M=75, $SD2_M$=5, SD_M=2.24, shape = normal.
Z score for sample on comparison distribution = 1.34.
Do not reject the null hypothesis; study is inconclusive.

47. A school counselor was interested in checking the effect of a new program designed to reduce adjustment problems in newly transferred students. From her years of working at the school, she knew that the average score on a scale of adjustment difficulties for a transfer student was 58 with a standard deviation of 10. After the new program had been implemented, she tested 50 students and found their mean to be 52.
   a. Was this difference significant at the .01 level?
   b. Explain your analysis to a person who is familiar with hypothesis testing for studies in which the sample consists of a single case, but is unfamiliar with hypothesis testing involving a sample of more than one case.

   Computation answer:
   Cutoff (.01 level, one-tailed) = -2.33.
   Distribution of means: M=58, $SD2_M$=2, SD_M=1.41, shape = normal.
   Z score for sample on comparison distribution = -4.26.
   Reject the null hypothesis; the research hypothesis is supported.

48. A researcher was interested in whether corporate executives who exercised regularly scored lower than did corporate executives in general on a scale of stress symptoms. For corporate executives in general, the average on this test is 80 with a standard deviation of 12. The distribution is normal. The researcher then measured 20 exercising executives and found them to have a mean score of 72.
   a. Is this difference significant at the .05 level?
   b. Explain your analysis to a person who is familiar with hypothesis testing for studies in which the sample consists of a single case, but is unfamiliar with hypothesis testing involving a sample of more than one case.

   Computation answer:
   Cutoff (.05 level, one-tailed) = -1.64.
   Distribution of means: M=80, $SD2_M$=7.2, SD_M=2.68, shape = normal.
   Z score for sample on comparison distribution = -2.99.
   Reject the null hypothesis; the research hypothesis is supported.

49. A private school promoted itself by advertising that its graduates had an average SAT verbal score of 550 (with the usual standard deviation of 100). At the end of the school year the Parent-Teacher Association (PTA) decided to test this contention and obtained the SAT verbal scores for 80 graduating seniors. The average score was 532.
   a. What should the PTA conclude in regards to the school's claim if a .05 level of significance is used?
   b. Explain your analysis to a person who is familiar with hypothesis testing for studies in which the sample consists of a single case, but is unfamiliar with hypothesis testing involving a sample of more than one case.

   Computation answer:
   Cutoff (.05 level, two-tailed) = ±1.96.
   Distribution of means: M=550, $SD2_M$=125, SD_M=11.18, shape= normal.
   Z score for sample on comparison distribution = -1.61.
   Do not reject the null hypothesis; study is inconclusive.

50.   A researcher was interested in finding out how many previously-studied
      items subjects would be able to recognize within a "sound-salad" (many
      different sounds mixed together) type of presentation if the subjects
      had been given an auditory, as opposed to written, presentation of the
      items. The researcher had data from previous experimentation regarding
      the norms for the written condition and found that the subjects in the
      auditory condition scored significantly higher at the .01 level ($\underline{Z}$ score
      of 6.73). Explain this result to a person who is familiar with
      hypothesis testing for studies in which the sample consists of a single
      case, but is unfamiliar with hypothesis testing involving a sample of
      more than one case.

51.   An organizational specialist working for a large company was asked to
      find out if a newly proposed customer relations program would
      significantly reduce the number of written customer complaints. She
      implemented the program for a month in several branches and found that
      the number of complaints submitted was not significantly lower than the
      company average for that month ($\underline{Z}$ score = .10). What should she report,
      and how should she explain this result to her supervisors if they are
      familiar with hypothesis testing for studies in which the sample
      consists of a single case, but are unfamiliar with hypothesis testing
      involving a sample of more than one case.

52.   A researcher was studying the reaction time for recognizing previously
      studied ambiguous pictures. He then wanted to know if a visual acuity
      training program he had designed would speed up this time. He tested 15
      individuals that had gone through his program and found that they scored
      significantly higher than the mean ($\underline{Z}$ score = +2.25) at the .05 level.
      How would he explain this result to a person who is familiar with
      hypothesis testing for studies in which the sample consists of a single
      case, but is unfamiliar with hypothesis testing involving a sample of
      more than one case.

53.   A researcher in a mental health clinic wanted to evaluate the
      effectiveness of a new form of short-term therapy on a particular group
      of patients. He knew, from previously compiled data, the mean score on
      a scale of psychological functioning for patients who have completed the
      standard short-term therapy. He then randomly selected 20 patients to
      participate in the new therapy, waited until they had completed it, and
      then compared their mean psychological functioning score to the normal
      average after therapy. He found that the test group was not
      significantly different ($\underline{Z}$ score -.04) from the mean. How would he
      explain this result to a person who is familiar with hypothesis testing
      for studies in which the sample consists of a single case, but is
      unfamiliar with hypothesis testing involving a sample of more than one
      case.

Chapter 7
Making Sense of Statistical Significance:
Error, Power, and Effect Size

Multiple-Choice Questions

1.   Setting the significance level cutoff at .10 instead of the more usual
      .05 increases the likelihood of
*   a.   a Type I error.
      b.   a Type II error.
      c.   failing to reject the null hypothesis.
      d.   accepting the null hypothesis when, in fact, it is false.

2.   A Type I error is the result of
      a.   improper measurement techniques on the part of the researcher.
      b.   failing to reject the null hypothesis when, in fact, it is true.
*   c.   incorrectly rejecting the null hypothesis.
      d.   incorrectly accepting the null hypothesis.

3.   Setting the significance level at a very high cutoff (such as 20%)
      increases the chances of
      a.   getting a nonsignificant result.
      b.   failing to reject the null hypothesis.
*   c.   a Type I error.
      d.   a Type II error.

4.   Failing to reject the null hypothesis when the research hypothesis is
      true is referred to as
      a.   the probability of rejection.
      b.   the error term.
      c.   a Type I error.
*   d.   a Type II error.

5.   Failing to determine that the research hypothesis is supported by the
      evidence of the sample when in fact the research hypothesis is true is
      called
      a.   a Type I error.
*   b.   a Type II error.
      c.   a strong experimental design.
      d.   a lack of foresight on the part of the experimenter.

6.   Type II errors concern scientists because
*   a.   it could mean that a good theory or beneficial practice is not used.
      b.   it means that the experiment must be repeated to confirm the
           positive result.
      c.   rejecting the null hypothesis should only occur when the research
           hypothesis is true.
      d.   future researchers might build entire theories based on a
           mistakenly significant result.

7. Conventional levels of significance have been set at 5% and 1% in order to
   a. maximally protect against Type I error.
   b. maximally protect against Type II error.
 * c. compromise between the risk of a Type I or Type II error.
   d. none of the above--these levels were set historically in an arbitrary way without regard to issues associated with Type I or Type II error.

8. It is useful to understand statistical power for which of the following reasons?
   a. Determining the number of subjects to use in an experiment.
   b. Making sense of psychological findings in the literature.
   c. Understanding why results that are not statistically significant may still be important.
 * d. All of the above.

9. Even if the research hypothesis is true, an experiment may fail to yield significant results because
   a. sampling error and other uncontrolled variables may cause too little variance in the population.
 * b. the sample that happens to be selected from the population being studied may not be extreme enough to provide a clear case for rejecting the null hypothesis.
   c. there is always a 5% (or 1%) chance of rejecting the null hypothesis in any given population, and finding a sample that falls within that small percentage by chance is fairly rare.
   d. just as there is a probability of rejecting the null hypothesis, there is always a chance that it must be accepted.

10. In the situation where the null hypothesis is true, the distribution from which the sample was taken is
 * a. the same as the known population's distribution.
   b. to the right of the original population distribution.
   c. to the left of the original population distribution.
   d. either to the right or left of the original distribution, depending on whether the mean of the sample is higher or lower than the mean of the original population.

11. Standard power tables are useful for
 * a. directly determining the power of an experiment.
   b. determining the predicted score (but not the variance) for the group exposed to the experimental manipulation.
   c. determining the predicted effect size of a proposed experiment.
   d. determining the probability of falsely accepting the research hypothesis.

12. The effect size and the number of subjects are two important determinants of
   a. the minimum significant result.
   b. experimental significance.
 * c. power.
   d. alpha.

13. Having a very small amount of overlap between the experimental and the comparison distribution
    a. reduces the power.
  * b. increases the power.
    c. does not affect the power.
    d. indicates that the two cannot be effectively compared.

14. Effect size can be defined as
    a. the amount of statistical importance a particular finding carries in the psychological community.
    b. the sum of squared deviations divided by the mean.
    c. the mean divided by the sum of squared deviations.
  * d. the degree to which the experimental manipulation separates the two populations.

15. The degree to which the experimental manipulation separates the two populations of individual scores is called
    a. experimental effectiveness.
    b. power.
  * c. the effect size.
    d. the significance level.

16. One way of affecting power of a planned experiment by altering the amount of variance within the two distributions is to
    a. use the variance of the experimental group instead of the variance from the comparison distribution.
    b. plan to exclude any scores in the sample that are not outliers.
  * c. use more precise measures.
    d. reduce the number of items on any questionnaires employed.

17. When the standard deviation of the original population is small, the experiment tends to
  * a. have a higher level of power.
    b. have a lower level of power.
    c. show a less significant difference between the two populations.
    d. have a high level of Type II error.

18. The formula for calculating effect size for a study comparing the means of two populations is Effect Size=
    a. (Population 1 $\underline{M}$ + Population 2 $\underline{M}$)(Population $\underline{SD}$).
    b. (Population $\underline{SD}$)(Population 2 $\underline{M}$) / Population 1 $\underline{M}$.
    c. (Population 1 $\underline{M}$ + Population 2 $\underline{M}$) / Population $\underline{SD}$.
  * d. (Population 1 $\underline{M}$ - Population 2 $\underline{M}$) / Population $\underline{SD}$

19. (Population 1 $\underline{M}$ - Population 2 $\underline{M}$) / Population $\underline{SD}$ is a formula for calculating
    a. power.
  * b. effect size.
    c. the variance of the distribution of means.
    d. the combined standard deviation.

Test Bank

20. One important advantage of using effect sizes is that
    a. they tell us all the relevant parameters of an experimenter's data set.
    b. they are frequently reported along with the means of samples.
    c. they are related to the level of statistical significance in an experiment, allowing us to create meta-studies.
    * d. they are a standardized score, making study-to-study comparisons easier.

21. Cohen has proposed some effect-size conventions based on the effects observed in psychology research in general because
    a. researchers frequently need to assess whether the effect size that they have obtained will allow them to reject the null hypothesis.
    * b. it is usually difficult to know how big an effect to expect from a given experiment.
    c. Cohen developed these scales and knows everything about them.
    d. they are more accurate than calculating a minimum meaningful difference.

22. The effect size conventions proposed by Cohen are useful to researchers for
    a. predicting the value of the dependent variable to use for the experimental condition.
    b. evaluating previous research to determine the likelihood it is statistically significant.
    c. predicting the effect their independent variable will have on various populations.
    * d. determining the power of a planned experiment.

23. According to Cohen's conventions, for research that compares means, a large effect size, in which only about 53% of the populations overlap, would be
    a. .5
    b. .7
    * c. .8
    d. .9

24. Effect size is one of the two major factors that contribute to power. Another factor is
    a. the sample's standard deviation.
    b. the minimum meaningful difference.
    * c. the sample size.
    d. the mean of the known population.

25. An experimenter may not be able to manipulate the effect size of an experiment to increase power. Another variable that the experimenter can usually easily manipulate to increase power is
    * a. the sample size.
    b. the beta level.
    c. the population parameters.
    d. the sample mean.

26. In actual practice, the usual reason for determining power before conducting a study is to
   a. eliminate the possibility that a mistake may occur.
   b. ensure that regardless of whether the research hypothesis is true, the experiment will yield a significant result.
 * c. determine the number of subjects needed to achieve a reasonable level of power.
   d. recognize the likelihood that the experiment will need to be repeated.

27. By starting with the effect size and the desired level of power, a researcher can work backwards through the power formula to determine the
   a. minimum meaningful difference.
 * b. number of subjects needed.
   c. population distribution.
   d. the alpha level of the experiment.

28. What effect will using a one-tailed test over a two-tailed test have on power (presuming the true population difference is in the expected direction)?
 * a. It will increase power.
   b. It will have no effect on power.
   c. It will decrease power.
   d. Power can not be calculated if a one-tailed test is used.

29. If the research hypothesis is true, but the study testing it has a low level of power,
   a. there is a high probability that the study will have a significant result.
 * b. the probability of obtaining a significant result is low.
   c. the null hypothesis will almost certainly be rejected.
   d. beta is necessarily low.

30. For an experiment to be worth conducting, Cohen suggests that a general rule is that it should have an 80% level of power. However, if an experiment is costly or difficult to conduct, a researcher would probably
 * a. want a higher level of power.
   b. settle for a slightly lower level of power.
   c. not calculate power levels.
   d. give up psychology and take up surfing.

31. One way of decreasing the standard deviation of the distribution of means in a planned study, thereby increasing power, is to have a larger number of subjects. Another would be to
   a. use a more stringent alpha level.
   b. use the sample variance in place of the variance of the population.
   c. change the minimum meaningful difference.
 * d. use a less diverse population.

Test Bank

32. Effect size is an important tool for evaluating effective research
   because
   a. it indicates the degree to which a result is statistically
      significant.
* b. it allows us to assess the magnitude of the statistical effect.
   c. it limits variance and therefore increases power.
   d. it is always smaller than the variance.

33. Practical significance is a combination of statistical significance and
* a. effect size.
   b. sample size.
   c. the population parameters.
   d. the amount over or under that level that the sample scored.

34. In statistics, we cannot state that the research hypothesis is ever
   definitely false. However, if one fails to reject the null hypothesis
   in a study which has a high level of power, this allows us to
   a. suspect that the research hypothesis may still be true.
* b. conclude that the research hypothesis is most likely false.
   c. make no statements about the research hypothesis.
   d. reject the notion that the effect size has anything to do with
      statistical significance.

35. A statistical method, developed in the past couple of decades, for
   combining the results of independent studies is called
* a. meta-analysis.
   b. power analysis.
   c. regression analysis.
   d. retrospective analysis.

36. A meta-analysis on the effect of relaxation techniques on anxiety
   levels found that
   a. all relaxation techniques yielded similar effects.
* b. there were clear differences in the effect sizes associated with
      different relaxation and mediation procedures.
   c. progressive relaxation was the most effective.
   d. relaxation techniques do not affect anxiety levels significantly.

Fill-In Questions

37. Rejecting the null hypothesis when in fact it is true is a(n)
   _____.

   Answer: Type I error

38. A Type I error occurs when you obtain a statistically significant result
   when in fact _____.

   Answer: the research hypothesis is false, the null hypothesis is true

39. p < .05 means that there is less than a 5% chance of making a(n) _____.

   Answer: Type I error

40. Using the .01 level of significance instead of the .05 level decreases the chance of making a(n) _____.

    Answer: Type I error

41. A(n) _____ occurs when you fail to reject the null hypothesis when in fact it is false.

    Answer: Type II error

42. Researchers try to avoid making a(n) _____ because it could mean failing to make use of a practical procedure or useful theory.

    Answer: Type II error

43. A researcher determines the _____ of a planned experiment in order to determine how likely it is that the result will be significant if in fact the research hypothesis is true.

    Answer: power

44. Most of the time researchers determine the power of a planned experiment by using a(n) _____.

    Answer: table, power table

45. The _____ of a study is the difference in the population means divided by the population standard deviation.

    Answer: effect size

46. Changing the procedures of a study so that it decreases the _____ of the population increases the effect size.

    Answer: standard deviation, variance, variation

47. The effect size of a study is a good indicator of its practical importance because, unlike statistical significance, it is not affected by _____.

    Answer: the number of subjects, sample size, $\underline{N}$

48. The _____ is a statistic that combines two of the main influences on power, the expected difference between populations and the population standard deviation.

    Answer: effect size

49. One way of understanding _____ is in terms of the degree of separation between populations due to the independent variable.

    Answer: effect size

50.   Effect Size = (Population 1 $\underline{M}$ - Population 2 $\underline{M}$) / _____ .

Answer: Population $\underline{SD}$

51.   Cohen's effect-size conventions for $\underline{d}$ for a small, medium, and large effect are _____, _____, _____ .

Answer: .2; .5; .8

52.   Cohen's _____ for effect size are based on what is typical in psychology research.

Answer: conventions

53.   According to Cohen, a good general rule for when it is worthwhile to conduct a study is when power is at least _____ %.

Answer: 80

54.   Power is affected by sample size, effect size, whether a one- or two-tailed test is used, ___, and type of hypothesis-testing procedure used.

Answer: alpha, significance level

55.   Increasing sample size _____ power.

Answer: increases

56.   In studies using a very large number of subjects, it is common to get statistically significant results that have a very small _____ .

Answer: effect size

57.   A researcher would use _____ to combine results of several different studies.

Answer: meta-analysis

Problems and Essays

    The essays called for in many of these problems ask students to explain the logic behind the analysis to someone who is familiar with the material covered in previous chapters. Instructors may prefer, particularly on a final exam, to ask for an explanation "to a person who has had no exposure to statistics at all." (Of course, such essays take students much longer to write.)

58.   A researcher is interested in comparing the SAT scores of a group of gifted children (who are expected to score higher) with the population mean. Explain what a Type I and Type II error would be in this study. (Be sure to state your answer in terms of the variables of this particular study.)

Test Bank

59. A study is conducted of whether students with fewer extracurricular activities have a higher GPA than students in general. Explain what a Type I and Type II error would be in this study. (Be sure to state your answer in terms of the variables of this particular study.)

60. A study examines whether students who have been in a theology class score higher on a scale of religious beliefs than the average person. Explain what a Type I and Type II error would be in this study. (Be sure to state your answer in terms of the variables of this particular study.)

61. An education researcher conducts a study of whether children with a large vocabulary scored higher on an intelligence test than the average. Explain what a Type I and Type II error would be in this study. (Be sure to state your answer in terms of the variables of this particular study.)

62. A study was designed to compare two ethnic groups on a measure of a particular personality trait. It used a large number of subjects in order to obtain a high level of power. The study did find a significant result, but the difference between the means was very small (small effect size). What conclusion could you make regarding the difference between the two groups on the personality scale? (Keep your answer to a sentence or two.)

63. A public school system wanted to know whether the reading levels of the students at two of its schools were different. The ensuing study tested an enormous number of students and concluded that School A's students did score significantly better than those of School B. The difference between the means of the two schools, however, was very small. What should you conclude regarding the difference in reading levels between the two schools? (Keep your answer to a sentence or two.)

64. A journalist was interested in college students' knowledge of current events. He compared a large group of college students to the general public using a questionnaire about recent items in the news. In this study, he tested large numbers of people and had a very high level of power. No significant result was found, and the null hypothesis was not rejected. What should you conclude about the current events knowledge of college students in comparison to the general public? And why? (Keep your answer to a sentence or two.)

65. A political consulting firm designed a study to test whether fans at a rock concert (held in the U.S.) would rate the President's performance lower than the general public. They were able to poll a vast number of subjects, so the study had a very high level of power. Surprisingly, however, there was not a significant difference and the researcher was unable to reject the null hypothesis. What should you conclude regarding the fans' rating of the President's performance? And why? (Keep your answer to a sentence or two.)

66. The human-factors department at a large corporation was asked to find out if ergonomically designed workstations really improved the speed and accuracy at which employees were able to perform their work. Thus, the department was planning to test a group of employees with the new workstations and compare measures of their speed and accuracy to the means for the company. What are three things that the human-factors department can do to keep the power of their experiment high?

67. A researcher is planning a study to test whether people are more likely to call events "natural" that are otherwise frequently attributed to "supernatural forces" if they have seen a particular film critical of "superstitions." What are three things that the researcher could do to keep the power of the study high?

68. A study is reported in which 15 professional artists were compared to the general population on their ability to solve 3-dimensional puzzles. There was not a significant difference at the .01 level, so the researchers were unable to reject the null hypothesis. Later, an analysis indicated that the power level had been quite low for the study. What are three things that could have improved the power for this study?

69. A study was designed to test whether high-level executives possess a greater motivation for success than the population average. The result was that the null hypothesis was not rejected at the .01 level and no significant difference was found. A later analysis of the experiment indicated that there was a very low level of power. What are three things that could have improved the power for this study?

Test Bank

Multiple-Choice Questions

1. In the formula for estimating the population variance from the
    sample, the sum of squared deviations is divided by
    a. the number of subjects in the sample.
    *   b. the number of subjects in the sample minus one.
    c. the number of subjects in the population.
    d. the number of subjects in the population minus one.

2. If a sample has 27 cases, the degrees of freedom used in the formula to
    estimate the population variance would be
    *   a. 26.
    b. 27.
    c. 27^2.
    d. $\sqrt{27}$.

3. When estimating the variance of a population from the sample, you can
    not use the sample's variance directly because
    a. it is based on using absolute deviations.
    b. it is based on using squared deviations.
    c. it tends to be slightly too large.
    *   d. it tends to be slightly too small.

4. All of the following apply to estimating the population variance (as
    opposed to knowing the population variance) EXCEPT
    a. in the formula to compute the population variance, the sum of
        squared deviations is divided by N-1 instead of N.
    b. to test hypotheses, you use a t test.
    c. on the curve of the comparison distribution, (i.e., the curve for
        the t test), extreme means are more likely than when using a normal
        curve.
    *   d. greater accuracy can be obtained from fewer samples.

5. Which of the following is true about t distributions?
    a. There are exactly 10 categories of t distributions.
    b. For any given sample size, there are between two and N-1 appropriate
        t distributions.
    *   c. The larger the sample size, the more a t distribution resembles a
        normal curve.
    d. t distributions are generally bimodal.

6. When estimating the population's variance from the scores in the sample,
    you should
    a. look on a special table to find the estimated variance.
    b. proceed normally, but interpret the results with caution.
    *   c. divide the sum of squared deviations by N-1 instead of N.
    d. multiply the sample's variance by the degrees of freedom.

7.   If you know the sample's variance but not the population's variance,
      a. you can look the population's variance up on a table.
      b. you can conduct a t test anyway, because variance is unrelated to
          the process.
      c. you should avoid making inferences based on your data.
  *   d. you can estimate the population's variance from the scores in the
          sample.

8.   Which of the following is true regarding biased and unbiased estimates
      of the population variance?
      a. An example of an unbiased estimate is the variance of a sample; a
          typical biased estimate is the researcher's initial expectation,
          prior to sampling.
      b. There is only one biased estimate--the researcher's expected
          findings; there are several unbiased estimates.
      c. A biased estimate is preferred to an unbiased estimate when the
          population is not normally distributed.
  *   d. A sample's variance is a biased estimate of the population's
          variance, but a slight change in the variance formula yields an
          unbiased estimate.

9.   What is the main difference between Z score and a t score?
      a. t scores are used when data are analyzed using a one-tailed test.
  *   b. t scores are used when the population variance is unknown.
      c. t scores are used whenever the sample size is greater than 30.
      d. t scores are only used when inferences are made about other samples.

Test Bank

10-13 A school counselor is interested in whether the level of depression in fourth graders in a particular class of 20 students differs from that of fourth graders in general at her school. On the test, a score of 10 indicates severe depression, while a score of 0 reflects the absence of depression. From reports, she is able to find about past testing. Fourth graders at her school usually score 5 on the scale, but the variation is not known. Her sample of 20 fifth graders has a mean depression score of 4.4.

10. If she calculates the unbiased estimate of the population's variance to be 15, what is the variance of the distribution of means?
   * a. 15/20 = 0.75
   b. 15/19 = 0.79
   c. 225/20 = 11.25
   d. 225/19 = 11.84

11. If the counselor were testing the null hypothesis that fourth graders in this class did <u>not differ</u> from fourth graders in general at the school in level of depression, and, based on her data, she calculated a t score of -.20, what decision should she make regarding the null hypothesis?
   a. Reject it
   * b. Fail to reject it
   c. Postpone any decisions until a more conclusive study could be conducted.
   d. There is not enough information given to make a decision.

12. Suppose the counselor had wanted to test the null hypothesis that fourth graders in this class were <u>less</u> depressed than those at the school generally. If she calculated her t score to be -.20, what decision should she make regarding the null hypothesis?
   a. Reject it.
   * b. Fail to reject it.
   c. Postpone any decisions until a more conclusive study could be conducted.
   d. There is not enough information given to make a decision.

13. If the standard deviation of her sample was 0.85, what was the effect size ($\underline{d}$)?
   a. 5/.85 = 5.88
   b. .85/5 = 0.17
   * c. (5-4.4)/.85 = 0.71
   d. .85/(5-4.4) = 1.42

14-16 Professor Juarez thinks the students in one of her classes this quarter are more creative than most students at this university. A previous study found that students at this university had a mean score of 35 on a standard creativity test. Professor Juarez finds that her class scores an average of 40 on this scale, with an estimated population standard deviation of 7. The standard deviation of the distribution of means comes out to 1.63.

14. What is the t score?
   a. (40-35)/7 = .71
*   b. (40-35)/1.63 = 3.07
   c. (40-35)/7² = 5/49 = .10
   d. (40-35)/1.63² = 5/2.66 = 1.88

15. What effect size did Professor Juarez find?
*   a. (40-35)/7 = .71
   b. (40-35)/1.63 = 3.07
   c. (40-35)/7² = 5/49 = .10
   d. (40-35)/1.63² = 5/2.66 = 1.88

16. If Professor Juarez had 30 students in her class, and she wanted to test her hypothesis using the 5% level of significance, what cutoff t score would she use? (You should be able to figure this out without a table--only one answer is in the correct region.)
   a. 9.635
*   b. 1.699
   c. -0.113
   d. -2.500

17. In which situation below would you use a t test for dependent means?
   a. To compare the level of honesty (based on an honesty scale) in politicians to the level of honesty in students.
*   b. To compare the level of reading comprehension of students at the beginning of a speed-reading class to their level of reading comprehension at the end of the class.
   c. To determine the correlation between liking for coffee and tendency to be a "night person" among a group of students.
   d. To compare the scores on a tolerance-of-diversity measure between two sororities.

18. Difference scores are usually used with
   a. a t test for a single sample.
*   b. a t test for dependent means.
   c. a t test for independent means.
   d. all of the above.

19. If 15 subjects take a pretest and a posttest with a mean change score of 1.5, and if the standard deviation of the comparison distribution is calculated to be .5, what is the t score?
   a. 1.5/(15-1) = 0.11
   b. 1.5/15 = 0.10
*   c. 1.5/.5 = 3.00
   d. 1.5/(.5*(15-1)) = 0.21

20-22 A school counselor claims that he has developed a technique to reduce pre-studying procrastination in students. He has students time their procrastination for a week and uses this as a pretest (before) indicator of procrastination. Students then attend a workshop in which they are instructed to do a specific warming up exercise for studying by focusing on a pleasant activity. For the next week, students again time their procrastination. The counselor then uses the time from this week as the posttest (after) measure.

20. If the counselor wants to examine whether there is a change of any kind (either an increase or decrease) in procrastination after attending his workshop, what would be the appropriate description of "Population 2" (the population to which the population his sample represents is being compared)?
   a. People whose posttest scores will be lower than their pretest scores.
   b. People whose change scores will be 0 or greater than 0.
*   c. People whose change scores will be 0.
   d. People whose change scores will be less than their pretest scores.

21. Presume the counselor wants to examine whether there is a change (either an increase or decrease) in procrastination after attending his workshop. If the counselor tests 10 subjects using the 0.05 level, what cutoff t score(s) will he use? (You should be able to figure this out without a table.)
   a. -2.62, 0, +2.62
   b. +2.262
   c. -2.262, 0
*   d. -2.262, +2.262

22. Suppose the counselor found the sum of squared deviations from the mean of the sample to be 135. Given that he tested 10 people, what would the estimated population variance be?
   a. 135/10 = 13.5
*   b. 135/9 = 15.0
   c. 10/135 = 0.07
   d. 9/135 = 0.07

23. A researcher conducts a t test for dependent means with 10 subjects. If the estimated population variance of the change scores is 20, what would the variance of the distribution of the means of change scores be?
*   a. 20/10 = 2.0
   b. 20/9 = 2.2
   c. 400/10 = 40.0
   d. 400/9 = 44.4

24-26.   Suppose a researcher conducts a t test for dependent means in which
         it is predicted that there will be a decrease in unemployment from
         before to after a particular job-skills training program. The
         cutoff t needed is -1.833. The standard deviation of the
         distribution of means of change scores is 2.0 and the mean change
         score for the sample studied is an <u>increase</u> of 5.2.

    24.   What is the t score?
           a. 5.2/-1.833 = -2.84
           b. 2/5.2 = .38
    *   c. 5.2/2 = 2.60
           d. 2²/5.2 = .77

    25.   What is the effect size?
           a. 5.2/-1.833 = -2.84; large
           b. 2/5.2 = .38; approximately medium
           c. 5.2/2 = 2.60; large
    *   d. It can not be determined without also knowing the
               population standard deviation or its estimate.

    26.   What is the appropriate conclusion?
           a. Reject null hypothesis.
    *   b. Do not reject null hypothesis.
           c. It can not be determined without also knowing the
               population mean.
           d. It can not be determined without also knowing the
               population standard deviation or its estimate.

27. Which of the following poses a serious problem when using a t test for
     dependent means, one-tailed?
     a. The population of difference scores is even moderately different
         from normal.
     b. The sample consists of less than 40 subjects.
 *   c. There is a ceiling effect in the test, which is likely to make the
         population of difference scores highly skewed.
     d. Pretest and posttest scores are highly correlated with each other.

28. Suppose you are interested in whether you can train subjects to remember
     more dreams per night. Based on preliminary research, you have reason
     to expect your training technique will produce a slight increase in the
     number of dreams per night (that is, a small effect size). Based on
     Table 8.8 in the text, if in fact it is true that you can train subjects
     to remember more dreams per night, and you conduct the study using 50
     subjects, what is your probability of getting a significant result?
     Assume you are conducting a one-tailed test at the .05 significance
     level and using a t test for dependent means.
     a. .09
     b. .29
     c. .32
 *   d. .40

29. What is considered a medium effect size when conducting a t test for
     dependent means?
     a. .20
     b. .40
 *   c. .50
     d. .80

30. Refer to Table 8.8 in the text. If you want to conduct a study in which you hope to detect a small effect size at the .05 level, using a $\underline{t}$ test for dependent means, how many subjects do you need for 80% power if you conduct a two-tailed test?
*   a. 196
    b. 156
    c. 14
    d. 12

31. Why do studies using difference scores tend to have larger effect sizes than studies using other research designs?
    a. There is a long-standing procedural bias in psychology to set up studies involving dependent means in such a way as to artificially favor large effect sizes.
*   b. The standard deviation of difference scores is usually low.
    c. Because subjects provide their own baseline, variance becomes a wildcard, causing the effect size to increase.
    d. Because studies with dependent means usually use a large number of subjects, larger effect sizes are easily detected.

32.   Counselor Troi wants to see if she can improve the level of ESP (Extra Sensory Perception) in subjects by instructing them in methods of relaxation. She designs a study in which 50 subjects are shown the back of a card and asked to "guess" what symbol (a triangle, square, or circle) is on the face of the card. Each subject will see a series of such cards, and the accuracy rate will be recorded. Then all subjects will attend Counselor Troi's relaxation seminar. Finally, they will be tested once more with the cards. To check if her seminar improves ESP, Counselor Troi plans to subtract post-seminar scores from pre-seminar scores, then conduct a t test for dependent means. Suppose Counselor Troi decides to conduct a one-tailed test in which she predicts an increase in ESP. The cutoff t score in her situation is 2.540 and her t test yields a t score of -4.8 (pretest minus posttest--that is, this is represents a decrease). Would her result be significant?
      a. Yes, -4.8 is clearly significant.
*   b. No, the research hypothesis indicates that only positive t scores would be significant
      c. Can't say without also knowing the number of subjects.
      d. Can't say--the null hypothesis is too vague.

33.   Which of the following is the most likely way for results of a t test to be presented in a research article for a study with 25 subjects?
      a. t test (25) < significant.
      b. t test(25) = 3.01, p <.05.
*   c. t(24) = 2.94, p < .01.
      d. t(24) < significant.

34.   A research article reports results of a study using a t test for dependent means as "t(16) = 2.67, p < .05." This means
      a. the result is not significant.
      b. there were 16 subjects.
      c. the t score was 16.
*   d. the t score was 2.67.

35.   A research article reports results of a study using a t test for dependent means as "t(38) = 3.11, p < .01." This means
*   a. the result is significant.
      b. the result is not significant.
      c. you can assume a one-tailed test was used.
      d. there were 39 degrees of freedom.

Test Bank

36-37 A research article included the following table:

Mean Score on Four Questionnaire Scales Before and After Exposure to the Experimental Manipulation.

Questionnaire	Before	After	Change
Dominance	18.42	16.31	-2.11
Independence	17.25	21.38	4.13**
Conformity	18.97	17.20	-1.77*
Nurturance	16.11	13.89	-2.22*

*$p < .05$ **$p < .01$

36. Which of the following differences was NOT significant?
*   a. Dominance.
    b. Independence
    c. Conformity and Nurturance.
    d. None--all were clearly significant.

37. Which of the following is most likely to be true given the information on this table?
    a. The hypothesis testing probably used one-tailed tests.
    b. The various scales all probably had just about the same population variances.
    c. The t scores are all larger than the raw change scores.
*   d. The hypothesis testing probably used a t test for dependent means.

38. Who invented "Student's" t test?
    a. Dr. Phil Guinness.
*   b. William Gosset.
    c. Jacob Cohen.
    d. Joan Guinness.

39. What was the main criticism of the Lankeshire Milk Experiment by the inventor of the t test?
    a. He or she was not consulted in planning the project.
    b. Forcing children to drink milk was unethical.
*   c. The same results could have been found with far fewer subjects.
    d. An additional posttest needed to be conducted to justify the government's conclusions.

Fill-In Questions

40. A _____ test is used to reach a decision about the null hypothesis when the population variance is NOT known.

Answer: t

41. The variance of a sample is a(n) _____ estimator of the population variance.

Answer: biased

Test Bank

307

42. If in a particular study the sum of squared deviations from the mean for the sample is 12 and there are 4 subjects, what is the estimated population variance? _____

    Answer: 4

43. Given a particular number of degrees of freedom, there is(are) _____ t distribution(s).

    Answer: one

44. The more degrees of freedom, the closer a t distribution is to the ____.

    Answer: normal curve, normal distribution

45. To find the score at which the null hypothesis will be rejected, you look on a table of t distributions. But first, you need to know the significance level, the degrees of freedom, and _____.

    Answer: whether it is a one- or two-tailed test

46. When calculating the variance of the distribution of means based on an estimated population variance, you divide the estimated population variance by _____.

    Answer: the sample size, N ($N-1$ is wrong)

47. When calculating the variance of the distribution of means based on an estimated population variance in a study with 20 subjects, you divide the estimated population variance by _____.

    Answer: 20 (19 is wrong)

48. Using the formula, (Sample M - Pop M)/S_M, you can calculate the _____.

    Answer: t score

49. In the formula (Sample M - Pop M)/S_M, S_M is the _____.

    Answer: standard deviation of the distribution of means, standard deviation of the comparison distribution

50. In a single-sample t test, suppose the mean of your sample is 95, the mean of Population 2 is 75, and the standard deviation of the distribution of means is 5. What is the t score? _____

    Answer: 4

51. Testing subjects before and after an experimental manipulation is called a _____ design.

    Answer: repeated-measures, within-subjects, pretest-posttest

Test Bank

52. If pretest and posttest scores are obtained from subjects, before conducting a t test for dependent means, you must first combine the two sets of scores into one set by computing _____.

Answer: difference scores, change scores

53. The _____ is assumed to be 0 when a t test is conducted using difference scores.

Answer: mean of Population 2, mean of the population to which the population represented by the sample is being compared, mean of the distribution of means, mean of the comparison distribution, μ_2, μ_M

54. In a t test for dependent means in which 10 subjects are each tested twice, making a total of 10 before scores and 10 after scores, what are the degrees of freedom? _____

Answer: 9

55. In a t test for dependent means, if the mean change score is 12 and the standard deviation of the distribution of means is 6, what is the t score? _____

Answer: 2

56. When conducting a t test for dependent means, an effect size of _____ is considered to be medium.

Answer: .5

57. When conducting a t test for dependent means, an effect size of _____ is considered to be small.

Answer: .2

58. The most common circumstance that creates a serious problem (in terms of meeting assumptions) when using the t test for dependent means is when the population is highly _____ and you are conducting a one-tailed test.

Answer: skewed

59. When the results of a t test are presented in research articles, the _____ directly follow(s) the "t" and is(are) in parentheses.

Answer: degrees of freedom, df

60. Student's t was created by _____.

Answer: William S. Gosset

Problems and Essays

Note. The essays called for in these problems ask students to explain the logic behind their answers to someone unfamiliar with the material covered since Chapter 7--that is, they are only asked to cover material relating to the t test. Instructors may prefer, particularly on a final exam, to ask for an explanation "to a person who has had no exposure to statistics at all." (However, such essays should be used sparingly in exams as they will necessarily take students much longer to write.)

61. A consumer researcher was asked to test a claim by a franchise swimming instruction program that they could teach the average 7-year-old to swim across an Olympic-size pool in less than 2 hours. The researcher arranged for eight randomly selected 7-year-old children to take instruction at this school and kept careful record of how long it took each child. The times (in minutes) were 60, 120, 110, 80, 70, 90, 100, and 130. What should the researcher conclude?
   a. Conduct a t test for a single sample (120 minutes is the "known" population mean) using the .05 significance level.
   b. Explain your analysis to a person who fully understands hypothesis testing involving a single sample and a known population, but has never been exposed to t tests of any kind.

Computation answer:
t needed (df = 7), p < .05, 1-tailed = -1.895.
M=95; S^2=600; S_M=8.67; t=(95-120)/8.67=2.88.
Reject Null hypothesis.

62. An industrial researcher is a consultant to a large chain of frozen yoghurt stores. Industry reports show that the average number of complaints received by management for a one-month period at this time of year is 6.5 (the variance is not known). Seven of this chain's stores are randomly selected to keep records of complaints received over a one month period. The numbers of complaints are 4, 8, 9, 0, 3, 5, and 6. Does this chain get a different amount of complaints than yoghurt stores in general?
   a. What should the psychologist conclude (use the .05 level)?
   b. Explain your analysis to a person who fully understands hypothesis testing involving a single sample and a known population, but has never been exposed to t tests of any kind.

Computation answer:
t needed (df = 6), p < .05, 2-tailed = ±2.447.
M=5; S^2=9.33; S_M=1.15; t=(5-6.5)/1.15=-1.30.
Do NOT reject the null hypothesis; results are inconclusive.

Test Bank

63. It is known that on a particular laboratory task, it takes the average person 2.5 s. Wondering whether older people are slower (take longer) on this task, the researcher tested 30 randomly selected 80 year olds. Their mean time was 2.7 s, with an estimated population standard deviation of 1.4 s.
   a. What should the researcher conclude (use the .05 level)?
   b. Explain your analysis to a person who fully understands hypothesis testing involving a single sample and a known population, but has never been exposed to t tests of any kind.

   Computation answer:
   t needed (df = 29), $p < .05$, 1-tailed = 1.699.
   $M=2.7$; $S^2=1.96$; $S_M=.07$; $t=(2.7-2.5)/.07=2.86$.
   Reject the null hypothesis.

64. As part of a larger cross-cultural study on the development of infants, a researcher compared 20 Brazilian 10-month-olds to an average of 10-month-olds from a number of other countries. He measured the amount of time the infants spent examining one of three objects--a fuzzy teddy bear, a pacifier, and a stick of sugar cane. Then he conducted three t tests, one for each object, comparing the two populations.

   As it turned out, the packets the researcher had mailed to the various countries had not contained clear directions for this portion of the study. As a result, many of the countries reported only the mean times to him, omitting the raw data. Thus he was forced to estimate the population variance from the data of the Brazilian sample, which contained complete information, since he had conducted it himself. The table and his descriptions of the results as he presented them in his report are presented below:

   Mean Time (in Seconds) Infants Spent Examining Objects

Object	Brazil	Average for Other Countries	Difference
Teddy Bear	85	83	2
Pacifier	46	41	5
Sugar Cane	18	37	-19*

   *$p < .05$

   This study does not support the notion that Brazilian 10-month-olds differ from other 10-month-olds as far as the amount of time they spend examining pacifiers and teddy bears, $t(4)=.67$, ns; $t(4)=1.03$, ns, respectively. However, Brazilian babies examined sugar cane for a significantly shorter amount of time, $t(4)=5.81$, $p < .05$. One possible explanation for this finding is that Brazilian babies might spend more time studying sugar cane because they have never or rarely seen it before.

   Explain and interpret these findings to a person who understands hypothesis testing involving a single sample and a known population, but has never been exposed to t tests of any kind.

65. A study was designed to test the effects of science fiction movies on subjects' belief in the supernatural. A scale was designed to measure the degree that a subject believes in the supernatural (high scores indicate high levels of belief). Seven subjects responded to the scale before and after watching Blade Runner, a popular science fiction movie. Subjects' scores are listed below. Assume that the researcher had reason to expect subjects to believe less in the supernatural after watching the movie.

Belief-in-Supernatural Scores, Before and After Watching
Science Fiction Movie

Subject	Before	After
A	3	3
B	5	3
C	9	6
D	6	8
E	7	8
F	5	2
G	4	1

a. Conduct a t test for dependent means (using the .01 significance level).
b. Explain your analysis to a person who fully understands hypothesis testing involving a single sample and a known population, but has never been exposed to t tests of any kind.

Computation answer:
t needed ($df = 6$), $p < .01$, 1-tailed = 3.143.
Difference scores = 0, -2, -3, +2, +1, -3, -3
$M = -1.14$; $S^2 = 4.48$; $S_M = .8$; $t = -1.43$.
Do NOT reject the null hypothesis; results are inconclusive.

Test Bank

66. An organizational specialist is hired as a consultant to a person planning to open a coffee house for college students, who wants to know if her customers will drink more coffee if she decorates in a Paris motif or in a San Francisco motif. To test this, the researcher sets up two similar rooms, but with the two different motifs, then arranges to have eight students spend an afternoon in each room while being allowed to drink all the coffee they like. (The order in which they sit in the rooms is rotated, so that half do their first afternoon in the Paris room and half in the San Francisco room.) The amount each subject drinks is recorded below:

Cups of Coffee Consumed by Motif

Subject	Paris	San Francisco
A	8.5	8.4
B	4.3	4.6
C	2.0	1.7
D	7.8	7.3
E	7.0	7.2
F	9.1	7.4
G	3.3	3.0
H	3.5	3.5

a. Determine whether there is a significant difference (use the .05 level) between the number of cups of coffee consumed in the two rooms.
b. Explain your analysis to a person who fully understands hypothesis testing involving a single sample and a known population, but has never been exposed to t tests of any kind.

Computation answer:
t needed ($df = 7$), $p < .05$, 2-tailed = 2.365
Difference scores = .1, -.3, .3, .5, -.2, 1.7, .3, 0
$M=.3$; $S^2=.39$; $S_M=.22$; $t=1.36$.
Do NOT reject the null hypothesis; results are inconclusive.

67. A researcher administered a scale measuring concern for farm workers (high scores mean high concern) to seven subjects before and after they attended a film about union organization of farm workers. Results are shown below:

Scores on the Concern Measure, Before and After Film

Subject	Before	After
A	17	20
B	7	4
C	10	11
D	13	15
E	8	5
F	9	8
G	11	14

a. Do the data support the hypothesis that the class affected concern for the lives of farm workers (use the .05 level)?
b. Explain your analysis to a person who fully understands hypothesis testing involving a single sample and a known population, but has never been exposed to t tests of any kind.

Computation answer:
t needed ($df = 6$), $p < .05$, 2-tailed = ±2.447.
Difference scores = 3, -3, 1, 2, -3, -1, 3.
$M=.29$; $S^2=6.90$; $S_M=.99$; $t=.29$.
Do NOT reject the null hypothesis; results are inconclusive.

68. A researcher working at a particular company wants to know if workers' health would improve if they were given extra days off. In this company, all workers undergo a standard physical exam twice a year and an overall health rating (higher scores mean better health) is automatically provided to the company. Thus, to conduct the study, the researcher selected five workers at random, arranged to have them receive an additional 2 days off every month over the period between health exams, and then compared the health scores on the two exams.
   a. Do the data shown in the table below support the notion that extra days off improves health (use the .05 level)?
   b. Explain your analysis to a person who fully understands hypothesis testing involving a single sample and a known population, but has never been exposed to t tests of any kind.

Health Rating, Before and After Period of Extra Days Off

Subject	Before	After
A	75	81
B	66	67
C	44	46
D	86	88
E	89	89

Computation answer:
t needed ($df = 4$), $p < .05$, 1-tailed = 2.132
Difference scores = 6, 1, 2, 2, 0
$M = 2.2$; $S^2 = 5.2$; $S_M = 1.02$; $t = 2.16$.
Reject the null hypothesis.

69. A researcher studied the effect of television violence on concentration of a particular blood chemical. In this study, 40 subjects were measured over a period of an hour prior to watching a violent show and then immediately after. In the results section, the researcher writes: "There was a significant decline in blood concentration from a mean of 13.41 (SD=2.48) to 12.38 (SD=2.69), $t(39) = 3.38$, $p < .01$ (one tailed)." Explain this result (including the underlying logic of the computations) to a person who understands hypothesis testing involving a single sample and a known population, but has never been exposed to t tests of any kind.

70. A psychologist tested a group of junior high school students when they were starting seventh grade, then again two years later when they were starting ninth grade. The students were measured on a number of personality traits at both testings. In the results section of the research report, the psychologist provided the following table:

Scale	7th Grade	9th Grade	Difference
Anxiety	132.21	114.61	-17.60**
Depression	112.15	109.13	-3.02*
Rigidity	108.14	111.90	3.76
Neuroticism	142.16	120.11	-22.05**

* $p < .05$ ** $p < .01$

Explain these results (including the underlying logic of the computations) to a person who fully understands hypothesis testing involving a single sample and a known population, but has never been exposed to t tests of any kind.

Chapter 9
The _t_ Test for Independent Means

Multiple-Choice Questions

1.   Which of the following is an example of a situation in which you could
     conduct a _t_ test for independent means?
     a. A comparison of the SAT scores of a group of 10 students who
         completed a special SAT preparation course compared to how people do
         on the SAT in general (based on the norms for the general
         population).
     *   b. A comparison of scores of subjects in a memory study in which one
         group of subjects learns the words in alphabetical order and another
         group learns the words in order of length of the word, from shortest
         to longest.
     c. A comparison of subjects' scores on a skills test before and after
         attending a training session for improving the skill.
     d. None of the above are suitable for a _t_ test for independent means.

2.   The comparison distribution for a _t_ test for independent means is
     *   a. a distribution of differences between means.
     b. a _Z_ distribution (that is, a normal curve).
     c. a binomial expansion.
     d. a distribution of proportional variance scores.

3.   A "distribution of differences between means" can be conceptualized as a
     distribution of
     a. difference scores, in which the difference scores are found by
         subtracting a series of sample means from the population mean.
     b. the differences you find when you use several methods, in sequence,
         of estimating the population mean.
     *   c. the differences you get when you repeatedly draw a sample mean from
         one population and one from another population and subtract one mean
         from the other.
     d. the differences between a single sample from Population 1 and all
         possible samples from Population 2.

4.   When conducting a _t_ test for independent means, if the null hypothesis
     is rejected, you are basically saying that
     a. the samples were drawn from populations that were actually dependent
         rather than independent.
     b. the variance of one sample is so much larger than the variance of
         the other sample that we decide that the variances of the parent
         populations must not have been the same after all.
     *   c. the mean of one sample is so far from the mean of the other sample
         that we decide the samples must come from populations with
         different means.
     d. the mean of one sample is statistically the same as the mean of the
         other sample, so they probably come from populations with equal
         means.

Test Bank   315

5.   When conducting a $\underline{t}$ test for independent means, a typical research
        hypothesis might be
    *   a. the mean of Population 1 is greater than the mean of Population 2.
        b. the mean of Sample 1 is greater than the mean of Sample 2.
        c. the mean of Sample 1 is the same as the mean of Sample 2.
        d. the mean of Population 1 is the same as the mean of
            Population 2.

6.   All of the following are true for both the $\underline{t}$ test for independent means
        AND the $\underline{t}$ test for dependent means, EXCEPT
        a. population variances are estimated from the information in the
            sample of scores actually studied.
    *   b. pretest-posttest experimental designs are common.
        c. the population means are unknown.
        d. the sample data (in some form) are eventually compared to a $\underline{t}$
            distribution.

7.   When determining the pooled population variance estimate in a $\underline{t}$ test for
        independent means,
        a. the variance of at least one of the original populations must be
            known (as opposed to estimated), but the other can be estimated from
            sample data.
        b. the variance of BOTH of the original populations must be known (as
            opposed to estimated).
    *   c. the estimates based on each of the samples are averaged in such a
            way as to give more influence to the estimate based on more
            subjects.
        d. the data from both samples are combined to form a single sample, and
            the estimated variance is computed in the usual way, but using this
            combined sample (that is, using the usual formula of the sum of
            squared deviations from the overall mean of these scores, divided by
            the degrees of freedom).

8.   Which of the following is the best way to reduce the variances in the
        distributions of means when conducting a $\underline{t}$ test for independent means?
    *   a. Increase the size of the samples.
        b. Raise the study's level of significance.
        c. Use the true population variance.
        d. Treat the two samples as one sample.

9.   When conducting a $\underline{t}$ test for independent means, once the variances are
        known for each of the distributions of means, the variances can be added
        together to yield the
        a. pooled estimate of the population variance.
    *   b. variance of the distribution of differences between means.
        c. $\underline{t}$ score.
        d. power of the study.

10.   In the formula "$S_{Difference}^2 = S_M1^2 + S_M2^2$," the "$S_M1^2$" refers to
        a. the estimated mean of the distribution of variances of Population 1.
        b. the variance of the difference scores for Population 1.
        c. the estimated variance of Population 1.
    *   d. the variance of the distribution of means for Population 1.

Test Bank

11.	The variance of a distribution of differences between means equals
	a. the difference between the variances of the two distributions of means.
*	b. the sum of the variances of the two distributions of means.
	c. the difference between the two estimated population variances.
	d. the sum of the two estimated population variances.

12.	The comparison distribution for a $\underline{t}$ test for independent means is a $\underline{t}$ distribution (as opposed to a normal curve) because
	a. tables are not available for the normal curve.
*	b. the population variance is estimated.
	c. $\underline{Z}$ distributions were not used at the time the $\underline{t}$ test for independent means was invented.
	d. there are more degrees of freedom for a single sample than when you are using two samples.

13.	When using a $\underline{t}$ table, the degrees of freedom you should use for a $\underline{t}$ test for independent means is
	a. the degrees of freedom for Sample 1 divided by the sum of the degrees of freedom for both samples.
	b. the average of the degrees of freedom for the two samples.
	c. the sum of the two sample sizes, minus one.
*	d. the sum of the two samples' degrees of freedom.

14.	In the formula $\underline{t} = (\underline{M}_1 - \underline{M}_2)/\underline{S}_{Difference}$, the "$\underline{S}_{Difference}$" refers to
	a. the sum of the standard deviations of the distribution of means.
	b. the pooled estimate of the populations' standard deviation.
*	c. the standard deviation of the distribution of differences between means.
	d. the average standard deviation of the two samples.

15.	Based on the following data, which would be the correct use of the formula $\underline{t} = (\underline{M}_1 - \underline{M}_2)/\underline{S}_{Difference}$?
	Sample 1: Mean = 60; Variance of the distribution of means = 2.
	Sample 2: Mean = 50; Variance of the distribution of means = 7.
	a. $\underline{t} = (7-2)/\sqrt{(50+60)}$.
	b. $\underline{t} = (60-50)/\sqrt{[(2^2+7^2)/2]}$.
*	c. $\underline{t} = (60-50)/\sqrt{(2+7)}$.
	d. $\underline{t} = (60-50)/(2+7)$.

16.	A researcher hypothesizes that people of personality type K score higher than people of personality type R on an intelligence test. The $\underline{S}_{Difference}$ turned out to be .9, while the mean score of type K people was 18.8 and the mean score for type R people was 21.3. What is the $\underline{t}$ score?
	a. $\underline{t} = (18.8-21.3)/.9^2 = -3.09$.
	b. $\underline{t} = (18.8-21.3)(.9) = -2.25$.
*	c. $\underline{t} = (18.8-21.3)/.9 = -2.78$.
	d. $\underline{t} = (18.8-21.3)/[(2)(.9)] = -1.39$.

Test Bank	317

17. Each of the following is part of conducting a t test for independent
    means, EXCEPT
    *
    a. difference scores are found for each subject.
    b. the population variances are estimated.
    c. a comparison is made against a t distribution.
    d. the variance of the distribution of differences between means is
       computed.

18. When conducting a t test for independent means,
    a. the medians of the two populations are assumed to be equal.
    *
    b. the null hypothesis is rejected if the t score you compute is more
       extreme than the cutoff t score.
    c. only the .01 significance level should be used because of the
       greater power compared to a t test for dependent means.
    d. all of the above.

19-21 A sociologist interested in cultural differences in women compared women
    of two ethnic groups on a Role Approval Index (high scores mean high
    degrees of approval of one's social role). The results were as follows:
           Ethnic Group A: $\underline{N}$=15 $\underline{M}$=55 $\underline{S}^2$=6.5
           Ethnic Group B: $\underline{N}$=23 $\underline{M}$=51 $\underline{S}^2$=4.5

    19. If you were to compute a t test for independent means, how
        many degrees of freedom are there in the t distribution?
        *
        a. (15-1) + (23-1) = 36
        b. 15+23 = 38
        c. (15+23) - 1 = 37
        d. (15+23)/2 = 19

    20. What is the pooled estimate of the population variance?
        *
        a. [(14/36)(6.5)] + [(22/36)(4.5)] = 5.28
        b. [(15/38)(6.5)] + [(23/38)(4.5)] = 5.29
        c. [(15/23)(6.5)] + [(23/15)(4.5)] =11.14
        d. [(14/22)(6.5)] + [(22/14)(4.5)] =11.21

    21. If the standard deviation of the distribution of the
        difference between means is .76, what is the t score?
        a. (15-23)/.76 = -10.53
        b. (.76)(15-23) = -8.00
        c. [(6.5+4.5)/2][.76] = 4.18
        *
        d. (55-51)/.76 = 5.26

22. One of the assumptions for the t test for independent means is that
    a. sample means are not significantly different.
    b. the mean of the distribution of differences between means is 1.
    *
    c. the variance of each of the parent populations is the same.
    d. the means of each of the parent populations vary by no more than 1
       standard deviation.

23. Which of the following is the MOST serious violation of an assumption
    for the t test for independent means?
    a. The sample size is smaller than 15.
    b. The populations are both dramatically negatively skewed.
    c. The populations are both dramatically positively skewed.
    *
    d. The populations are dramatically skewed in opposite directions.

24. If a study has 18 subjects in the experimental group and 7 subjects in
     the control group, what is the harmonic mean of these sample sizes?
     a. $18/(18+7) + 7/(18+7) = .6$.
     b. $(2)(18)/(18+7) + (2)(7)/(18+7) = 2.0$.
*   c. $(2)(18)(7)/(18+7) = 10.01$.
     d. $(18+7)^2/(18+7) = 25$.

25. In an experiment involving 40 subjects, which study would have the most
     power?
     a. A study with 10 in the experimental group and 40 in the control
        group.
     b. A study with 40 in the experimental group and 10 in the control
        group.
*   c. A study with 25 in the experimental group and 25 in the control
        group.
     d. All would have the same power. (Power depends on the total number of
        subjects, and how they are divided between groups makes no
        difference.)

26. If a research article reports a result as "$\underline{t}(28) = 4.21$, $\underline{p} < .01$."
     a. the result was statistically significant.
     b. there were 30 subjects in the study.
     c. the $\underline{t}$ score was 4.21.
*   d. all of the above.

27. Which of the following is an example of the most common way for a $\underline{t}$ test
     for independent means to be reported in a research article?
     a. $\underline{t}(i:29) < .05$.
     b. independent $\underline{t}(15): 30.16$, $\underline{p}$: significant.
     c. $\underline{t}(independent) = 2.93$, significant.
*   d. $\underline{t}(45) = 3.52$, $\underline{p} < .05$.

Fill-In Questions

28. In a study of the effects of a particular drug on creativity, 15
     subjects took a creativity test twice--once in a normal mental state and
     once under the influence of the drug. A $\underline{t}$ test for _____ would be
     conducted to analyze the data.

     Answer: dependent means

29. In a study of the effects of smell on concentration, 20 subjects
     performed a standard task while exposed to an unpleasant smell and
     another 20 subjects are tested on the same task but without being
     exposed to the unpleasant smell. A $\underline{t}$ test for _____ would be
     conducted to analyze the data.

     Answer: independent means

30. In a $\underline{t}$ test for independent means, once the two estimates of the
     population variance are obtained, the next step is to combine these to
     form a(n) _____.

     Answer: pooled estimate of the population variance, $\underline{S}_{Pooled}^2$

31. Because Sample 1 is sometimes bigger (or smaller) than Sample 2, a(n) _____ is used to combine the two estimates of the population variance into an overall pooled estimate.

Answer: weighted average

32. $\underline{df}_1 + \underline{df}_2 = $ _____. (Give a symbol.)

Answer: $\underline{df}_{Total}$

33. When conducting a $\underline{t}$ test for independent means, a typical null hypothesis is that the mean of Population 1 equals the mean of _____.

Answer: Population 2

34. "$\underline{S}_{Pooled}^2/\underline{N}_1$" is the formula to find the variance of the _____ associated with Population 1.

Answer: distribution of means

35. If you take a mean from a population's distribution of means and subtract it from a mean from another population's distribution of means, and do this repeatedly many times, you would be constructing a(n) _____.

Answer: distribution of differences between means

36. In a $\underline{t}$ test for independent means, the difference between the means of your two samples is divided by the standard deviation of _____ to yield the $\underline{t}$ score.

Answer: the distribution of differences between means

37. "$\underline{t}$=(Sample $\underline{M}$ – Population $\underline{M}$)/$\underline{S}_M$" is used to conduct a(n) _____.

Answer: $\underline{t}$ test for dependent means

38. "$\underline{t} = (\underline{M}_1 – \underline{M}_2)/\underline{S}_{Difference}$" is used to conduct a(n) _____.

Answer: $\underline{t}$ test for independent means

39. In a $\underline{t}$ test for independent means, if the null hypothesis really is false, the closer together the population means are, the more likely it is that a(n) _____ error will be made.

Answer: Type II

40. To conduct a $\underline{t}$ test for independent means, ideally the populations should both be normally distributed and have the same _____.

Answer: variance

Test Bank

41. If the populations are highly _____ in opposite directions, the standard t test for independent means should not be used.

Answer: skewed

42. Hypothesized effect size for a study involving a t test for independent means is the difference between the hypothesized population means, divided by _____.

Answer: σ, the standard deviation of the population

43. In a t test for independent means, an effect size of _____ is considered large.

Answer: .80

44. In a t test for independent means, an effect size of _____ is considered medium.

Answer: .50

45. In an experiment involving 48 subjects, you are most likely to detect a result with a small effect size if you assign _____ [give a number] to the experimental group and _____ [give a number] to the control group.

Answer: 24; 24

46. When sample sizes are unequal, the _____ tells you the equivalent size that two equal-sized samples would need to be for a study to have the same amount of power.

Answer: harmonic mean

47. "$[(2)(N_1)(N_2)]/[N_1 + N_2]$" is the formula for the _____.

Answer: harmonic mean

48. A study with two groups of 10 subjects each, using a t test for independent means, yielded a t of 2.21, which was significant at the .05 significance level. The standard way of describing these results in a research article would be as follows: _____.

Answer: $t(18) = 2.21$, $p < .05$.

Note. The essays called for in these problems ask students to explain the logic behind their answers to someone unfamiliar with the material covered since Chapter 8--that is, they are only asked to cover material relating to the t test. Instructors may prefer, particularly on a final exam, to ask for an explanation "to a person who has had no exposure to statistics at all." (However, such essays should be used sparingly in exams as they will necessarily take students much longer to write.) Alternately, if students have been tested separately on the t test for dependent means, instructors may prefer to ask for an explanation that assumes the reader is familiar with the t test for dependent means.

49. A (fictional) manager of a small store wanted to discourage shoplifters by putting signs around the store saying "Shoplifting is a crime!" However, he wanted to make sure this would not cause customers to buy less. To test this, he displayed the signs every other Wednesday for 8 weeks, for a total of 4 days displayed. He recorded the store's sales for those four Wednesdays, then recorded the store's sales for the four alternate Wednesdays, when the signs were not displayed. On the Wednesdays with the sign, the sales were 83, 73, 81, and 79. On the Wednesdays without the sign, sales were 84, 90, 82, and 84.

   a. Do these data suggest that customers buy less when the signs are displayed? (Use the .05 significance level.)

   b. Explain your analysis to a person who fully understands hypothesis testing involving a single sample and a known population, but has never been exposed to t tests of any kind.

Computation answer:
With Sign: $N=4$; $df=3$; $M=79$; $S^2=18.67$.
No Sign: $N=4$; $df=3$; $M=85$; $S^2=12.00$.
$df_{Total} = 6$; $S_{Pooled}^2 = [(3/6)(18.67)] + [(3/6)(12)] = 15.34$.
$S_M1^2 = S_M2^2 = 15.34/4 = 3.84$.
$S_{Difference}^2 = 3.84+3.84 = 7.68$; $S_{Difference} = 2.77$.
t needed ($df=6$, $p<.05$, 1-tailed) $= -1.943$.
$t = (79-85)/2.77 = -2.17$. Reject the null hypothesis.

Test Bank

50. A (fictional) team of psychologists conducted a study of the effects of sleep deprivation on decay of short-term memory. Eight subjects stayed in a lab for two days. Four more were randomly assigned to not sleep during that period, and the other four were allowed to sleep when they want to. At the end of the two days, the subjects completed a short-term memory task. Here are the data:

Mean Time (Seconds) for Remembering

Sleep Deprived	Normal Sleep
7	9
8	8
7	11
9	7

a. Based on these data, does sleep deprivation reduce short-term memory? (Use the .05 significance level.)

b. Explain your analysis to a person who fully understands hypothesis testing involving a single sample and a known population, but has never been exposed to t tests of any kind.

Computation answer:
Sleep Deprived: N=4; df=3; M=7.75; S^2= .91.
Normal Sleep: N=4; df=3; M=8.75; S^2=2.91.
df_{Total} = 6; S_{Pooled}^2 = [(3/6)(.91)] + [(3/6)(2.91)] = 1.91.
S_M1^2 = S_M2^2 = 1.91/4 = .48;
$S_{Difference}^2$ = .48+.48 = .96; $S_{Difference}$ = .98.
t needed (df=6, p<.05, 1-tailed) = -1.943.
t = (7.75-8.75)/.98 = -1.02.
Do not reject the null hypothesis; experiment is inconclusive.

51. Does training in a particular memory program affect memory for spontaneously observed events? A (fictional) researcher had arranged to train four of eight volunteers in a memory program and the other four served as a control group. A week later, as part of their psychology class, all eight subjects watched a film showing a bank robbery and afterwards were questioned about the events. The number of accurate responses for the subjects who had taken the memory course were 20, 25, 24, and 23. The number of correct responses for the control subjects were 14, 22, 18, and 17.

a. Do the data in the table below support the contention that those trained in this particular memory program are more accurate at recall for spontaneously observed events? (Use the .05 significance level.)

b. Explain your analysis to a person who fully understands hypothesis testing involving a single sample and a known population, but has never been exposed to t tests of any kind.

Computation answer:
Memory Program: N=4; df=3; M=23.00; S^2= 4.67.
Control Group: N=4; df=3; M=17.75; S^2=10.91.
df_{Total} = 6; S_{Pooled}^2 = [(3/6)(4.67)] + [(3/6)(10.91)] = 7.80.
S_M1^2 = S_M2^2 = 7.80/4 = 1.95.
$S_{Difference}^2$ = 1.95+1.95 = 3.90; $S_{Difference}$ = 1.97.
t needed (df=6, p<.05, 2-tailed) = ±2.447.
t = (23.00-17.75)/1.97 = 2.66. Reject the null hypothesis.

52. A (fictional) consumer researcher wanted to know if customers really are influenced to buy more by sales clerks who smile more. To test this, clerks at eight stores in a large Canadian clothing chain were given special instructions at the start of a week and then sales over the week were recorded. Four of the stores were randomly selected to have the clerks receive instructions to be especially courteous and be sure to smile a lot. Clerks at four other stores were simply instructed to be especially courteous. Sales (in thousands of dollars) for the four stores in the Smile condition were 36, 40, 36, and 44; sales for the four stores in the control condition were 40, 31, 27, and 30.

   a. Do these data suggest that customers might buy more if they encounter smiling sales clerks? (Use the .05 level.)

   b. Explain your analysis to a person who fully understands hypothesis testing involving a single sample and a known population, but has never been exposed to t tests of any kind.

Computation answer:
Smiling: $N=4$; $df=3$; $M=39$; $S^2=14.67$.
Control: $N=4$; $df=3$; $M=32$; $S^2=31.33$.
$df_{Total} = 6$; $S_{Pooled}^2 = [(3/6)(14.67)] + [(3/6)(31.33)] = 23.00$.
$S_M1^2 = S_M2^2 = 23/4 = 5.75$.
$S_{Difference}^2 = 5.75+5.75 = 11.5$; $S_{Difference} = 3.39$.
t needed ($df=6$, $p<.05$, 1-tailed) $= 1.943$.
$t = (39-32)/3.39 = -2.06$. Reject the null hypothesis.

53. A (fictional) political scientist was able to obtain recordings of election-night acceptance speeches of seven newly elected representatives to the U.S. Congress, and counted the number of minutes devoted to urban problems in these speeches. The four of these representatives from rural districts devoted 5, 0, 3, and 4 minutes to urban problems. The other three representatives studied, who were from urban districts, devoted 11, 11, and 14 minutes to urban problems.

   a. Do these data suggest that the amount of time devoted to urban problems in acceptance speeches of newly elected representatives to the U.S. Congress differ according to whether they come from rural or urban districts? (Use the .05 level.)

   b. Explain your analysis to a person who fully understands hypothesis testing involving a single sample and a known population, but has never been exposed to t tests of any kind.

Computation answer:
Rural: $N=4$; $df=3$; $M=3$; $S^2=4.67$. Urban: $N=3$; $df=2$; $M=12$; $S^2=3$.
$df_{Total} = 5$; $S_{Pooled}^2 = [(3/5)(4.67)] + [(2/5)(3)] = 4$.
$S_M1^2 = 4/4 = 1$; $S_M2^2 = 4/3 = 1.33$;
$S_{Difference}^2 = 2.33$; $S_{Difference} = 1.53$.
t needed ($df=5$, $p<.05$, 2-tailed) $= \pm2.571$.
$t = (12-3)/1.53 = 5.88$. Reject the null hypothesis.

54. A (fictional) health researcher conducted an experiment in which subjects watched a film that either did or did not include a person being injured because of not wearing a seat belt. A week later, as part of a seemingly different study, these same subjects reported how important they thought it was to wear seat belts. The 16 subjects who had seen the injury film gave a mean rating of 8.9 with an estimated population standard deviation of 2.1. The 36 subjects in the control condition had a mean of 7.0 with an estimated population standard deviation of 2.4.

    a.   Do these data suggest that seeing a movie with a person being injured due to not wearing a seat belt makes attitudes more positive (higher ratings) towards seat belt usage? (Use the .01 level.)

    b.   Explain your analysis to a person who fully understands hypothesis testing involving a single sample and a known population, but has never been exposed to t tests of any kind.

Computation answer:
Injury Film: $N=16$; $df=15$; $M=8.8$; $S^2=4.41$.
Control Film: $N=36$; $df=35$; $M=7.6$; $S^2=5.76$.
$df_{Total} = 50$;
$S_{Pooled}^2 = [(15/50)(4.41)] + [(35/50)(5.76)] = 5.35$.
$S_M1^2 = 5.35/16 = .33$; $S_M2^2 = 5.35/36 = .15$;
$S_{Difference}^2 = .48$; $S_{Difference} = .69$.
t needed ($df=50$, $p<.01$, 1-tailed) = 2.404.
$t = (8.9-7.0)/.69 = 2.75$. Reject the null hypothesis.

55. A theater arts department enlists the help of a (fictional) social science professor to design a study to see if being surrounded by highly attractive people affects the performance of young actors. Each of 30 student actors is provided a script and asked to enact a particular scene with a group of other performers, and their performance is rated by a panel of judges. This enacting of the scene, however, occurs under one of two conditions, to which the subjects are randomly assigned: For 13 of the actors, all the other performers are dressed and made up to look very attractive; for the other 17 actors, all the same other performers are dressed and made up to look very unattractive. With attractive co-performers, the mean performance ratings for the actors with attractive co-performers was 4.3 ($S = .86$); with unattractive co-performers, the mean was 5.4 ($S = 1.30$).

    a.   Do these data suggest that acting with attractive co-performers affects performance? (Use the .05 level.)

    b.   Explain your analysis to a person who fully understands hypothesis testing involving a single sample and a known population, but has never been exposed to t tests of any kind.

Computation answer:
Attractive Co-Performers: $N=13$; $df=12$; $M=4.3$; $S^2= .74$.
Unattractive Co-Performers: $N=17$; $df=16$; $M=5.4$; $S^2=1.69$.
$df_{Total} = 28$; $S_{Pooled}^2 = [(12/28)(.74)] + [(16/28)(1.69)] = 1.28$.
$S_M1^2 = 1.28/13 = .10$; $S_M2^2 = 1.28/17 = .08$;
$S_{Difference}^2 = .18$; $S_{Difference} = .42$.
t needed ($df=28$, $p<.05$, 2-tailed) = ±2.049.
$t = (4.3-5.4)/.42 = -2.62$. Reject the null hypothesis.

56. A (fictional) psychotherapist wanted to know if his clients self-disclosed more while sitting in an easy chair or lying down on a couch. All clients had previously agreed to allow the sessions to be videotaped for research purposes. The therapist randomly assigned 10 clients to each condition. The third session for each client was videotaped, and an independent observer counted the client's disclosures. The therapist reported that "clients made more disclosures when sitting in easy chairs ($M=18.20$) than when lying down on a couch ($M =14.31$), $t(18) = 2.84$, $p < .05$, two-tailed." Explain these results to a person who fully understands hypothesis testing involving a single sample and a known population, but has never been exposed to t tests of any kind.

57. A (fictional) researcher wanted to know if caffeine lowered the threshold at which sound could be detected. He conducted an experiment with 30 subjects and found that subjects who drank 2 cups of coffee could detect a tone of 1000 cps at a mean intensity level of .283 dyne per cm². Subjects who did not drink coffee could detect the same tone at a mean intensity of .291 dyne per cm². A t test for independent means found the two intensity levels to be significantly different, $t(28)=2.11$, $p<.05$, two-tailed. Explain these results to a person who fully understands hypothesis testing involving a single sample and a known population, but has never been exposed to t tests of any kind.

58. A (fictional) researcher conducted a study comparing adjustment of adolescents who had been raised in homes that were either very structured or very unstructured. Thirty adolescents from each type of family completed an adjustment inventory. The results are reported in the table below. Explain these results to a person who fully understands hypothesis testing involving a single sample and a known population, but has never been exposed to t tests of any kind.

Means on Four Adjustment Scales for
Adolescents from Structured Versus Unstructured Homes

Scale	Structured Homes	Unstructured Homes	t
Social Maturity	106.82	113.94	-1.07
School Adjustment	116.31	107.22	2.03*
Identity Development	89.48	94.32	1.93*
Intimacy Development	102.25	104.33	.32

*$p < .05$

59. A (fictional) psychologist was interested in whether men with higher levels of a particular hormone show higher levels of assertiveness. Levels of this hormone were tested for 100 men. The top ten and the bottom ten were selected for the study. All subjects took part in a lab simulation in which they were asked to role play a person picking his car up from a mechanic's shop. The simulation was videotaped and later judged by independent raters on each of four types of assertive statements made by the subject. The results are shown in the table below. Explain these results to a person who fully understands hypothesis testing involving a single sample and a known population, but has never been exposed to t tests of any kind.

Mean Number of Assertive Statements

	Type of Assertive Statement			
Group	1	2	3	4
Men with High Levels	2.14	1.16	3.83	0.14
Men with Low Levels	1.21	1.32	2.33	0.38
t	3.81**	.89	2.03*	.58

*$p <.05$ **$p < .01$

Chapter 10
Introduction to the Analysis of Variance

Multiple-Choice Questions

1. An analysis of variance differs from a t test for independent means in that an analysis of variance
   a. is usually used to compare two groups, but a t test for independent means is not.
 * b. can be used in any situation in which a t test for independent means would be used, but a t test for independent means can not be used in any case in which an analysis of variance would be used.
   c. is conducted before the experiment, whereas a t test for independent means is conducted after.
   d. computes variances as part of the analysis, whereas a t test does not.

2. Analysis of variance should only be conducted when
   a. sample sizes are greater than 30 per group.
   b. there are less than 30 subjects per group.
 * c. population variances are equal.
   d. population sizes are equal.

3. Because of the assumption that the population variances are equal, when an analysis of variance is conducted
   a. fewer degrees of freedom are required.
   b. sample variances are not important.
 * c. an averaged estimate of the population variance can be calculated.
   d. population parameters (such as σ and μ) are used in place of sample statistics.

4. When an analysis of variance is conducted,
   a. fewer subjects are required than when a t test for independent means is conducted.
 * b. two estimates of the population variance are compared.
   c. difference scores are computed, as in a t test for dependent means.
   d. all of the above.

5. In an analysis of variance, if the null hypothesis is true, then
   a. the research hypothesis is also true.
   b. fewer subjects are needed for the experiment.
 * c. there should be less variance among means of samples than if the null hypothesis were not true.
   d. the within-group estimate of the population variance is smaller than the between-group estimate.

6. For one-way analysis of variances, if the null hypothesis is true, then
   a. the analysis of variance will never produce a significant F ratio.
   b. estimates of the population variance will be easier to calculate.
   c. the variance between sample means is significantly larger than the variance within each sample.
 * d. any difference among sample means reflects variance within the populations.

Test Bank

327

7. When conducting an analysis of variance, if the within-group variance estimate is about the same as the between-group variance estimate, then
   a. the null hypothesis should be rejected.
 * b. any difference between sample means is probably due to random sampling error.
   c. an error in the calculations was made, because within-group variance estimate must always be smaller than the between-group variance estimate.
   d. any difference between sample means is probably due to a real difference caused by experimental conditions.

8. When conducting an analysis of variance, if the null hypothesis is false, then
 * a. the variation between sample means reflects the variation within the populations and the variation between the population means.
   b. the within-group variance is significantly larger than the between-group variance.
   c. the variance within each sample is larger than if the null hypothesis were true.
   d. the variance between sample means is no greater than the variance within the population with the largest variance.

9. When conducting an analysis of variance, when the null hypothesis is true, then all of the following are true EXCEPT
   a. occasionally an F ratio will be significant anyway.
   b. within-group and between-group variances are estimating the same population variance.
 * c. the F ratio will generally be significantly larger than 1.
   d. the variance between samples is due entirely to random sampling variance.

10. When conducting an analysis of variance, the null hypothesis is rejected when
   a. the t score is significantly larger than the cutoff t.
 * b. the F ratio is significantly larger than 1.
   c. the t score is significantly smaller than the F ratio.
   d. the F ratio is significantly smaller than the t score.

11. In an analysis of variance, the population variance can be estimated within any one group by
 * a. finding the sum of squared deviations of the scores in that group from that group's mean, and dividing that sum by that group's degrees of freedom.
   b. finding the sum of squared deviations of the scores in that group from that group's mean, and dividing that sum by the numerator degrees of freedom.
   c. finding the sum of squared deviations of the scores in that group from the overall mean of all the scores (in all groups), and dividing that sum by that group's degrees of freedom.
   d. finding the sum of squared deviations of the scores in that group from the overall mean of all the scores (in all groups), and dividing that sum by the numerator degrees of freedom.

12. "$\underline{S}^2{}_{within}$" equals
   a. the sum of squares within each group.
   b. the square root of the standard within-group deviations from the mean.
   c. the squared variance within groups.
 * d. the population variance estimate based on the variation with each of the groups.

13. When sample sizes are equal, $\underline{S}^2{}_{within}$ is calculated by
   a. summing the population variance estimates computed within each group, and dividing by the total number of subjects.
 * b. summing the population variance estimates computed within each group, and dividing by the number of groups.
   c. multiplying the within-group sum of squares ($\underline{SS}_w$) by the size of each sample ($\underline{n}$).
   d. dividing the within-group sum of squares ($\underline{SS}_w$) by the size of each sample ($\underline{n}$).

14. What is $\Sigma(\underline{M}-\underline{GM})^2/\underline{df}_{Betweem}$?
   a. The $\underline{t}$ score for a $\underline{t}$ test for dependent means.
   b. The between-group sum of squared deviations.
 * c. The estimated variance of the distribution of means.
   d. The between-group estimate of the population variance.

15. In the formula, $\Sigma(\underline{M}-\underline{GM})^2/\underline{df}_{Between}$, the "$\underline{GM}$" means
   a. general multiple.
 * b. grand mean.
   c. group mean.
   d. guess of maturation.

16. In an analysis of variance where sample sizes are equal, when extrapolating from the estimated variance of the distribution of means to an estimated variance of the population of individual scores,
 * a. the estimated variance of the distribution of means is multiplied by the number of cases in each sample.
   b. the estimated variance between groups is divided by the number of groups.
   c. the estimated variance of the distribution of means is divided by the number of cases in each sample.
   d. the estimated variance of the population of individual cases is divided by the number of groups.

17. For an analysis of variance, if the between-group estimate of the population variance is 30 and the within-group estimate is 25, then the $\underline{F}$ ratio is
   a. 25/(30-25) = 5.00.
   b. (30-25)/30 = 0.17.
   c. 25/30 = .83.
 * d. 30/25 = 1.20.

18. If the within-group variance estimate is 8.5 and the between-group variance estimate is 5.3, what is the $\underline{F}$ ratio?
 * a. 5.3/8.5 = 0.62
   b. 8.5/5.3 = 1.60
   c. $\sqrt{5.3}/8.5$ = 0.27
   d. $\sqrt{8.5}/5.3$ = 0.55

Test Bank

19. A study has three groups, each with an equal number of cases. The population variance is estimated from the variance within each group, yielding three estimates, 54.4, 48.6, and 50.9. What is the within-group estimate of the population variance?
   a. (54.4+48.6+50.9)/(3-1) = 76.95
 * b. (54.4+48.6+50.9)/3 = 51.3
   c. (54.4+48.6+50.9)/(3+1) = 38.48
   d. (54.4+48.6+50.9)/(3+2) = 30.78

20. If you had four populations with equal means and equal variances, you could construct an F distribution for situations with samples of 10 cases each by
   a. applying the t test formula to each pair of samples and squaring, then repeating this process a large number of times.
   b. applying the analysis of variance formula to a set of four samples (one from each of the four populations) of 10 cases each, computing the degrees of freedom, and repeating this process a large number of times.
   c. taking 10 samples from each of the four populations, computing the F ratio, and repeating this a large number of times.
 * d. taking samples of 10 cases from each of the four populations, computing an F ratio for each set of samples, and repeating this a large number of times.

21. One characteristic of an F ratio is that
   a. when looking up the cutoff F on a table, the degrees of freedom are needed from the numerator, denominator, and the sum of squares calculation.
 * b. it is never less than 0.
   c. it is negatively skewed (the long tail to the left).
   d. the standard t distribution (for 30 df) is used as a comparison distribution.

22. For analysis of variance, the effect size is based on
   a. the size of the groups times the distribution of sample means.
   b. the sum of the population means, divided by the variance within each of the populations.
 * c. the standard deviation of the means of the populations, divided by the variation within each of the populations.
   d. the difference between the largest and smallest population mean divided by the variance within each of the populations.

23. In terms of estimated values, Estimated Effect Size =
   a. $(F2)(\underline{n})$.
   b. $S_M2/S2_{Within}$.
   c. $S2_{Between}/S2_{Within}$.
 * d. S_M/S_{Within}.

24. When examining effect size for the analysis of variance, a medium effect size is
   a. .10.
 * b. .25.
   c. .40.
   d. .90.

25. Which of the following most accurately reflects how the results of an analysis of variance would be reported in a research article?
   a. F < p(.01)
 * b. F(3,50) = 4.33, p < .01
   c. F(4.33) = p(.01)
   d. F = 4.33, significant

26. Which of the following would be most likely to appear in a research article to report the results of an analysis of variance?
   a. F(44) = 3.40, significant
   b. F(2,44) < .05
 * c. F(2,44) = 3.4, p < .05
   d. F = 3.40, p <.05

27. If a research article presented the results of an analysis of variance as "F(2,38) = 3.60, p < .05," how many groups were there in the study?
   a. 2
 * b. 3
   c. 40
   d. 41

28. A research article reports the following: "The mean performance scores for the Normal Sleep, Reduced Sleep, and No Sleep groups were 18.0, 16.6, and 15.6, respectively, F(2,36) = 2.95, p < .05." Based on this information, which conclusion is most accurate?
   a. People who get no sleep perform significantly worse than people who sleep a reduced amount.
   b. People who sleep a reduced amount perform significantly worse than people who sleep a normal amount.
 * c. The three groups do not all come from populations with the same mean, although it is not clear which population means are different.
   d. This study cannot conclude that amount of sleep is related to performance.

29. Ronald A. Fisher was noted for
   a. the creation of the t test for independent means.
   b. his charming personality, which inadvertently helped popularize the statistical tests he developed.
 * c. the creation of the analysis of variance.
   d. his overcoming of great physical disabilities.

30. All of the following are true about the creator of the analysis of variance EXCEPT
 * a. his name was Karl Pearson.
   b. he supported the idea of eugenics.
   c. he wrote 300 papers and 7 books.
   d. his work was first popularized in agriculture.

Test Bank

31. A consumer researcher is interested in the effects of Annual Income and Motivations To Shop on shopping patterns of consumers. If Annual Income (broken into two levels: High and Moderate) and Motivation To Shop (with three levels: Escape, Necessity, and Socializing) are considered in one study, how many cells will there be?
    a. 2
    b. 3
    c. 4
  * d. 6

32. An interaction effect in a two-way factorial research design
    a. is the effect of one variable, ignoring the influence of other variables.
  * b. occurs when the influence of one variable changes according to the level of another variable.
    c. almost never occurs when more than one variable is considered at a time.
    d. is rare in a well-designed study, and usually indicates some error in computation.

33. A two-way factorial design
  * a. is "two-way" because the influence of two separate variables is being studied.
    b. varies only in name from a one-way analysis of variance.
    c. considers two levels of a single variable.
    d. considers a single level of two variables.

34 In a two-way factorial design, you are testing
    a. one interaction and one main effect.
  * b. one interaction and two main effects.
    c. two interactions and one main effect.
    d. two interactions and two main effects.

35. In a factorial design, a "cell" is
  * a. each combination of levels of the variables.
    b. the combination of different levels of one variable, ignoring any other variables.
    c. a study with a single 1-level variable.
    d. the same thing as a "main effect."

36. In a factorial design, the mean score for all the subjects at a particular level of one of the variables is a(n)
    a. interaction effect.
    b. cell.
    c. cell mean.
  * d. marginal mean.

37. You can identify interaction effects in all of the following ways EXCEPT
    a. through inspecting cell means.
  * b. through inspecting marginal means.
    c. by using graphs.
    d. by a verbal description of results.

Test Bank

by

*   a. comparing the pattern of cell means across one row to the pattern of cell means across another row.
    b. conducting a series of <u>t</u>-tests.
    c. dividing each cell mean by its marginal mean.
    d. dividing each cell mean by a weighted marginal mean.

39-42 The effects of the amount of time spent shopping, Short (under 15 minutes) or Long (over 15 minutes), and the age of the shopper, Young (under 22) or Old (over 22), were studied to see their relation to the amount of money spent by shoppers in a record store. Consider these scenarios while answering the following questions:

Dollars Spent on Purchases

	SCENARIO A				SCENARIO B				SCENARIO C		
	Time Shopping				Time Shopping				Time Shopping		
Age	Short	Long		Age	Short	Long		Age	Short	Long	
Young	20	25	22.5	Young	20	30	25	Young	20	20	20
Old	25	30	27.5	Old	30	10	20	Old	10	40	25
	22.5	27.5			25	20			15	30	

39. Which statement is true about Scenario A?
    a. There is a moderate interaction effect.
*   b. Older buyers spend more in general, and the longer people shop, regardless of age, the more money they spend.
    c. Older buyers who shop a long time buy more than younger buyers who shop a long time, but older buyers who shop a short time buy less than younger buyers who also shop a short time.
    d. General trend is for buyers to buy more and shop for less time.

40. Which of the following interpretations are consistent with the interaction effect in Scenario B?
    a. People who spend more time shopping buy more if they are older than if they are younger.
    b. When there is a long time to shop, younger shoppers outspend older shoppers; but if there is only a short time to shop, age makes no difference.
*   c. Older people typically shop for records only when they know what they want, so that if they are going to purchase anything, they can do so in a short time. Younger shoppers are more likely to buy only after carefully examining all their possible purchases for a long time.
    d. Younger shoppers enjoy browsing (which means taking a long time)-- it puts them in the mood to buy. Older shoppers prefer to carefully consider their options and come to a sound decision--a process which typically takes a long time.

41. Which of the following statements is consistent with the data in Scenario C?
    a. The row means show that those who shop a long time spend twice as much money as those who shop for less time.
    b. Taken on their own, the marginal means indicate that there is an interaction effect.
    c. Younger shoppers were not affected by the amount of time they shopped, but older people bought more if they just shopped for a short time.
*   d. Regardless of how long they shopped, younger people bought the same amount. However, older people bought more if they shopped a longer time.

Test Bank

333

42. A store manager said, "How much money people spend isn't related to age. All that matters is how long they shop." If she said that after seeing the results of one of these studies, which scenario was she probably looking at?
   a. Scenario A
   b. Scenario B
   c. Scenario C
 * d. None of the above

43-46 The scenarios below are possible results of a study in which subjects completed a measure that assessed how important religion was to them personally. Subjects were either from a Rural or an Urban area and were either Poor or Rich.

Importance of Religion

	Scenario A				Scenario B				Scenario C		
	Rural	Urban			Rural	Urban			Rural	Urban	
Poor	50	50	50	Poor	50	80	65	Poor	40	50	45
Rich	80	80	80	Rich	50	50	50	Rich	40	70	55
	65	65			50	65			40	60	

43. Which statement is true about Scenario A?
   a. There is a moderate interaction effect.
 * b. Religion is consistently more important for rich people than for poor people, regardless of where they live.
   c. Religion is more important to people who live in the city, regardless of their wealth.
   d. Religion is particularly important to people who are both poor and live in rural areas.

44. Which of the following interpretations is consistent with the interaction effect in Scenario B?
   a. Religion is more important to poor people when they live in rural areas. In the cities, they are socialized to be more like the rich, who are less religious, regardless of where they live.
 * b. Rich people, regardless of where they live, belong to a cultural elite which values religion moderately. Poor people value religion more in urban centers than in rural areas, because it is more easily accessible.
   c. People who live in the city need religion more than people in the country, regardless of how rich or poor they are.
   d. Poor people in urban areas have a harder time than people in rural areas, so they value religion more. Rich people who move to the country are trying to get away from their materialistic lifestyle and tend to be more religious.

45. Which of the following statements is true, based on the information presented in Scenario C?
 * a. The row means show that, overall, religion is more important to rich people than to poor people.
   b. The column means show that religion is more important to poor people.
   c. The row means show that there is no difference between rich and poor in their interest in religion.
   d. There is a clear interaction effect in which poor people value religion more in urban areas while rich value it more in rural areas.

46. A sociologist said, "As far as how important religion is to

Test Bank

people, it doesn't matter where they live. What matters is
how much money they make." If her conclusion was based on
one of these scenarios, which one was she probably looking
at?

*   a. Scenario A
    b. Scenario B
    c. Scenario C
    d. none of the above

47. When the cell means of a factorial design study are graphed, if the lines
are not parallel,
    a. marginal means should also be plotted.
    b. there are more subjects in one of the conditions.
*   c. there is an interaction effect.
    d. a rounding error was made or the means were plotted improperly on the
graph.

48. In research articles, the reporting of the results of a factorial
analysis of variance
    a. rarely includes a textual description.
    b. are often shown in table format only.
*   c. are usually presented with a combination of table and textual
description.
    d. typically give brief explanations of the underlying logic of the
factorial analysis of variance.

Fill-In Questions

49. To test the null hypothesis that three populations have equal means, a(n)
_____ should be conducted.

Answer: analysis of variance

50. When conducting an analysis of variance, the null hypothesis is that the
_____ means are equal.

Answer: population

51. The "between-group population variance estimate" is symbolized as
_____.

Answer: $\underline{S2}_{Between}$

52. The "within-group population variance estimate is symbolized as _____.

Answer: $\underline{S2}_{w}$, $\underline{MS}_{w}$

53. The between-gropu population variance divided by the within-group
population variance estimate is called the _____.

Answewr: $\underline{F}$ ratio, $\underline{F}$

54. To conduct an analysis of variance, one assumption that must be met is that each population distribution is _____.

Answer: normally distributed

55. When conducting an analysis of variance, one assumption that must be met is that the _____ is the same in each population.

Answer: variance

56. When conducting an analysis of variance, _____ different estimates of the population variance are compared. (Give a number.)

Answer: two

57. When conducting a(n) _____, two different estimates of the population variance are compared.

Answer: analysis of variance

58. In an analysis of variance, if the null hypothesis is false, then the _____-group estimate of the population variance is larger than if the null hypothesis were true.

Answer: between

59. In an analysis of variance, if the null hypothesis is false, then the _____-group estimate of the population variance reflects this.

Answer: between

60. For a specified number of groups, each with a specified number of cases, if you took a sample, computed the F ratio, plotted it on a graph, and then repeated the process for an infinite number of samples, computing and plotting F ratios each time, you would have created an F _____.

Answer: distribution

61. In a one-way analysis of variance, when there are equal sample sizes, the within-group population variance estimate is found by taking the _____ of the estimates of the population variance computed from each sample.

Answer: average

62. For one-way analysis of variances,
"$(S_1^2 + S_2^2 + \ldots + S2_{Last}) / N_{Groups}$" is the formula for _____. (Do not give a symbol.)

Answer: the within-group population variance estimate

63. For one-way analysis of variances, when sample sizes are equal, "$(S_M^2)(n)$" is the formula for _____. (Do not give a symbol.)

Answer: the between-group population variance estimate

64. In an F ratio, the denominator is always the _____-group estimate of the population variance.

Answer: within

65. Complete the formula: S_M/S_{Within} = _____.

Answer: estimated effect size

66. Complete the formula: Estimated Effect Size = _____.

Answer: S_M/S_{Within}

67. When calculating the effect size for a one-way analysis of variance, _____ is divided by the population standard deviation, or its estimate (S_{Within}).

Answer: the standard deviation of the distribution of means, the estimate of the standard deviation of the distribution of means

68. According to Cohen's conventions for effect size of one-way analysis of variance, .40 is a _____ effect size.

Answer: large

69. If a research article reported an analysis of variance as $F(4,45) = 3.82$, $p < .01$, then there were _____ groups in the study.

Answer: five

70. In a study with 3 groups, each with 20 subjects, if a one-way analysis of variance yielded an F ratio of 6.21, which was significant at the .01 level, a research article would report the results as _____.

Answer: $F(2,57) = 6.21$, $p < .01$

71. A(n) _____ is when the influence of one independent variable changes according to the level of another independent variable.

Answer: interaction effect

72. A study of 50-year-olds found that, overall, women spend more time at home than men. However, a(n) _____ was found between education level and gender, such that the difference between men and women was less for college educated subjects than it was for those with only a high school education.

Answer: interaction, interaction effect, pattern of cell means

73. In a two-way analysis of variance, a difference between the means on one independent variable ignoring the effects of the other independent variable is known as a(n) _____.

Answer: main effect

74. Interaction effects can be described verbally, _____, and numerically.

Answer: graphically

75. In a graph of the results of a two-way analysis of variance, the vertical axis shows income level while the horizontal axis is labeled as "marital status." Two lines are drawn on the graph, one for women and one for men. If the lines are _____, then marital status has one relation to income for men and another effect for women.

Answer: not parallel

76. You can see an interaction effect numerically by looking at the pattern of _____ means.

Answer: cell

77. In the top row of a 2 X 2 table of cell means, there was a 6 and a 6. In the bottom row, there was a 4 and a 4. This pattern indicates that there was a(n) _____ effect.

Answer: main

78. In a graph of a two-way analysis of variance, _____ indicate that there was NOT an interaction effect.

Answer: parallel lines

Note. The essays called for in these problems ask students to explain the logic behind their answers to someone unfamiliar with the material covered since the preceding chapter. Instructors may prefer, particularly on a final exam, to ask for an explanation "to a person who has had no exposure to statistics at all." (However, such essays should be used sparingly in exams as they will necessarily take students much longer to write.)

79. A (fictional) sports researcher was interested in differences in eating habits among professionals in different sports. Thus, she administered a standard written test of eating habits to 12 randomly selected professionals, four each from baseball, football, and basketball. The results were as follows:

Eating Habits Scores

Baseball Players	Football Players	Basketball Players
34	27	35
18	28	44
21	67	47
65	42	61

a. Is there a difference in eating habits among professionals in the three sports? (Use the .05 significance level.)
b. Explain your analysis to a person who understands the t test for independent means but is completely unfamiliar with analysis of variance.

Computation answers:
F needed ($df=2,9$; $p<.05$) = 4.26.
Baseball: $M=34.5$; $S2=461.67$.
Football: $M=41$; $S2=347.33$.
Basketball: $M=46.75$; $S2=116.25$.
$GM = 40.75$; $S_M2 = 37.56$; $S2_{Between} = 150.24$; $s2_{Within} = 308.42$.
$F = 150.24/308.42 = .49$.
Do NOT reject null hypothesis; the study is inconclusive.

80. To study the effectiveness of possible treatments for insomnia, a (fictional) sleep researcher conducted a study with 12 subjects. Four subjects were instructed to count sheep (the Sheep Condition), four were told to concentrate on their breathing (the Breathing Condition), and four were not given any special instructions. Over the next few days, measures were taken of how long it took each subject to fall asleep. The average times for the subjects in the Sheep condition were 14, 28, 27, and 31; for those in the Breathing condition, 25, 22, 17, and 14; and for those in the control condition, 45, 33, 30, and 41.

    a. Do these data suggest that the different techniques have different effects? (Use the .05 significance level.)
    b. Explain your analysis to a person who understands the t test for independent means but is completely unfamiliar with analysis of variance.

    Computation answers:
    F needed ($df=2,9$; $p<.05$) = 4.26.
    Control: M= 37.25; $S2$ = 48.25.
    Sheep: M= 25.00; $S2$ = 56.67.
    Breathing: M= 19.50; $S2$ = 24.33.
    GM = 27.25; S_M2 = 82.56; $S2_{Between}$ = 330.24; $S2_{Within}$ = 43.08.
    F = 330.24/43.08 = 7.67. Reject the null hypothesis.

81. High school juniors planning to attend college were randomly assigned to view one of four videos about a particular college, each differing according to what aspect of college life was emphasized—athletics, social life, scholarship, or artistic/ cultural opportunities. After viewing the videos, the subjects took a test measuring their desire to attend this college. The (fictional) results were as follows:

    | | Desire to Attend this College | | |
Athletics	Social Life	Scholarship	Art/Cultural
68	89	74	76
56	78	82	71
69	81	79	69
70	77	80	65

    a. Do these data suggest that the type of activity emphasized in a college film affects desire to attend that college? (Use the .01 significance level.)
    b. Explain your analysis to a person who understands the t test for independent means but is completely unfamiliar with analysis of variance.

    Computation answer:
    F needed ($df=3,12$; $p<.01$) = 5.95
    Athletics: M=65.75; $S2$=42.91.   Social Life: M=81.25; $S2$=29.58.
    Scholarship: M=78.75; $S2$=11.58.   Art/Cultural: M=70.25; $S2$=20.91.
    GM = 74; S_M2 = 55.41; $S2_{Between}$ = 209.64; $S2_{Within}$ = 26.24.
    F = 209.64/26.24 = 7.99. Reject the null hypothesis.

82. A (fictional) team of psychologists designed a study in which 12 psychiatric patients diagnosed as having Generalized Anxiety Disorder were randomly assigned to one of three new types of therapy, here labeled X, Y, and Z. One year after therapy, the patients' overall mental health was assessed on a special scale by interviews with several counselors otherwise uninvolved in the study and blind to which type of therapy the patients received. The results were as follows:

Mental Health Assessment		
Therapy X	Therapy Y	Therapy Z
85	78	79
79	81	83
84	68	75
67	75	74

a. Do these data suggest that the different therapies have different effects on mental health? (Use the .05 level.)
b. Explain your analysis to a person who understands the t test for independent means but is completely unfamiliar with analysis of variance.

Computation answer:
F needed (df=2,9; p<.05) = 4.26
Therapy X: M=78.75; S^2=68.25.
Therapy Y: M=75.50; S^2=31.
Therapy Z: M=77.75; S^2=16.91.
GM = 77.33; S_M^2 = 2.78; $S^2_{Between}$ = 11; S^2_{Within} = 38.72.
F = 11/38.72 = .28. Do not reject the null hypothesis.

83. A (fictional) researcher compared the absolute olfactory thresholds of gourmet chefs, workers in a garlic processing plant, and office clerks. ("Olfactory" refers to the sense of smell and "absolute threshold" refers to the minimum stimulation a sense can detect.) Here are the results:

Detection Levels of Vanilla		
Chefs	Processors	Clerks
1.6	2.4	2.1
1.5	2.1	2.0
1.8	2.5	1.7
2.1	2.0	2.3
1.9	2.2	1.9

a. Do these data suggest that there is a difference in olfactory thresholds among these three types of people? (Use the .05 level.)
b. Explain your analysis to a person who understands the t test for independent means but is completely unfamiliar with analysis of variance.

Computation answer:
F needed (df=2,12; p<.05) = 3.89.
Chefs: M=1.78; S^2=.057.
Processors: M=2.24; S^2=.043.
Clerks: M=2.00; S^2=.050.
GM = 2.01; S_M^2 = .053; $S^2_{Between}$ = .265; S^2_{Within} = .05.
F = .265/.05 = 5.3. Reject the null hypothesis.

84. A (fictional) researcher examined the effect of different kinds of music on concentration while doing a particular kind of math task. Forty-eight subjects were randomly assigned to do a series of math tasks under one of three conditions: 16 while listening to soft gentle music, 16 while listening to loud intense music, and 16 while in silence. The means and estimated population standard deviations for the three groups were: Soft-gentle: $M = 33$, $S = 5$; Loud-intense: $M = 42$, $S = 6$; Silence $M = 42$, $S = 4$.

a. Do these data suggest that there is a difference in performance on this kind of math task under these three conditions? (Use the .05 level.)

b. Explain your analysis to a person who understands the t test for independent means but is unfamiliar with analysis of variance.

Computation answer:
F needed ($df=2,45$; $p<.05$) = 3.21.
$GM = 39$; $S_M2 = 27$; $S2_{Between} = 432$; $S2_{Within} = 25.7$.
$F = 432/25.67 = 16.83$. Reject the null hypothesis.

85. A (fictional) health researcher conducted a study comparing the effectiveness of three different programs to encourage people who have been prescribed high blood pressure medication to actually take their medication regularly. Twenty high blood pressure patients were randomly assigned to each condition (that is, there were a total of 60 subjects). A questionnaire administered to these patients 2 weeks later found that the mean number of days those in Condition A had taken their medication was 9 ($S2 = 4.5$); the mean number of days for the Condition B subjects was 12.3 ($S2 = 5.5$); and the mean number of days for the Condition C subjects was 11.7 ($S2 = 5.0$).

a. Based on these data, is there any difference in the effectiveness of the three programs? (Use the .05 level.)

b. Explain your analysis to a person who understands the t test for independent means but is unfamiliar with analysis of variance.

Computation answer:
F needed ($df=2,57$; $p<.05$) = 3.17 (actually based on 2,55 df).
$GM = 11$; $S_M2 = 3.09$; $S2_{Between} = 61.8$; $S2_{Within} = 5$.
$F = 61.8/5 = 12.36$. Reject the null hypothesis.

86. In the morning, before any subjects had had breakfast, a memory test was given to subjects after eating either a large meal, a small meal, or nothing at all. There were 25 subjects in each condition. The (fictional) results were as follows:

	Memory Test Score		
	Large Meal	Small Meal	Nothing
M	2.1	2.5	2.9
$S2$	1.0	1.2	.8

a. Based on these results, does amount of breakfast eaten affect memory? (Use the .05 level.)

b. Explain your analysis to a person who understands the t test for independent means but is completely unfamiliar with analysis of variance.

Computation answer:
F needed ($df=2,72$; $p<.05$) = 3.13.
$GM = 2.5$; $S_M2 = .16$; $S2_{Between} = 4$; $S2_{Within} = 1$.
$F = 4/1 = 4.0$. Reject the null hypothesis.

87. A (fictional) sociologist found a difference in the way subjects responded to a questionnaire on ethics in the medical professions, depending on what the subject was wearing when completing the questionnaire. (Subjects were randomly assigned to wear different outfits.) He reported his results as follows: "A subject's responses were clearly different according to whether he or she wore a doctor's uniform (M=38.8), a mechanic's uniform (M=47.6), a cooking apron (M=44.6), or no special uniform (M=42.9), $F(3,42)$ = 4.53, p<.05." Explain and interpret these results to a person who understands the t test for independent means, but is completely unfamiliar with analysis of variance. Assume there were 15 subjects in each condition.

88. A (fictional) article reported that in a particular type of American family, "first-borns have higher GPA's in high school (M=3.15) than either second-borns (M=3.01) or last-borns (M=2.87), $F(2,27)$=3.49, p<.05." Explain and interpret these results to a person who understands the t test for independent means, but is completely unfamiliar with analysis of variance. Assume each group had 10 subjects.

89. A (fictional) research article compared intelligence scores of workers in three different industries (labeled I-1, I-2, and I-3). The authors provided the table below and noted in the text: "The three groups of workers did not differ significantly in their intelligence scores, $F(2,21)$ = 1.12, ns." Explain and interpret these results to a person who understands the t test for independent means, but is completely unfamiliar with analysis of variance.

Mean Fluid Intelligence Test Scores for
Workers in Three Different Industries

	I-1	I-2	I-3
M	75.2	69.8	70.0
SD	8.4	6.9	9.1

90. A (fictional) health researcher was interested in helping smokers quit smoking. She wanted to know if there was a difference in success rates between three methods of quitting: X, Y, and Z. She designed a study with 15 subjects, 5 in each group, and asked subjects to track how many cigarettes they smoked in a 2-week period. In the results of her study, she reported as follows: "The means of the groups (Method X: M=156, SD=33.6; Method Y: M=163, SD=34.4; Method Z: M=145, SD=48.4) did not differ significantly, $F(2,12)$= .27, ns." Explain and interpret these results to a person who understands the t test for independent means, but is completely unfamiliar with analysis of variance.

91. a. Create a study using a 2 X 2 design and fill in a table of cell means so that there is an interaction effect.
   b. Make a graph showing these results.
   c. Explain the pattern of the cell means you created.

92. a. Create a study using a 2 X 2 design and fill in a table of cell means so there is a main effect and no interaction effect.
   b. Make a graph showing these results.
   c. Explain the pattern of the cell means you created.

93. In a study on memory, subjects were divided into older (15-18 years old) and younger (11-14) subjects. Some of each age group were instructed to remember a list of 20 words by relating the words to themselves. A second set of subjects from each age group was not given any special instructions, other than to memorize the 20 words.

a. Create a table showing all the cells and make up means for the cells such that an interaction effect exists.

b. Describe the pattern of the cell means.

Chapter 11
Chi-Square and Strategies when Populations Are Not Normal

Multiple-Choice Questions

1.   In a chi-square test, the variables are
      a. rank-order (ordinal).
      b. ratio-scale.
      c. continuous (quantitative).
*   d. categorical (nominal).

2.   The inventor of the chi-square test was
*   a. Karl Pearson.
      b. W.S. Gossett.
      c. Ronald Fisher.
      d. Sir Francis Galton.

3.   The main idea of a chi-square test is that you
      a. test the estimated degree of fit (proportion of variance
         accounted for) of one variable to the other variable.
      b. compare the estimated population means, to see if they vary from each
         other more than by chance.
      c. compare estimated population variances, to see if they vary from
         each other more than by chance.
*   d. test how well an observed frequency distribution fits some expected
         pattern of frequencies.

4.   All of the following are steps in computing the chi-square
      statistic EXCEPT
      a. determine the expected frequencies in each category or cell.
      b. determine the actual, observed frequencies in each category or cell.
      c. divide each squared difference by the expected frequency for its
         category or cell.
*   d. compute the overall $\underline{F}$ ratio, by computing, for each category or cell,
         the observed minus expected, and squaring this difference.

5.   The formula for the chi-squared statistic is
*   a. $\Sigma[(O-E)^2/E]$.
      b. $\Sigma[(O-E)^2]/E$.
      c. $O/\Sigma(O-E)^2$.
      d. $E/\Sigma(O-E)^2$.

6.   The degrees of freedom for the chi-square test for goodness of fit is
*   a. the number of categories minus one.
      b. the mean number of scores per category, minus number of categories.
      c. the mean number of scores per category, minus one.
      d. the total number of scores, minus the number of categories.

7.   The values in a chi-square distribution are always greater than 0 and
      a. are normally distributed.
      b. less than 1.
*   c. can be quite large.
      d. are negatively skewed.

8.   One distribution that is always greater than 0 and positively skewed
      (most scores clumped on the left, with a tail on the right that
      stretches out a long ways) is the distribution of
      a. Z.
      b. t.
 *   c. X^2.
      d. all of the above.

9.   In a chi-square test for goodness of fit, the null hypothesis is that
      a. the number of cases in one category is no greater than the number of
         cases in the other.
      b. the variances of the populations of categories are the same.
 *   c. the proportion of cases over categories breaks down the same for the
         two populations.
      d. the means of the two populations of categories are the same.

10.   A contingency table is a table in which
 *   a. the distributions of two nominal variables are laid out so that you
         have the frequencies of their combinations as well as the totals.
      b. chi-squares for each category are displayed over each level of the
         independent variable.
      c. F distributions are translated into t distributions.
      d. X^2 distributions are translated into F distributions.

11.   In a 3 X 4 contingency table, there are
      a. four levels of each variable.
      b. two levels of one variable and three levels of the other.
 *   c. three levels of one variable and four levels of the other.
      d. four levels of one variable and five levels of the other.

12.   In a contingency table, the word "independence" means
      a. the distribution of one variable varies over different levels of the
         other.
      b. the variables in the table should not be compared.
      c. the observed frequencies are larger than the expected frequencies.
 *   d. there is no relationship between the variables.

13.   One way to determine the number of cases expected in any one cell of a
      chi-square contingency table is to
 *   a. multiply the number of cases for the cell's column by its row
         proportion, its row proportion being computed as the number of cases
         for the cell's row divided by the total number of cases.
      b. divide the total number of cases by the number of cases in the cell
         and multiply this result by a row proportion, its row proportion
         being computed as the number of cases for the cell's row divided by
         the total number of cases.
      c. multiply the number of cases in the cell's row times the number of
         cases in the cell's column.
      d. divide the number of cases in the cell's row by the number of cases
         in the cell's column.

14. When conducting a chi-square test for independence, a good check on your arithmetic in computing the expected frequencies is to make sure that
   a. the expected frequency of each cell is no larger than the observed frequency.
   b. the sum of all the expected frequencies times the degrees of freedom equals the sum of all the observed frequencies.
 * c. for each row and column, the sum of the observed frequencies and the sum of the expected frequencies come out to be the same.
   d. for each row, the sum of all the expected frequencies equals the observed frequencies, minus 1, for each column.

15. In a chi-square test of independence, the term "expected frequency" generally refers to
   a. the distribution of cases over categories on the measured variables under the assumption of equal numbers of cases in all cells.
 * b. the expected distribution of cases over categories on one variable if the distribution of cases over categories on the other variable is completely unrelated to it.
   c. the spread of the independent variable, to see if it is a truly independent variable.
   d. the population's distribution of the scores on the dependent variable, as estimated by the sample data.

16. The degrees of freedom for the chi-square test for independence is
   a. the number of categories minus one.
 * b. the number of columns minus one, times the number of rows minus one.
   c. the total number of category levels minus one.
   d. the number of subjects minus the number of cells.

17. "$(N_{columns}-1)(N_{Rows}-1)$" is the formula for the degrees of freedom for
   a. the chi-square test for goodness of fit.
 * b. the chi-square test for independence.
   c. the within-group estimate of a two-way analysis of variance.
   d. the sum of the between-group effects in a two-way analysis of variance.

18. In a chi-square test for independence, the null hypothesis is that
   a. the two population variances are independent.
 * b. the two variables are independent in the population.
   c. the means of the populations are not equal.
   d. the means of the populations are equal.

19. Which of the following would NOT be allowed in an ordinary application of the chi-square tests?
 * a. Subjects' preference for studying sitting or lying down are assessed as sophomores and then again as seniors.
   b. Tall and short people are compared on their religious affiliation.
   c. The number of people of different ethnicities working in a particular company is compared to the proportions of those ethnicities in the general public.
   d. The number of successes of an advertisement is compared for three different groups of consumers to see if the number of successes is equal for the three groups.

20. The phi coefficient is
    a. always less than 0.
  * b. $\sqrt{(X^2/\underline{N})}$.
    c. always greater than 1.
    d. $(\sqrt{X^2})/\underline{N}$.

21. All of the following are true about the phi coefficient, EXCEPT
    a. it is very closely related to the correlation coefficient.
  * b. it is the same as the correlation coefficient squared ($\underline{r}^2$).
    c. it is the Greek letter "ϕ".
    d. it equals $\sqrt{(X^2/\underline{N})}$.

22. "$\sqrt{(X^2/\underline{N})}$" is the formula for
    a. δ.
    b. α.
  * c. ϕ.
    d. μ.

23. According to Cohen's conventions for the phi coefficient, a large effect size is
    a. .10.
    b. .15.
    c. .40.
  * d. .50.

24. In a study with 100 subjects, if an analysis yields a X^2 of 3.15, what is the phi coefficient?
    a. $\sqrt{(3.15)/100} = .02$
    b. $\sqrt{(3.15^2/100)} = .32$
    c. $\sqrt{[3.15/(100-1)]} = .18$
  * d. $\sqrt{(3.15/100)} = .18$

25. The formula for Cramer's phi statistic is
    a. $\sqrt{(X^2/(\underline{N})(\underline{df}_{Smaller})}$.
    b. $\sqrt{(X^2/df)}$.
    c. $\sqrt{(X^2/\underline{N})}$.
  * d. $\sqrt{[X^2/(\underline{N})(\underline{df}_{Smaller})]}$.

26. In a study with a 3 X 2 design, ϕ and Cramer's ϕ
  * a. are equivalent.
    b. are equivalent if ϕ is divided by 2.
    c. are equivalent if ϕ is divided by $\sqrt{2}$.
    d. are unrelated.

27-30 In a (fictional) developing country, 100 people were randomly selected and their socioeconomic class and religious affiliation were ascertained. Here are the results and an excerpt from the results section of this fictional study:

Observed (and Expected) Frequencies

	CLASS			
Religion	Poor	Middle	Total	%
agnostic	(7.9) 4	(4.1) 8	12	12
atheist	(8.6) 6	(4.4) 7	13	13
Protestant	(20.5) 21	(10.5) 10	31	31
Catholic	(14.5) 17	(7.5) 5	22	22
other	(14.5) 18	(7.5) 4	22	22
Total	66	34	100	100

Excerpt: "Based on a chi-square test for independence, the poor differed from the middle class in the distribution of religious identification, $X2(4, \underline{N} = 100) = 11.73$, $\underline{p} < .05$."

27.   Of the total population, agnostics, atheists, and others made up what percent?
* a. (12+13+22)/100 = 47%
  b. (4+6+18)/100 = 28%
  c. (8+7+4)/34 = 56%
  d. (12+13+22)/66 = 71%

28.   What percentage of the middle class was Catholic?
  a. 7.5/34 = 22%
  b. 5/100 = 5%
* c. 5/34 = 15%
  d. 7.5/100 = 8%

29.   One finding of <u>this</u> study was that
  a. being poor caused subjects to be Catholic.
* b. poor subjects tended to be Protestant, Catholic, or other, while middle class subjects were most likely to be Protestant.
  c. poor subjects valued religion more than middle class subjects.
  d. being Catholic caused subjects to be poor.

30.   The phi coefficient for this study is
  a. $\sqrt{(11.732/100)} = 1.17$.
  b. $\sqrt{(11.73)}/100 = .03$.
* c. $\sqrt{(11.73/100)} = .34$.
  d. $\sqrt{(11.732)}/100 = .12$.

31-34 A (fictional) study reported: "A chi-square test for independence was conducted to explore the relationship between whether a subject had or had not sought psychological counseling and the profession of the subject (lawyer, car dealer, postal worker, high school teacher, and college professor). A significant relationship was found, $X^2(4, N=100) = 11.1$, $p < .05$, such that...." Here are the data:

Observed (and Expected) Frequencies

Profession	Had Subject Sought Counseling?		Total	%
	Yes	No		
Lawyer	12 (15)	10 (7)	22	22
Car Dealer	19 (15)	4 (8)	23	23
College Prof.	22 (19)	7 (10)	29	29
High School Tch.	4 (8)	8 (4)	12	12
Postal Worker	9 (9)	5 (5)	14	14
Total	66	34	100	100

31. Compared to high school teachers, 33% of whom had sought counseling, what percent of college professors had sought counseling?
    a. 22/66 = 33%.
  * b. 22/29 = 76%.
    c. 19/66 = 29%.
    d. 19/29 = 66%.

32. What percentage of postal workers had NOT sought counseling?
    a. 5/34 = 15%.
    b. 5/100 = 5%.
    c. 5/9 = 56%.
  * d. 5/14 = 36%.

33. One finding of this study was that
  * a. high school teachers tended to seek counseling less than the other professions studied.
    b. car dealers sought counseling less than other professions in the study.
    c. car dealers and college professors had the most stressful jobs, since they had had to seek counseling more than people in other professions.
    d. car dealers were about evenly split on those who had and those who had not sought counseling.

34. The phi coefficient for this study is
    a. $\sqrt{(11.1)/100} = .03$.
  * b. $\sqrt{(11.1/100)} = .33$.
    c. $\sqrt{(11.1^2/100)} = 1.11$.
    d. $\sqrt{(11.1^2)/100} = .11$.

35. All of the following are true about the inventor of the chi-square test EXCEPT
    a. his name was Karl Pearson.
    b. he also invented the method of computing correlation used today.
  * c. he stole most of his ideas (or "borrowed heavily") from other statisticians and mathematicians.
    d. he also did work in the now discredited field of eugenics.

Test Bank

36. In general, the $\underline{t}$ test and the analysis of variance are
    a. dependent on five basic assumptions.
    b. free of assumptions.
    c. sensitive to violations of assumptions.
    * d. adequate if there are only slight violations of assumptions.

37. When the normal-curve assumption is strongly violated, the ordinary $\underline{t}$
    test
    a. resembles an analysis of variance.
    b. is conducted using $\sqrt{t}$ instead of $\underline{t}$.
    * c. yields an incorrect result.
    d. is adequate.

38. Assumptions for statistical procedures are about
    * a. populations.
    b. samples.
    c. inferences.
    d. hypotheses.

39. A sample that comes from a normally distributed population
    a. might have more members than the population.
    * b. is sometimes approximately normally distributed.
    c. is always approximately normally distributed.
    d. is never approximately normally distributed.

40. A sample that comes from a population that is NOT normally distributed
    a. is never approximately normally distributed.
    b. is always approximately normally distributed.
    * c. is sometimes approximately normally distributed.
    d. is distribution-free.

41. A population is usually NOT normally distributed if
    a. a small sample drawn from the population is positively skewed.
    b. two dependent variables are simultaneously measured.
    c. a scale or index is used to measure the dependent variable.
    * d. a ceiling or floor effect exists.

42. When conducting a statistical test, a single outlier can
    a. make the test more robust to violations of the assumption of
       normality.
    b. reduce the sample's variance, making significant results easier to
       achieve.
    * c. lead to a significant result, when the other numbers, considered
       without the outlier, would not have led to a significant result.
    d. improve the reliability of the statistical procedure.

43. A widely used procedure when the sample data do not appear to come from
    a normal population is to
    a. duplicate data that will make the sample more normal.
    b. sample only members of the population who will make the samples
       normal.
    * c. transform the data.
    d. normalize the data by deleting the data that make the distribution
       nonnormal.

44. All of the following are true about data transformations EXCEPT that
    *
    a. measures like number of siblings, income, and number of hospitalizations are usually more accurately understood after being transformed.
    b. higher scores are still higher, lower scores are still lower.
    c. they are usually justified because precise scores on most psychological scales do not have direct meanings.
    d. transformations are applied to all scores.

45. In a square-root transformation,
    a. high numbers become lower and low numbers become higher.
    b. moderate numbers remain unchanged, but low numbers become slightly higher.
    c. low numbers become much lower, but high numbers remain basically unchanged.
    *
    d. moderate numbers become only slightly lower, but high numbers become much lower.

46. Which of the following represents the correct scores if 1, 4, 25, and 81 were transformed using the rank-order method?
    a. 1, 2, 5, 9
    b. 1, 4, 25, 81
    c. 4, 4, 25, 25
    *
    d. 1, 2, 3, 4

47. Which of the following represents the correct scores if 4, 25, 25, and 100 were transformed using the rank-order method?
    a. 2, 5, 5, 10
    *
    b. 1, 2.5, 2.5, 4
    c. 1, 2, 3, 4
    d. 1.5, 2, 3.5, 4

48. The data for a procedure that is "distribution-free" would be probably transformed using the
    a. reflection transformation.
    b. antilog transformation.
    *
    c. rank-order method.
    d. inverse transformation.

49. Because the distribution of rank-order data is known exactly rather than estimated, rank-order tests
    *
    a. do not require estimating any parameters.
    b. are used in most real studies.
    c. are almost always preferred over square-root transformations.
    d. require drawing additional samples.

50. Which of the following is a nonparametric test?
    a. analysis of variance
    b. t test for dependent means
    *
    c. chi-square
    d. t test for independent means

51. Of the following rank-order tests, which corresponds to a t test for independent means?
    a. Wilcoxin signed-rank test
*   b. Wilcoxin rank-sum test
    c. Kruskal-Wallis H test
    d. Spearman Rho

52. Recently some statisticians have shown that instead of using the special computational procedures involved in the rank-order tests, you obtain about the same results if you transform data into ranks and then
    a. compute a Spearman Z.
    b. find the mean of the scores' inverses.
*   c. apply all the usual arithmetic for calculating an ordinary parametric statistic, such as a t test.
    d. apply all the usual arithmetic for calculating a typical nonparametric test, such as a Wilcoxin signed-rank test.

53. In research articles, data transformations are usually mentioned in the
    a. Discussion section.
    b. Introduction.
    c. Materials section.
*   d. Results section.

54. What type of test was conducted in a study for which the Results section noted, "Comparisons of desire to swim and parental expectations were made using Wilcoxin rank-sum test"?
*   a. rank-order test
    b. analysis of variance
    c. computer-intensive test
    d. t test for independent means

Fill-In Questions

55. The chi-square test was invented by _____.

    Answer: Karl Pearson

56. One difference between a chi-square test and an analysis of variance is that in a chi-square test all variables are _____.

    Answer: nominal, category-type

57. The chi-square test for _____ lets you test how well an observed frequency distribution over categories fits some expected pattern.

    Answer: goodness of fit

58. The formula for computing chi-square is _____.

    Answer: Σ (O-E)2/E]

Test Bank

59. The formula for _____ is Σ (O-E)2/E] .

Answer: X2, chi-square

60. In the chi-square test for goodness of fit, the degrees of freedom are _____ minus 1.

Answer: the number of categories

61. Chi-square distributions are _____ skewed.

Answer: positively

62. A _____ is a chart in which the distributions of two nominal variables are laid out so that you have the frequencies of their combinations as well as the totals.

Answer: contingency table

63. _____ is the term usually used to refer to a lack of relationship between two nominal variables.

Answer: Independence

64. A student at a (fictional) Canadian university conducted a survey of the food preferences (vegetarian, vegan, or neither) and the country of origin (Canada, U.S., or other) of 100 students at her university. To test the significance of a relationship between food preference and country of origin, she should conduct a _____.

Answer: chi-square test for independence

65. The formula for finding the degrees of freedom for a chi-square test for independence is the number of columns minus one, _____ the number of rows minus one.

Answer: times, multiplied by

66. "($\underline{N}_{Columns}$-1)($\underline{N}_{Rows}$-1)" is the formula for the degrees of freedom for the chi-square test for _____.

Answer: independence

67. In a chi-square test, it is important that each observed case be _____ all the others, that is, that selecting any one particular subject can not in any way make it more likely that some other particular subject will be selected.

Answer: independent of, unrelated to

Test Bank

68. The effect size for the chi-square test for independence is measured by
_____.

Answer: the phi coefficient, ϕ, Cramer's phi, Cramer's V, ϕc

69. Complete the following formula: $\phi =$ _____ .

Answer: $\sqrt{(X2/\underline{N})}$

70. The power of a study testing hypotheses using the chi-square test of independence is determined by significance level, degrees of freedom, sample size, and _____ .

Answer: effect size, phi, Cramer's phi

71. The _____ of a chi-square test is determined mainly by effect size and sample size.

Answer: power

72-75 A researcher posed the question, "Does Smith's rehabilitation program decrease the rate of prisoners who re-offend?" The researcher conducted a (fictional) study and published her findings, from which article the following excerpt was taken:

A chi-square test for independence was conducted to test whether Smith's rehabilitation program differed from the old system in the number of repeat offenders. Results indicated that a difference did exist, $X2(1, \underline{N}=68) = 8.74$, $\underline{p} < .005$, such that under the Smith program . . .

Observed (and Expected) Frequencies

Program	Re-Offend? No	Re-Offend? Yes	Total	%
Smith's	(14) 8	(20) 26	34	50
Standard	(14) 20	(20) 14	34	50
Total	28	40	68	100

72. Of prisoners under Smith's program, _____ % DID re-offend.

Answer: 76

73. Prisoners under the standard program represented _____ % of the repeat offenders.

Answer: 35

74. According to this study, _____ appeared to be less effective in reducing the number of repeat offenders.

Answer: Smith's program

75.   The phi coefficient for the above study was _____.

        Answer: $\sqrt{(8.74/68)} = .36$

76-79 A researcher conducted a study in which he asked women to rate their
       sense of humor as low, medium, or high, and then to answer whether they
       believed they were or were not generally well-liked. The results of the
       (fictional) study were published in a psychological journal. Here is an
       excerpt from the result's section:

        A chi-square test for independence was conducted
        to see if the extent to which a subject found
        herself to be a funny person was related to how
        well-liked she thought she was. Results were
        significant, $X2(2, \underline{N}=68) = 8.90$, $\underline{p} < .05$, such
        that subjects who rated themselves as having a
        strong sense of humor . . .

	Well Liked			
Humor	No	Yes	Total %	
High	(11) 7	(11) 15	22	32
Medium	(9) 7	(9) 11	18	27
Low	(14) 20	(14) 8	28	41
Total	34	34	68	100

76.   According to these results, _____ % of the people who
        thought themselves to be highly humorous also thought they
        were well-liked.

        Answer: 68

77.   Of the people who reported that they were not well-liked,
        _____% also reported that they had a low sense of humor.

        Answer: 59

78.   The effect size for this study is computed using _____.

        Answer: Cramer's phi

79.   The effect size for this study comes out to _____, which
        is a _____ effect size.

        Answer: .36; medium

80.   When a distribution appears to be nonnormal, based on observation of the
      data, one solution is to apply a(n) _____, and then, having met the
      normal-curve assumption, carry out an ordinary parametric test.

      Answer: data transformation

81. If data are skewed right, _____ transformations may be used to normalize the data.

    Answer: square-root

82. A square-root transformation might be used to normalize a distribution that is _____ skewed.

    Answer: positively

83. If a ceiling or floor effect exists, the distribution will probably be _____.

    Answer: skewed, nonnormally distributed

84. An extreme score that is at the far end of a sample's distribution is called a(n) _____.

    Answer: outlier

85. _____ allow data from nonnormal populations to be analyzed using the standard parametric procedures such as t tests and analyses of variance.

    Answer: Data transformations, Converting the data to ranks

86. In a rank-order procedure, scores of 6, 10, 17, and 25 would be converted to _____.

    Answer: 1, 2, 3, and 4

87. The general name for a test that can be performed on data from a population with any shaped distribution is _____.

    Answer: distribution-free, nonparametric, rank-order

88. _____ have the advantage of permitting the use of the familiar, precise parametric techniques.

    Answer: Data transformations, Converting to ranks and then using the ordinary procedures

89. Data transformations are usually described in the _____ section of a research article (though sometimes in the Methods section).

    Answer: Results

90. If a research article reported that "level of intensity was compared to reaction time using a Wilcoxin rank-sum test," then a _____ test had been conducted.

    Answer: rank-order, nonparametric, distribution-free

> **Note.** The essays called for in these problems ask students to explain the logic behind their answers to someone unfamiliar with the material covered in this chapter. Instructors may prefer to ask for an explanation "to a person who has never taken a course in statistics"--thus requiring the student to explain the principles of hypothesis testing from scratch. (However, such essays should be used sparingly in exams as they will necessarily take students longer to write.)

91. Design a three-category study to be analyzed by the chi-square test for goodness of fit.
    a. Make up data.
    b. Analyze these data. (Use the .05 significance level.)
    c. Describe the underlying logic of the analysis and interpret your "findings" to a person who is familiar with hypothesis testing in general, such as with the t test for independent means, but knows nothing about chi-square tests.

92. A (fictional) researcher planned a study in which a crucial step was offering subjects a food reward. It was important that three food rewards were equal in appeal, so a pre-study was designed in which subjects were asked which of the rewards they preferred. Of the 60 subjects, 16 preferred cupcakes, 26 preferred candy bars, and 18 favored dried apricots.
    a. Do these data suggest that the different foods are differentially preferred by people in general? (Use the .05 significance level.)
    b. Explain your analysis to a person who is familiar with hypothesis testing in general, such as with the t test for independent means, but knows nothing about chi-square tests.

Computation answer:
$X2$ needed ($df=2$, $p<.05$) = 5.992.

	O	E	O-E	(O-E)2	(O-E)2/E
cupcake	16	20	-4	16	.8
candy bar	26	20	6	36	1.8
apricots	18	20	-2	4	.2
	60	60	0		X2=2.8

Do not reject the null hypothesis; the study is inconclusive.

93. A (fictional) high school principal wanted to know if the racial make-up of her teachers mirrored that of the student body, which broke down into 47% white, 28% Latino, 15% African-American, and 10% other. Of the 65 teachers, 42 were white, 4 were Latino, 15 were African-American, and 4 were some other race.
   a. Do these data suggest that the racial make-up of the faculty members is different from that of the students? (Use the .05 significance level.)
   b. Explain your analysis to a person who is familiar with hypothesis testing in general, such as with the t test for independent means, but knows nothing about chi-square tests.

   Computation answer:
   X2 needed ($df=3$, $p<.05$) = 7.815.

	O	Expected	O-E	(O-E)2	(O-E)2/E
White	42	(47%)(65)=30.55	11.45	130.10	4.29
Latino	4	(28%)(65)=18.20	-14.20	201.64	11.08
African-American	15	(15%)(65)= 9.75	5.25	27.56	2.83
Other	4	(10%)(65)= 6.50	-2.50	6.25	.96
	65	65.00	0.00		X2 = 19.16

   Reject the null hypothesis.

94. Design a 2 X 2 study to be analyzed by the chi-square test for independence.
   a. Make up data.
   b. Conduct the hypothesis test (use the .05 significance level)
   c. Compute a measure of association (and indicate whether it represents a small, medium, or large effect size).
   d. Describe the underlying logic of your analyses and interpret your "findings" to a person who is familiar with hypothesis testing in general, such as with the t test for independent means, but knows nothing about chi-square tests.

95.   A (fictional) new school district superintendent was preparing to
       reallocate resources for physically impaired students. He wanted to
       know if the schools in his district differed in the distribution of
       physically impaired. He drew samples of 20 from each of his five
       schools, and found 4 impaired (and 16 unimpaired) students at School 1;
       1 impaired (and 19 unimpaired) at School 2; 6 (and 14) at School 3; 3
       (and 17) at School 4; and 7 (and 13) at School 5.
       a. Do these data suggest that the distribution of physically impaired is
          different at different schools? (Use the .01 significance level.)
       b. Compute a measure of the effect size and indicate whether it is
          large, medium, or small.
       c. Explain your analyses to a person who is familiar with hypothesis
          testing in general, such as with the t test for independent means,
          but knows nothing about chi-square tests.

Computation answer:
X2 needed (p < .01, df=4) = 13.277.

Physically Impaired

School	Yes	No	Total	%
1	(4.2) 4	(15.8) 16	20	20
2	(4.2) 1	(15.8) 19	20	20
3	(4.2) 6	(15.8) 14	20	20
4	(4.2) 3	(15.8) 17	20	20
5	(4.2) 7	(15.8) 13	20	20
Total	21	79	100	100

X2 = .01+.00+2.44+.65+.77+.21+.34+.09+1.87+.50 = 6.88.
Do not reject the null hypothesis; the study is inconclusive.
Cramer's phi = $\sqrt{(6.88/[100][1])}$ = .26,
about a medium effect size.

96. A (fictional) advertising firm wanted to target television advertisements for people who eat out often. So a study was conducted in which 75 randomly selected people noted what they watched for a week, and then they were categorized according to the type of show they watched most. They also completed a questionnaire about how often they eat out, and were divided into those that do and do not eat out often. The results were that those in the group that eat out often included 3 who most watched quiz shows, 9 who most watched situation comedies, 7 who most watched movies, 8 who most watched news shows, and 3 who most watched soap operas. Of those who ate out rarely, the figures were 8 quiz show, 6 situation comedy, 13 movie, 3 news show, and 15 soap opera.
   a. Do these data suggest that the distribution of type of shows watched is different for those who eat out often versus rarely? (Use the .05 significance level.)
   b. Compute a measure of the effect size and indicate whether it is large, medium, or small.
   c. Explain your analyses to a person who is familiar with hypothesis testing in general, such as with the t test for independent means, but knows nothing about chi-square tests.

Computation answer:
$X2$ needed ($\underline{p}$ < .05, $\underline{df}$=4) = 9.488.

Type of Show	Eat Out Often	Eat Out Rarely	Total	%
Quiz Shows	(4.5) 3	(6.75) 8	11	15
Situation Comedies	(6) 9	(9) 6	15	20
Movies	(8.1) 7	(12.2) 13	20	27
News Shows	(4.5) 8	(6.75) 3	11	15
Soap Operas	(7.2) 3	(10.8) 15	18	24
Total	30	45	75	100

$X2$ = .5+.23+2.45+1.63+1.5+1+.15+.05+2.72+2.08 = 12.31.
Reject the null hypothesis.
Cramer's phi = $\sqrt{(12.31/[75][1])}$ = .40;
medium to large effect size.

97. Do people think diversity in a large population is healthy or damaging? At a particular (fictional) college, responses of a randomly selected group of students found that 10 majoring in behavioral sciences thought it healthy, 3 damaging; in natural sciences, 4 healthy, 8 damaging; arts, 18 healthy, 7 damaging; languages, 6 healthy, 7 damaging; and history, 4 healthy, 9 damaging.

   a. Do these data suggest that opinions about diversity vary over different majors? (Use the .05 significance level.)
   b. Compute a measure of the effect size and indicate whether it is large, medium, or small.
   c. Explain your analyses to a person who is familiar with hypothesis testing in general, such as with the t test for independent means, but knows nothing about chi-square tests.

Computation answer:
X2 needed (df=4, p <.05) = 9.488.

| | Diversity Effect | | | |
Major	Good	Bad	Total	%
Behavioral Science	(7.14) 10	(5.78) 3	13	17
Natural Science	(6.72) 4	(5.44) 8	12	16
Arts	(13.86) 18	(11.22) 7	25	33
Language	(7.14) 6	(5.78) 7	13	17
History	(7.14) 4	(5.78) 9	13	17
Total	42	34	76	100

X2 = 1.15+.18+1.38+1.1+1.24+1.2+1.59+1.34+.26+1.79 = 11.23.
Reject the null hypothesis.
Cramer's phi = $\sqrt{(11.23/[76][1])}$ = .38;
medium to large effect size.

98. A (fictional) study on the effects of lack of REM sleep on the ability to recall a list of words found that, of subjects who did not get normal REM sleep, 4 scored high on memory recall, 7 scored moderately, and 9 scored low. Of subjects who got normal sleep, 10 scored high, 9 moderately, and 1 low.
   a. Do these data suggest that REM sleep is related to how people score on the memory recall? (Use the .01 significance level.)
   b. Compute a measure of the effect size and indicate whether it is large, medium, or small.
   c. Explain your analyses to a person who is familiar with hypothesis testing in general, such as with the t test for independent means, but knows nothing about chi-square tests.

Computation answer:
$X2$ needed ($\underline{df}=2$, $\underline{p} < .01$) = 9.211.

Recall	Sleep Condition Normal	Deprived	Total	%
High	(7) 10	(7) 4	14	35
Moderate	(8) 9	(8) 7	16	40
Low	(5) 1	(5) 9	10	25
Total	20	20	40	100

$X2$ = 1.29+1.29+.13+.13+3.2+3.2 = 9.24.
Reject the null hypothesis.
Cramer's phi = $\sqrt{9.24/[40][1]}$) = .48; large effect size.

99. A (fictional) economics department surveyed those graduating in the major to see whether they were going on to graduate school in the same proportions as those from similar colleges. Their conclusion was reported as follows: "Compared to those from similar colleges, far fewer of our students are going on to graduate school in economics, more of our students are going on to graduate school in other fields, and fewer of our students are not going on to graduate school at all; $X2(2, \underline{N} = 275) = 13.24$, $\underline{p} < .01$." Explain this result to a person who is familiar with hypothesis testing in general, such as with the t test for independent means, but knows nothing about chi-square tests.

100. A (fictional) survey was conducted of the incidence of five kinds of anxiety disorders among people who were being treated with a particular medication. The study reported the results as follows: "The relative incidence of the five disorders among the patients taking the medication was not significantly different from the incidence in the general population; $X2(4, \underline{N} = 651) = 2.09$, $\underline{ns}$." Explain the results of the study, including what conclusions might be drawn, to a person who is familiar with hypothesis testing in general, such as with the t test for independent means, but knows nothing about chi-square tests.

101. A study was conducted in which unemployed workers were randomly assigned to either receive a special job-finding training program or to a control group program (involving developing more personal skills). After the program, the workers were followed up as to whether they obtained a job in the next year. The results of this fictional study included the following statement: "Those in the job-finding program were significantly more likely to have found a job in the following year, X2(1, $\underline{N}$ = 380) = 4.21, $\underline{p}$ < .05."
   a. Compute a measure of association and indicate whether it represents a small, medium, or large effect size.
   b. Explain the results of the study (including the effect size result) to a person who is familiar with hypothesis testing in general, such as with the $\underline{t}$ test for independent means, but knows nothing about chi-square tests.

   Computation answer: ϕ = .11; small effect size.

102. For the scores 5, 190, 8, 6, 21, 18, 11, 13, 16, and 10:
   a. Carry out a square-root transformation.
   b. Convert the original scores to ranks.

   Computation answers:

Raw	Square-Root	Rank
5	2.24	1
190	13.78	10
8	2.83	3
6	2.45	2
21	4.58	9
18	4.24	8
11	3.32	5
13	3.61	6
16	4.00	7
10	3.16	4

103. A (fictional) sports researcher wanted to test whether imagery could improve the bowling game of junior bowlers. Five bowlers who were randomly assigned to concentrate on pleasant settings for 10 seconds before each turn scored 141, 157, 160, 167, and 172. Five bowlers who were randomly assigned to bowl in their normal manner scored 76, 83, 88, 94, and 198.

    a. Conduct a t test for independent means (at the .05 level) using the scores as they are (untransformed).

    b. Conduct another t test using square-root transformed scores.

    c. Explain the reasons for using the transformation and the implications of the difference in results of these two methods. (Write your explanation to a person who is familiar with the t test for independent means but not with data transformations.)

Computation answers:
t needed ($df=8$, two-tailed, $p < .05$) = ±2.306.

Untransformed Score Analysis

	Image	Normal
M	159.4	107.8
S2	140.3	2586.2

$S_P2 = 1363.25$ S_M2 272.65

$S_D$ifference2=545.3; $S_D$ifference=23.35; t=2.21.
Do not reject the null hypothesis.

Square-Root Transformed Data

	Image	Normal
	11.87	8.72
	12.53	9.11
	12.65	9.38
	12.92	9.70
	13.11	14.07
M	12.62	10.20
S2	.23	4.82

    $S_P2 = 2.52$

S_M2 .50   .50

$S_D$ifference2=1.0; $S_D$ifference=1.0; t=2.42. Reject the null hypothesis.

104. A (fictional) psychologist compared infants of three different temperaments on their ability to recognize faces. The scores for the infants with Temperament I were 508 and 131; the scores for the infants with Temperament II were 577 and 483; and the scores for the infants with Temperament III were 1,907 and 1,104.

    a. Do these data suggest that among infants in general, these kinds of temperaments make a difference in ability to recognize faces? (Conduct a standard one-way analysis of variance--but using ranks. Use the .05 level.)

    b. Explain and justify your analysis to a person who is familiar with the one-way analysis of variance but has never heard of using rank-transformed data.

Computation answer: F needed (df =2,3; $p < .05$) = 9.55.

Temperament I		Temperament II		Temperament III	
Raw	Rank	Raw	Rank	Raw	Rank
508	3	577	4	1,907	6
131	1	483	2	1,104	5
M	2		3		5.5
S2	2		2		.5

$S2_{Within}$=1.5; $S2_{Between}$=6.5; F=4.33.
Do not reject the null hypothesis.

105. A (fictional) research article reported eye-blink rate for subjects lying or telling the truth during a short interview. In the Results section, the author reported that "the number of blinks were not normally distributed, so an inverse transformation was performed. All subsequent analyses were based on the transformed number of blinks." Explain this quote to a person who is familiar with ordinary parametric statistics, but who has never heard of data transformations.

106. A group of teachers whose classes were either very authoritarian (i.e., they placed a high emphasis on rules) or very non-structured were compared on their satisfaction with their careers. In the Results section of the (fictional) research article, the author stated that "the satisfaction scores were ranked and then analyzed using the Wilcoxin rank-sum test." Explain why the researcher might have used the Wilcoxin rank-sum test instead of an ordinary t test for independent means. (Write your explanation to a person who is familiar with the t test for independent means but not with the data transformations or rank-order tests.)

Multiple-Choice Questions

1. What is multiple regression all about?
   a. Association of one independent variable with one dependent variable.
   b. Association of one independent variable with two dependent variables.
   c. Association of one predictor variable with the combination of two or more dependent variables.
   * d. Association of one dependent variable with the combination of two or more predictor variables.

2. Which of the following describes a situation where hierarchical multiple regression should be used?
   a. If you want to know the correlation between two dependent variables over and above some other dependent variable.
   * b. If you want to know the correlation between a predictor variable and a dependent variable and then how much is added by including another predictor variable.
   c. If you want to know which combination of variables has the highest correlation coefficient.
   d. If you want to know the correlation between a predictor variable and dependent variable and then how much is added by including another dependent variable.

3. Suppose that a researcher wants to know the correlation between product recognition and television advertising. Suppose that the researcher then wants to know how much is added by adding print advertising to the correlation. What procedure should be used?
   * a. Hierarchical multiple regression
   b. Stepwise multiple regression
   c. Factor analysis
   d. Multivariate analysis of variance (MANOVA)

4. A researcher wants to determine which of several predictor variables has the highest correlation with the dependent variable; then which of the remaining predictor variables when added to that first predictor variable creates the best overall prediction; then which of the still remaining predictor variables ... etc.--continuing this process until either no predictor variables are left or adding the best remaining variable does not make a significant addition. The process to use is called
   a. hierarchical multiple regression.
   b. path analysis.
   c. factor analysis.
   * d. stepwise multiple regression.

Test Bank

5.   Which of the following statements best describes stepwise multiple
     regression?
*
     a. Every predictor variable is looked at individually and the one with
        the highest, significant correlation with the dependent variable is
        chosen. Then each remaining predictor variable is looked at in
        combination with this variable to see which combination has the
        highest multiple correlation with the dependent variable. Then this
        process is continued with the next remaining predictor variables.
        And so on.
     b. A correlation is done with the dependent variable using one predictor
        variable and then progressively adding the other predictor variables,
        step-by-step in a systematic, planned order. As each predictor
        variable is added, the additional contribution it makes is computed.
     c. Correlations are computed among all pairs of variables (ignoring
        which are predictor and which dependent variables), and then they are
        ordered from smallest (most negative) to largest (most positive).
     d. Correlations are computed using each predictor variable separately
        and then all of the ones that are significant are put together and a
        multiple regression is conducted.

6.   The degree of association between two variables, over and above the
     influence of one or more other variables, is called
     a. hierarchical multiple regression.
     b. stepwise multiple regression.
*   c. partial correlation.
     d. factor analysis.

7-8 Suppose that you want to know the relation between depression and how
     lonely the person feels, over and above any possible genetic factor that
     may play a role in depression.

     7. What procedure would you use?
        a. Stepwise regression
*   b. Partial correlation
        c. Factor loading
        d. Factor analysis

     8. What approach would be taken?
        a. A stepwise regression, ignoring genetic factors
        b. Loneliness would be partialled out
*   c. The genetic factors would be partialled out
        d. A hierarchical regression, without adding any genetic factors

9.   When a researcher administers the same test twice to the same people in
     order to check the accuracy of the test, the researcher is assessing
     a. face validity.
*   b. test-retest reliability.
     c. split-half reliability.
     d. construct validity.

10. When a researcher correlates the responses of half of the items on a
     questionnaire to the other half to check the accuracy of the measure,
     this is called
     a. face validity.
     b. test-retest reliability.
*   c. split-half reliability.
     d. construct validity.

11. Cronbach's alpha can be thought of as
   *
   a. the average of the correlations between two halves of a test based on every possible split of the items into two halves.
   b. the average of the largest and smallest correlation among test items.
   c. the square root of the standardized path coefficient.
   d. the standardized path coefficient squared.

12. To be considered useful, a test should have reliability of
   a. .1 to .3.
   b. .3 to .5.
   c. .5 to .7.
   * d. .7 to .9.

13. When are reliabilities most likely to be discussed in research articles?
   *
   a. When a new measure is developed.
   b. When results of the study being reported are significant.
   c. Reliability is almost never discussed in research articles.
   d. Reliability is almost always discussed in research articles.

14. Suppose that a researcher has administered to a large group of fathers a questionnaire about how frequently they do each of 40 activities with their children. The researcher then wants to know if there are some groupings of activities, such that within each grouping if a father does one he is likely to do the other, but in which there is little association between activities in other groupings. Which procedure should this researcher use?
   a. Partial correlation
   b. Hierarchical multiple regression
   * c. Factor analysis
   d. Stepwise multiple regression

15. The relative connection of each of the original variables to a factor is called the variable's
   a. factor analysis.
   * b. factor loading.
   c. partial factor.
   d. path factor.

16. If a researcher had twenty different variables that seemed to affect investment choices and she wanted to try and simplify this by grouping them, what procedure should she use?
   * a. Factor analysis
   b. Partial correlation
   c. Path analysis
   d. Multiple regression

17. What is the goal of path analysis?
   a. To group variables
   b. To eliminate unnecessary variables
   c. To arrange variables from most to least influential
   * d. To analyze the causal structure of a group of variables

18. If researchers said that they were making a diagram with arrows connecting the variables, you would know that they were probably using
   a. factor analysis.
   b. partial correlation.
   * c. path analysis.
   d. multiple regression.

19. There is another technique that also uses a path diagram with arrows between variables, but has some advantages over path analysis. What is this technique called?
   a. Partial correlation
   b. Multiple regression
   c. Factor analysis
 * d. Structural equation modeling

20. Suppose that someone is assessing school status as indicated by a combination of GPA, activities, and involvement in school government. In latent variable modeling, school status is called a(n)
 * a. latent variable.
   b. manifest variable.
   c. measurement variable.
   d. causal variable.

21. Which of the following is an advantage of structural equation modeling over ordinary path analysis?
   a. Significance tests are not needed.
 * b. It analyzes the links among latent variables.
   c. It analyzes the links among manifest variables.
   d. It can handle both endogenous and exogenous variables.

22. Suppose that a researcher is interested in the influence on depression of amount of sleep, number of activities the person is engaging in, and how much the person is eating. In structural equation modeling, depression in this example is called a
   a. measurement variable.
   b. manifest variable.
   c. causal variable.
 * d. latent variable.

23. What is a limitation of causal modeling?
 * a. Even when all predicted paths are significant, there is an overall
      good fit, and the significance test comes out right, it is possible
      that there are other patterns of causality that work better.
   b. Only the cause is looked at and you are not able to compare and link
      the different variables to each other.
   c. It cannot be done very easily on a computer.
   d. The path diagrams are rarely accurate and often portray a false picture--in
      particular, they tend to suggest that the true linkages
      are among the manifest variables whereas in fact they are usually among the latent
      variables.

24. Suppose that a researcher wanted to study the effect of three different teaching programs on students' learning, and wanted to eliminate the effect of initial differences in learning ability among the students. What procedure should the researcher use?
   a. Multivariate analysis of variance (MANOVA)
   b. Analysis of variance (ANOVA)
 * c. Analysis of covariance (ANCOVA)
   d. Latent variable modeling

25. Which of the following is the best description of a covariate?
   a. A dependent variable that is correlated with an independent variable.
 * b. A variable that is controlled or partialled out.
   c. A variable that is thought to be an effect of all variables measured.
   d. A variable that does not seem to have any effect on the others.

Test Bank

26. What makes multivariate analysis of variance (MANOVA) different from multiple regression, correlation, or ordinary analysis of variance?
* a. There can be more than one dependent variable.
  b. There can be more than one independent variable.
  c. It can be done with hand computation.
  d. It can be done on a computer.

27. If a researcher wants to be able to have more than one independent variable, more than one dependent variable, and the researcher wants to partial out a variable, what procedure must the researcher use?
  a. This cannot be done.
  b. Analysis of covariance (ANCOVA)
  c. Multivariate analysis of variance (MANOVA)
* d. Multivariate analysis of covariance (MANCOVA)

28. What is the difference between a multivariate analysis of covariance (MANCOVA) and a multivariate analysis of variance (MANOVA)?
  a. A MANCOVA can have more than one dependent variable, whereas a MANOVA cannot.
  b. A MANCOVA can be done with a computer and a MANOVA cannot.
  c. With a MANOVA, variables can be partialled out.
* d. With a MANCOVA, variables can be partialled out.

29. What is the difference between an analysis of covariance (ANCOVA) and a multivariate analysis of covariance (MANCOVA)?
  a. With a MANCOVA variables can be partialled out, whereas with an ANCOVA they cannot.
  b. With an ANCOVA variables can be partialled out, whereas with a MANCOVA they cannot.
* c. A MANCOVA can have more than one dependent variable, whereas an ANCOVA cannot.
  d. A MANCOVA can have more than one independent variable, whereas an ANCOVA cannot.

30. If you are reading a research article and the statistical procedure looks unfamiliar, what should you look for to get a basic understanding?
  a. Some indication of the q coefficient, or if that is not available, some indication of power.
* b. The p level (that is, whether the result is significant or not) and the effect size.
  c. The path diagram or contingency table (depending on the level of measurement of the variables involved).
  d. The regression line.

Fill-In Questions

31. _____ is an approach to multiple regression in which predictor variables are added to the prediction rule, one or a few at a time, in a planned sequential fashion, permitting the researcher to determine the relative contribution of each successive variable over and above those already included.

    Answer: Hierarchical multiple regression

32. The first step in _____ is that each of the various predictor variables that have been measured are correlated with the dependent variable to see which has the highest correlation.

    Answer: stepwise multiple regression

Test Bank

33. _____ is a procedure for finding the correlation between two variables, over and above the influence of one or more other variables.

Answer: Partial correlation

34. When a correlation is computed between two variables, over and above the influence of one or more other variables, these other variables are said to be _____.

Answer: held constant, partialled out, controlled for

35. Another name for partialling out or a holding a variable constant is _____ that variable.

Answer: controlling for, removing the influence of

36. _____ is the extent to which, if you were to give the same measure again to the same person under the same circumstances, you would obtain the same result.

Answer: Reliability

37. A problem with using _____ reliability for a test of knowledge (such as a vocabulary test) is that when people take it the second time, their performance is likely to be different as a result of having taken the test once.

Answer: test-retest

38. Probably the most widely used measure of reliability is called _____; it is equivalent to the average of the split-half correlations from all possible splits into halves of the items on the test.

Answer: Cronbach's alpha

39. _____ is an exploratory statistical procedure, applied in situations where many variables are measured, that identifies groupings of variables correlating maximally with each other and minimally with variables in the other groupings.

Answer: Factor analysis

40. In factor analysis, a(n) _____ is a subset of variables all correlating with each other but not with variables not in the subset.

Answer: factor

41. A factor loading is the correlation of a factor with a(n) _____.

Answer: individual variable, variable

42. In factor analysis, a variable is considered part of a factor if its _____ is above some cutoff, such as .30.

Answer: factor loading, correlation with the factor

Test Bank

43. _____ is a method of analyzing the correlations among a group of measured variables in terms of a predicted pattern of causal relations; that is, it is a type of causal analysis.

Answer: Path analysis

44. In a path analysis, each arrow has a(n) _____, which shows the degree of relation of the variables at the two ends of the arrow in the context of the entire causal model.

Answer: path coefficient

45. LISREL is the name of a computer program often used for _____; in fact, LISREL is often used as a shorthand name for this technique.

Answer: latent variable modeling, structural equation modeling

46. _____ is a sophisticated version of path analysis that includes paths involving unmeasured, theoretical variables.

Answer: latent variable modeling, Structural equation modeling, LISREL

47. Unlike ordinary path analysis, _____ permits a kind of significance test and provides measures of the overall fit of the data to the hypothesized causal pattern.

Answer: latent variable modeling, structural equation modeling, LISREL

48. A(n) _____ variable is an unmeasured theoretical variable assumed to be the underlying cause of several variables actually measured and used in the analysis.

Answer: latent

49. A(n) _____ is an analysis of variance conducted after first adjusting the variables to control for the effect of one or more unwanted additional variables.

Answer: analysis of covariance, ANCOVA

50. A variable partialled out in an ANCOVA is called a(n) _____.

Answer: covariate

51. A multivariate statistical technique is a statistical procedure involving more than one _____.

Answer: dependent variable

52. A(n) _____ analysis of variance is an analysis of variance in which there is more than one dependent variable.

Answer: multivariate

Test Bank

53.   ANOVA is to MANOVA as ANCOVA is to _____.   (Spell out, do not just use the acronym.)

        Answer: multivariate analysis of covariance.

Problems and Essays

Notes.
    1.   Problem 54 asks the student to make up and discuss research examples corresponding to the various techniques introduced in this chapter. Asking the student to do this for all of the ten techniques listed will be more than is reasonable within a typical exam period. Thus, if this item is used, it is recommended to either (a) list only a subset (even just one) of these or (b) list them all (or a large subset) and give the student a choice of some number to be done.
    2.   The essays called for in problems 55-63 ask students to explain the results of a study that uses one of the procedures covered in this chapter, writing their explanation to a person who is familiar with the procedures covered in previous chapters. Instructors may prefer, particularly on a final exam, to ask for an explanation "to a person who has never taken a course in statistics." (However, such essays should be used sparingly in exams as they will necessarily take students much longer to write.)

54.   Make up a plausible study for each of the following statistical procedures, indicating how it would apply and what results you would predict.   (Do not use a study covered in class or in your textbook, but you may use a real study you have read about elsewhere.)
        a. Hierarchical multiple regression.
        b. Stepwise multiple regression.
        c. Partial correlation.
        d. Reliability tests.
        e. Factor analysis.
        f. Ordinary path analysis.
        g. Structural equation modeling.
        h. ANCOVA.
        i. MANOVA.
        j. MANCOVA.

55.   A personnel director conducted a study of job satisfaction among clerical workers in her company. She reported the results as follows: "A forward stepwise regression analysis was conducted for predicting job satisfaction which led to a solution with two predictor variables, liking for coworkers (ß=.25) and status among coworkers (ß=.21), with an overall $\underline{R}2$ of .37. Three other variables were measured (pay, benefits, status with supervisors) but were found not to add significantly to the prediction." Explain what this result means to a person who is generally familiar with multiple regression but not with stepwise multiple regression.

56. A (fictional) study is conducted in which strangers are put in pairs and given a chance to get to know each other for a half hour. Then they are given a questionnaire. The researchers report the following results:

A hierarchical regression analysis was carried out. Consistent with previous findings, the first variable considered, physical attractiveness, significantly predicted degree of attraction ($R^2 = .16$). As predicted by our theory, adding perceived liking of the other person for the self to the model significantly increased the prediction (overall $R^2 = .28$; R^2 increment = .12, $F_{(1, 107)} = 6.21$, $p < .01$). Also as expected, adding the extent to which subject felt there was a lot in common with the other person did not add a significant increment (overall $R^2 = .30$; increment = .02).

Explain the logic of this procedure and what this result means to a person who is generally familiar with multiple regression but not with hierarchical multiple regression.

57. A (fictional) research article reports the following result: "The correlation between marital satisfaction and self-esteem ($r = .36$, $p < .05$) remained substantial even after controlling for income (partial $r = .34$, $p < .05$)." Explain this result to a person who is familiar with correlation but not with partial correlation.

58. A research article describing a newly developed (fictional) measure of lawyers attitudes towards their profession and attitudes towards clients includes the following: "For the Attitudes Towards Profession Scale, reliability was strong--Cronbach's alpha = .89 and test-retest correlation (over 2 weeks) = .94. However, for the Attitudes Towards Clients Scale, reliability results were mixed--there was an adequate alpha of .73, but the test-retest correlation was only .48." Explain this result to a person who is familiar with correlation but not with reliability and the ways it is assessed.

59. As part of a market analysis of a new product, trial customers were asked to evaluate the product on eight rating scales. The researcher then subjected these ratings to a factor analysis which produced the results shown in the following table.

Rating Scale	Solidity	Appearance	Utility
Sturdiness	.71	–	–
Likelihood to last	.69	–	–
Safety	.41	–	–
Style	–	.72	–
Personal appeal	–	.43	–
Attractiveness	–	.42	–
Usefulness	–	–	.54
Efficiency	–	–	.47
Value at planned price	–	–	.32

Note: Loadings less than .30 are left blank.

Write a report to the product manager explaining this table, assuming the product manager is familiar with correlation but not with factor analysis.

62. A study was done examining influence on how well students do on statistics exams based on a questionnaire given to a group of students just before the exam (and also using the exam score). The following variables were measured: (a) score on the exam, (b) hours studied, (c) overall GPA, and (d) strength of desire to do well on this exam.
   a. Draw a plausible path diagram (that is, with the arrows and path coefficients) for the results of such a study.
   b. Explain the meaning of your diagram to a person who is generally familiar with correlation and regression but not with path analysis.

Test Bank

375

63. A psychologist conducts a (fictional) study of the relation between physiological age and mental health. The data are analyzed using structural equation modeling. The psychologist reports:

> The latent variable for physiological age had three measured variables as indicators--age in years (path coefficient=.77), cellular age index (.83), and anatomical age index (.69). The latent variable for mental health had three indicators--self-esteem (.81), absence of anxiety (.84), and absence of depression (.60). The crucial path from the age latent variable to the mental health latent variable was .34, which was significant ($p < .05$). The overall fit of the model was very good (Bonnet-Bentler NFI = .91) and the model could not be rejected ($p=.36$).

a. Make a diagram of these findings using the standard conventions for drawing latent variable path diagrams.

b. Explain the diagram and these results (in a general way) to a person familiar with correlation and regression, but not with path analysis or structural equation modeling. Be sure to note the limitations of any conclusions that can be drawn.

64. A (fictional) sociologist analyzed court records as part of a study of how long it takes jurors to come to decisions in criminal versus civil court cases and in the federal vs. state courts in the U.S. The results section of the research report included the following:

> A 2 X 2 analysis of covariance was conducted with type of court system (Federal vs. State) and type of trial (Criminal vs. Civil) as the independent variables and length of jury deliberations as the dependent variable. Length of the trial was included as a covariate to control for variation due to different amounts of information that the juries might have to consider. There was a main effect for type of trial, $F(1, 95) = 4.38$, $p < .05$, with juries typically deliberating longer in civil trials. Neither the main effect for type of court system nor the interaction were significant.

Explain these results to a person who is familiar with factorial analysis of variance and correlation and regression analysis, but not with analysis of covariance.

65. A researcher conducted a (fictional) experiment in which subjects were presented factual questions on a computer screen, which the subject was instructed to answer as quickly as possible by pressing either the A key (for yes) or the L key (for no). Subjects were randomly assigned to carry out the task under one of three conditions--a very hot room, a very cold room, or a normal-temperature room. The research article reporting the results included the following:

> A one-way MANOVA was carried out comparing performance in the three conditions using the two dependent variables of speed of response and accuracy of response. The result was a significant multivariate effect . . . Follow-up univariate analyses showed a significant effect only for speed, $F(2,87) = 6.21$, $p < .01$. As shown in the table [not included here], post-hoc multiple comparisons indicated that speed was slower in the hot room than in either of the other two rooms, but there was no difference between speed in the normal-temperature versus cold room.

Explain these results to a person who is familiar with analysis of variance and multiple comparison procedures, but not with multivariate analysis of variance.

This section does not include answers given in the Answers to Practice Problems section of the text. This section also does not include essays or graphic answers. Some chapters are not included here because they contain no unanswered computation problems.

Chapter 1

2a. Frequency table:

X	f	%
38	1	3.33
37	0	0
36	0	0
35	1	3.33
34	0	0
33	0	0
32	1	3.33
31	0	0
30	0	0
29	0	0
28	2	6.67
27	0	0
26	4	13.33
25	8	26.67
24	5	16.67
23	0	0
22	3	10
21	2	6.67
20	2	6.67
19	0	0
18	0	0
17	0	0
16	0	0
15	1	3.33

Chapter 2

3. Governors: $\underline{M} = 172/4 = 43$; $\underline{SD} = \sqrt{(140/4)} = 5.92$.
   CEO's: $\underline{M} = 176/4 = 44$; $\underline{SD} = \sqrt{(480/4)} = 10.95$.

6. Verbal Ability: $\underline{Z} = (81-50)/20 = 1.55$.
   Quantitative Ability: $\underline{Z} = (6.4-0)/5 = 1.28$.

Chapter 3

2c.

TV Hours		Violence		
Raw	Z	Raw	Z	$Z_X Z_Y$
14	1.27	9	.97	1.23
8	-.63	6	0.00	0.00
6	-1.27	1	-1.62	2.06
12	.63	8	.65	.41
Σ 40		24		3.70
M 10		6	$r = .93$	
SD 3.16		3.08		

3c. $r = -4.95/10 = -.50$.

4c. $r = .57/10 = .06$.

7.

Subordinate	$(-.66\underline{H})$	+	Prediction Rule $(.14\underline{S})$ +	$(.09\underline{R})$	Predicted Manager Effectiveness
A	.66		-.14	-.09	.43
B	0.00		0.00	0.00	0.00
C	.66		-.14	-.09	.43
D	.66		0.00	0.00	.66
E	0.00		-.14	0.00	-.14
F	0.00		0.00	-.09	-.09
G	1.98		-.14	-.09	-1.75
H	.66		-.42	-.09	.15
I	1.98		-.14	-.27	1.57

Chapter 5

5. Cutoff $(p < .01, \text{1-tailed}) = -2.326$ $Z = +1.2$
   The experiment is inconclusive.

Chapter 6

7. Distribution of means will have a mean of 5.5 and a standard deviation of .2. Cutoff $(p < .05, \text{1-tailed}) = 1.64$. Sample's mean rating of 5.9 is 2 standard deviations above the mean. Null hypothesis is rejected.

Chapter 8

2. t needed ($df = 9$, $p < .05$, 1-tailed) = -1.833
    $S^2 = 13.78$; Sample $M = 28$; Population $M = 30$, $S_M = 1.17$;
    $t = (28-30)/1.17 = -1.71$; do not reject null hypothesis

5. t needed ($df = 4$, $p < .05$, 1-tailed) = -2.132.
    Difference scores: -7,3,-4,-4,-8. $M = -20/5 = -4$. $S^2 = 74/4 = 18.5$.
    $S_M = \sqrt{(18.5/5)} = \sqrt{3.7} = 1.92$. $t = (-4 - 0)/1.92 = -2.08$.
    Do not reject the null hypothesis.
    $d = M/\sqrt{(S^2)} = -4/\sqrt{(18.5)} = -4/4.30 = -.93$; large effect size.

Chapter 9

4. t needed ($df = 9$, $p < .05$, 2-tailed) = +/- 2.262
    Normals: $M = 6$; $S^2 = 5.6$; Own-name: $M = 9.6$; $S^2 = 19.3$; $S^2_{Pooled} = 11.69$
    $S_{M1}^2 = 1.95$; $S_{M2}^2 = 2.34$; $S_{Difference}^2 = 4.29$; $S_{Difference} = 2.07$ $t = -1.73$

Chapter 10

3. F needed ($df = 2,72$; $p < .05$) = 3.13 (df for 2,70 used).
    $S^2_{Between} = (1)(25) = 25$. $S^2_{Within} = 2.0$. $F = 25/2 = 12.5$.
    Reject the null hypothesis.

5. F needed ($df = 3,8$; $p < .05$) = 4.07.
    Engineering: $M = 11$, $S^2 = 1$. Marketing: $M = 6.67$, $S^2 = 1.34$.
    Accounting: $M = 5$, $S^2 = 3$. Production: $M = 14.33$, $S^2 = 2.34$.
    $S^2_{Between} = [(11-9.25)^2 + (6.67-9.25)^2 + (5-9.25)^2$
    $+ (14.33-9.25)^2]/3\}(3) = 53.59$.
    $S^2_{Within} = 1.92$. $F = 53.59/1.92 = 27.91$. Reject the null hypothesis.

Answers to Practice Problems

Chapter 11

2. $\underline{X^2}$ needed ($\underline{df}$=4-1=3,5%)=7.815

Season	$\underline{O}$	Expected	$\underline{O-E}$	$(O-E)^2$	$(O-E)^2/E$
Winter	28	(1/4)(128)=32	-4	16	.50
Spring	33	(1/4)(128)=32	1	1	.03
Summer	16	(1/4)(128)=32	-16	256	8.00
Fall	51	(1/4)(128)=32	19	361	11.28
Total	128		128 0		$\underline{X^2}$=19.81

Conclusion: Reject the null hypothesis.

5. $\underline{df}$=(3-1)(3-1)=4; $\underline{X^2}$ needed ($\underline{df}$=4,5%) = 9.488

	Community			
	A	B	C	Total
For	12 (9.8)	6 (4.2)	3 (7)	21(23.33%)
Against	18 (16.8)	3 (7.2)	15 (12)	36(40.00%)
No opinion	12 (15.4)	9 (6.6)	12 (11)	33(36.67%)
Total	42	18	30	90

$\underline{X^2}$=.49+.77+2.29+.09+2.45+.75+.75+.87+.09=8.55

8. Score: 201 523 614   136 340 301   838 911 1,007
   Rank: 2   5   6   1   4   3   7   8   9
    $\underline{M}$: 13/3=4.33 8/3=2.67   24/3=8 $\underline{GM}$=5
    $\underline{S^2}$: 8.67/2=4.34 4.66/2=2.33   2/2=1

$\underline{F}$ needed ($\underline{df}$=2,6; p < .05) = 5.14
$\underline{S^2}_{Between}$={[(4.33-5)^2+(2.67-5)^2+(8-5)^2]/(3-1)}(3)=22.32
$\underline{S^2}_{Within}$=(4.34+2.33+1)/3=2.56; $\underline{F}$=22.32/2.56=8.72
Reject the null hypothesis.